HOLY MOLY MACKEROLY

From 3 Art Stamps to the Smithsonian

Reflections on the Business of Art and the Art of Life

GLORIA PAGE

MESA POINT PUBLISHING

For information/permission contact:
Gloria Page: www.holymolymackeroly.com
Mesa Point Publishing: www.mesapointpublishing.com

■

Art stamp images from "Curtis' Collection" (pgs. 154, 237, 240) are reproduced with permission from the Uyeda family.
Watercolor (in gray tones) by Kate Gray (pg. 247) is reproduced with permission of the artist.
Rights to the use of the handcarved stone image (pg. 6) by Mr. Ming Quan Wang belong to the author.

"Decalogo del artista" by Gabriela Mistral
From the book: *Selected Poems of Gabriela Mistral* translated and edited by Doris Dana
Copyright © 1961, 1964, 1970, 1971 by Doris Dana
The Johns Hopkins University Press, Baltimore, Maryland
The Johns Hopkins University Press Ltd., London
Reprinted with permission from the Joan Daves Agency/Writers House, Inc., New York, NY

■

Cover art by Gloria Page
Cover design by Elizabeth Howard
Text / graphics layout by Gary Page
Photography credit: David Vargas (photo of the author)

■

Publisher's Cataloging-in-Publication

Page, Gloria.
    Holy moly mackeroly! : from 3 art stamps to the
    Smithsonian : reflections on the business of art and the
    art of life / Gloria Page. -- 1st ed.
      p. cm.
      Includes index.
      LCCN 2002102554
      ISBN 0-9718901-0-2

    1. ImpressionsArt Design. 2. Page, Gloria.
    3. Home-based businesses--United States. 4. Design--
    Economic aspects--United States. 5. Art--Marketing.
    6. Women-owned business enterprises--United States.
    I. Title.

HD2336.U5P34 2002   658'.041
                           QBI02-701314

Published and Printed in the USA
on quality Recycled Paper

Dedication and Appreciation

I would like to dedicate this book to my husband Gary,
    and together we dedicate this book to the best works of Art and Heart in our lives,
    our sons Brandon and Bryan. We love you both so much.

To my Mom, Ida: "Je t'aime beaucoup."

This book is also dedicated to

- Carolyn McLaughlin Birkes, whose supportive and adventurous spirit will always sparkle my way.

- Curtis Uyeda, a person I never met, but then again, I did.

I extend my sincere appreciation to all of the people whose stories are woven into the fabric of these pages and my life: without you, no story.

Thank you to all of my customers and buyers over the years, the ones I've had the pleasure to meet and the vast number I haven't met yet: without you, no business.

And last, but certainly not least, I dedicate this book to *you*, the person with this book in your hands, reading this right now: without you, what's the point of writing it all down?

Heart-to-heart, I thank you all.

A Special Thanks to…

My Art Critique Group friends for their Creative Contributions:

Susan Taylor Glasgow	Taylor Glasgow Studios	Glass / Mixed Media Sculpture
Janet Ghio	Janet Ghio Designs	Art Quilts
Kate Gray	Gray Studios	Graphic Design / Watercolor
Josephine Stealey	Jo Stealey Paperworks	Handmade Paper
Lisa Christian	Lisa Christian Designs	Jewelry

The following friends for their Personal Business Stories:

Lara K. Birkes	Sendable Wearable Art	Handmade Cards
Kay Foley	Ampersand Cards	Handmade Cards
Janet Ghio	Janet Ghio Designs	Art Quilts
Ken Logsdon	Post-a-Quote	Handmade Cards
Brenda (BJ) Thompson	I'd Rather Be Stamping	Stamp / Stencil Store

To Sharilyn Miller, for being happy to write the Foreword, and for helping me to expand my vision through your own—thank you so much. You are special to many people.

Thank you to Janet Ghio, for your constant encouragement as this book was being written and for being my first "friendly reader." It made all the difference in the world, truly.

Jana Emory, thank you for being the final "friendly reader." Your way with words makes me laugh, think, and shows me new ways of looking at life.

Thank you, Mr. Wang, for carving the Confucian stone stamp for me to use in this book, and for the depth of artistry and tradition infused in it. I will use it with deep respect.

The Uyeda family, for giving your permission to include beautiful art stamp images from "Curtis' Collection," my gratitude is yours.

To Gary: I appreciate the great design work on the websites, the fabulous show displays, and computer tech support. For always supporting my dreams—hugs. You're the best.

Contents

Words are the Voice
of
the Heart.

CONFUCIUS

FOREWORD
by *Sharilyn Miller*

Just about every artist and craftsperson I know is desperate for one thing: more time for art. This is true of serious artists with M.F.A.s as well as stay-at-home moms who make greeting cards at the dining-room table. Their quest often leads to self-examination, calendar juggling, and, inevitably, to the tantalizing thought of turning their passion into a self-supporting endeavor. A job. Imagine doing what you love all day long and being paid for it, too. That's the dream—and it's heady.

Then reality intrudes with a heavy tread. We begin to ask important questions, like how do I get started? Doesn't it take a lot of money? What do I do first? Which papers do I file? Do I need a bookkeeper, an accountant, an attorney, and a nanny for my kids? Where do I fit this business into my house, my lifestyle, and my time schedule? Our self-esteem begins to erode under an avalanche of doubtful questions. Maybe starting a home-based art business wasn't such a good idea after all. Gee, all I wanted to do was make money from my artwork ... because I want to spend more time doing what I love.

At this point, many of us simply give up. We trudge each morning to our jobs, secure in the knowledge that we have health-care coverage and a bi-weekly paycheck. The dream of making a living from our art still festers inside, but it seems too difficult to get started. If only...

This is where Gloria Page steps in. She knows all about the pitfalls of starting a business that's based on a passion for art. She's really been there. Today, Gloria is a successful art-business owner whose creative endeavors have graced the pages of *Somerset Studio* and *Belle Armoire* magazines, *The Stamp Artist's Project Book* and *The Complete Guide to Rubber Stamped Jewelry* (to be released in early 2003). How did she get started? Did a rich uncle bankroll her fledgling business? Did she have special connections with the art world? No. Gloria started her art business with $25 and three rubber stamps.

Such humble beginnings quickly blossomed into a wealth of creative opportunities. Gloria has sold thousands of artwork pieces, published articles on her craft, written chapters for books from leading craft publishers, and sold cards to the Gift Shop at The Renwick Gallery of Contemporary Arts and Crafts—at the request of the *Smithsonian*, no less! And that's just a taste of her creative experiences so far.

For all of us who yearn to follow a similar path, Gloria says, "I firmly believe that with the simplest of tools and a pioneer sense of adventure, anyone can... test the waters of what it would be like to have your own business with handcrafted items..."

We all need more of this type of encouragement, and you'll find it here in her new book. Can you go from three rubber stamps to the Smithsonian? Gloria did. Is it uphill drudgery all the way? It doesn't have to be. Can anyone make a business from her art or craft? Anyone can try. And, as Gloria says, "you have nothing to lose but an opportunity."

This is not a how-to book with to-do lists and spreadsheets and advice on collecting overdue bills. Plenty of such art-business books abound. Gloria goes a step further with this endeavor, sharing a large portion of her overfilled life with her readers while answering the really tough questions, like "what's it like making thousands of handmade cards for a company that just wants duplicates of the same thing?" She offers an artist's perspective, a wealth of experience and an abundance of personal anecdotes to glean from. She's honest, encouraging, gentle, and full of hope for you and me. If you're an artist or craftsperson who could use a little encouragement with your coffee in the morning, then this book is a great place to start.

FORWARD: *the Introduction*

"You miss 100 percent of the shots you never take."

- Wayne Gretzky, Hockey Player

Quotes. Concise little gems, aren't they? Like crystals on the chandelier of life… You can find them sparkling, tucked into the most interesting places where you least expect to be enlightened. You can find quotes in a *Reader's Digest* in your bathroom library or on a car bumper speeding by, as well as in the Great Books of Western Civilization. There are Quotes by *Women*, Quotes by *Zen Masters*, Quotes by *Kids* who may even be your own. In a few words, a human being of whatever age and from whatever period in history, has encapsulated a bit of wisdom with a temple bell ring of truth to it, offering a chance for the reader to reflect, laugh, change and grow. Someday I will organize and compile my floating collection of quotes captured on whatever scrap of paper presented itself to me in the moment, from dinner napkins to checking account deposit slips. Someday. When I was considering what thought I would like to present to begin this book, I had this vague memory of a quote with a reference to "taking shots," and sure enough, I found it on a little paper tucked into the vastness of my studio collection of things that are "keepers." Perfect—it says it for me: the beauty of a quote.

If I were to say it in my own words, it would come out something like: "Go for it. There's nothing to lose except an opportunity." And *that* is not something to lose lightly.

Eight years ago, I had three rubber stamps and not a clue as to what a heat gun was or how to use it. I used a kitchen toaster for the heat to do my first embossing. I made 18 bookmarks and sold them. If anyone had told me at that time that in a few years I would be getting a call from the Smithsonian to design cards for them, I would have considered it *more* likely to be pursuing a career in the NHL, since I could skate better than I could stamp. Hockey is a gene-thing. Stamping had a learning curve. Nevertheless, I did take a shot at this business-of-art idea and have been moving forward with it ever since.

Over the years I have read so many articles, books, editorials, letters-to-the-editor, etc. addressing this topic of making money from stamp art and home businesses in general, in vastly different fields. The entrepreneurial spirit is sweeping the world and with the onset of the Internet and inter-connectedness, the sky is no longer the limit. But do you know what? We've had a computer for only a few years. I used my 1940 Underwood typewriter for many years before that. Even now, for the "genuine article" look, instead of a computer-generated font, I take out my Underwood. It has all been a process over time. I firmly believe that with the simplest of tools and a pioneer sense of adventure, anyone can take steps, venture out and test the waters of what it would be like to have your own business with handcrafted items, whatever they may be. My venue happens to be cards at the moment—a *lot* of moments and cards over the past eight years. I started with stamps, and so my vocabulary will dance around in that lingo-language, but hopefully the themes will be useful and applicable in wider circles, too.

I would like to say, right here and now, that in no way am I committed to making a push for anyone *to do* a business. I see a lot of interest out there in printed material with many people asking, wondering, and hoping to hear stories of what it is like to develop a personal passion-based lifestyle. I have been personally asked again and again to share my stories, so use them as you like. It may simply be a fun or interesting read; it may be a springboard to start something you've secretly dreamed of pursuing. Perhaps this book can be for you a point of encouragement, an arm around your shoulder from someone who's been there before, friendly help from a stranger when there is this street that looks scary to cross. My intuition tells me that there is a place for this book. I sure would have appreciated reading something along these lines way back when myself.

In 1998 I began entertaining the idea of writing things down, as in "a book." Talk about a street that looks scary to cross—that was one for me. An interesting thing started to happen as I harbored that secret thought: I started to see *everything* as "a good chapter," "a good story," or "something for the book."

Way back, when I was 19, I got my first car, a compact, cute, sky-blue automatic Volkswagen Fastback. The *minute* I drove my car out of the Used Car Lot, I couldn't believe how many people bought Volkswagens the same day I did. They were everywhere. In reality, of course, it was simply a matter of focus; I was "seeing" them now as if I had some special glasses on that filtered out every other type of car. The same kind of thing happened once I began to focus on putting my story down on paper. I noticed that these and similar questions were popping up all over the place in different forms and forums, and I was keenly aware of how they were being addressed:

- How can I make money from my vast rubber stamp collection so that I can at least support my habit of collecting infinitely more?
- What's best: Retail or Wholesale, Reps, Consignment, maybe a Website…?
- Would you speak about your experiences developing a home-based business?
- "Dear Editor: Thank you for your fabulous magazine. You have inspired me to believe that I could try the business of art… just one small question: how on earth do I get *started*?" …and on and on in that light.

The same and related questions have been around for a long time, obviously. Now with my new focus, I found myself wondering how the experts were answering these questions and what I would say myself. I studied the situation from different vantage points by role-playing various positions: as Gloria the Wanna-be Artist, with no art background and very few supplies who wants to quit her job and start a card company; as Gloria the Hobbyist, with zillions of stamps who wants to find a way to make a little money on-the-side to buy more… I read books and articles, trying on the shoes of the author, the reader, and the "wonderer," to see how they would fit. I came to the realization that there is a lot of information out there and a lot that I don't even know exists. Multiple layers of issues are addressed in a highly informative manner. We are presented with typical problems and pointers, warnings about consignment and copyrights, the legalities of getting your registered company name, tax and accounting issues, and always the sage advice to read more in order to be better informed. And with all the different shoes and hats I tried on, I would find myself saying: "Thank you. But something is missing." I would find myself wondering: How does all or any of this apply to *me*? There is so much, almost too much information. How do I sort it all out and determine what I basically need to know without getting inundated and depressed? Some of these people actually seem to be on a mission to discourage me, for some strange reason. What is valuable and what needs to be tossed or at least delayed for a while?

Where do you go with the barrage of information that seems to keep accumulating as mountains of paper threatening to avalanche your workspace and your confidence? I don't know about you, but there is a point for me when I have crossed the border from learning-land to overwhelmed-city. I get into this weird space between being sleepy and being scared. Mental wandering replaces the research-mode. Can I use any of this information right now? My mind drifts… Well, maybe I'll just flip through this magazine here and think about that business-stuff later… As I browse, gaze at and drool over the artwork and masterpieces of "the pros," I logically and rightfully figure that *they* are the ones who have figured it all out, *they* are the ones who must be making tons of money from their fabulous stamp art or whatever art they're doing. They have the background. They have the connections. It is all *too complicated*, anyway. I might as well forget it. Believe me, I understand. To this day, after having sold tens of thousands of cards and other things, I still get avalanched and bombarded in my head. I do not want to study myself into a stupor. It would be much nicer to have a conversation with fellow travelers.

Let me be more than completely honest. In retrospect, (such an intriguing world-view), if I had known *then* what I know *now*, would I have started a home-based card business? I don't know; I am not completely sure. I'd like to believe about myself that I would have the guts to tackle all the issues. I will say that I am very glad that I didn't know "too much." There are times when I do believe with all my heart that "ignorance is bliss." Crawling out of ignorance towards the light *slowly* tends to work for me. I hope to give enough information that will be deemed useful and supportive, yet not so much that it would blow anyone away, or dash any hopes to the ground. Hope is powerfully fragile.

And speaking of ignorance: when I was a kid, my Mom sat me down for a chat about "the facts of life." I received the information and gentle advice and had one question: "Mom, you talked about what you *do*, but I want to know: how do you *feel* when you love someone?" I need *more than the external facts here, please*. I sensed that the mechanics needed to be fleshed out with tenderness and poignancy: with the experiential. The talk got much deeper at that point. Tension was replaced by smiles, as I recall.

I would like to draw a direct analogy here to "the facts of home business life." I truly appreciate all the well-written and meticulously researched work that is available. My respect for the authors and the material presented grows over time. I have a lot more to learn. But knowing myself, I also know that I need more than facts, and I am not at all interested in hype. During the course of reading, I find myself saying things out loud like: Yes, that's true. Good point. Whoops, didn't know that. Okay, but c'mon, c'mon, *COME ON!* I get the basic drift. Apparently there are methodical steps to success. But I need something more. I need stories, personal-real-examples; *I need drama!* I want to laugh, to cry, and to connect. Put some flesh on the bones, please. How does it *feel* when:

- …you sell your very own artwork for the very first time?
- …you decide to act as your own rep and walk into an Exclusive Shop with your humble little products tucked under your sweaty, trembling arms?
- …a shop owner humiliates you and rejects your work?
- …you decide to make the leap and quit your "real job" and commit to your dream of an art business?

- How does it feel when… "respectable types" think you are nuts for doing it? (And then you turn around and sell tons of artwork anyway?)
- …your family and friends walk into your art booth crowded with customers? Their pride, hugs and smiles—what happens when you see that?

How about these questions:

- Is it boring with a capital-B to make tens of thousands of cards over and over again? Is wholesale worth it?
- What is it like to count up your checks and cash after a two-day show and find $1500 is sitting in front of you?
- What happens internally when the Smithsonian calls you and asks you to design cards for the Gift Shop at the Renwick Gallery of Contemporary Arts and Crafts? And then *orders* them over and over again for years?

Here are a few big questions: How much background do I need to even begin thinking of starting my own business or is it possible to jump in and learn along the way and feel comfortable with that? What is the cost of getting started? What are the risks?

And now for my favorite question of all: "Is any of this any *fun*?" Trust me—it is.

The plan is for this book to be fun as well as helpful. For checklists of "business do's and don'ts," this is not the place. For stamping techniques, thousands of luscious books will help you out. For memoir-style personal experiences, this is where I hope I can give you something of value. This is my cozy niche. If people can feel encouraged and find they are laughing along the way, we are headed in a positive, up-beat direction. Who needs more reasons to be intimidated or overwhelmed? I certainly don't. Just relax.

As I mentioned before, the seed of this book was planted in 1998. The exact location was during a hot-bath-in-the-middle-of-the-night-so-I-can-*think* kind of time. It wasn't exactly Ten Thousand Waves Japanese Spa in Santa Fe standards, but it was quiet and the vanilla candle was pleasant. It was a stream of consciousness manner of thinking that led me from mentally planning the stack of orders on the drafting table to be done ASAP, to reflecting on ways to expand my business. Next we floated to the dreamy thought of how nice it would be to be able to do something "one-time" for a change, instead of starting everything from scratch every single time… grateful for my business, mind you, yet at the same time wishing for a way to expand the experience beyond what I had been able to do up until that point. What could I do that could be "printed?"

The more I thought and reminisced, the more I saw my business as "a story," and more specifically, a series of stories. Chapter titles and story titles popped into my head like thought-bubbles. I had spoken at the University every semester for years and had my talk mapped out in "stories" already. There was: "Carolyn Birkes and My Very First Art Show Ever," and "On Fire or Ice-Berged? Do the Hardest Thing First. Scars. Kindness…" In all of the titles I saw in my mind, there was a point to be made or a point of gratitude to be expressed. It made sense to me in that form. There are defining moments, influential people and pivotal decisions. They are not all flashy and monumental. No matter how small, they were and are significant. So, right then and there, in the steam-and-dream state that I was in, I started to see how all of the things I had done, tried to do, spoke about and hoped to do, took the form of a book. By writing I could thank all the people who co-wrote those experiences with me. Things I had learned and inherited could have an extended life past me. Maybe I could inspire some people. Maybe I could figure out and finally *get* a few of the infinite things people have been trying to teach me along the way by writing it down. Things started to fall into place and the structure of this book was born then and there. Even the title was crystal clear, although I hesitated because it wasn't sophisticated in the least. So many people had asked me over the years to "tell the story." I had done it with my voice, gestures, an outline, tears and laughter in person. A new voice could be on paper, a book in print: "Holy Moly Mackeroly!" It is time.

During the course of 1999, I thought about the idea—a lot. Story titles were lining up like terra cotta Chinese soldiers buried for centuries underground that finally surfaced. On January 1, 2000, I started to write. I also started reading about writing: authors like Natalie Goldberg (*Writing Down the Bones*), Julia Cameron (*The Right to Write*), and Ann Lamotte (*Bird by Bird*)... A big question for me has always been: who has "the right to write"? I am not a trained writer and I am not a trained artist either. So, I am going to sit down and write a *Book* about my *Art* business. Right. That makes a whole lot of sense, doesn't it? I have made seemingly millions of things that I have sold, but I have not made millions of dollars. Now, someone like Mary Engelbreit (card artist/Designer), wouldn't you agree that *she* has the right to tell her story in a glossy, four-color hardcover book of how her "Life is Just a Chair of Bowlies" Empire came into being? But what about me? What *are* the bottom-line measures of success that grant a person credibility and not the uncomfortable label of being incredibly arrogant to think that your story is worth writing, let alone publishing? I did a lot of thinking and reflecting as well as working full-time and raising a family during that year of 1999. Was this my own next level of adventure, the next "shot" that I needed and wanted to take, ready or not here I come? Was this my time? Had I paid enough dues in the world of business and life in general?

"To be or not to be"... To think or not to think. To do or not to do: at one point there wasn't any question. As with most steps in my business-life, the bottom-line translates into "*just do it.*" Try. See what happens; see where it all leads. The chance is here if I want to take it. The door is open if I want to walk through it. I know that I absolutely do not want to look back years from now and regret the fact that I didn't try. Nothing will be lost except an opportunity if I don't dive in and write this thing. I want to be able to look in the mirror and in my kids' eyes. The year 2000 held a kind of promise in my heart and I used it to empower myself to higher levels of change and challenge. I picked up a pen.

On January 1, 2000, I started writing and writing and...writing. Do I have the *right to write*? Sure I do. Everybody does. I am the only one who can tell my story and you are the only one who can tell yours. With confidence under my belt and gratitude in my heart, I would like to say: "Thank you, Natalie, Julia and Ann." I have a lot to learn and, darn it, I'm going to learn by doing, not waiting and wishing.

I do tend to like to be good at the things I do. For many years that translated into holding back until I was accomplished enough at whatever it was before venturing out "in public." Show my *art* when I'm an Artist. Publish my *book* when I'm a Writer. It seems like it would be nice to be at the peak and pinnacle of some endeavor and then step into the spotlight—to be an expert, credentialed, acclaimed: *then* let people see me and whatever it is that I do. It has been a very rewarding experience to tear that thinking down in my life, rip it to shreds and toss it—to actively and happily set myself up as a beginner time and time again: A beginner stamper. A beginner printmaker. A beginner tilemaker. A beginner artist. A beginner Mom. A beginner businesswoman and writer. A beginner *human being*, for heaven's sake... to value the process as much, if not more, than attaining the goal itself. I love those National Geographic Magazine photos of the victory at the summit—Everest conquered against great odds. I love even more the whole story of getting up there—the process to the top. And when it is a group-shot, not just a lone victor, that is what I find to be especially heartwarming and moving. A smiling bunch of ecstatically weary, sun-and-ice wind-whipped folks, arms around each other, celebrating life, the quest, nature, the peak experience with a view on top of the world and of each other: that is the best of all. To share the big adventure—an extreme experience of camaraderie and triumph in the face of life-threatening dangers—your life and mind are changed forever. You made the decision to reach the summit and you did it—together.

In my business, *ImpressionsArt Designs,* I have had countless adventures on my own personal mountain-climb and would like to share them. None were life-threatening or dangerous, but many were scary and there were risks that challenged me from the inside out. These will be touched upon:

- Developing wholesale accounts with reps
- Working my own wholesale house accounts
- Applying for and entering Juried Fine Art Shows
- Selling retail at Craft Fairs in my own booth
- Placing artwork for sale on consignment
- Teaching beginning stamping and handcarving classes
- Being a founding and participating member of a Fine Arts Gallery
- Designing a logo for a state-wide organization
- Jurying into a highly regarded Fine Crafts organization as an Artisan
- Speaking as a guest-speaker/artist at the University and for other groups
- Going on TV as a local artist and giving arts/crafts demos
- Getting lots of media play in newspapers that advanced my business
- Making submissions to internationally distributed magazines / getting in
- Going back to school and taking my first college-level art class—at 45
- Having my artwork published as part of another person's book(s)
- Selling on-line with a website and personal domain name
- Writing and self-publishing my first book (this one)…

And the list goes on, interlaced with personal past experiences, inspirations and the sense that the journey and climb continue.

There is value to each of these venues and I am glad that I have explored them all, knowing that it is the beginning of much more to come. Some of these ventures are more comfortable for me than others; some are more lucrative than others. At times it has been confusing trying to balance and juggle all of these aspects of my business and have any semblance of a tranquil life in the process. Mostly it has been stimulating and fun. I like being my own boss. I like controlling the flow and making decisions that affect this aspect of my destiny, my business life. I truly love this lifestyle.

You might connect to one or more of these ideas and want to give it a try yourself. You may have an entirely different approach, and find it interesting to read about someone else's style. And this might just be another angle to the ever-expanding World of Stamp Arts and the Business of Arts and Crafts, and your curiosity is piqued. Wherever you and I are coming from, I am glad we are meeting here.

One of my many hopes in writing this book is to de-mystify the challenges that are real yet not insurmountable in the creation and development of a home business. Another book will direct you to make an appointment with a card buyer—I am going to tell you what happened when I did. Stories are the yarns and the colors on the tapestry of our personal lives. Stories weave us together as human beings. I want it tight and warm.

If you were to explore all eight Pueblos in Northern New Mexico, particularly Cochiti and Jemez, you would find a tradition of creating the image of a "Storyteller." The clay figure is a person seated on the ground with all of these little people gathered around to hear stories from a grandfather, grandmother, father, mother, teacher, elder. Many are depicted, each is unique. The Storyteller's mouth is usually open in an oval shape, eyes are oftentimes closed, head tipped back, and the listeners are attentive and gathered closely together, sometimes, literally, all over the Storyteller! Perhaps it is a legend being told, perhaps a song being sung, wisdom of the Ancient Ones, a lesson of life, the story of Great Medicine, the Great Spirit, of nature, tales to empower one's own spirit—a story to delight or a story to transport us to a realm of contemplation. The Storyteller is the central figure of the pottery scene; the Story is center-stage. Everyone is very present and awake—we are going to receive something and we don't want to miss a word. I listen to all storytellers. I believe that if we listen, "there are sermons in stones."

In my family we have always told stories. The Family Slide-Show/Home Movies Event happens whenever we make it to Santa Fe. We usually start late at night. The popcorn is *not* microwaved for these events, since we will only allow the genuine article. Every slide gets a response of some sort, from a running commentary to howls, inside jokes to yawns-to-get-on-with-it and on to the next shot. The visuals create the basis for what becomes a very long night that goes way past the time it takes for the old slide projector to cool down. We are just getting warmed up. The Pichenotte Board and the Cribbage Board may come out. The stories that are more in the Independent Film Genre get rolling. And the funny thing is: we don't have slides, movies or videos of these—they are strictly oral tradition exclusives. Yet they are so vivid in our minds that I swear I can see them more clearly than if they were home movies. There are *The Classics* that are always included: My brothers David and Norman tell: "How the Crazed Mad Dog of Bristol was Hot on Our Heels the Day of Our First Major Bike Expedition," followed by Norman's "How the Bear Almost Ate Me and My First Wife in the Tent at Smoky Mountain National Park; She Snored and Didn't Even *Wake Up!*" We will visit the stories of little Michael, the cutest Army Recruit in U.S. History, 5-year-old Paul dressed up as Uncle Louie and his stints as the family therapist seated at his "Lucy's Psychiatric Booth." We will re-visit slides of Gloria with the Ringo Starr haircut at Gillette Castle and of the *entire* family disastrously early one Christmas morning in the 60's, all looking like rejects from the bar scene in *Star Wars*. Only when I became a parent myself could I relate to how wigged-out my parents looked. How many times can you tell the same story and still have it be funny? I don't see an end in sight for any of ours. My business stories are simply an extension of this family storytelling trait. Believe me, laughing is good.

A "book about business" doesn't usually conjure up the image of reflections and memoirs in the narrative sense. Usually we would think of a business text as being more in the checklists/formulas mode. My angle is more along the lines of the fact that my business *itself* has its own story: the human-face-side. That is the alive-side for me, the pulse. It is not mechanical. It is a way of living and thinking. My business grew with me, of course, yet in some ways it has a life of its own, with unpredictable factors and other people woven in. My children are connected to me and at the same time are absolutely unique and independent from me. When my business was born in 1993, I had absolutely no idea what was being set in motion... one rubber stamp and then three...

I have woven together "Reflections on the Business of Art and the Art of Life." There are thoughts, memories, struggles, victories, flubs, hopes, dreams and my ever-present gratitude to people who live lives that I am seeking to learn from, those precious folks whose sparkle makes a statement to the world that Life *itself* is meant to be our ultimate work of art. This is my tribute to them.

Having friends who have also made the decision to start different art businesses is a point of comfort and inspiration. They have gifts in store for you in this book as well.

Please do not expect a chronological order in the writing sequence, but know that the overall thrust is the development of my business, *ImpressionsArt Designs*, from the time I started out in 1993, to the writing of this book in 2000-2001. I grab memories from the way-back machine and fuse them to situations that have presented themselves during the course of these years. Conversations that happened a few minutes ago, as well as ten or thirty years ago, are always a challenge to re-create, trying to keep the words and the heart behind the words as close to the original as possible. I have tried.

Seeing this book as a collection of self-contained short stories will serve you well.

It is not a tiny book for several reasons. I learned to use the computer so that I could write it and this is the format I learned in. I wanted a book that would fit in nicely with my other arts and crafts books and magazines. Finally, I wanted room around the edges of the text. Add your own quotes, notes, doodles, stamp art, etc. if you like that sort of thing. Personalize it, use it, work with it. I never did envision this in a "pocket edition."

As for sentence structure, I've been told that I oftentimes speak in incomplete sentences. No. Really? Can't imagine. I noticed it about myself when I started to write and the computer kept doing this squiggly red-underlining thing telling me something was definitely wrong that sounded perfectly fine to me. Sometimes I took the computer's advice and more often than not I clicked "ignore all." I write like I think like I talk—a kind of stream-sequence. Commas do not always get the attention they might deserve. I am less interested in a formal literary look and correctness and more interested in a conversational feel and tone. This is memoir, not a term paper. All ye English majors and grammar fanatics: beware and cringe or lighten up and have a good time. Let's play!

Having started with a quote, I'd like to wrap this up with two more. From a hockey player to a holy person to an entrepreneur, from Gretzky to Gandhi to Conrad Hilton, when something is true, it is true in the raucous arena, the hushed ashram, a luxury hotel, or your own home. True things resonate in our hearts. They are a universal experience. Get real. Get enlightened. Get rich. Get inspired. But whatever we do, let's get *on* with it.

If, at the end of the day and the end of this book you whispered to yourself even once "I can *do* it!" and you actually go and do it, whatever *it* means to you... *bravo!*... for you.

You may never know what results will come from your action,
but if you do nothing, there will be no result.   - *Gandhi*

Success seems to be connected with action. Successful people keep moving.
They make mistakes but they don't quit.   - *Conrad Hilton*

HOLY MOLY MACKEROLY!
…. what on earth does *that* mean?

Growing up, long, *very long* ago according to my kids, before words like *awesome*, tight and sweet, cool and neat, even before groovy, far-out and other assorted retro-speak were in vogue, this little Connecticut Yankee (New Mexican wanna-be) that I was, actually spoke French before I spoke English. I think that is pretty "cool." Language has always fascinated me. At times it has frustrated me as well, especially when, as a little person, I moved into the confusing world of learning English around the age of five and made a tossed salad out of my sentences. "Waterfall" became "l'eau-l'eau fall" in my way of thinking, and when corrected, promptly explained to my taken-aback mother that "my mouth doesn't talk that way!" so *there*. And to this day I delight in exploring my poetic license with French/English phrases that stretch the rules and challenge the ears.

As words poured into my world, some were particularly fun, like "holy moly!" and "holy mackerel!" when things were *very* way cool, even though I never could and still can't figure out what is holy about mackerel—I gave my mackerel a halo, regardless. These words were fun to say and they got your point across.

Eventually, over time, I did grow up (still working on it), and studied French formally in school, speaking English for the everyday-talk. In first grade at St. Ann's, I took a little hand-held mirror to French Class to study my own mouth, practicing those lovely rolling "r"s and the different "u"s and "oo"s. The mirror routine was pretty much unnecessary in my case since I already had that stuff down since crib-time. Later on, Latin, Ancient Greek, a few Japanese Kanji and Chinese characters made their way into my word-world and my love for Ancient Words from all cultures was born and grew with me. In time, at age 36 and then 40, my kids were born and in no time at all they started talking, rarely stop, and it gets more interesting by the day. We talk, laugh, yell, tell jokes and stories, play with silly words, make some up even, and then one day it happened…

We were walking home from school and my son Brandon was telling a great story about his day in a very funny way. The details are lost to me now, but I do remember blurting out immediately after laughing:

"HOLY MOLY MACKEROLY!!!" It fit the occasion and stuck in our memories.

Nobody thought it was too weird, at least no one said anything in the moment, and now it is part of our family's vocabulary—here's to passing it along. During the course of developing my business, I have had my "HMM moments," like the day the Smithsonian called me, being an excellent example; getting an e-mail from *Somerset Studio* Magazine saying that my first submission "knocked (their) socks off" being another.

"Talking business" can be serious stuff. Of all the titles this book could possibly have, I chose this one so that we could all lighten things up and have some fun from the very beginning. You may love it, you may hate it, but you probably won't forget it.

I hope that in your reading of my storytelling, in the process of doing that along with reflecting on your own stories, you will find yourself saying:

"Holy Moly Mackeroly!" with me, once or twice along the way.
And please, don't forget to smile.

Part One

beginnings

"Let's start at the very beginning, a very good place to start.
When you read you begin with A-B-C
When you sing you begin with DO-RE-MI…"

(*Rodgers and Hammerstein*)
from: *The Sound of Music*

When you start a business, when you start anything at all, you begin with… a thought.

Whether it is as simple as starting the day, or as complicated as starting a new life, including everything in between, the beginning point is in our minds. "I have this idea…" That original thought, insight, inspiration, insane impulse, whatever you want to call it—*that* is the seed of creation. It may come as a bolt of lightning or in the mist of a dream. It may seem like divine intervention that tastes like enlightenment, or it may feel like a rush of madness that needs tempering. What we do with that seed—where we plant it and how we nurture it in the very beginning—is extremely significant.

When our vision is crystal clear and we are filled with confidence one day, it is disconcerting when the fog descends and we find ourselves afraid the next. Beginnings can be bold and dramatic; they can also be gentle. Dealing with fear, listening to "first thoughts," carefully directing them—these make for beginnings that develop into change.

The silent fear of failure can be the single thought that stops us dead in our tracks. The hope for change (notice I did not say *success*) can empower us to take one step. No matter how small it is, that is a beginning.

A thousand mile journey begins with one step. – *Chinese* Proverb

Start-up Costs:

- 3 Rubber Stamps @ $ 5.00 ea. $15.00
- 1 Ink Pad $ 7.00
- 1 Piece of Good Paper $ 3.00
- 1 Pair of Scissors (pre-owned)   ————
                              TOTAL $25.00

The guts to *just try it*.................*priceless*!

Many times I've read articles about the start-up costs of home businesses in different fields, and I am generally blown away and wonder how on earth anyone can manage the investment and handle the risk. We are usually talking in the hundreds, and more often, many thousands of dollars. So, how on earth can I realistically come up with the outrageously low dollar amount of $25.00 to start-up a stamp business? First of all, because I already owned the scissors, and well, simply enough, because I did it.

For those of you who have never stamped before, this may sound reasonable and quite manageable. For those of you who own so many stamps that you have separate insurance policies on your collections and have serious addictions amassing stamping tools and toys, this sounds nuts. *Nobody* can start a stamp business selling things that you have made with only $25.00 worth of "equipment." A heat gun costs more than that. I would be more than willing to bet that for some people, with all of the incredible resources at your fingertips, you still don't think that you have anywhere near enough of whatever it would take to even *think* about starting a business, let alone doing it. Am I right? Or close? Here is your chance to think again—and perhaps, to relax a bit, too.

Whenever there is the prospect of something new on the horizon, a number of things start popping up, usually all at the same time. Some are good and helpful; others are not. The vision, creative energy, the adrenalin that makes it hard to sleep with all the hope and excitement pounding in our heads and emotions, these are the stuff of dreams. It gets contagious, too, as you tiptoe out and start telling very close friends your very wild ideas. "I have this idea…what do you think?" (Make sure you ask very close, very safe friends.)

Here's the hard part: along with the fire of enthusiasm, something else tends to start creeping in: fear. A big one, in terms of starting your own business has to be the money-factor. Is this going to cost so much to start-up that the risk is more than I can take on? It is a fair and responsible question that needs to be asked. The problem is the answer: we might inflate the basic needs to get to the starting line, thereby throwing everything into a tailspin of self-doubt and discouragement and decide to never even give it a try. This may well be "Roadblock #1" for you, and I would personally like to pick up the darn thing and get it out of your way—that's what friends are for. If you start simply, it doesn't have to cost a fortune. (Enjoy watching the conversations you have with yourself over this topic.)

Sometimes I find it hard to believe that I actually did what I did, knowing that I jumped in when I was far from ready. I also know that if I had waited until I was ready, I'd still be waiting. There is a balance to be achieved between the ideal and the practical and each person finds it and lives with it. I'd like to share how this all got started for me.

You already possess everything necessary to become great. – *Crow* Proverb

The "way-back machine"

…the earliest beginnings of my business…

Mr. Peabody and his boy Sherman, the dog and kid combo on the *Rocky and Bullwinkle Comedy Hour*, cruised history as observers and participants with a tendency to tweak events and impart a bit of insight at the end—no famous quote would ever quite be the same. I'd like to borrow their "way-back machine," cruise a bit, and promise not to tweak. The moral of this story is: "The smallest step gets you to a new place. So take it."

The first entrepreneurial enterprise of my life: 2-cent paper airplanes. My brother David and I made and decorated the planes, set up our "booth" in front of our house on Center Street in Bristol, Connecticut, and sold our wares on Sunday mornings after Mass so we could catch the church traffic. It was great. People would be sitting in their cars waiting for the traffic light to change and we would be making sales. The going rate was 2-cents, so when we were given a nickel or sometimes even a quarter and told to "keep the change," we were in financial heaven. Hey, some of those planes had glitter work and some mighty fine graphic designs—we deserved every cent we got.

Once you get the taste of selling your own handmade "things," you want more. Paper airplanes were the appetizers. Over the years, I would try a little of this and a little of that as far as selling went—nothing was serious or full-time—more for enjoyment than anything else. In my twenties, I made God's eyes (Ojos de Dios) out of yarn and whittled sticks, selling them on consignment in Santa Fe shops on Canyon Road. In my early thirties, my husband Gary and I ran a flea market booth to make money for a project in Guatemala—he brought back hand-woven clothing, bracelets, purses and other accessories that were handmade. He set up an area in the booth where we could design and create customized jewelry using beautiful beads from Greece. We came up with the name *Folklands* for this mini-business. All proceeds were donated—I loved doing it.

Later in that decade, we were living in upstate New York in a Hobbit cottage and I was the director of a daycare center. I had another business brainstorm. In my spare time, I made miniature grapevine wreaths and sold them locally. And then one fateful day, it happened. Gary came home with a little paper bag in his hand and said: "Here. This is for you. What do you think of this idea?"

Always up for a surprise or gift, I opened the tiny bag and pulled out a small block of wood with a picture of a heart/wreath on it. "What's this for?" I asked, trying to be nice and grateful. "Take out the other things inside. You'll see." Reaching in again, out came two flat plastic boxes, one green, and the other one red. "What are these for?" I brilliantly asked again. "It's a rubber stamp and these are the colored inkpads. Here, I'll show you. You just tap the stamp a few times and then stamp the design on the paper. It's easy. I thought maybe we could use this idea so you could make the hang-tags for the grapevine wreaths…" At that very moment, I got my first rubber stamp demonstration and class from my husband in our Hobbit cottage among the trees. Life would never be the same…

The stamp worked perfectly for the price tags, primitive as they were. At the daycare center, my friend and assistant Naoko, just happened to happen upon stamps at the local crafts store, independent from my close encounter. During naptime for the children, we both brought in our few stamps one day and had to laugh at how much we didn't know about this new hobby. She had gotten hooked and had a few more stamps than I did. Our afternoon routine included "teacher creativity activity." Naptimes for the kids quickly became stamping times for us. We were helping each other understand the most basic fundamentals. All of our supplies for our new hobby easily fit into one plastic shoebox.

A few Christmas stamps were added to my one wreath. Naoko and I made Holiday cards for friends and family, humble efforts for sure. I decided to buy a couple of stamps for Mother's Day in the spring and stuck my toe into the business waters—a handful of cards put on a cafeteria table. They sold, but that was as far as I wanted to take it at that time. It was going to stay a "hobby" as far as I was concerned.

Enter my Mom on a visit from New Mexico. We had a great time and then as her tradition is to give me a fun gift at the end of a visit, she asked me what I would like…? "Let's see, you know, it would be fun to have a few new stamps, how about *Southwest* ones to commemorate your visit?" "Sounds great to me. Get us to the store and we'll get shopping." This was in upstate New York, the land of George Washington-did-this-and-that-here-there-and-everywhere, so my request for Southwest stamps was met with an interesting stare. "Do you have a catalogue that I can look at and order from?" Sure enough. I ordered three from a very small selection, and unbelievably to me now, one was actually a very cliché coyote howling at the moon. Hey, it was as close as I could get to the Southwest at the time. It seemed like it took forever for those stamps to arrive.

Mom was back home in Santa Fe by the time they did come in. We chatted on the phone, ideas flew back and forth and then a bolt of lightning struck—bookmarks. I was going to take those three little stamps and make bookmarks. I bought one sheet of nice quality paper from an art store and started cutting—with scissors. My son's hole-punch worked great at the top. I stamped the three images in a vertical row—dink/dink/dink. I didn't know what else to do except to make a ribbon "thing" at the top. A little marker touch-up for color was added at the last minute. I counted them—there were eighteen. With a makeshift piece of clear plastic for a protective cover, I lined them up on the table and felt proud. Handmade Southwest Bookmarks—they were wrapped and shipped to my Mom. This is the Way-back Machine of all way-back machines for me. Those simple bookmarks were about to launch an enterprise. I really didn't have a clue.

My Mom's boss, Jo Glicksberg, ordered three-dozen bookmarks for the La Fonda Newsstand, our first account. We gratefully received many lessons from her along the way about business forms, reps, and other helpful topics such as business in general. Jo's big word was always "refine." You get things rolling, learn how to improve, *refine* and advance. There is no way to put a value on that very first businessperson who says, "Yes. I want your product. I like it enough to commit money and retail space to showcase it." There were many more to come, but only one can be the first. Thank you, Jo, so very very much. You saw more than what you were looking at, those very first attempts…

Three little Southwest stamps were not, however, going to get us very far, so the hunt was on: find new stamps, quickly. The stamp store in Santa Fe is in the middle of the downtown plaza area and has a very long name that, I believe, has been somewhat abbreviated to *Guadalupe's*. Over the years, the store has changed hands a number of times, but my connection goes back to the 1993 era. Thank goodness for the kind crew who were willing to help me out by stamping dozens of samples so that I could order long distance. My Mom was the go-between for everything including my first stamping lessons, a kind of correspondence course, you might say. The stamp store ladies would give my Mom mini-lessons, product descriptions and samples to illustrate the points and I would learn and order based on the information I was receiving. A heat gun came as a surprise out of the blue and sure beat using the toaster in the kitchen for embossing. My birthday and Christmas presents for quite a while were stamps and more stamping supplies than I knew what to do with. We were building a business. In time, I would connect to magazines, catalogs, books, classes and individuals who knew a lot, but these humble roots were how a fledgling business was sustained and expanded for quite some time. Remember: your viewpoint is the major determining factor for a beginning point.

The original eighteen bookmarks were used as samples for a very short time, since one store insisted on buying *those*, right then and there. My Mom's personal rep technique was to put the bookmarks in a non-descript paper bag, tuck it under her arm, walk into a shop and asked if the stationary buyer "might like to see what my daughter makes…" That was one quiet technique—effective, too. The pace of development at that time was an extremely long and slow learning curve. Looking back on those first stamping efforts that were actually, unbelievably being *purchased* of all things, I cringe with delighted amazement that anything at all got off the ground. The fact that there were no other handmade bookmarks at that time around Santa Fe meant that we had found a niche, especially since great bookstores abound in the area. Add to that my mother's enthusiasm and willingness to walk around with that paper bag, coupled with my willingness to jump in there, ready or not, and the ingredients were there for Stage One.

Did I intend to start a handmade card business? Did I have this big plan in place to quit my job and start an art business? No, I really didn't in the beginning. The idea of making bookmarks was an extension to my very small miniature wreath "business." I wanted to have hobbies on the side that could generate a little extra money that I could put aside for my children's future. As I started to get more and more accounts with the bookmarks, I let the wreaths go. When I acted upon advice from my "professional" rep (later on) to try handmade cards since the market was much broader, I was beginning to see the bigger possibilities. The bookmarks receded, cards became the point of emphasis, and at that point, I began to entertain the notion that perhaps I should consider doing this as my "day job." It was a gradual transition, not a dramatic leap or plunge.

Having a job at the daycare center provided stability of sorts and a steady income situation. I love being with children. Having my own was a dream come true. What it all came down to was the fact that I wanted a home business so that I could be with my sons. A lifestyle choice was placed before me when my husband supported me in my desire to try and make it work, this home-based art business idea. It meant sacrifice, it meant we would have to find our way in the dark, so we each lit a candle and started walking. I know that we have no regrets. My children have me home and that makes us all happy. They have told me how proud they are of the life we have built—together.

The course of my business is similar to a meandering river: it keeps moving from the source. There have been high points and low, white water rapids and dry parched times, yet all the time there is this sense that we are going somewhere, getting to some destination, come crazy hell or high water. The farther I go and the longer I stick with it, the more scenery along the way and the more I can clearly see gets carved out of me and comes to the surface. It is like the gorges and canyons surrounding my own personal, internal Rio Grande. This life path cuts a swath of Grand Canyon in me. It is not so much the dramatic vistas the tourists love to photograph—more like the view from the base of the canyon, looking up and seeing all the layers cut through and exposed in the colors of time, quiet in the evening light. You look up, you look back, and it is a total wonder.

"You're kidding... I made that?"

"In the Beginning there were 18 bookmarks, and it was good.
And so it was, the First Stage..."

And there were a heck of a lot of stages after that—they were good, too. At one point, someone said, "Watch out! Whatever doesn't move, she will stamp. If it does move, she'll catch it, pin it down and then stamp it." True enough. Wanting to spread my wings and experiment with my own creation story, I was simultaneously timid about the ever-widening "canvases" I was challenging myself to work on. It took some time to get to the Second Stage. It is called "product development." Here's how that unfolded...

My bookmarks measured 2¼ x 7½-inches, so my graphic design world was that size for quite some time—over a year at least. That's pretty small. I carried around a blank bookmark in my purse in order to make sure that any stamp I considered buying would squeeze into that space. It had to do that—I was committed to those dimensions. Thousands of pieces of cardstock had been cut to that size and thousands of custom-made plastic sleeves had been purchased as well. Everything was lined up in order by color, stacked in plastic shoeboxes. I didn't have any play money. The stamps I bought were the stamps I needed and they needed to *fit*.

My rep and friend, Gini, called one day and said, "Gloria, Tommy and Kittie at Marcy Street Card Shop told me to tell you that they love your bookmarks and your designs. They made another order yesterday. They said that there is, however, a limited market for them. They would like you to consider *cards*. Please think about it. There is a huge card market compared to bookmarks. It is wide-open, lots of motion, constant turnover. When you decide to do it and make some cards, they would like to be your first customers and carry them in their shop. Marcy Street is big time cards... let me know..."

Cards. Oh, my. I hadn't even thought of that, I really hadn't. Not for selling on a big scale. I had made cards for family and friends since I was a kid, but now, for a *store*? One time I made a dozen Mother's Day cards, put them on a table in a cafeteria with a little sign saying: "$2.00 each, leave money in the basket." To my surprise, at the end of the week there was $24.00 in the basket. It was nice. I bought a few more stamps, but a card *business*? This was an entirely different matter. I took some time to think about it...

The bookmark thing was going along okay. Orders came and I was able to get them made by working part-time late at night, continuing with my full-time day job as director of a child care center. The supplies I needed, I had. It was a comfortable little hobby that happened to make a little extra money each month. Cards... *CARDS?* What size are they talking about? Where do I get the paper for them? The envelopes? And the biggest, most pressing question that I had was: "How on earth am I going to fill up all that *space*?" I pulled out cards that I had and measured them. The size I liked best was the standard A-6 as I would later discover it was called. The face of the card was 4½ x 6¼—that's *big* when you put it side-by-side with my bookmarks. I don't know about this...

Anyway, there's nothing to lose by trying a couple of things to see if I could come up with ideas. After cutting some paper and folding it poorly, I took out my collection of teeny tiny stamps and dinked away. Oh, brother. They were awful. Plain white paper with these little floater things—not at all cohesive. The darn paper was just too *big*. It looked stupid. But the challenge was on and I could see my gears turning internally. Business. A card business. That thought had crossed my mind at different points in my life. It had always remained that: just a thought. Now there were these people in Santa Fe saying that if I did actually *do* it, they were interested. There's power in that. It propelled me at least to the point of sending my first efforts once again to my Mom, first rep and general source of inspiration and support. She gave a kindly review of the first efforts and immediately started sending me handstamped images from the local stamp store there in Santa Fe—possibilities—they were *big*. It seemed that we were heading straight into Stage Two. I wondered about it and knew it was right at the same time.

My family moved to New Mexico with the idea of being there for about a year in order to develop my business, giving it my best shot before heading to the Midwest. This card thing was now apparently the way to go. The stamp collection expanded along with the stamp size and my mind. If you can believe it, I was just finding out that there were publications like *Rubberstampmadness* out there, and I had not as yet seen any books on stamping cards, etc. Pretty isolated and insulated. I knew where to get my paper and my plastic sleeves and now I was discovering new and bigger dimensions.

One day down the road of time, I happened to be in Albuquerque at Ta-lin, a Chinese Food Market with my Mom shopping for noodles. Hot ones: the kind of spice that makes my nose and my children run: *that* kind. Perusing the shelves near the noodle department, my eyes caught the glint of gold—like gold leaf. Picking up several packages, I noticed that these papers were bundled in packs of 100 sheets of various shapes and sizes. They reminded me of Origami sheets in a way, but they were not all squares. These were called "Joss paper." It was so cheap, too. I loved everything about it. But what is Joss paper and what do you do with it?

Years later I would end up buying this paper by the carton or the pound, but in the beginning I just wanted to know what it was for. I found a kind and patient Chinese woman in the store who was willing to take the time to share with me and explain at least as much as she felt I could handle and receive. I watched her carefully as she spoke; the words and phrases were measured initially. If I could take one level of explanation, she would move on. I was very open and the more "spiritual" she got, the more into it I was, so I got a lot of information for an outsider, I think. She spoke of Ancestral Worship and showed us how this paper was actually used as "money" in special ceremonies. Sometimes it was folded into paper "boats," and hundreds of them were stacked on top of each other and then set on fire. That sounded meaningful and dramatic to me! There were Joss papers for many purposes, occasions, ceremonies, rooms of the house, even Joss paper that could be used as clothing. I was fascinated.

Now that I had a general sense of what it was, the next question was whether or not I could use it in art projects, such as making cards and bookmarks. Would it be multi-culturally correct or would I be sacrilegious to use such paper in such a commercial way? She laughed and said: "Go ahead and use the papers for your art! That's a great idea! You will have good fortune if you do. And don't worry too much. There is a restaurant in Santa Fe that orders these Joss papers by the case in order to use them as the paper under their fancy desserts. When you make cards, come back and show us. We would love to see what you are doing." "I will. Thank you so much." (I did go back—great response.)

I bought a number of packages, still not really sure of what it was that I had in mind. The whole ride back to Santa Fe, I was thinking. I wondered about two things:
- Having never used any paper other than straight cardstock, I wasn't sure if the inks would bleed all over the place after stamping.

- Having never layered any papers before, I wasn't sure about glue. I did have paper cement to try out…

At that point the only thing to do is to sit down and make a card. So I did it. I glued down the Joss paper, held my breath, inked up a stamp, put it down, pressed hard, lifted up—and the result was wonderful! It worked and I was hooked. I knew it—my mother knew it. This was the beginning of the second stage, the card business.

I sent that original card to my friend Hannah. It was a thank you card. She got excited by it and sent me a thank you card for the thank you card. Hers was saved and so was mine from what I heard. That kind of encouragement and enthusiasm were catalysts to keep on going. Somebody actually liked my card!

The ink didn't bleed, but the glue wasn't the best. It just so happened that on the very same day I made that first "real card," I went out to check the mail and the latest *Rubberstampmadness* magazine was waiting for me. Sitting at the table, I happened to open to the page with an advertisement for the Daige Rollataq adhesive system. It sounded like the solution to my glue problem. I called the art supply store Artisan on Canyon Road and sure enough, they carried the handheld version. It was in my hands within the hour and gluing to me, from that point on, meant Rollataq. My styles of bookmarks changed, but more importantly, I could now envision making cards.

This all may be much-ado-about-not-so-much. This is one very elongated story about getting from one little product to another slightly different, slightly bigger product. It's true that it was this labored. The point is that it was pivotal, and many steps in my business were taken in increments as slow and labored as that transition. I felt at times like Indiana Jones contemplating taking that step over the chasm. Once he committed to it, the optical illusion was broken and he could see the rock bridge. Before that, it was a matter of a leap of faith with a lot more at stake than my going from bookmarks to cards. As silly as it may sound, the bigger "canvas" was a challenge for me. It proved to be foundational in contemplating future hurdles. I would tell myself over and over again: "It's just a bigger piece of paper—*jump*." "It's just fabric or clay instead of paper…"

A selection of some of my original card samples is kept in a three-ring binder. I look them over from time to time. I smile. It's a good thing to do now and then. Revisit where you've been and reflect on how far you've come. Have a laugh and heave a big sigh of relief that there were folks kind enough to buy your things along the way. I can guarantee that a year from now when I look back on what I am doing now in my business it will be a similar experience. How kind of *Somerset Studio* to publish all those *rocks*.

A couple of years into the card-making phase, I was in Santa Fe on a business trip to write up orders on my house accounts and also to meet as many of the card buyers as I could. My rep would describe people to me, but meeting them was much better. I made appointments for my accounts and decided to make casual visits to hers, since I wouldn't be writing up orders, just saying hello. It was going well.

One day, however, it got glitchy. I dropped in for a friendly visit, and saw that my whole business idea had been hijacked by someone I thought was a friend as well as a customer—a tough story coming later. After buying a stamp or two to make myself feel better, I almost called it quits for the day, and then decided, oh, what the heck, I'm downtown, why not pop over to Marcy Street Card Shop around the corner and see if I can meet the owners. Maybe one of them will be there. My rep always speaks so highly of them. Probably I can't lose by finishing up my day with a visit there.

I dashed around the corner and then started dragging my feet. Maybe this wasn't my lucky day, maybe they weren't there, wouldn't have time if they were, should have made an appointment; it's rude to just walk in... *Just open the door and face it*. Nice shop. Wonderful shop! Great cards... whoa, some of mine right over there. That's a nice feeling. "Hello, my name is Gloria Page, I'm a cardmaker and I was hoping to meet..." "*Gloria!* Gloria Page from Missouri, I knew it must be you! I am Kittie and this is my husband Tommy. We love your artwork! It sells so well here in the shop, your prices for handmade cards are so reasonable so we can carry a big variety. Come on, do you have a minute to chat in the backroom?" I was moved and at the same time a little worried because I hadn't made an appointment, and I knew from my rep that these people were extremely busy and packed their days full. My idea was to shake hands and leave. I didn't want to take their time so I said that. Well, enough of that. She was so happy that we were finally meeting face-to-face and there was time to chat. There we were squished in with tons of products from all over the planet. Now I could really look at her. This was the person who started something very big for me. We are sitting here together.

I started to speak: "Kittie, I came today because I just had to thank you personally for buying bookmarks right from the beginning and for being the person to encourage me to make cards..." All of a sudden I started to cry, and she put her arm around my shoulder and let me get through what I needed to say. "Why did you buy those first things I made? They were terrible, really. Looking at all the beautiful things in your shop, how come you bought mine before I was ready?" She had tears, too, and said, "We didn't look at what you were making and just see what was there. We saw where you were headed, your potential, and we wanted to be part of that, and help you on your way." Then we cried together. A few funny stories, some inspired card ideas, a hug, and I was on my way once again. I sure was glad to be in Santa Fe that day. It was a good decision to turn the corner.

Some business relationships are simply that: all business. That's fine. Some are difficult and others are delightful. It is one big patchwork quilt of experiences. Kittie's patch in my quilt shimmers. I try as much as possible to keep my heart open to such possibilities, knowing that they are rare, but wanting to be 100% present when they do happen. The spirit of what she gave and taught me that day is something I hope to be able to give and be for other people. To believe in and actively engage in supporting each other's potential, the more we all gain. We nurture this fabulous garden of blossoms exploding in all their glory right before our very eyes. It isn't all "just business." It's life.

Card production started to catch up with bookmarks, surpassed them, and became the main menu. Then I "glorified" the cards, put them in frames, 5x7 and 8x10, mind you, reminding myself "it's just a bigger piece of paper." More reading, more exposure to the stamp art world and art world in general, inspired me to experiment more, to stretch my thinking and creative horizons. It wasn't so much a matter of taking these veritable giant leaps anymore. Progressive steps were the replacement. When people ask me "What do you make?" or "What do you do?" I wonder how to answer. It's not just cards anymore. There are quite a few etceteras such as: jewelry, handmade tiles, cloth Masu boxes, fabric scrolls, clay ornaments, wood magnets, New Mexican tinwork, hand-dyed / block-printed scarves, ceramics... all with a wide range of designs within each of those categories. I constantly create my own handcarved tools and there is no lack of ideas.

One time a while back I was visiting my friend Betty Scott and we were jamming some ideas about a new product line that I envisioned calling "Ancient Words." It was getting very late, but we were on a roll, so we moved our discussion upstairs to a room that has tons of books, Aboriginal art, crystals, carved gourds and stories galore attached to *everything*. We were looking at some Sanskrit text, it was about 1:30 in the morning, I was looking around the room, glanced up high and saw this wonderful long piece of paper with Chinese and Japanese characters printed on it. Beautiful paper. Nice design overall. "Betty, speaking of Ancient Words, that piece up there is really nice. Where did you get it? What's the story behind that one?" "Gloria, are you serious? *You* made it— don't you remember?" "You're *kidding…I* made that?" I reached up and took it down off the shelf… sure enough, I did.

We laughed and the story came back. Betty had asked me months before to stamp out some of my Oriental character stamps on any old paper with translations—I couldn't possibly do that. Instead, I layered handmade papers and made a gift out of it. But I had forgotten all about it… Strange to be complimenting yourself in the middle of the night.

Here is a suggestion for whatever it is worth: take photos along the way. Not of every single thing you make, but catch a lot of it on film—at least categories of creations, booth set-ups, whatever you might want to look back on in time. It is invaluable to me to have these four little 4x6 photo albums, basically chronological, chock full of pictures of things I actually made with my own two hands. I am shocked when I open them up and look through. "I can't believe I made all that stuff." I get reminders and inspiration. When I am kind of dry in the creativity arena, I open them up. When I feel stuck, looking at photos from times when I wasn't stuck does help. At other times, it is just nice to remember making the artwork and wondering now where on earth, literally, it all is because it sure isn't in my house anymore. I hope it made people happy along the way.

Once you make the leap and start making "new things," it can become more than an interesting experiment, play or relaxing escape—it can become a way of life. The card business took off and when it got to the point of making sometimes 10,000 cards a year, then I wanted to always check in with myself and make sure that I wasn't going to get bored or boxed into a new world view: the size of the face of a greeting card. I would buy bigger and bigger frames for art shows. Those sold very well. I decided to try cloth scrolls and made those bigger over the years, too. It was like a process of stretching my perspective. I had to carve images to fit the expanded canvases, so I didn't buy 4x6-inch blocks anymore; I bought 12x18-inch instead. As for styles, I decided to have fun with that as well. I purposely made designs that I figured no one in Missouri would buy just to watch what would happen. Sure enough, those would be the first to go at the gallery! I decided to try and fit into my stereotyped concept of a more classical Midwest style which was a stretch for me and those things did well, too, and I received a bit of teasing for going in so many different directions at the same time. It has kept things fresh for me. I made a goal: I was determined to sell at least one of every different kind of product idea I ever came up with, and I did it. It was a good challenge that taught me a lot about breaking my own concepts of what people like and what sells where.

I still make bookmarks from time to time but not for wholesale. There is this new style that I developed using split bamboo and mat board. After thousands of the originals, I needed to move on, so they evolved. It's only natural to go to new places.

The art of life lies in a constant readjustment
to our surroundings.   – *Okakura Kubuzo*

Art sparks...influences and impressions along the way

From the little spark may burst a mighty flame.   - *Dante*

Biography on A&E is it for me—I am glued to the TV. I would never in a million years get the *Biography channel* because it would take on addictive proportions in my life and then I wouldn't have a life myself. I would sit all day—fascinated and vegetated. It is absolutely true that "every life has a story," and I love hearing it. Ever since reading Ann Frank's diary and Helen Keller's story when I was very young, biographies have held a grip on my heart and imagination. The past, the history behind a face or an image, is always different than what I would have expected. The twists and turns, pain and triumphs, seeing someone's baby pictures, all of it pulls me into another life. I sit there laughing, crying, wondering how someone could be so brave, creative, stupid, deadly, sick, powerful, beautiful, loving, visionary, generous, divine... or just plain human.

There I sit, transfixed, watching myself react to all that I am watching and simultaneously making comparisons to my own life. It's as if someone else's life is bouncing off the screen back in my own face—a mirror. If I am moved to tears by what I am seeing, I'd better start living a more "moving" life myself. If I am horrified by obvious greed and selfishness, I'd better watch my priorities. When I am awestruck by sheer courage, then how about it, Gloria? Have a brave heart and get a grip on those points of panic that do you in periodically. How would I look on the screen?

The stories that I particularly enjoy involve a person defying odds: going someplace from nowhere. I am impressed when great success is achieved by sheer determination and force of will, not tidy, predictable, comfortable paths: dire circumstances be damned! The attitude of: "I am going to make myself into somebody no matter what." I absolutely love that kind of person. Unconventional and quiet triumphs intrigue me and keep me awake even though I may be beat at the end of my day, folding laundry to justify the fact that I am watching too much TV. (If my kids find out, they will give me a hard time like I give them a hard time. "You are brain dead, Mom!") Getting famous or infamous enough to be featured on "Biography" is not necessarily because you were such an ideal human being. But every life can have at least one lesson for another life. I listen for my lessons.

I have been influenced by art and especially by people actively engaged in the Art of Life. We all have. It is called being alive from what I can gather. Choosing to be awake and interacting with our world puts us in touch with beauty if we are open to perceive it and willing to be touched by it. The simplest daily things deeply affect me. There are "art sparks" flying around everywhere, igniting our hearts and imaginations. I am watching.

At one point I entertained the thought of what it would be like to fabricate my autobiography—to fantasize away. I spent a couple of minutes trying to come up with ideas; it proved to be a total waste of time. My story is mine and that is good enough.

I actually have an *art business* at this time in my life. That is so outrageous to me and yet it is also the most natural thing I can think of at the same time. I have asked myself to reflect on what were some of the art influences in my life that I am aware of. Why do I have this thing for Oriental Art and why do I love combining Southwest petroglyph imagery with it? Why does it work so well? I love folk art and crafts. Where did that get started? As I go butterflying around the garden of my memories, I plan to catch glimpses of people and events that shaped my direction—a few of them, anyway.

A very early memory is walking around downtown Bristol, Connecticut and window-shopping with my Mom. The interesting thing about our window-shopping is that it had absolutely nothing to do with looking-to-buy; we were looking to enjoy the displays themselves: the props, lighting, design, color schemes, marketing appeal. (We certainly didn't use those terms. We were more in the ooo-aah-mode.) I enjoyed doing that especially at night when the stores were closed and people were not around. We could own the streets and peer into the stores with no pressure to buy or explain what we were doing. I learned to look, appreciate and walk away. I didn't have to own or possess what I admired; it was enough to enjoy the sight of beautiful things and leave it at that.

One night my little brothers were with us and we cracked up because there was this unusual lamp in the window display at Funk's Furniture Store where my grandfather used to work selling furniture. The lamp had some kind of mechanism that made the lampshade appear as if it the entire scene was moving! This was in the days of black-and-white TV, please remember, and this lamp was in *color*. It showed a little Tom Sawyer look-alike using a scenic stream as a potty. You only saw him from the back, of course, but it still was the most risqué-naughty thing we had ever seen and we asked to go back and see it in the window again, which we did. The times when we took bus trips all the way to Hartford, the displays at G. Fox & Co. kept us enchanted for hours. The windows were huge and in the winter they were animated and sparkling beyond imagination.

Window magic, display art... To this day, whether we find ourselves on Canyon Road or on the plaza in Santa Fe, her stomping grounds, or bicycling around Rocheport, Missouri together, Mom and I will always find a window, study it, ooo-and-aah-it, take notes, draw sketches, and always "tip our hats" to the quiet geniuses of display art. You won't see a signature, the work is temporary, but the impression is lasting. Now that art shows and gallery displays are a part of my life, I know that I draw upon those early experiences. My Mom sends the most wonderful and unexpected props for me to work with, from yards of glittering fabric for the Holidays to 25-year-old weathered fence posts from her backyard. The UPS deliveryman and mailman can't believe what makes its way to my door: bones, rocks, cholla cactus, dried-up juniper trees, and rusted barbed wire for starters. There are times at shows when the talk centers more on my displays than what it is I am trying to sell, so I have sold displays, too. Why not? I can always come up with something new and keep the look as fresh as those changing window displays of old.

I can't draw—not yet anyway. Ask my kids—they will tell you because they tell me: "Hey, Mom, you have your own art business, but you just can't draw. Your dinosaurs, monsters, Pokémon, your Holy Mackerel, and everything else ends up with a silly smile, so we are just going to ask Dad to draw from now on..." Thanks, guys. It's absolutely true. Look at the cover of this book for proof: Exhibit A. I did, however, draw this puppy in 1st grade that was terrific and got all kinds of rants and raves: a brown dog on manila paper with a red tongue sticking out. Unfortunately, I recently heard from my mother that she honestly believes that she still has that picture, 40 years after the fact, and I wish I could just remember how great I think it is rather than face reality upon seeing it come out of some old box. (A bit of an aside is in order here: I want to say: "Hurray for rubber stamps for all of us drawing-challenged people.")

Now there was talent in my family. My brother David had the famous learn-to-draw set, the one with the charcoals that showed all about shading and making things look real.

My husband had the same set in Missouri. These guys had people *framing* their stuff. My brother Norman was this cool little designer-type dude who fashioned racecars out of erasers, the white and pink kinds that have tapered ends. Michael, the cartoonist, with that pencil flying, caught the motion of a hair-cutting session, making you laugh and think with his insights produced with basic yellow No. 2 pencils on white paper. You could find Paul, the model-builder-genius-entertainer-type, re-creating Star Trek environs with cast-off boxes, sound effects and all. I found myself the oldest and eventually shortest of all these guys, and my thing became "crafts." My hands became very busy at a very young age. The Chapman sisters made sure of that.

Our house was white on the bottom, maroon on the top. Across the street was a big green house where the Chapmans lived—three sisters who called themselves "the old maids." We called them Ruthie, Billie and Eleanor, and the story was that they were descendants of the legendary John Chapman, better known to all as "Johnnie Appleseed." There was a menagerie of dogs and cats; big Duke is the one I remember. There was a wealth of New England arts-and-crafts in their home because they were each experts in an array of traditional creative arts and they had this desire to share their knowledge. My brother David and I were "adopted" as craft-apprentices and we learned and we did whatever we did the *right* way, let me tell you. We weren't allowed to be sloppy, stupid or lazy just because we were kids. If my knitting was crumby, it was pulled apart, not in a mean way, just in pursuit of perfection, that's all. Braided rugs were done evenly or they were done over. This wasn't a feel-good-session, a bolster-your-self-esteem experience. My self-esteem and confidence were built on solid ground. When Ruthie, Billie or Eleanor said that what I made was "good," it *was* good and I was proud that I met their standards. It also wasn't always precision work that we did, so things could loosen up, too. Our winter pinecone wreaths with nuts and acorns were creative adventures that started out with collections of materials from under trees at Rockwell Park and in our own neighborhood. Tons of glue on a cardboard pizza circle served as the base—the wreaths were beautiful—Martha Stewart was a nobody. Every season meant new crafts. Every Christmas meant that our family would receive a fabulous gingerbread house made by the Chapmans. I can't remember ever eating the houses, just taking pictures of them.

Ruthie gave me a copper bracelet with a leaf design that was too big for a tiny arm but I didn't care and wore it anyway by shoving it high on my arm so I wouldn't lose it. It was from Arizona and the Chapmans always gave us their past issues of Arizona Highways magazines. I inhaled them. Ruthie told me tales of "The West," and the real Arizona highways that she had seen and about this place called New Mexico that was actually, remarkably, enchantingly, part of the United States. Visions of cactus, turquoise, sunsets and cowboy boots and hats danced in my head. I would go to the Great Southwest someday. She knew she was planting that in me. I knew I would grow-up and do it.

My first "trip" outside of my home territory, even past *Hartford*, was going with Ruthie to Pennsylvania Dutch country: Lancaster County, PA. My journal logged every town we passed through on the turnpike that all looked the same, mile after mile. Every five minutes I logged in: We are now entering… we are now entering… and even though it all looked the same I was so excited to write the unfamiliar names, especially when we entered a new *state* and got closer to a land unknown to me—my whole world changed.

Such a lovely new world! We ate fresh peach ice cream made by an Amish family on their farm and the cows where the milk came from were in the barn with us. That struck me as being so wonderful and I hoped that the cows didn't mind. The clothes of black and blue, the horse-drawn carriages and wagons… this was a real lifestyle, not a movie, not fiction. There was a warmth and genuineness in the atmosphere, a kind of secret in their simplicity and separateness. The hex signs and the massive barns of wood and stone forged an image of folk-art-in-real-life, especially when I met Amos Zook, an elderly Amish artist whose hex signs protected and graced many structures and homes. I was given some spending money and bought a package of circular reproductions of his art work and taped them to my bedroom door where they remained for years.

Travel, folk art, meeting people from an "exotic" world outside of my own little Connecticut Yankee Catholic girl-world existence opened me up. The Pennsylvania-Dutch Farmers' Market with frizzed beef, shoo-fly pie, peaches as big as grapefruits and sweet as candy dribbling to your elbows with every bite, and smorgasbord for dinner. These were new words and experiences that made me forever want to taste more.

Having come from that Johnnie Appleseed stock, the Chapmans had the inclination to plant things in me, it seems. It bore fruit. Crafts became very significant in my life. Since the three sisters were older when I was quite young, we never spoke as adults with each other. Reflecting on what they did for me, I have some planting to do, too.

When the Smithsonian asked me this past year to design cards with an Amish quilt theme for the Renwick Gift Shop, the memories of Amish Pennsylvania Dutch were as fresh as those peaches had been. Researching cloth designs and coming up with prototypes, I felt a joy in creating something with my hands with a connection to the past. I think Ruthie, Billie and Eleanor would have liked the cards. Had they been across the street, I definitely would have asked for their input. This time I was on my own.

Let's cross my childhood street from their green house back to our maroon and white one and head to the basement. My Uncle Norman had a "studio" there. That is the place where I learned the value of burlap, egg crates and paper towels with watercolor tracings. I learned that you could be an artist in an unfinished basement.

He was a graduate of RISD: Rhode Island School of Design. My brother Dave and I have these memories that go on and on. Our uncle was "cool." He had a beard and had an apartment in Providence. There was a huge, funky stuffed chair and drawings everywhere and from this small place he took off for a year of study in Italy. We would get postcards with foreign stamps and when Mon Oncle Norman came back, he had sketches by his (also cool) friend Andy that got framed for our house, a gi*gantic* (empty) Chianti bottle, and he started driving a motorbike around town. One time he took us to Greenwich Village. We were 9 and 10 and we saw Mrs. Kennedy slowly come out of a dark car all dressed in black going to a restaurant just down the way from ours. She looked at us. We waved in a quiet, sad, shy way. It was 1964. Then we had dinner and there were small Chianti bottles on all the tables with very drippy, colored candle wax all over them. It seemed that the ceiling was black, the food was Italian, and the whole experience of that night was etched forever in memories that held tight to such new ways of being alive.

For a while my uncle worked for an architectural firm and lived in his mother's apartment, which was part of our house. He needed a place to work, so he made an arrangement to fix up part of our basement and turn it into a "studio." It was wonderful because he used things that were so cheap and there was style and class to it. He showed us the value of burlap, bulletin boards he made himself, and cardboard egg crates for design elements. Since my uncle knew how to mat and frame pictures, our house started to have "real artwork" around. At some point I inherited an original Oriental piece that had been done as an example by an artist visiting RISD. It was of bamboo on extremely fragile rice paper—I had it for years. All of these small things wove a big picture of impressions in a sensitive mind. I knew that I wanted to have my own "style" someday…

One time my Uncle Norman told me a story that I have used in my own thinking many times: as an art student, he was given an assignment in watercolor. He worked at it for hours, crumbling up and tossing out countless efforts that were failures. Into the night, through the night and into the morning and nothing; nothing except the paper towel that he had used to blot all of the brushes with, which he decided was better than anything he had produced on the expensive watercolor paper. So, he submitted the paper towel as his project and did okay with it! I was so affected by that story. How could he *do* that? Whether he got a "good grade" on it or not was not the point for me—it was the fact that he would have the guts and the very idea to hand a scrap towel in to a college professor. There was a confidence, a freedom, an exhaustion and daring that I love about the simple act of seeing the art in what was truly and honestly toss-able.

A few years ago I had to prepare for a photo shoot in order to get into a Fine Arts Show. I needed a good set of slides and had made an appointment with a professional photographer in town, Peter Anger. Everything seemed to get down to the wire as far as time was concerned and I was scrambling to put together a decent set of my work before this appointment. At the final moment I needed one last card and I couldn't think of anything. I was at a total loss as to what to do. Then I remembered my uncle's story about the blotted paper towel and looked at my own drafting table in an unfinished basement with burlap and bulletin boards all over the place and noticed this piece of scrap paper that had been blotting dye-based inks—it was perfect. I cut it up, glued, stamped, and presto: the final card. At the end of the photo shoot, Peter asked if he could buy one card that he really liked. Of course it was the one with the scrap paper. He said to just put a price on it because he wanted it even when, *especially* when, I told him the story of how it came to be. In the end, I suggested that he take $3.00 off from my bill and it worked well for both of us. He got a rather unique card and I got a story connected to my uncle.

So much filters into us as we grow up and engage in the world. Going to museums, parks, on hikes, riding a bike fast on cold dark nights, snow in your face, sunburn on your back, people's faces, their words and their silence—it all impacts the people we become. Neighbors across the street, a map of the Wild West, a good documentary about Egypt… a book, a teacher, friends and enemies, places we've seen and places we dream to see, the smell of fresh bread, the smile of a child, the tears that flashed and shattered light into diamonds in our own eyes because of love or tragedy—we are the accumulation of all of these experiences. The four seasons, stars in the sky… a warm hug when the whole universe seemed so cold. Go ahead—try to grab it. What is it? What are those moments that add up and make you who you are? If we have been given much, we have much to give. If we have been denied, it is not too late to be nourished. For all of the vibrant and powerfully pure and simple sparks in my life, countless ones, I am grateful. I hope that together with my children, we can create the next generation of story "sparks."

I used to sketch, paint, and embroider mountains, mesas and the sun all the time. Very simple, quiet designs. And it was never the sunset—it was always the sunrise on the horizon, that sublime place where heaven and earth apparently meet. I want to stand in that place. There is always the possibility of something new—right there.

"Excuse me, who *are* you?"

"Excusez-moi, mademoiselle, vous êtes américaine?"
("Excuse me, Miss, are you American?")
"Pardon?"
("Whatever gave you that idea?)
"Vous êtes américaine, n'est-ce pas?"

There I was, a light rain misting my army-green plastic poncho. Underneath, one could find a heavy and neatly packed and stuffed blue JanSport soft-framed backpack, tent included. All around one could find France that happened to be very wet at that moment, drenched in a "French way," which translates into something far more romantic than plain old rain. Imagine musty liquid lavender and then you are getting closer… Hefty hiking boots that were usually in high gear were temporarily in neutral. Out of the mist, a figure was appearing, approaching, and then stopped. Right before me stood the quintessential Frenchman—an absolute classic. My little man, my petit bonhomme, was old and fuzzy-white around his head and bushy moustache. A gray sweater on a gray day, the style that you would expect to see—the pockets sagging, the worn wooden buttons, black beret and umbrella. He stopped me with his eyes first and then with his question: "…are you American?"

In the middle of nowhere really, the villages were tiny and scattered about far from the next city that I was heading towards, Tours. Twenty-six years ago, I am twenty. Am I an American? I am trying extremely hard *not* to be and that is precisely what I am doing here in the Middle-of-Nowhere, France, attempting to hide and secretly pretending to be "one of them" since my ancestors were from here and it wasn't anybody's business where I was from as far as I could tell. I look rather French. If I could keep my mouth shut long enough, I could keep them guessing. But this gentleman was standing in front of my face and he was *in* my face asking me until I gave an answer. So, I gave some hippy-dippy winger non-answer in French and then he knew for sure by my accent and content exactly where I was from. I gave in. "Oui, je suis américaine." His smile warmed the core of me; a splash of Monet poppies came to mind.

Standing at attention, he saluted me, military-style. I was stunned. He explained, in his purest, simplest French so that I could receive every word and all the heart embedded in each word, that I was the first American that he had met since The War. Because of the brave Americans who came and gave their lives for the liberation of France, his village was spared. His life had been good and long. And he had made a promise to an American soldier many, many years earlier—he would memorize the English words to the song "I am a Yankee Doodle Dandy," and sing it to the first American he met—a tribute of gratitude. I was that first American and he sang the song for me, for America, with all the glory of his divine French accent, with all his heart, saluting while his tears and the rain washed the soil that was soaked with tremendous sacrifice. Joining in with my own tears and cracking voice, I never was more "American" than at that exact moment, expatriate that I thought I was and never would be again. I am so proud to be an American.

He hugged me. We went in our opposite directions, waving, saluting, and glancing back… in time.

"Howdy, little lady, are you an Indian?" Am I a *what*? Oh, brother, it was a Texas tourist, and there I was leaning against an adobe pillar off the plaza in Santa Fe. He had a mighty fine looking camera aimed in my direction and I was so tempted to raise my hand, and solemnly say: "How," thinking of my Native American friends smiling in the background. I can imagine that I was picture-perfect with extremely long dark hair parted in the middle, single-braided down the back, bright red Guatemalan shirt and sash. But really now. I looked more like a hippy than anything else. I resisted the urge to do the hand/"How" routine and instead, I extended my hand and said: "Hi! My name is Gloria Lagasse and I am from Connecticut. I live here in New Mexico now. Where are you from? *Texas*? Really. Have a wonderful visit…" I don't think he took the picture.

"Excuse me, are you an *artist* here in town?" I was sitting on a blanket with my husband and sons, Missouri 1996, waiting for the Fourth of July fireworks to get started. The question flew straight past me, and someone on my blanket made me aware of the fact that the question was mine to answer. "Oh, sorry, what was that again? I really didn't think you were talking to me… an *artist* here in town? Well, uh, I guess, well…" "Didn't you have a booth last month at Art in the Park? You mentioned that it was your first time doing an art show." "Oh, that, yes I did." Click. Click. Mind starts working. "We bought two pieces from you and we really like them. So do our friends. We hope you will be doing more shows in the future. Do you have a store locally where we can buy your things on a year-round basis and we were wondering…"

Once we started talking, I remembered their faces and the fact that they had bought something from me. I remembered the exact frames finally and I recalled talking with these kind people, some of my very first customers at my very first art show only one month before sitting on that blanket in July. Their opening question and the fact that I was recognized "in public" was a totally new experience. The fact that they had a definition for me, a title of sorts, was interesting. There I was looking behind and around me for the "artist" they were talking to…

A number of months ago, a fiber artist, Rebecca Bluestone, came to Columbia from Santa Fe and gave a presentation with her husband Robert, a classical guitarist. I attended the Reception. Those events are usually a bit much for me and I prefer to know they are happening rather than sipping the wine and balancing the finger-foods in person. But I couldn't help myself, she was from Santa Fe and I was starving for a connection, so I ventured to the Art League for a bit of schmoozing. My friend Susan, who loves these events as much as I don't, was sharing with Rebecca and motioned me over. Oh great. I want to, don't want to, "Hello, Rebecca, welcome to Columbia." Then she asks me the inevitable: "…are you an *artist* here in town?" Susan took over answering the question after my awkward lapse in timing, and we had a very nice evening, even though I don't ever seem to know quite who or what I am.

Dr. Betty Scott put me through this little exercise after my first presentation to her Creative Process Class at the University of Missouri. All I needed to do was answer a "simple question":

"Who are you?"

"Gloria Page."

"Who are you?"

"Gloria Ann Page."

"Who are you?"

"Gloria Ann Therese Lagasse Page."

"Who are you?"

"Can I say what I *do*?"

"Who are you?"

"Okay, I am a mother, wife, sister, friend, a person trying to do an art business."

"Who are you?"

"I like the color turquoise, I am from Connecticut, I wish I came from New Mexico, and I am really tired of your question."

"Who are you?"

"Who are *you*? And why are you doing this to me?"

"Who are you?"

"I don't have a clue."

"Who are you?"…   And this is the short take on the actual experience.

Don't you love it? You are in a place and someone walks up to you and says either "And who are *you*?" or "What do *you* do?" I can nail the name by now, but *what do I do*? What is the definition? I resist answering. That appears to be a lifetime habit at this point. What I do and what I have done in the past are not the definitions of who I am. It is a platform, a springboard from which I will propel myself to become more, not a box which contains the sum total of my value as a human being, case closed. Am I an American? Obviously. Am I a Native American? Not really, but there is this story that we have a way-back-great-grandmother from a Northeastern Tribe and I want to believe it is true so I don't research it in case it's not. Am I an artist? Sure I am. Why not? I would be the first to argue that case for everyone else on the planet, so I might as well accept it for myself. We are all artists in one way or another—I love to philosophize on that subject. Perhaps it is with a brush or pen as a tool, a rubber stamp, surgeon's laser, computer, camera or clay on the wheel. A piece of wood polished to perfection, transformed from exotic trees to a game board—a work of art to play with, generation after generation— that is art. A bowl of rice cooked and served with love is a work of art. Interior design, public speaking, dance, music and magic are art, too, as well as a beautiful smile, hands that heal, landscaping, lifescaping. When I look around searching for the spirit of art, I see it in children, the un-checked artists, free spirits that they are. They are my favorite crowd. The artist arena is vast. Okay, let's say that I am an artist.

Why resist a name? Perhaps it is the narrowing down that I find objectionable along with the expectations inherent in definitions. I may be an "artist," having this card business and a business card, but I sure don't want to stop there and be only that and whatever it is that artists are supposed to be and do. I want to write, too, learn to play the hammered dulcimer, dance the polka and travel the globe with my crew among infinite other things. I think that there are times when we jump and we know exactly where we are going to land or at least have the goal and expectation in mind. And then there are those leaps of faith into the unknown that make life really exciting with an edge and cliffs all over the place. That is pioneer territory, a place without definition, on the uncharted map. I like going there, even at the risk of getting lost. I did get lost for two days in the mountains in New Mexico once. I found my way out and I found out a lot about myself. It was supposed to be an afternoon hike. Finally, in the light, a path out of the dark…

Who am I? Who are you? What do we want? Where are we headed? Good questions. As for the *answers*, how about shouting a few declarations and affirmations out there to the listening as well as non-listening universe: "I am an artist! I am a writer whose pen is pulsating and computer is quaking at the keys! I am a musician and a dancer itching to stomp. I am an entrepreneur, world traveler and a literary explorer, whatever that means. I am at the beginning of figuring it all out and the further along I get, the more I have to laugh. It's not all about accomplishments and milestones—those can actually get in the way. The more I see, the more there is to see. The more I know, the more I want to learn. It is a quality of life that I am after, not things or titles or final destinations. The journey, that great trek into the eternal unknown—that is where the best stories come from. You mentally wear hiking boots on a daily basis.

And when I need quiet and distance from all the definitions and grand proclamations, I will shut my mouth and eyes and smile. I am all of the above and more, I am none of the above, and above all else, I want to be and I am simply: me.

Here is a piece of good news: we can re-invent ourselves whenever the heck we decide we want to. So, when will it be: now, later today, before I turn 50, or before I…

So, excuse me, I really don't want to miss this one: "Who, may I ask, are *you*?"

You know, your career is just your career.
Your life is your *Life*!
- *Sissy Spacek*

The almighty "BUT"

(Note: the "inconsequential BUT" is this one: I thought it was purple, but it was blue.)

I swear that the month of January must be the biggest "BUT per capita" month of the year. For the New Year, these resolutions might sound familiar:

"I am (we are) going to clean out the nasty garage… BUT: it is *too cold*!" Strange: in the Spring it is too wet, in the Summer it is too hot and in the Autumn it is too perfect so why would anyone want to waste time doing something like *that?*

"I am going to lose a few pounds… BUT: I wouldn't want to see all of this beautiful Holiday food go to waste, so I'll wait until February." All sounds like solid logic to me. I've heard it or said it enough to be convinced.

How about "I will walk a mile a day," etc… you get the idea. The list goes on and the creativity of the reasoning after using the word "but" is astonishing.

"I would love to be an 'artist'… BUT: I can't draw even if my life depended on it." This can go on forever and in some cases, it does.

Now, let's approach this from a slightly different angle. Let's find a way to employ the almighty "but" to our advantage and get somewhere for a change. How about:

"I can't draw BUT I sure as heck can *stamp*!"

"I can't finish my book if everybody around here keeps jumping for the computer BUT if I take out the typewriter, I can save my inspiration and sneak in computer time later." It works—I just did it.

Whatever is on the other side of "the almighty but" is either an excuse or a solution. No buts about it.

The dress-up box

Costumes were not reserved for Halloween in our family. The dress-up box was a permanent fixture in the toy department of our lives. Dive in there and you might come out a Nurse, a Cowboy, Indian, Majorette, Mr. Sensation, an Old Lady, Uncle Louie, or Raggedy Ann among infinite others. The box itself was originally a padded vinyl toy box, white with sparkle-chip designs on it, and it too, had a disguise. It had become our Magical-Transformation-Vehicle. Once you bent over and started digging in, no telling who would come out in your place. Just who are you going to be today, anyway?

I don't know that I ever outgrew "dressing-up." The box fell apart and faded away, but there have always been costumes in my life. In high school, my friends would comment on the fact that there would be "*no way* to have all of Gloria's friends in one room at the same time and expect them to get along with each other the way they did with her." My clothes were the same: how could they get along with each other in the closet? From "Miss New England" with my L.L. Bean clothes which were few (expensive) and cherished for their simplicity of style and classic quality, make a sharp left to hippy clothes embroidered and beaded, a fast right into Izod Lacoste and Fred Perry tennis whites, a Catholic school girl's uniform decked with U.S. Army buttons and boots (just to rile them), all the way to cute and cool aqua coordinates from Sears. There was the basketball team uniform, the field hockey duds, and there were Sunday church dresses worn with nylons and shiny shoes. All in the same closet and drawers, all mine, all me. That never seemed schizo to me—it just seemed natural. I was all-of-the-above-and-more-to-come. It is the way I have always seen it.

"Dressing for the occasion" in life is simply another form of diving into the dress-up box, as far as I can tell. To this day it is still the very same thing for me, except that I don't need to get on the old lady wig to get the white hair effect—it's real now. I work at home and generally sport sweats, t-shirts, Reeboks and aprons: mint green or blue denim. Ink, paint, glue, and similar substances are imbedded in the denim and it is my working-artist uniform of choice. When an Art Show comes around, then a new costume is in order—perhaps a long flowing skirt, dark colors, artsy jewelry, dark shades and a hat with a statement attached. Off to campus to meet the students and tell my story? Black jeans and a turtleneck, dark leather vest handmade by my brother Norm, and a sprinkling of silver and turquoise will do nicely, thank you. The Opening Reception for my Gallery Show? A long black dress, a power necklace of black and peacock blue dichroic glass, black velvet shoes and a touch of *make-up* even! Time to pick my kids up from school? We're back to the sweats... a One Woman Everyday-is-Halloween Fashion Show.

It is a pretty wide range, and it is all in the same closet and drawers because it is *all me*. The Navajo-made crushed green velvet broomstick skirt and traditional shirt are hanging right next to a Guatemalan shirt-dress tailored for gringos with the texture and feel of hand-woven cloth. A Miss Retro-1972 tiny-flowered number is next to that, a black, slick turtleneck with pinstripe gray tunic right after that for some business appointment on Madison Avenue, I guess. A dusty rose rhinestone-studded sweater from the Jewish Women's Organization Thrift Store in Chappaqua, New York, the long African mud-cloth tunic vest, my favorite... what's *next???* Now to the point:

I just read another piece written on the subject: "So you are considering a Career Change and are wondering if you should try to develop a home-based art business based on your craft?" subliminally entitled: ("CAUTION: Do you really want to give up your great job and take the risk of living the life of an *artist*? Do you have any idea at all what that *means*?") The red flags are up all over the place and this is supposed to be *helpful* and *inspirational*? I understand, I really do, but hang on a minute. Just give me a second here because I am going to jump right into my little girl dress-up box on your behalf and put on a cheerleader's outfit, and that is more of a stretch than I am usually willing to make, but extreme times call for extreme measures. Here we go, wiggle-wiggle-twist-and-pull. Okay. The warning flags are presently replaced by colorful pom-poms and this is what I have to say: *Who says* that you have to give up *anything* to just simply "try on" the idea of having an art business? You don't have to hang up your three-piece suit forever. You don't have to gamble away your security and comfortable benefits for the crapshoot of a lifetime. And you also don't have to be scared of how ignorant you are of the unknown. Experience is the best teacher and everyone has to start somewhere.

Just play around in the dress-up box! Here's a thought: How about starting with a Clown Suit so that we don't get so serious here that we forget what this is all about, namely the pursuit of doing what we love doing. Honk your own nose and then step out into new territory. You probably don't want to make a fool of yourself and yet you also probably don't want to kick yourself in the backside years down the road of regret because you didn't give this three-ring circus a try just for the fun of it.

Perhaps you wondered if anyone would ever buy any of your handmade cards, so stop wondering and stick them in a pretty basket, put a price on them, a tin can for the cash will do and see what happens at that office that you still want to work in. *Just do it* and see if there is any money in the can at the end of the week to add to your safe and consistent paycheck. See what happens and see what you do with what happens. Maybe you always wanted to try one of those Craft Shows at your local Fall Festival. Great! Try it on and see how it fits. A Holiday Bazaar with you sitting at a card table hawking your wares? How about a few art items on consignment at a nice gift shop downtown? These are all temporary ventures, no huge risks. If you discover that you are encouraged, then take another step. If you find that some particular aspect of the Art Business Life is uncomfortable, take another direction. Throw that particular costume back in the box. You might surprise yourself by taking it out again much later, with a new feather in your cap from some other experience. It might fit better and feel more comfortable later. Who knows? You can't know until you try it on.

There is a woman here in town who decided that she loves making cards and probably was complimented enough times that she took a business step with them. Her lovely cards are now selling at a very nice gift store downtown: Poppy. I finally met the artist and she is such a sweetheart. The owners of the shop love her work and sell lots of it. As a card artist, Connie is not interested in expanding her business. She is content to put a lot of time into each card, satisfied with the experience of having one shop, and doesn't want to venture into high pressure, high volume production and sales. I admire her cards and her decision. We can all put on what fits for us.

I have "dressed-up" as an artist for eight years in different outfits and don't see an end in sight anytime soon. In the past two weeks alone, I have blasted to new levels defying logic as I know it. It took some serious costume-changing dynamics on my part, and I was up for it. If I had seriously pondered whether or not I was ready, I know that I would have floundered and lost my footing. When I was eight years old and wanted to be a Nurse, I put on my costume and I *was* a Nurse: instantly and completely. My dolls were extremely lucky to have me. I wasn't worried about what I didn't know or the fact that I did not have a degree in Nursing, that I was too young or too short. Who cared? My dolls needed me; *that* was the important thing. My Aunt Rhea had over *2,000* dolls—I would have needed a whole Hospital Staff to take care of all of them. I got dressed-up for me and for my dolls and rose to the occasion. I played Nurse until that game was finished.

When I was asked two weeks ago to submit artwork for publication in a book that will have international distribution and instant prestige by its connection to the Author/Editor, I put on my blue denim apron and went to work. Did I feel ready? Did I know what I was doing completely? No, but I dressed for the occasion, rose to it, did my best and it worked. The results were way beyond my expectations or wildest hopes. I may be exhausted, behind in my orders and life in general, but I will have a new costume for the box (or closet): Published Artist "Who is Very Grateful." I folded this new outfit up carefully and set it aside. Then I simply put on my sweats and inky apron once again and got back to work. Costume switching can be a hassle or fun—fun is better.

Is a *home* business a good thing for me? You bet. Did I ever think of chalking the whole thing up to "an interesting experience," chucking the dress-up box out the window and applying somewhere, *anywhere* for a "real job"? You bet. I started very-part-time and have pulled out and tried on many articles of clothing from my art business box, tossed a few, added, re-arranged, went on shopping sprees, did sackcloth and ashes, switched things back and forth between the real stuff in the closet and the pretend stuff in the box. At the moment, I am sporting this Writer's get-up, and I'm not quite sure where to hang it up at the end of the day—it's a new category in my closet.

How many times we dressed-up and played the *Wizard of Oz* as kids I couldn't possibly say. My own personal adult-size "Yellow Brick Road" has had some interesting twists and turns, believe me. There have been friends to trek with, and in lonely times, I've had my fair share of very personal lions and tigers and bears to contend with. Should I keep going with this adventure? Should I get off the Road completely? Inevitably I find myself, time after time, bending down and digging into that dear old Dress-Up Box, reaching for those sparkling, red ruby slippers, slipping them on over lace anklet socks, with eyes closed, clicking my heels together, whispering ever so gratefully and softly… "There's no place like home, there's no place like home…"

In all of the safe places we know and have, we can take refuge and find comfort. And best of all, when we are ready to come out and play, we can do that, too.

"…Somewhere over the rainbow,
skies are blue,
and the dreams that you dare to dream
really do come true…."

- *Dorothy* in *The Wizard of Oz*
"Over the Rainbow"
Lyrics by E. Y. Harburg

"There's no place like home"... no place.

First there was Meadow Street. Then Lillian Road. Next: 16 Center Street. Those street addresses were in Bristol, Connecticut. It was my life; those were my homes until I was 18. I can remember my first telephone number, 40 years ago. It was Ludlow 25410. Moving around, all over the place, I have had many addresses and telephone numbers over the years. The location of the mailbox, the coordinate on the globe, that place we sometimes call *home*, at other times house or apartment, the block, the Camp, crash pad, Gerry tent, dorm, youth hostel, "escape," an array of names to say I am here *right now*. My stuff is here. I am planted for the time being. Send my mail, preferably not bills, *here*. And if there is a change of address, please forward anything that is worth the postage.

Home... a powerful word with powerful implications in the imagery and memories attached to it. I know that my art is attached strongly to my sense of home. Holding on to it, searching for it, longing for it, re-creating it, running from it and racing towards it. Notice that I take pride and comfort in the fact that I have a *home* business. I made a point of putting that center stage in this book. I can be "at home" in the most bizarre places, the most ordinary places, or no place in particular. Home can be totally alone without being lonely or it could be with special people, too. It can be the smack of a kiss from my kids that brings me a cozy home feeling or I can find myself right smack dab in the middle of insanely alive New York City where the smile of an old stranger warms me from my fright of being there in the first place. A certain smell can bring home to my nose and closing my eyes "I'm there" once again. I can be perfectly at home in a daydream, a song, or a foreign country that can feel as familiar as my favorite pajamas. Give me a chair, a book, a candle and a cup of tea: home.

And when times are tough or just in transition, and it feels hard to feel at home anywhere, especially inside my own skin, then I can go for a long walk or a bike ride until I am ready to head inside again. Maybe what would help is to pick up a pen and start writing. This is a newfound home for me—I have to "go there" every day or I feel lost. Far away, half-a-lifetime ago, there was just me, myself and I, the three of us, in a two-man tent in the French Alps in the snow—now that was one of my sweetest addresses and it was for one night only. I wrote in my journal by flashlight gazing up at mountains that cut the sky apart. I am at home doing my artwork in the middle of the night in a basement in the middle of mid-Missouri in the Midwest, pretending sometimes to be someplace else, when I need to be. There are many forms and methods, vehicles, to get back home.

I love the fact that what I create with my hands goes to other people's hands and oftentimes ends up displayed in someone's home or tucked into a special drawer because my cards are "keepers." It is meaningful for me to know that there is a home in New Zealand that has a petroglyph design framed piece that I made hanging on a wall. It delights me to hear that a couple bought several framed pieces with New Mexican chile designs because they just did their kitchen over and wanted to have a "touch of New Mexico" here in Missouri. My friend Julie has a Raku piece that she insisted on buying before a show. It looks so beautiful and it is a special treat for me to be able to see it hanging on her wall, beautifully displayed; most destinations are a mystery to me.

The first geographical "place" called "home" for me was on Meadow Street. I have no memories of those early times as far as living there myself. I remember visiting years later because it was also in the same brick block that was my grandmother's home. My Mom would have the real Meadow Street stories because that is where she grew up—a massive brick block, owned by her parents. Their Grocery Store was on the ground level. Apartments were above. My truest "home memories" begin at our second house on Lillian Road: the little white house with the very cool real life-size outdoor playhouse and a big field that stretched way the heck out there. Tall grasses like a New England prairie, if there ever was such a thing. My mother would have these recurring dreams of "the Russians rushing the field in invasion-mode or the Indians descending from the plains" in surround-sound-mode. It was, after all, the 1950's, mind you, and the Cold War was hot on our heels and in our fears and obviously, our nightmares, too. "The Wild, Wild West" for our family at that time in our lives was the stuff of Movies and TV and all the stereotypes and hypes that go along with that. Who would have guessed at that time that we would eventually live out in the Great Southwest at the end of the Old Santa Fe Trail, only to find us "gringo white guys" in the minority. Now my kids are wearing the same dress-up box Cowboy and Indian costumes that my brothers wore way back when…

Bristol in the 50's… We did have some genuine excitement and terror when lightning bolts dug up the ground and started a fire that burned down our neighbors' garage one stormy day. The weather was crazy there sometimes. When I was about 4-years-old, I became furious during one thunderstorm and started throwing toys at the lightning, yelling at it to *go away* and to leave my brother and me *alone! We want to play!* My Mom ran out and picked up this little wet yelper of a wild child, me, dashing into the house, both of us shaking. We huddled in a corner and she sang: "Who's Afraid of the Big Bad Wolf…no, no, not me…my Mommy won't let him come in, no, no…" That helped so much that to this day, I still sing or at least hum that tune when shaky things happen. The storms would pass and there were many more peaceful days than tumultuous ones, but the dramatic ones are more fun to remember and write about.

So, I was born a Connecticut Yankee. White clapboard houses and shutters, maple sugar candy and the like. There was a postcard-picture-perfect Congregational Church on the village green nestled in history right at the top of my street, to the left. There were churches everywhere, come to think of it, and directions around town were often given with them as points of reference. "Go down West Street, past St. Stanislaus, and take a right…" As far as color and seasons are concerned, New England autumn for me is up there. Turtleneck-sweater-weather. Leaves blazing, tumbling on your head to the ground just so that you can bury yourself in mountains of them or sink deeply into cushiony nests. Maple tree crunchies were in your ears, up your back and in your underwear, for heaven's sake, by the time you went inside for Nestlé's Hot Chocolate with marshmallow floaties. Baths came later in the evening and you had more leaves to shed there. The trees eventually lost all of theirs and that meant raking, but that kind of work was okay, even for kids. Work and play lines were blurred. With barren trees you could see more of the sky. There were times in New England, distinctly imprinted in my memory, when I recall this gesture of raising my hands over my head, motioning how much I would like to *push* all the hills and foliage away—just out of my line of vision so that I could get a sense of the Big Picture, the Vista. I never could see far enough for my taste.

Where is home? Where am I from? Is home a place? The clichés of home being "Where the Heart Is, Where your Family Is, a Place to Hang Your Hat, Home is a State of Mind…" all of these well-used concepts have a ring of truth to them, definitely. I don't want to go cosmic on anyone here, but all of this is something I like to grapple with in a down-to-earth wrestling/reflecting kind of way. I think that my art is a way for me to create a sense of home by allowing me to pull together different elements that I love: places, cultures, colors, textures, memories and dreams, put it on paper, push it into clay, carve it, stamp it, frame it. (Sell it!) I have always felt at home when I am making things.

One of my all-time favorite "homes" in my life was an olive green Gerry two-man tent that got used by one lady: me. It was my "address" for months in France. (It saw many-a-night in the Sangre de Cristos, too, and got set up in England and Wales as well as Arizona and California.) My Gerry "house" and all that I needed to survive pleasantly was transportable on my back. It is amazing how much we don't need in order to live on this planet and how much I've accumulated since then. That kind of dwelling gets set up and taken apart every single day. It is a nomadic life and I have always held a fascination and sensed a kinship with tent-dwelling cultures. The impermanence of home is physically a fact of life. It strips things down to simpler forms. You seriously consider how much you and your camels are going to have to carry, and think more than twice about accumulating anything other than the necessary.

Being "at home" is for me, more often than not, a state of mind, in a place for a moment or for a very long time. I don't think the time factor matters to me a whole lot. The place itself may or may not be relevant: the state of being is. There are times when I am perfectly at ease in the least expected place—a personally designed and tailored comfort-zone in the middle of nowhere. At other times, the environment, frankly, is *everything*. In the case of New Mexico, the place was relevant and the comfort-zone was everywhere I took my next step. The first time I flew in an airplane away from the nest of my early years was to go to New Mexico for my interview at St. John's College in Santa Fe. I was 18. Destination: Albuquerque. Couldn't spell it easily, but I was going there anyway. I left the flying to the pilots so I could have a window seat. I wanted to be alone. I wanted to be 100% present. The land changed gradually from my vantage point up in the clouds. I rarely blinked, intent upon drinking it all in, every drop. The young cocoon-girl was breaking out and spreading her wings in the thinning atmosphere of freedom and space. "Go West, Young Girl!" and in going West, things got browner and earthier, rougher in a tangible hands-in-the-dirt way. Less green, less tame, more me.

I wanted to land in New Mexico, to get on the ground and step on it, sinking those negative-heel Earth shoes in that dry dust, smelling the sage by walking straight into it. (Never mind that I did that eventually and walked straight into a cactus on the other side, an involuntary Penitente experience.) "Get this bird down, why don't you!" We finally landed. Albuquerque *International* 1972. The International part seemed a bit exaggerated back then. You had to walk to the terminal from the plane. Usually I am one of those nice people who let others go ahead of me in lines. That day I wasn't rude exactly, but I also wasn't in my sweet little let-everyone-on-earth-go-before-me mode either. I had to get out of that plane! I will never forget standing at the top of the mobile stairway, breathing New Mexico for the first time. There was no air, but I could finally breathe! That Breath was deeper and the Expanse wider than anything I had ever seen before. Slowly, slowly I turned not just my eyes but also my whole body around so I could *see*. I didn't have to push anything out of the way. I kept turning and gazing, squinting in the rarified light, and in the vastness I felt so "at home." Down the stairs to the ground, pushing my feet into the tar to make sure I landed. I asked someone where the air was and the way to the shuttle bound for Santa Fe. St. John's arranged the trip to the College. A trip from one town to another, from one life to another... my state of being was forever altered. This experience wove its way into my life many times in different ways over the years.

Years later, finding myself in upstate New York starting this little business venture, there came a point when once again I found myself at a crossroads in the decision-making process. Where to hang my hat next... It was time to move on, but this time not alone with a backpack and a tent, not alone on a plane to the Southwest. This time with a husband, two children and too much stuff. We would head west, sort of. To the Midwest. To Missouri, the *beginning* of the Old Santa Fe Trail, Gary's hometown of Columbia. For a number of reasons it seemed like it was time for a new start in old territory for Gary. There were more reasons, less reasons, let's just go.

But there would be a detour of about a year first—Santa Fe, the *end* of the Old Santa Fe Trail, my family's home. Yes, they had uprooted, that Yankee family of mine, years earlier. *They* were now the New Mexicans and I was doing the yo-yo thing. They had settled in the Land of Enchantment, thank God. Because of that, "going home" meant Santa Fe—lucky me. The idea was that we would live with my Mom for a number of months so that I could get my business off the ground by immersing myself in the area this time as a "businessperson." Different orientation, different place by now, too. It was good that our address was Camino Carlos Rey for that time. It is a safe and fun place. My kids have wonderful memories of that time, short as it was, young as they were. I made good inroads for my business foundation during the time we were there. It was a window of opportunity that I used to the best advantage that I could at the time.

Then the time came for a change of address, once again. Detour-time was over. Gary and Brandon loaded themselves into the yellow Ryder truck, setting off for Missouri and specifically for Columbia in Boone County. I lingered a bit in Santa Fe with the baby and we flew a couple of weeks later. We had a new address I heard, on Count Fleet Court, near Derby Ridge School. It is off of Smiley Lane. Strange names to me. I liked Camino de la Cruz Blanca, Don Diego, Cerrillos Road, Canyon Road and the adobe, chamisa, sage and prairie dogs that went with that territory. What were these streets called Count Fleet, War Admiral, Seattle Slew, in this Derby subdivision? In time I came to learn that these names were all prized Kentucky Derby caliber horses, dead or alive I couldn't tell you. As we were driving to our house for the first time, I was in a state of shock, withdrawal, and disbelief, fighting an attack of depression because somehow everything looked the *SAME!* Oh my God, what have we done? We just came from "the City Different" and now here everything all looks the same! I was way out of my element. But here we were. I got out of the car and wanted to walk around the house that was still in the process of being built and I started to sink into thick, sticky, rain-drenched clay—it was an unusual feeling to say the least. I wanted to be happy for me and for my guys and for the possibilities that were as yet unknown. So I laughed at myself for literally being "stuck-in-the-mud" and washed the gloop off my shoes a little later. It was limbo-land for a while. I enrolled my son in school, had a good feeling about that, and it helped. Day by day I started to make friends, one by one, and that helped a lot.

We haven't changed addresses for 6 years. This place became home.

I have lived in and visited many different places in this country and in a number of foreign countries, and I can say that each place, each town or village has given me something. Even places that I would never want to go to again as long as I live made some impression on me and I can remember something, however small, that I did love; some kind of cherishable memory or story, bar none. As I brush the dust or soot or mud off my shoes going from one place to another, I am more because of having been there. Take this Missouri place, for example.

I love the people I've met here. I love the art community here. This has been a great place for me to expand my business and believe me I was worried about that a lot at one point. Could my rather quirky style find a place here? The answer is a kindly "yes."

For a person like me who finds delight in interesting words, this place is a total blast! My husband knows the state of Missouri quite well and he told me some town names and I was sure that he was joking. He also told me that he has relatives whose first and second names were: Estella Ella, Orly Gorly, Chester Lester, and Golda Viola. "Stella," his Grandma, was the *best* huggable sweetheart you could ever hope to meet, and her fried chicken and garden-fresh tomatoes would make Emeril Lagasse's mouth water. Gary's family even has some ancestral connection to Daniel Boone. And come to find out, he wasn't joking about any of the names in his family or in Missouri. I bought myself a state map and checked out the lists of towns and it is such a *hoot*. In the Missouri way-back machine there were many Native American tribes, French settlers and other European settlements as well. The history of this state is so interesting to me as I pick things up from my son's 4th grade Social Studies book. As far as names go, it is sometimes downright comically delightful. And I thought that some street names in Columbia seemed a little unusual when I first came here. There was a lot more in store for me. *Missouri*, the word itself, originally is an Indian word meaning "town of the big canoes." The "ee" sound at the end came from the French later on, probably. I still can't bring myself to say "Missour-ah," but I do give in at MU football games.

No matter where I live in the future, there will always be something that I will remember in an endearing kind of way about Missouri. From Frankenstein to Plato, Versailles to Japan, from Tightwad to Success to Peculiar, and a whole lot woven in and around, the state map of Missouri will definitely make me smile. And that's a fun and good thing to cherish...

Remember that great scene from *It's a Wonderful Life* where "Mary" decorated the abandoned house with travel posters from all over the world, the ceiling is leaking, the policemen are serenading in a downpour and Jimmy Stewart walks in and takes his hat off and sees the *bedroom*? That double take: priceless. They had just saved Bedford Falls with two bucks left in the till, "Momma Dollar and Papa Dollar." They were going only as far as leaky, drafty 320 Sycamore for their honeymoon, the local "Waldorf Hotel." The fireplace was ablaze, chickens were roasting on the phonograph-turned-rotisserie and I don't know of a more wonderful depiction of "home." I don't know of many more romantic movie scenes either.

Perhaps you have a Home and you are rooted there forever and ever. That is good. Perhaps you have a Home and are *not* rooted there forever and ever. That is good, too. If I am present enough in each place that I choose to be, for however long that may be, I receive something because I made room inside of myself. And hopefully, I will take what

I love with me and leave something behind that I have added before moving on. God knows life is a journey, whether we stay put or not.

Looking at my own artwork, I see many places that I love. In my little studio I can touch a place through design and color. Yet there is nothing like being there for me. Someday I am going to take my family to France so that I can take them to the towns I walked through and the vineyards I worked and bled in. We have to go to Athens, not the one in Missouri, the one in Greece. We will walk the steps of the Acropolis and find a dusty street so that I can bend down and write in the dirt, wondering if possibly Socrates etched here, too. I have to sit on the ground with a back-strap weaving teacher in Guatemala weaving with colors that make you dance inside. Once in a while I will stand up and move to another position, adding some yarn or re-adjusting my thoughts. I will sit at Ryoan-Ji Temple Zen Garden in Kyoto and do absolutely nothing at all. I will enter many worlds. I will go to Nepal and Tibet and India somehow or other. I will go to Canada, so that my ancestors can feel my footsteps on their soil and my sort-of-Canadian way of speaking French can be laughed at by me and the folks up there. Australia has too many crazy animals to miss and it just sounds like too much fun. Finding a place to hang out in Australia and Texas in order to have the time to listen to people talk is my idea of a great time—wonderful sounds… These are among the must-visits and the must-re-visits.

So many places in my wishful-thoughts feel so "home" to me even though my feet haven't sunk into the soil yet or for a very long time. If someone asked me right now, if I could live anywhere in the world, where would it be, I would pause first… Then I'd have to say that it seems to me that my husband and I have this Southwest thing in our hearts almost as if our mutual genetic coding reads "SW" or something. We seem destined for our own personal "mesa point." Today we are here, and there are a lot of ways for me to be at home right where I am sitting and writing, thank you for asking. The quest for home is a way of life. It plays into my art, work and quirky philosophical perspectives. The address is incidental. There's no place like home, and there are a lot of places I'd like to give that name to, at least for a while.

…And even though they fell in love with Paris,
when they went home in May to their own small town,
fragrant with honeysuckle,
they discovered, to their immense happiness,
that it is possible to have TWO great loves, after all.

- *Kay Foley*
(American Cardmaker/Writer)

He wanted to run away to the
Circus
but felt he was (alas!) too old
& the Circus was (sigh!) too far from……….home.
He went to the movies instead & it turned out
that he was pretty happy about it after all.   - *Kay Foley*

Each place that I have loved I'll keep with me. - *Don Blanding*

44

A tiny little Play

Cast of characters:
- My uncle and aunt, Phil and Julie
- An antique shop owner
- A glass vase

Setting/Scene(s):
- New England, 1960-ish, a road trip north, an out of the way shop, then back in the kitchen in Connecticut…

(Antique collectors are treasure hunters. They can be individuals; they can come in pairs. My aunt and uncle and my husband's aunt and uncle, Dorothy and Don, come to mind. Our tiny little "play" opens at Phil and Julie's dining room table, just before I leave for France when I was twenty. I am listening to a story… a true story)

"We were driving around northern New England, stopping at antique shops along the way, wherever the road took us. We saw one rather rundown, not very impressive place, but decided to stop there anyway. There was a point very early on when it seemed like it was not the place to be, but something caught our attention. It was a very dusty vase on a dusty old shelf. It had a pretty shape and it cost $2.00. We bought it. That was that. When out trip was complete, we headed home.

Taking our purchases out of the boxes, they needed to be cleaned, so the vase was taken to the kitchen sink to be washed. It started to sparkle as the layers of dust peeled away and then its secret came to light—underneath the base, there it was: a signature. This lovely vase was a *signed Steuben!* For $2.00, can you believe it? And do you know what, even if it wasn't "valuable," it still had such a pretty shape, like a fan…"

This little story has rolled around in my head for all of these years ever since. Whenever I find something of value—cheap—like my dining room set for $25.00 that someone later offered me $800.00 for—I said "no, thank you," I think of the vase story. But I do more with it than that. I role-play the different members in the cast and the scene itself—the journey to unlikely places, for example—that is my life. First, I put myself in the shoes of the shop owner who doesn't have a clue as to the value of what is in front of his own face, in his hands, in his dusty world—I know I miss things. Then I'll slip into the role of my aunt and uncle standing at the kitchen sink making their discovery, drying that $2.00 vase ever so carefully, placing it in a lovely mahogany and glass showcase—some things I don't miss. And what about the artist who made the vase in the first place, signed it and sent it on its merry way to untold homes and hands: who was he and could he ever have imagined the stories etched into the glass he created? What about the things that I've created? What fates have they experienced? And finally, the dusty vase—in hard times I feel like that lonely vase on the old shelf, all but abandoned, with a cheap price tag attached, feeling like a piece of junk—we've all had those moments. We get picked up, washed and appreciated, and sparkle like never before. Sometimes you just need to be loved and cared for—I know I do. You try to give and give and then there is this point of needing to be filled up… I have been and will be all these characters, over and over again.

"All life is a stage." We are the characters, the props, the scenery, the laughter, tears, applause, and the silence as everyone exits the theater. It was a tiny little story told long ago about a pretty glass vase in a cabinet—the kind of story you just always remember.

Always, all ways a beginner

In the beginner's mind there are many possibilities,
but in the expert's there are few.

- Shunryu Suzuki
Zen Mind, Beginner's Mind

A student from the University here in town has been working on an article about my business. It is a "profile." We've met downtown for taped interviews, e-mail each other, and the whole process is interesting to me. Stacy has interviewed people in my life and the article should be finished soon. The other day we met for our final official "chat," and during that time she asked me a simple yet profound question: "What exactly is it that you learn from your children? You have mentioned that you learn from them, and I was wondering if you would elaborate on that…" Brandon is 10; Bryan is 6. Yes, I did say that to her and I do say that quite often. Now I was being asked *what*. Name it—exactly. Not generalized feel-good stuff; what specific things do you learn from those young people in your life. Say it clearly in words, one after the other.

I stumbled around searching for the words. There is this eager person sitting across the table from me, pen poised, waiting for something: an answer; hopefully with insight, wisdom and depth attached. I sat there having "this feeling" about what I mean when I say that, but where are the words to nail the feelings down on paper? I gave a few weak examples of characteristics I admire about each of them, but I couldn't put my finger on it, I couldn't grab it. What do my children teach me? It haunted me that I couldn't verbalize something that I had tossed out into the universe countless times for years: "I am always learning from my children, from all children." But *what exactly is it that I am learning*? If I don't know, I obviously haven't learned, after all. It isn't easy to admit that.

I came home with a different set of ears and eyes attached to my head in order to listen and to watch. Not for whether or not they are "behaving well." Listen and watch for what it is that I am learning. The whole answer is not to be had in a few days; I know that much for sure. But a couple of things have jumped out at me, and I'd like to start there.

Children experience an unbelievable number of *firsts* in their lives all the time. The first time I tried pineapple, the first time I rode a bike without training wheels, the first time I lost a tooth, the first time my heart was broken by kids at school; it goes on and on. It is their way of life. There is a freshness, exhilaration, pain, bewilderment, love, all new, all intense, very much "in the moment." No points of reference. Not jaded or encumbered or numbed by having been there before. I love that about all children. It is springtime to my autumn. If the pineapple is delicious it is *deeee-licious!* the first time. After falling off a bicycle again and again, bloody knees and all, that look of sheer pride and victory is eternally captured in the camera of happy memories when a child glides and rides independently: for that first time. Personally, I like pineapple. I like riding my bike. I tried these things out long ago and now they are automatic—I take them for granted. I don't eat and feel the same way as the *first* time. That *Be Here Now for the First Time Freshness* is one of the things I learn and need to constantly re-learn from my children.

The second of two things I want to mention now is *playing*. Not just with toys. That is one aspect of playing and I love to watch my kids be creative with the store-bought stuff and I especially love to watch how they get creative with junk and simple things like a box or piece of paper. For as long as I can remember, we have used the phrase "getting the artist-feeling" when an idea was bubbling over internally. "Mom, I need paper." "Do you have 'the artist-feeling'?" "Yes." Wonderful things are transformed from a plain piece of paper and a No. 2 pencil, guided by that "artist feeling." I asked Bryan recently about what happens to him as he is getting the artist-feeling. Straight-on little man that he is, a straight, quick answer: "I get a picture in my head and then I have to go and put it on paper right away." It is the same with projects: "I get an idea in my head of something I want to make and I have to go and make it. Now." Right away. And what if it's 10:00 at night? It has to be done even if he is scared of the dark. It is play but a mission as well.

There are infinite methods and mediums of play. Playing with art, with people, with toys, with ideas, with language. You can play with time and numbers, dirt, rocks, flowers; you can play with your own face, making it do outrageously cool contortions. Watch kids play with water; better yet, play in water with kids. Playing. Joking. Just this morning from Bryan: "Knock. Knock." "Who's there?" "45." "45, who?" "You are 45!" A roar of laughter from the little man, and when he realized that I was now *46*, it was all the more funny. Jokes are a new way to play and the rules are not set in stone—yet. There is no risk, no judgment from me. I didn't say "that was a dumb joke; it didn't make a whole lot of sense." Just the opposite: it was cute and funny and so is my son. We laughed together in genuine enjoyment of the newness of the whole experience and of each other. When kids are building with blocks, no Lego construction is ever "unacceptable." There is no right way or wrong way to finger-paint. Actually, the more mess the better. There is the kind of freedom in play that liberates the constrictions of too much training, too many criticisms, and way too many rejections in all forms. I have a friend who happens to be a grandmother as well as an artist. Janet calls me up and says: "Hey, Gloria, do you want to come over and *play*?" It's wonderful to hear that. Sure, let's do fabric-dyeing, bleach discharge, anything. Let's just play! She gives me toys that are different than mine—she won't let me play with black and brown too much because that is where I go. Janet puts out pink and orange and purple. I stretch my horizons when we play at her house.

Children have a beginner's mind, because they are beginners. They don't have to work at it or philosophize about it. Children play because they are children and that is how they "work" in the process of learning. So, where does that leave us older types? How about with the option available to choose to get back to basics, re-start as a beginner, liberate the child within and play so that we, too, can work at the learning process once again. I look in the mirror and I can see all the white hair. I just turned 46 and realized that that is closer to 50 than it is to 40. But I am still *inside* the little kid who threw toys at lightning bolts to chase them away so that we could keep on *playing!* I am so grateful to have my children in my life, not just to watch but also to grow up with. I get another chance to see life as new—together with them.

A pearl starts out as a grain of sand, an aggravator clamped inside a shell. Not a very glamorous beginning, but a stunning development. We, as adults, have pearlized aspects of ourselves and that is lovely. I am not suggesting here that we throw away all the layers of beauty and wisdom gained over a lifetime. I am, however, reminding myself that stripping away certain veneers is healthy. When I was growing up, people wanted to modernize everything and painted the lovely dark hardwoods in their homes all white. Later on, being modern translated into being natural, so it meant getting back to the original wood. That was painstaking strip-work. The results made it worth it, because getting back to the original was important—the genuine article once again. Keep what is real; strip away what is not. I have friends who are trained artists—degrees in graphics, fine arts: very impressive "stuff." Several of them have not "done art" for years. I mean nothing but a few careful sketches, tightly rendered and hidden in secret notebooks. These are successful people in the jobs they took on to make money. But their art is like a lost love. I've heard how their art was so trained into them that they lost the sense of childlike wonder at their own creativity, and hunkered down in knowledge, technique and fear of criticism to the point of immobility. The more they seemed to know, the more they knew they would never measure up to the standards of the masters or, more importantly, to the standard they expected of themselves. That is sad. Pablo Picasso said, "Every child is an artist. The problem is how to remain an artist once he grows up."

I know other people who are fulfilled and challenged in their fields and that is inspiring. We could all gain from looking at the very late-in-life work of Henri Matisse: his paper cuts. After all of his incredible masterpieces, a lifetime of creation, sitting in a wheelchair he could cut paper in joyful colors and simple shapes, covering walls in delight. If only I could cut paper like that—I wish. I am not coming from an art historian's perspective—I don't have the background. I just know that when I lugged home a 10-lb. library book about Matisse and saw an old photograph of him cutting paper with scraps cascading all over his lap, all over the floor, I was moved. He was like my kids with their junior Fiskars scissors, very simply expressing that "artist feeling."

When I was looking for a college to go to more than half a lifetime ago, I was moved when I read the first line of the St. John's College catalog at that time: "What is truth?"… It doesn't get any more fundamental or cosmic than that. The process suggested was to get back to Socratic methods. (A pretty pricey version of getting down on the ground and writing in the sand, engaging in conversations based on simple and direct questions.) Go directly to the literary personages of Western Civilization and ask your questions. I love the ideal. Go to the heart of the matter; go to the beginning. I am simply underlining my long-held desire and belief that learning is not simply a matter of piling up, it is also a process of stripping down. Good luck attempting to manage that balancing act.

Going to France a few years later, I allowed myself only one book in English. My self-imposed rules: Thou shalt *not speak* English, tough luck that your French is lousy. Thou shalt *not read* anything in English except one book: Suzuki-Roshi's *Zen Mind, Beginner's Mind*. I subsequently added to my limited traveling library and bought Jack Kerouac's *Desolation Angels* in French: *Les Anges Vagabonds*. Oh, brother. I wanted so much to be enlightened by the Zen book, but I just couldn't get it. *On the Road* had worked in English, but Kerouac sounded really strange in French, so I felt a bit stranded. That was good for me. I had been on Mount Olympus at St. John's, and in France, put myself in the position of literally writing in the sand and using hand-sign-language and emergency dictionaries to say even the simplest of things. It was baby-babble time, completely back-to-basics time. Months later when I had my first dream totally in French, I was ecstatic! When I went to England after that and stumbled and mumbled my way with English, I threw my head back in laughter. Stripping away fundamentals gave me the opportunity to know the joy of getting them back. Something basic: like talking.

We are going to be cleaning our basement soon—oh, horror and joy at the same time. I am going to keep my eyes wide open in search of my Suzuki book—I wonder if I'll "get it" this time. It will be interesting to open it up. It will be extremely rewarding to get-back-to-basics in organizing my house-world, too. My life seems to be an endless cycle to new beginning-points. (Found the book—that's where the quote came from…)

In my business life as a stamper/printmaker/tilemaker/whatever-er, I am a *beginner* in every sense of the word, and I am content. For me, *learning* is a total action verb, a motion that propels me. Having started with nothing but a love of making things with my hands, I am grateful to learn along the way, and feel genuinely excited with the freshness of being like a kid elbow-deep in finger-paints. I don't know about different mediums working together or not, so I experiment. Sometimes it works, sometimes not, but always I come away new. I have not learned so much about what *not* to do, so it is okay for me to just give things a try. Who cares? What is there to lose by trying? So many times I have been completely surprised. What seemed to me to be a small and fleeting idea turned into something big down the road. The twists and turns take us to places we never would have planned for or anticipated. We cannot always see the results of actions in the moment. Events get layered. Usually, I am pleasantly surprised, but this one weird day…

I did something strange with some tiles. There was a chemical reaction of some sort between sealers that I used and when I opened my booth up on the second morning of a major show, to my horror, there were a few tiles with the entire surface design peeled away and curled up like a sheet of Saran Wrap! My heart was pounding as I bundled them up, headed to the trash and heard a loud crash as they hit the bottom—how many of those had I sold yesterday? How many un-delighted customers were going to storm my tent for refunds on these fraudulent tiles? As it turned out, no one came back for a refund, but one woman came back to actually buy more! I explained my fear that she might have one from the "experiment that went awry" and gave her a "gift credit" just in case. She was excited and picked something out and I never did get any complaints—my 800-number was on everything. I never made that kind of tile again and I also never stopped trying new ideas. A little more research, perhaps, before heading to market…?

Whenever I've found myself getting too "heady," I've always gravitated to a place where I could be around kids for a while—like a playground, for example. When I was in college and had my fill of the big words, I'd hop on my bike in search of kid-world. With a book in hand, a pretense, I would sit there listening, not reading a single word. The inter-changes between children—that directness, simplicity, the honesty, possessiveness, the imaginative-twists, the rudeness, the cuteness, the joy were all heart-warming and revealing, if I was willing to look in my personal mirror. Children play games, but not the same games we play as adults. Their games are honest and in the open.

I never want to become so polished that I lose the rough edges of naturalness. Mexican river stones are about as smooth as I'd ever like to be. With eyes open, ears tuned in and heart listening, my challenge to myself: don't let the child within fade away.

I will conclude with a story of my oldest son as a preschooler, a sweet 4-year-old who was burned one day in an accident at school... scalding water on his leg and foot, my tender, soft baby. While I rushed there, he sat in pain, in water. As I held him, his teacher in tears apologized and said that Brandon had calmly looked around the room before I arrived and said, "Don't worry, Teachers, early in the morning it was a wonderful day." The teachers had to take turns leaving the room in tears, and I cried with his pain and because of his beautiful heart. How could such a little boy think of others like that when he was hurting so badly? What *exactly* is it that I am trying to learn from my children? Brandon's heart that day is my goal in life.

The Great Art Heist at the Camp

My maternal grandparents, Lucien and Antoinette, owned a small grocery store in Connecticut. They bought a piece of lakefront property up north a little, just over the border into Massachusetts, on the Congamond Lakes. This wonderful place became known as "the Camp" for the three generations connected to it. My mother Ida and her two younger brothers, Marcel and Norman, were very young children when their father passed away. In his all-too-short lifetime, with his own hands, hands that had grabbed hockey sticks and hugged his family, he created two things that would remain for us who had never met him: "the Camp," not quite finished, and a wooden game board (called a "Pichenotte" board), which he fashioned out of starch crates from their grocery store. Both were such happy legacies—heirlooms, an inheritance that money could never buy.

The Camp was yellow with white trim and the lake water sparkled like diamonds. It was so clear you could see the tiniest rocks on the bottom. You could see fish, too, and when you swam underwater, the sun streamed through, down into the water, refracting light and warming your vision. There was a dock and a small motorboat that my uncles maneuvered like flying fish chasing wild tsunamis. My uncle Marcel's smile and laughter were contagious even as he scared the living daylights out of us as he slammed into waves, making us fear for our lives! It was the thrill of a lifetime; we laughed until it hurt. If there weren't enough waves, he made more. We spun around and caught them *all*. Our butts were sore after that for *hours*. It is a major treat to have a "big teaser" in your life.

The Camp was Grand Central Station for barbecues and countless gatherings and vacations over generations. It had its own "smell," especially when the door was opened for the first time each year. Musty. Homey. Ours. All ours. Climbing a wooden ladder got you to the single big bedroom upstairs with exposed beams, four double, bouncy, creaky, squishy beds. Each time we started the summer, all my brothers and I raced upstairs to lay claim to the bed of our choosing—sometimes negotiable, at other times parental intervention was necessary. We also picked out our favorite bathrobes, the camp-style fuzzy-type with Indian designs on them that you pay a fortune for now, but at the camp were hanging all lined-up in different sizes on a pole ready for the picking. They were perfect for a cool late night chat on the long front porch.

The toilet was flushed with pails of lake water for many years. There wasn't anything particularly romantic about that whole situation and I vaguely remember talk of putting in a septic tank and a huge smelly hole in the back "yard" for a little while. But these things were grown-ups' problems. They solved them in short order and we were always free to just be kids. We could go exploring in the swamp behind the Camp, dash past "problems" holding our noses, and jump off the dock into the lake in front of the Camp. Life was a splash. One year the men in the family built the coolest changing room and storage shed—it even had showers. It was all so wonderful. I still have beautiful dreams of the Camp. They are always lovely, peaceful, happy, bonsoir dreams, and I always feel refreshed when I wake up and try to snuggle back to dreamland. The water sparkles like diamonds in the center of my being. The gentle sounds of lapping lake waves in the evening and at dawn, the fragrance of water lilies in the pond, hearing the oars cutting the water approaching the lilies… all parts of real dreams. To this day, we still have in the family a stone in two pieces that my brothers discovered in the hillside of sand that bordered our land—we were totally convinced it was a dinosaur egg. ("Lucky me" has it for my kids.) I don't care what the museum curators said in Hartford—it is still very real to us. There are only a few "things" remaining from life at the Camp. The dinosaur egg is one—it has a special place of honor in the Archives of Family Lore (inside a safe box.)

At one point during, I believe, my early teen years, my grandmother, Mémère, decided that for a number of her own reasons, she was going to sell the Camp. It was hard for me, but I really had no idea what it was like for all the adults, especially for my mother, to experience this loss. It happened. It was a chapter in our lives that was over. Summers were never the same. You move on, and we looked back, but there was no going back—until many years later. It was about 15 years ago, give or take a couple of years. I was about 30, my Mom 50-something, my Grandmother 70-something. It was many years after the Camp had been sold to who-knows. It was just the three of us. The two of them had come to the East Coast for a wedding and I was living in upstate New York. I picked them up in Connecticut and we drove together to see the Camp and re-visit our memories. What a trip.

Just getting there was nutty because after all those years, landmarks had changed. I had never driven there because I was a kid when the Camp was ours and I couldn't drive way-back-then. My mother had screwed-up once when we were little when she got brave and took to the driving wheel without my Dad. We got lost and couldn't seem to get out of Bristol, Connecticut for a long time. She was striking out on her own, taking the driver's seat. I always did admire her for persevering and getting us there no-matter-what. But as far as that trip in 1980-whatever, she was not the most confident navigator. My grandmother basically just took over with the directions and sure enough we got there. It was so interesting. Three generations of Gagne/Rajotte/Lagasse women pulling into the Camp, each of us with deep wells of our own, looking, walking, touching parts of our lives by touching things around us, filling those wells in our own ways.

The house was still yellow, but it had aged. Me, too. The people who owned the property were not there, no answer at the door. It was still very early in the season for lake folks and it felt abandoned in a peaceful sort of way. We had some personal time, reflection-space. As I walked on the side porch, I couldn't believe it—oh my God, the lake—it had shrunk! What on earth happened? I had "just gotten bigger," my Mom informed me. It was always like this. In my mind's-eye it was oceanic. The diamond-water-sparkles still made me squint and that was the beauty of it. Mom went to the water and held it, caressed it, splashed it, and I'm sure she doused herself. Born again. I picked up rocks for skipping, unhappy that the water was so green-looking now and smelled like gasoline. The soft sound of distant Johnson motors wasn't there that day—my uncles' boat was a mirage at best. Mémère was sitting where the picnic table had been. There was silence, then a few whispers. I knew that this was the only time in my life that this would happen and I wanted to hold it still. A slow song played over and over…

There was a point when it seemed like it was time to go—and my grandmother led that little expedition, la générale. But the troops were reluctant, since I think my Mom and I could have camped out and slept on the ground: anything to be there. We slowly marched back up the hill and stopped at the porch, looking in with cupped hands to see if we would recognize any remnant from our time. Maybe that ugly coconut-head, a table, metal chairs, something to say, "We were here" long ago. Then it happened. My mother fixed her gaze on something through the dark screen. She grabbed me and pointed. It was hard to make it out. Oh my God, there it was! This print, a picture of the "Indian Maiden by the Lake," *Our Lady of the Lake!* The picture was hanging crooked and you couldn't see the whole thing. Something was on top of the picture. A cloth? What was covering it? I couldn't believe it. It was actually a pair of men's underwear, Fruit of the Looms (Hanes, BVD's, you get the idea), stiff and dry after a winter of hanging on a nail, and desecrating our Work of Art! It was an outrage, and my grandmother, sensing that this whole little episode was starting to get out of hand, wanted us to get out of there faster than immediately. She started grumbling in French and my mother was ignoring her in a very amusing kind of way—not insulting or rude, just amusing.

All of a sudden, my mother tells me: "We are going to take that 'painting'!" As in *TAKE IT!* She starts fiddling with the porch screen, loosens, then opens it, and informs me that since I am the smallest, she will boost me up and I will get on that porch and *rescue* the Indian Maiden. Remove it, as in re-possess it—*steal* it, right off of the porch wall. I can't believe this is happening! My own mother is demanding that I be her partner in crime! (Side bar here: Please understand that this Indian Lady looks nothing like a Native American woman and it certainly is not a painting. It's more like something you would cut off from the top of an expired calendar. It is also the most romanticized picture you ever laid eyes on—this woman looks like a compilation of Disney's Pocahontas with Snow White's face framed with a wig of black-braided-hair, propped in a silent-movie set for *South Pacific Lake*, circa Flappers' era, 1920. It is serene, surreal, and no matter how silly it is in a way, I have always loved it, and apparently, so did my mother. It goes way past cartoon. It is so special. It shows how we ladies felt when we were at the Camp.)

My grandmother's grumbling got not a whole lot louder, but a whole lot racier. She was cursing up a French-Canadian blue streak, and I had a general idea of what she was saying, and got filled in later as to the details. Whew. Before I knew what was happening, my mother had her hands cupped, my foot was in this stirrup of sorts, and I was pulling back the screen, pulling myself up and onto the porch. My heart was pounding. What if those people were indeed inside and heard this "breaking-and-entering?" There are other cottages within seeing-distance—who was calling the police? I removed the stiff underwear and—there she was! Pound-pound-pound. I handed the picture to my Mom. And I actually carefully replaced the underwear on the nail—don't ask me why. We put the screen back in place, thank God it wasn't damaged, and high-tailed it to the car, Indian Maiden rescued and secure in my shaky little sweaty criminal hands. Generations of Catholic guilt descended upon me, and there was no confessional in sight. In the trunk, locked away, was this picture from a past life. Driving away, my grandmother is still going at it, my mother is beaming, and I can't believe I just did what I did.

My mother is so cool—she wants to do a little sightseeing in the area before we go home! I want to get out of the state of Massachusetts like yesterday. Guess what. We go sightseeing to another part of the lake. I could care less how lovely the view is and she is having a jolly time, my grandmother is fuming and then my dear mother decides that we couldn't possibly leave the good state of Massachusetts without making one last pit-stop. Why don't we go and buy some pies at this place we used to buy pies from? Why don't we *get out of here*?!!! I'm driving, so I get directions from my passengers and we drive to the pie place. All of a sudden, in the distance directly behind me, a Police siren is heard and the Police car is bearing down on *me!* It is speeding-up and getting closer and I am in a total panic, hands gripping the steering wheel white-knuckled style, eyes bugging out of my head, and my mother thinks the whole thing is hysterical! Let *her* tell you this story someday. All I can see is jail and Major Newspaper Headings, my reputation ruined for life. I'm losing my mind, totally freaked, and she is going nuts laughing! There was no way that I was going to look in the rear-view mirror and check out my Grandmother's expression. When I did look back, all I could see was flashing red lights and the siren was unnerving me. I slowed down, and the Police car pulled out and went around me... and just kept going. He was gone. All of this panic was for nothing. We pulled into the driveway and my hands were shaking badly. My mother gets out and saunters around, having a great old time picking out pies and I stay in the car trying to make some kind of reconciliation-connection to my grandmother and trying to calm down at the same time. I get her to reminisce about her husband and their early romance... That was nice, but I can't remember much of what she said. At one point I got out of the car and it somehow came out that the policeman is a friend of the owners of the pie shop and does his siren thing once in a while. It was all a joke. Ha, ha, ha.

Back to Connecticut we went, on to New York I went, and home to New Mexico the Indian Maiden went. And I haven't gone to jail yet.

My Mom's heart was broken when the Camp was sold. It was sold along with most of the contents. Probably my grandmother saw things for what they seemed to her—old, junk, "dust collectors," storage problems, etc. Maybe so for her, but maybe not for others. She wanted to leave it behind, my mother needed to take it with her; her Dad had built it. We didn't have the money to buy the Camp. It was gone. Having *Our Lady of the Lake* was a heart-healer. She was a symbol and priceless in a spiritual kind of way. And speaking of spiritual, my grandmother did tell me, years later, in her own interesting kind of way, that she forgave me for taking the picture, and her smile secured it for me. Did I catch a glimmer of amusement or perhaps even pride in that smile from someone whose own renegade stories raised my eyebrows more than once or twice? I can only speculate.

Living in Missouri, I frequent Antique Malls and one day (spacing around), I was stunned to see a picture that was very close in imagery to the Indian Maiden. Same look. Same kind of frame. I carefully took it off its nail (memories flooding back), looking for the price tag: $37.50. Hmmm. I guess I owe that to the owner, at least that much. I did try to find out who lived at the Camp in the 1980's, calling the Southwick Town Hall, but I couldn't get the address through my description, because we never had an address during those early years. I did try, but I didn't go overboard with the search either. My Mom and her best friend Elaine actually went a number of years ago for another visit—entirely different place physically by that point, probably the same people. She met them and they had a very nice visit and chat. The topic of "The Great Art Heist" was not brought up in the conversation, I'm sure of that. In speaking with my mother just today, she said that The Heist never even *occurred* to her when she was chatting with the nice people by the lake. It wasn't a matter of hiding the fact from them—she absolutely and genuinely believes that the Indian Maiden is *hers*. Oh, brother, and Amen to that at the same time.

If this ever gets to the point that this all comes back to haunt me, legally-speaking, then so be it. I will pay the price of the "Painting," offering to double the price or whatever it takes so that my mother can keep it, and if worse-comes-to-worse and I get hauled off to serve time for breaking-and-entering, and she has to give it up, I will beg for one thing—Please, *please*, let me go to Kinko's first and make the best color-photo-copy

I can for my Mom, because no matter what, she has to have a copy of that print. It is a part of the Camp, so it is a part of her. It is also this crazy story of three generations…

She assured me today that she will visit me in jail, and I assured her that she can serve time *with* me, sweetie-pie, or share community-service hours, or whatever comes down. I am *not* going down alone. Don't even think about it.

My grandmother passed away a few years ago in Santa Fe at the age of 89. We had a lovely memorial family gathering, and at my Mom's home there was a beautiful array of photographs from Mémère's life, candles and flowers, and prominently displayed: the picture of the Indian Maiden, "Our Lady of the Lake." The story was told to my younger cousins of how we did indeed "rescue" the Lady and my mother's heart as well in the process. In the midst of sharing some of her handmade hats, jewelry and other great assorted mementos, we had a "fashion show," prancing around the room in vintage classics, my cousins and I. My youngest son Bryan was a toddler and the hit of the show as he piled about seven of her crocheted hats on top of his head at the same time, waltzing around the room, making sure everyone got in on the act. We all performed "Mémère imitations" of her "profile-nose-pose" and roared ourselves to happy tears.

Another generation had just heard a Camp Story. I can just see my grandmother soaking up every minute of being in the spotlight of this story—the more you tell it, the wilder it gets, the more of a legend it becomes and the more we laugh. Add another one to the family archives. "Art" finds its way into our lives, one way or another.

Do these ambling stories have anything at all to do with my *business*? Yes, they do. Are they detailed accounts that amount to nothing more than aimless journeys into the vast past? I hope not. Artists live in the world of symbols. We are creators of work that is symbolic to others and symbolic to us—it is meaningful, it invokes an emotion, a memory, dream, a wish... I may create a piece that means one thing to me, and entirely something different to other people drawn to it for their own personal reasons. Our stories are the same—symbols of the bigger picture. That is how I see it.

Life is either a daring adventure
or nothing at all.   - Helen Keller

Generation after generation… ripples in the pond.
Water lilies go deep and hold strong, delicate on the surface.

"I think I'll skip the Louvre, merci."
Where to find art

"Anywhere I found wood I took it home and started working with it to show the world that art is everywhere, except that it has to pass through a creative mind."

- *Louise Nevelson*
Russian-born American Sculptor

It was the overnight train to Paris. For me it was the overnight train *through* Paris. I didn't have a plan to stop. This was the same train that had carried thousands of soldiers during The War. I wasn't going to war but I had my own battles and my own agenda.

Head bobbing, hopefully not on anyone, my vision blurred in the middle of the night in the middle of France somewhere, this Frenchman leans over and whispers: "Pardon, veux-tu visiter Paris? Veux-tu aller au Louvre?" (Loose translation: "Pardon me, don't you want to visit Paris and check out the Louvre?") My response, in my unique Connecticut-Yankee, touch of Canadian, hippy-traveler personal version of a valiantly attempted French sentence (in translation): "I think I'll skip the Louvre, merci. I came to France to see *art*, not Paris or museums. I came to look at people's faces and listen to their stories. I came to walk on the land, the earth of France."

Ouch. That was received with a look that was exactly what I relished—what a great face I got for that slanderous remark. The look was accompanied by a sniff, rolled eyes, and a mumbling of something about "those Americans" and I was off dozing again on my way north—straight through Paris, Mon Dieu…

In France, I wanted to tear my identity to shreds by taking away my own language, my comfort zone, first. Then the idea was to shake up ordinary, conventional thoughts, like going to museums to see art, and give that a toss as well. My last name is a French name—it comes from the Old French word for "stone mason." I sat on the stone walls of grand châteaus playing music on my recorder, connected and content. People smiled…

Today, twenty-five years later: Oh, wouldn't it be so wonderful to go back to France after all these years? This time I want to go with my whole family, not alone again. My son thinks Paris is way too much about romance based on all the cartoons he's seen, and I know that it is way over the top in terms of how much it would cost to pull it off, but I would love to go—*especially* to Paris and at least a whole week spent meandering in and gazing at the Louvre. Oh, to see all of the museums, galleries, cafes, flea markets, bakeries… How exhilarating to bicycle through the countryside brushing along the fields of lavender, poppies and sunflowers. The delicately massive stone houses with old wooden shutters, the ancient roads and grapevines… they would all wrap their secrets around my imagination. I want it all and I want to share it all.

And to this day, I would still look at all the faces of all the people, convinced even more strongly now than ever: *that* is the most beautiful art in the world to me: a face and the story behind it. In my personal reflections, whether discussing building the business or living daily life, I see people woven in, again and again. I smile at each one. There is no distinction in my mind between "what I do for a living" and living. They are one.

Customers... without them, no business

For the first couple of years in my business, I was rather detached from the idea and reality of "customers." I knew they existed because I was getting orders. People were buying my things to sell in their shops and other people were buying from the shops so the circle was complete—sort of, but not really. Who were all of these people anyway? My reps handled the buyers and the buyers handled their customers, and I sat at whatever table happened to be available making "the stuff." I always felt a sense of gratitude that somebody in the great "out there" liked what I was making enough to pay for it, yet I also experienced a strange sense of alienation from the whole process. My end involved designing, receiving purchase orders, production and shipping. At one point, it wasn't enough. I wanted faces and stories—real contact. "Hello. I want to shake your hand."

You say that out loud, the fact that you want this personal contact with customers and all that—it sounds nice and invigorating, warm and fuzzy. Once reality sets in, however, it can also sound a bit intimidating and threatening as well as potentially rewarding and heartwarming—a toss of the proverbial coin. I drew a line in the sand and made myself cross it—I made an appointment with the buyer for a Museum Shop—and met my first real live customer face-to-face. That whole story is coming very soon, but I had to re-visit these two moments from that experience: making the call and then shaking hands. Thank God it was a good experience in the end. Thank goodness I ventured out past the great wall of fear. I met many buyers after that first meeting who are my customers but also, on occasion, more than that. If I am open to it, I may get great advice, business-savvy insight and even a new friend. Sometimes it is all business—sometimes not: like my account at St. John's College Bookstore in Santa Fe—it goes way beyond.

I avoided approaching that particular bookstore for years. I had been a student there eons ago, never finished, and therefore had unfinished internal business there and didn't want to be embarrassed by being rejected as a "card vendor." Somehow the thought of going there to sell cards when so many of the graduates throughout *history* went on to become rich and successful, threw me a curve ball. So I put it off for years. How many times are we going to visit the procrastination scenario? Who knows.

One curious thing: the location of the bookstore has changed since my era and is now the former main college library where I had had a student aid job. The "old library" is now a successful business with one of the ultimate greeting card selections in Santa Fe, a place of many serious competitors—the compliment is well deserved. My Mom, the catalyst, got my behind up there one time under some ruse to go visit our friend Hannah, who just happened to be working in the bookstore and who just happened to have worked in the bookstore when I was a student as well—that was how we met. I wasn't prepared to make a card presentation, and I did not have an appointment. It was just a "visit." Now that I think about it, how convenient that my mother had me bring my card samples "just to have in case something strikes us during the day as we are out and about..." I see.

It was great to see Hannah, I met Craig and Andrea, and my fears were melting through their kindness. As I was chatting about how wonderful the bookstore was, all of a sudden the conversation shot back in my direction and the big question was asked: "Gloria, you make cards, don't you? Do you happen to have samples with you? We would love to see them..." "I didn't make an appointment or anything, so maybe some other time would be better for you?" "*Now* would be great if it works for you." "Well, okay, I'll just go out to the car and get my master set. I'll just be a minute…" that turned into years of a very special account for me. I am proud to say that I have had cards at St. John's College Bookstore in Santa Fe, New Mexico. It is way beyond business for me. They are beyond "customers" or "accounts."

It would be a very long list if I were to gather all the names of all the accounts I have ever had over the years. Are all of them close friends that bring me to tears whenever I visit? Some, but definitely not all. Most of the time it is strictly business, it is friendly and I am grateful. Through the buyers and the fact that I was acting as my own rep and speaking directly with them, I was receiving the benefit of their insights and getting an ego boost because of their approval and compliments about my work—they were putting money on the line to buy from me, and they were giving me shelf space in beautiful shops that pay a premium for every square inch. The appreciation and respect were going both ways. (I think my mother pulled a fast one on me, and I am so glad she did.)

In the less romantic and ideal scenarios, there were places that my cards did not do so well in, and over time and after experimentation, they were dropped. It makes business sense. I never feel sorry for having tried and I do not feel mortified because they didn't sell. It's just the way it goes sometimes—not the right product in the right place at the right time. Live and learn and on to the next place. I would rather have fewer, bigger accounts than to be spread thin making piddly numbers of cards to be sent all over the known universe. Give me substantial orders and a chance to focus.

Being my own rep took me closer to the feeling of connecting with "my customers," but there was one more layer to uncover and the way for me to get there was to do retail art shows and I knew that. It is there that you hear the "oooo's and ahhh's," and get asked all the questions about your intriguing techniques, style, and things like "how can you be so creative and come up with new things all the time?" You get to answer the questions, get to know people directly, wrap their purchases and see them writing checks directly to you and in your presence. It is all very "now" and genuine. It is also the time when you can be in a place where the sponsors swear that 50,000 people come with their wallets bulging with wads of money they can't wait to spend on art, and you happen to notice those tens of thousands of people walking right on by your booth. Being steady, hopeful and open hour after hour, day after day is good training on a lot of levels. Once you are there, you cannot just walk away. The customers that are streaming by may also turn around and come back. It is the handful that do get off the beaten path, come in, look around and connect with you and your work—and even buy it—they make it all worth it. Believe me. It goes way beyond a business deal for me—it is a matter of heart.

There is no such thing as a business without customers. There is no such thing as doing art without being sensitive to how it is received and perceived by other people. When someone loves what you do, shares a word or two, smiles, responds to your creative efforts, tells you where the piece is destined—it is so deeply rewarding. Just the other day, I ran in with my son to Poppy, a gift store downtown, delivering the last of my Christmas products on consignment. As we were heading to the backroom, my son and I noticed that a mother and daughter were standing in "my section" in the store, with a number of my things in their hands, obviously considering buying. My son shot me the greatest look of pride in his Mom and a few quiet words. Whenever this kind of thing happens, I usually savor the moment, and then walk on by, not wanting to bring attention to myself or in any way put pressure on the sale. This time, I couldn't help myself—the

Holiday spirit was everywhere, so I just quietly walked over and said a few words. What a sweet and gracious woman—she said all the lovely things that you could ever hope to hear—simple, honest, and cordial; as a Mom, she knew how to bring my son into the experience. I respected that. Whether they bought my things or not, I may never know, but the fact that they were clearly appreciating it as we walked in will always be with me.

There was the customer who came into my tent in the pouring rain. It was my last outdoor show; it had to close down. He bought some cards and reminded me that he had purchased one of my first tile "efforts" the year before, a very crazy-looking tile, an Aztec serpent of all things. We laughed and it brightened a rough morning. The day before, I had made over $1,000. The "storm day" I made $27. Because a kind man bought in the rain and made me laugh, the day was saved and memorable. It wasn't a disaster or a waste. He gave me a few dollars for a few cards and a heck of a lot more. Such is the power of "the customer" with heart, especially the ones who keep coming back.

Another show: Kit, the Professor of Geography who flew by the tent, handed me $10 and yelled, "Put that one on hold for me! I'll be back!" and did come back—these are all part of a personal treasure trove of experiences. I had to make a custom change on Kit's framed piece—he wanted a red "sun" to replace the black circle I had block-printed on. He was right—it needed to be red. Trying to get that done in the middle of the night the week after a show when you are exhausted past reality is not the best idea. I smudged the rice paper. It happened to be antique rice paper and the last piece I had, so I needed to be creative in terms of fixing it—just as soon as I stopped crying at 2:00 in the morning. An inspiration hit and the result was more beautiful than the original. I made silver "grass" out of Chinese Joss paper that covered the smudge and added a dimension. Of course I explained the alteration and Kit found the whole story inspirational enough to not only accept the revised artwork, but to tape my "confession" on the back of the piece as a point of added value. It is now hanging in Kit and Cathy's home on Breakfast Creek.

So many customers, so many stories. I can write hundreds of pages about the "business" in all of its myriad forms, but the art techniques and technical aspects mean nothing at all compared to the value of people who have entered my life and stayed there through the years. Whenever I hear or read the word "customer," I listen for what comes afterwards. There are marketing "techniques" to get people to buy your products. But customers can sometimes be discussed as if they are some kind of commodity themselves—not my style. I am not averse to learning how to communicate with customers and setting up the best environment for sales. I can respect that as a skill and even as an art in and of itself. This is what I know and believe strongly: my customers are people who respect my work, and me, and that respect is returned to them with gratitude. My customers are keeping my business alive, and because they are buying my creations, I am able to give more to my family, not only financially, but also emotionally because my customers are supporting my lifestyle of choice, which is so satisfying and rewarding.

I had to sit back with eyes closed for a minute here and found myself saying: "Don't blow this piece. You have thousands of experiences, so many people to thank. Make sure it is clear. You waited until the very end to write about this topic for a reason—it is so dear to your heart..." To say that I love these people is not an exaggeration. It is true.

Customers, and my connection to them, are the pulse of my whole business, the lifeblood. A few examples, a few pages, I can't put it all down here, yet I can say thank you to each special person who is part of this picture—we both know who you are.

Do the hardest thing first

and get it over with...

One of the biggest advantages of having a rep(resentative) for me is the fact that I am in a kind of "safety zone." I do not have to make appointments to set myself up for pain and rejection. Let the rep show my things; let the rep get rejected; it's not personal for them, anyway. It is *extremely* personal for me. "What do you mean you don't like my cards? Does that mean then that you don't like *me*?" On the other hand, I also do not have the opportunity to learn directly from the experience of dealing with buyers, absorbing their environments, jumping in there and co-designing for very specific design needs and requests. So, emotionally I may be protected from the uncomfortable position of hearing: "No thank you, we are not interested," but the fact is that I am missing more than I am gaining. At least that is how my thinking went about two years into the business. I had a great rep; that was in place. But what about "repping myself"? Could I get up the nerve to show up on my own and face the music? At the same moment that I knew it was the best next step to take, I simultaneously knew that it was the hardest.

Since I was going to be in Santa Fe for a limited amount of time before trekking to the Midwest, I was keenly aware of the fact that my window of opportunity was narrow. Contacting my rep about my idea turned out to be interesting. I sensed a hesitation on her part and wanted to understand what was going on. I learned about "territories," and I certainly didn't want to create any problems in our relationship, but I also was convinced by that time that there were places that I could get as customers/accounts, or at least try to get, that my rep had not attempted yet, for a variety of reasons. From my perspective, this was "Open Territory," and we worked out a congenial way of communicating which accounts were "hers" and which were "house accounts," in other words: "mine." Over time it served us both well, I believe. My business base expanded substantially.

Frankly, it was all cozy-jive-chit-chat-theory for some time, because I was too scared to do it. I was used to sitting at a table, dinking around with rubber stamps. I wrapped orders up and sent them on their merry way. I could wear t-shirts or pajamas if I wanted to because I worked at home and sometimes I worked in the middle of the night. No one saw me—I saw no one. I knew that I had to blast it wide open. Time was slipping through my fingers like sand through Dorothy's hourglass, and Toto, the Tin Man, Scarecrow and Cowardly Lion were not on their way to bail me out—it was all up to me. It was time to get "dressed-up and grow-up" and march straight into the business world whether I felt prepared or not. Waiting was not getting me any more ready; that was clear enough.

Where-to-go was the next big question. Northern New Mexico is filled to the overflowing with wonderful shops. I knew what I had to do—find the place that scared me the most, the nicest, hardest-to-get-into-shop I could come up with and make my first appointment there. There is a certain risk in doing that, but the need to get the hardest one behind me, no matter how it went, outweighed the morale-rationale of going easy on myself and starting with some potentially "safer" first attempt. I know myself—if I went soft, there would always be this lingering fear in the future of that "hardest place" until I finally built up the courage to try. I was in one of those "Go for Everest!" modes and knew what that translated into, as far as my business was concerned at that time and place: *The Museum of Fine Arts Gift Shop*, downtown Santa Fe. Oh, brother.

I had heard about it. It was described as a lovely place, quite small, exclusive and competitive. There is limited showing space; everything is carefully selected. I had cards and bookmarks; I knew that they carried cards. All I could do was try, so I called and made an appointment. That was quite a fumbling-around experience in its own right, since the terminology was not familiar to me and I did not have a name to connect to or a referral that could get me in the door. It took a couple of calls to connect personally to the card buyer, Linda. She was cordial and we set up an appointment. I tried my best to prepare some cards and bookmarks in a three-ring binder "portfolio" of sorts. I did not know about setting up a "deck" of cards, the preferred method of buyers. They want to have a stack of individually sleeved cards so that they can blitz through a line, pull out, layout, and see the selection in its entirety, as it would appear on their shelves. I had a little book with examples taped in on the pages. Oh well, we all start with something.

Arriving way too early, I needed to kill some time, so I waited in the hallway of the Fine Arts Museum, explaining to the guards why I wasn't paying money to actually go into the Museum. They gave me permission to sit in the courtyard and use the restroom. I was so nervous I was sweating and I was not climbing a mountain or doing anything more strenuous than sitting. It usually takes a serious vertical hike to get a sweat going for me there. It is extremely dry in New Mexico, but I was not that morning. The hourglass emptied and I approached the door of the Museum Shop. Opening the door, I couldn't help but notice how it sparkled in there. Walking to the counter, I introduced myself, explaining that I had an appointment with the shop manager, Linda. I had approached the right person and we exchanged a friendly handshake. She welcomed me and asked to see what I had brought. I opened my little book, slowly turning the pages and explaining that these were handmade cards and bookmarks, wondering if she would be interested in carrying them in the Museum of Fine Arts Gift Shop…

She kindly looked through everything, and then looked at me and said: "You have very nice work and I like your design-sense and presentation. However, as you can see, the theme in this particular Museum Shop is not centered on Native American Art, which is the heart of what you have shown me. These designs would do well perhaps, in our other shops…" and as she was talking, I felt this unstoppable wave of embarrassment ascend from my feet to my face and I completely turned red, as in *bright* red, and with my shock of white hair, I must have been quite a sight. I couldn't believe that I had been so worked-up about going there in the first place that I had never even ventured into the shop to see what they carried and to figure out that what I made was not appropriate there at all. Mortified and standing there, I was frozen in place, speechless.

And right then and there, as I will never forget and will always be grateful for, I was rescued by Kindness and an arm-around-my-shoulder. Linda quietly said, "I think the quality of your work is great. What if we walk around the shop together and see what ideas and inspirations come to you. Perhaps you could create something special for our shop, based on what you observe and get inspired by. Let's look together…" She held my arm for a moment and I felt steadied. It was quickly apparent that the main element in the marketing of the shop was "Georgia O'Keeffe." Posters, books, cards—this, after all, was, up until the creation years later of "The Georgia O'Keeffe Museum" in Santa Fe, *the* place to see originals in the museum's wonderful collection. Linda asked me what stood out and of course I simply said: "Georgia O'Keeffe." Bingo. Could I "possibly work up some prototypes of cards and bookmarks that we might like to carry with that theme in mind?" "I will try my best. Thank you." With that, she explained to me that I would need to make a presentation of ideas, send them to her, and then there would be a process of Review, before possible acceptance. No promises to be accepted and get in, but a lot of support to go ahead, be creative, and put it out there. See what happens. I left grateful and energized because of the way I was treated.

I learned so much that day, and probably have more to learn from the experience over time. First of all, I learned that it is wise, and makes a great deal of sense, to go to a possible account *in person*, if at all physically possible. Study the merchandise, the layout, the ambience, and the colors… I could have done that easily, geographically-speaking. It was a short drive from my house, but it was a long way from my thinking. It is interesting to reflect on that in retrospect—if I *had* gone in ahead of time, would I have figured that it was better to forget the idea entirely? I can't do a reverse-crystal-ball thing here—all I know is that I was entirely fortunate to have a kind person guide me through what could have been a humiliating, discouraging first-effort, leaving me in the dust. Someone wearing a lovely white lace blouse was willing to pick me up from the dust—to teach, not demean. I learned that "professional" business people do not have to be stereotypically cold and brusque. I hope a lot of people can learn that. That helped me to be able to go to a second shop and then a third… and have many stories from then on.

My mother, bless her heart, was waiting for me outside on a white iron bench on the Plaza. It had gone well. We were happy and relieved. And I had an idea. Let's go to the stamp store across the street and check out if there are any Georgia O'Keeffe images. I seemed to remember that they carried some. We headed over there and sure enough, there it was—the stamp I needed. I also found a stamp of a steer skull that could work (until I carved my own years later) and I was on the way to a new level of building my business. I wrote to the stamp company and got permission. I read about Georgia and learned that she collected Chinese Scrolls, so I designed cards and bookmarks using Chinese Joss paper. I did go on to make a presentation to the Fine Arts Review Committee or whatever they were called and my designs were approved. I then had to write to The Georgia O'Keeffe Foundation in Taos for *their* approval, and even though I stupidly misspelled "O'Keefe," forgetting the second-f, they kindly corrected me in the approval letter. (I try my darnedest not to make any spelling mistakes after that goofy, idiotic, dumb faux pas.) Blundering along the way, but not giving up, it took about six months to "get in." It was more than worth the time and effort. I was "in" the Museum of Fine Arts Gift Shop in Santa Fe, New Mexico, folks. That was behind me and ahead of me at the same time.

Over time, the bookmarks out-sold the cards, so the cards were phased out and I made many orders of the other. That went on for years and things changed within the system a number of times, so I find myself wanting to go back for another visit to see what is there now, and how I could possibly fit in once again. Some accounts stay and some fluctuate. Whatever happens in the future with this one particular shop is open in my mind, but what happened in the past opened me up to so much. From there, I went on to very different types of shops, from The Wheelwright Museum of the American Indian to The Museum of International Folk Art, to Ten Thousand Waves Japanese Health Spa, to the Santuario in Chimayo. My range of designs expanded along with the confidence that came from the experience of putting myself on my own frontline. Am I afraid to go anywhere and talk to anyone about what I do? No, I'm not. I'm serious about it and I get a little nervous because I want to make a good presentation, but that is light years away from fear. Can I give a formula for how to approach your own accounts? Not really, but I will say that sincerity and the willingness to listen are good starting points. I will also say that arrogance and pushiness don't have a place in my approach. Every single time I have met with a buyer, I have learned something about my business, business in general, my limits and potential. Now I look forward to the next encounter. If it helps to take a friend with you, do it. My Mom went with me a few times and my friend and cousin, Ann, went to an appointment that made me nervous. They were near—it helped—support does that.

Has it all been fun and games with no rejections? No, this is the real world. Is it the best idea in the world for everyone to do the hardest thing first? It's not the way I go every time, that's for sure. You have to know your tolerance level for pain and suffering. If you do get rejected, will you get blown out of the water and discouraged from ever knocking on another door? Then don't do it this time. When the place, timing and your courage are in sync, it is good to consider taking up the challenge. After facing the hardest place first, getting that over with and surviving it, resilience and confidence are easier to attain and maintain. Plus the experiences just make the best stories; trust me.

There is "do the hardest thing" and there is also "say the hardest thing." Strangely enough, that can mean for many people, putting words to their dreams. I went to a conference. It was a good one, especially because of the main speaker, Bill Hunt, a potter with many other credentials in the inspiration business. In the final moments, he put us into little groups and directed us to discuss different points "out loud" with members of the group—what I do, impediments in my way, realistic goals, etc. The big monster leap was that we were to say "the most outrageous dream we have"—to envision ourselves in the way-out-there realms of success. It was fascinating. Every person had his or her own experience with it. Mine was to avoid the topic in the beginning. I realized we were all avoiding it in one way or another by chatting, and I decided to push the issue. I made this one poor person *SAY IT!* She finally came out with it. It was a big dream and we all got excited for her; she beamed. Then, oh *no!* The group time was up and *I hadn't said mine.* I turned around, grabbed somebody, anybody at that point and said: "I want to sit down and talk with Oprah about my book." That sounded so nutty to me that I laughed—hard. There are other big crazy ideas that I have and now I just say them out loud. I'm learning. It doesn't hurt anyone, I enjoy just letting it rip, and I was shocked to find out that the right people to tell don't look at you funny at all—they smile back. My wildest ideas sound less crazy by the day, since some of them are real now. This is all very liberating.

As for re-enforcement for the concept of "doing the hardest thing first" and having the *courage* (meaning "believe in your heart") to do it, how about the following:

A person who has never made a mistake
has never tried anything new.   - *Albert Einstein*

Courage is being scared to death
but saddling up anyway.   - *John Wayne*

You've got to jump off cliffs all the time
and build your wings on the way down.   - *Ray Bradbury*

62

Credentials

The biography on the back of a card...

What makes me think that I have the qualifications to write a book and the credentials to proclaim myself an artist all at the same time? Who gave me permission? I did. After all these years I guess I just decided that it is what makes me happy so I am just doing it and learning along the way. It is working for me. I am making new agreements with myself. Definitions are open to change because I am open to change.

When I was a sophomore in high school, I made a fateful decision. After years of driving and pushing myself relentlessly in school for the almighty grade and the acceptance and adulation that accompanied success, titles and awards, I found myself floundering. I overheard a girl talking about me in the cafeteria, a sweet girl. She said to her friend: "Gloria is so smart. I wonder if she knows how hard it is for other people to learn. I think I would like her, but I am afraid to even see if she would like me. I am afraid of her." Soon afterwards I resolved to blow my grades out of the water and to, in effect, throw my credentials-to-the-future in the trash. My plan unfolded...

I struggled with my sophomore English teacher as much as I had loved my freshman one. So, I decided that I was not going to do any work in the class, not take any tests and therefore flunk English. Period. It was my best and one of my favorite subjects. I would sit there and not participate at all. She seemed bitter and uninspired as a teacher and I was going to reciprocate and take care of my "Gloria is so smart" image all at the same time. My teacher was fit to be tied.

Sitting there doing nothing at all was a novel experience. Getting glowered at instead of praised was new and my friends didn't know what to make of it. I was radical in some ways, but usually not stupid. I persevered and held firm until report card time and opened it up to find: English: A. "*A??? This is a terrible mistake*!" I went directly to my teacher and demanded to know why I had been given an "A," when I most clearly, definitely, absolutely, without question deserved an "F." "...because, Miss Lagasse, I know the game you are playing. If you had done the work you would have gotten an 'A,' so you have it on your record and that is final." Really. Well, next we paid a little visit to the Assistant Principal, the big gun nun who lived in the same convent with my English teacher. It didn't go so well there, either. She wouldn't go less than a "D." That became the record. The Principal wanted no part of this one.

My position in the hierarchy of the smart people was blown to bits and it was interesting to explain that grade at college interviews later on, although I enjoyed telling it as much as they seemed to be intrigued listening to it. It was a game of sorts; I did "damage" my credentials, sort of. The sweet, shy girl who was afraid of me ended up becoming a friend and we worked together on a Coffee House project later on in high school. All too soon, second semester English was upon us. My teacher did put the "D" on the report card and approached me the very first day of second semester in front of the whole class. Her announcement/pronouncement was as follows:

"Since you were not interested in being a *student* last semester, I thought you would prefer being the *teacher* this semester for our unit on Romantic Literature. (Something like that.) You may pick any author of your choosing and prepare a presentation for the class for this date... that is one month away. We'll see what you do this time."

I poured my heart and soul into this one, that's what I did this time. Gathering a group of friends, I asked each of them to prepare a chapter chosen from Kahlil Gibran's *The Prophet* for a multi-media presentation: music, stage lights, readings, the works. I wrote, directed and did the "sound board" (tape player). On the given day, my class, teacher included, were seated in the Auditorium for the Performance, my English class where I was the "teacher." My three friends, Jeanne, Paul and Win did a superb job with their readings. Many people were moved to tears, all applauded warmly and as it turned out the entire school would see the performance over the course of one week.

My rebellion was a bit unusual and it took different forms over the years since then. Wrestle, tussle and toss the status quo around and see who and what shakes out. My teacher was right in a way to say that I was playing a "game," but it was not according to her definition or rules. Her compliment after the performance of "good job" flew straight past me as I told her "thank you" and also to "please save it for someone who really worked hard, didn't get A's, and needed to hear that from a teacher." Looking into my classmates' eyes was my deep satisfaction. After my "D," I don't remember any of the grades I got from that point on; my value base was altered forever after.

I am an insecure person in a lot of ways as well as arrogant in some ways, too. The previous story illustrates both fairly well: insecure about what I overheard in the cafeteria, arrogant towards the power brokers. Actively working on humility at one point in my life, I was amazed at how proud I was of becoming humble. Some things take longer than others, I guess. And if you beat yourself up hard enough for too long, you do get insecure; what good is that? An acceptance of our natural selves is a tad healthier all around. That Gibran program really was a wonderful experience for all of us. It was a good class. Now, getting back to the "business of art" and speaking of credentials…

When I started out in this business of being my own rep at one point, I went to the hardest, most challenging place I could think of and did battle there. I learned and came out of the whole thing with a little more confidence. The second place on my list was The Case Trading Post of The Wheelwright Museum in Santa Fe. It is up on *the hill*—a classy section of town hosting a set of prestigious and well-visited museums with very nice gift shops attached. The Case Trading Post stood out for me—the décor, the quality of art, the products, displays, and friendly people who worked there—I checked it out first this time. Now that I had one experience under my belt, I thought I would give it a try, but nervousness still ruled the day. I made an appointment and my Mom came along for moral support. We were there a bit early, so we browsed around.

Do you know that feeling when you are in a kind of stupor and fog; your body is walking around but your mind has disengaged? The only thing that kept me grounded was the disconcerting sound of the creaky floorboards—the more I retreated into an insecurity/invisibility mindset, the noisier those boards became to the point of sounding like fingernails on a blackboard. When I was a customer there, I liked the ancient sound—it romanticized the atmosphere. As a scared little vendor, the sound unnerved me; it exposed the fact that I was actually there. The clock was ticking the time away to my appointment. When the time came, I left my Mom to peruse books, and headed to the backroom. Mom gave me the "thumbs up" signal and the secretary asked me to "have a seat." The main buyer for the Museum Shop, Robb Lucas, would be with me "shortly."

I remember being kind of fumbly, putting things here and there, not in any particularly logical sequence. Observing my uneasiness and wanting to help, the very kind secretary struck up a chitchat about what it is that I do, and how nice to be creative and things along those lines. I started to breathe semi-normally again. She motioned me to come and sit closer to her desk so I quickly and quietly scooted my chair over. Could she take a peek at my cards? Of course! She told me that she *loved* them! How much was I charging if I didn't mind telling her? Well, retail $2.50 each. "That's *all?*" This was starting to be a good day after all.

Then in hushed tones, this kind person (whose name I cannot remember) asked me if I had looked at the other cards out there on the racks. Yes, I had, because I came before this meeting to check it out, having learned a lesson or two at the Museum of Fine Arts. She advised me to take the time to study the handmade cards that were being made and sold in Santa Fe at that time and turn them over—study the *backs* of the cards. That seemed odd to me—why the backs? If I wanted to see the designs I'd be looking at the fronts, but the designs were clearly not the point in this discussion. "Why, you look for yourself. On the backs of many cards there are entire *biographies*, I tell you! The entire backs of some cards are completely filled with credentials, awards, honors, degrees, titles, you-name-it impressive stuff that gives them the right to glue a feather to the front of the card and charge $5.00 for it! Imagine—that kind of money for a feather glued to the paper. The biography on the back of the card and some fancy signature gives them the right to do that, I guess..." I laughed out loud and promised I would check out the competition now that I was truly in "the card business." It was now time to meet Robb.

Having been gently ushered out of my nervous stupor, I was now aware of my surroundings and sensitized to details. Out of the office came a powerful looking Native American jewelry artist, finishing up his appointment with Robb. They parted with friendly feelings and I was welcomed with a warm handshake, smile and shown to a seat. Someone has to be completely at home within himself and in his environment to make me feel as "at-home" as I felt there in that office immediately. Breathe again. Right away I liked him, his energy and enthusiasm. That has been confirmed time and time again over the years. Robb is a very good person.

He was quick flipping through my deck of card samples. He had pulled out a stack, had the basic ordering plan lined up in his mind and started talking: one dozen of this that and the other, cards and bookmarks, he left the door open for me to be creative with the order and I wrote up a $175+ first order on the spot. It was short and sweet, thank you so much, another artist was on the waiting chair and I was out in The Case Trading Post, creaking the floor, smiling at my relieved mother. It went well; very well. For the second time now as I was building this business, one step at a time.

It has been very inspiring to get orders from Robb over the years. He always says something like "I'd like 4 dozen bookmarks, 4 dozen cards, assort them the way you like, include Mimbres animals and you know what works here... New designs are great—have fun—thanks, and drop by whenever you make it to Santa Fe..." so perfect. He opened the way for my creativity and we both benefited from that. I wasn't always repeating the same thing and his customers could count on standards as well as fresh new looks. He asked me to try different products, too, like gift tags, and I learned along the way what worked and what didn't. Someone who actively encourages you (and is even willing to pay you) to experiment is giving you a gift.

Whenever I do an order for The Case Trading Post of the Wheelwright Museum, I find myself putting my whole heart-plus into it. Even though there is "net 30 days" on the invoice, Robb always pays earlier than necessary and includes a short, friendly note with news from Santa Fe, knowing that I miss being there, and a compliment about the order just sent. It makes my day every time. This account is technically a "house account" because I developed the account personally. My reps did handle it temporarily, but I almost always took the orders by phone personally. I try to visit there whenever I do get to town and I am always made to feel very much at home.

Over the years I have enjoyed turning greeting cards over and reading the "backs," especially the ones with "biographies." The backs of mine have gotten simpler and shorter over the years, rather than more "wordy." I have tailored them down to my small handcarved "hand stamp" and a personal signature. That's about it. I include an insert that describes the cards as being originals and handmade, and those have gotten simpler over time, too. Hopefully the fronts of the cards say all that needs to be said.

Even if I wanted to make a big long list of credentials, they don't exist in those terms anyway. I am honored by the people who buy my cards. That kind of honor is good enough for me. When I was on my way out the door that day years ago, the secretary at the Wheelwright wished me well and said that my attitude was "refreshing" in a competitive art scene that sometimes gets self-inflated. I laughed at that, too, and I appreciated it at the same time. My credentials: The University of Hard Work, with a Degree in *Just Trying It*. I like that. I would just like to say this, honestly from my heart, the most important thing is just to do our best, situation by situation, day by day, knowing darn well that our best will be different according to circumstances, but our best all the same. The credentials, the grades, the self-congratulating or self-flagellating: let them all go. I want to be attached to the meaningful: vision and perseverance come to mind.

To wrap this up, I would like to pause in reflection with a note of warning: Right at that lovely point where you feel liberated and have a certain amount of confidence in place, watch out for a subtle little devil-of-a-trick you just might play on yourself. It is called "dream sabotaging," how about that? I am not talking about what others may say or do to you. I am talking about little mental impediments, hurdles, you may put in your own way. Case in point, for the sake of illustration: "I am going to write a book."

The insecurities are at bay for a time; this is good. I start to write; this is very good. Wanting to bolster my confidence I look for, buy and read books on the writing life, books by Natalie Goldberg and Julia Cameron, for example. The more I read, the more charged up I get, the more I write and this is all on track to great things so far.

Then it happens—like the flu—it sneaks in when you are unaware. You get this bug in your thinking that says: "You are doing just fine, but there is *one thing* you need to do before you can publish—just *one little thing*, then you will be qualified and will have the credentials you need. *All you need to do is take a writing class with Natalie or Julia (preferably both) (preferably in Taos) and then you will be free to put yourself out there as an author and dare to publish.*" Oh. I see. Is that all… That is a self-sabotage mindset.

"Well, it just so happens that I can't afford to do that." That is hard to face and admit. It zaps too much of the power you were building up. It nags at you and opens the door for the insecurities to return, gleefully dancing on the end of your pen, on the keyboard, and on your sensitive shoulders every time you look in the mirror. Putting impediments in our own way? That is a definite no-no. Remember, spread those wings—and fly!

Minds are like parachutes—they only function when open. – *Thomas Dewar*

Competition vs. Camaraderie

Competition: a rivalry between two or more businesses (or people) striving
    for the same customer, market (or goal). A contest.
    (Compete: from the Latin "to strive together.")

Camaraderie: goodwill and lighthearted rapport between or among friends.
    (Comrade: a friend or companion; from the Old French for "roommate.")

The word "competition" is one loaded little collection of eleven letters, isn't it? It can get the adrenaline flowing with excitement and it can cause a bristling, furrowed-brow countenance all within the same moment. Think of the time you won an upset in a Tennis Tournament and then think of the person who stole your idea and made money from it. Both times you faced a competitor. The outcomes were pretty different, and so were your reactions. I've been in those two places—the win/lose drama plays out all the time, or at least as much as we choose to engage in it.

I enjoy a good challenge. I like to compete in certain ways. When I play, I play to win, whether it is a game of cribbage, Pichenotte, tennis or whatever contest I am engaged in. Forget this: "It doesn't matter if you win or lose, it's how you play the game" business. *Forget it*! I want to win, but I may lose, and of course I teach my kids the importance of "it's how you play the game." I do believe that. I may get skunked, get whooped or lose in all its varied forms, but I do have a good time trying my best and playing fair along the way. Interestingly enough, though, I sometimes have a hard time watching the Olympics or any sport on TV because I feel so bad for the skater that falls or the skier or team that loses. It hurts me. I guess I want everyone to win—a world with no "agonies of defeat" just a lot of "thrills of victory." Idealistic, yes; realistic, no.

There are most definitely some very inspiring aspects to competition in the world of business. It is a driving force to innovation and excellence in the best sense and use of the word, in the hands and consciences of ambitious people with some semblance of a moral compass. On the other hand, there are very ugly aspects to the competitive world of business, where crushing and annihilating others becomes the main sport—the Roman Coliseum comes to mind as a fitting image. My lessons of life in this subject area started pretty early on. My brothers and I competed, but that was (mostly!) friendly. The outside world was a whole different chariot race. I had a lot to learn.

When I was a kid, I participated in a number of sports and also found myself in competition for the position of #1 student in my elementary school. The weird problem was that my main competitor was also my very best friend in the world, Jeannie. We switched off the #1 position regularly and always stayed friends. I wasn't trying to beat her down. I was trying to beat my own record. None of the parents were "pushing." It wasn't personal against her and she felt the same way towards me. "The powers that were" in The System of the time pitted us "against" each other in that little scenario for 8 years. We were beyond it, and at the same time engaged in it. We congratulated each other along the way in a kind of stressed-out way. Jeannie was naturally much more "intelligent" in an intellectual sort of way than I was. I worked so hard memorizing; Math exams still have a distinct place in my worst nightmares. Jeannie loved to read and could read a book very quickly, absorbing knowledge beyond surface facts. Our different strengths contributed to the fact that we became an excellent team later on in high school. Back in grammar school, who "won" in the end? By some crazy one-tenth of one percent or something ridiculous like that, I did, and so we were Valedictorians *together* in my estimation. But I was the one given the certificate and the title. Hmm.

I paid for that, though. I may have "won" on one level, but I paid dues along the way. Especially in third grade. That is the place and that is the time when I learned the ugly side of competition. Jeannie and I shared the camaraderie side, the positive part of competing where you "strive together," but Colleen (name changed to be nice) chose the contest side, the win/lose/opposition aspect and chose me as her unknowing rival in the most negative sense. Jealousy is ferocious. I had not learned how to wear a gladiator's armor and helmet and I also had not learned how to take that strong, defensive stance in life yet. I was only in the *third grade*. The Coliseum of my childhood played out on the playground of St. Ann's Catholic School. The surface was all tar. The definition of recess took on a totally different meaning from this day forward and forever after.

Report cards had been given out. I was quietly happy with mine. I always looked at it by barely opening it so that no one else could see… just my parents could, later. I got a nickel for every "A" and that was fun. I must have been taking my report card back to school in the morning, because I had it in my hand at the morning recess. The lioness approached, on the prowl. Colleen and her cronies surrounded me and this is how it went:

"So, Gloria, did you get all A's again this time?"
(Silence)
"I asked you if you got all A's again, Teacher's Pet."
"No."
"I can't hear you. Did you say 'NO'?"
"I said no."
"So let's see your report card and see what you got."
"I don't want anyone to see it. Just my parents."
"GET IT!"

And so the chase began. I ran all over the schoolyard and they chased me to the point of exhaustion and then Colleen stuck out her leg and tripped me. My face smashed on the tar and I lost my grip on my Report Card. It flew out of my hand. I crawled to reach it, but she stepped on it and picked it up. Standing over me, bloody face and broken nose and all, she proceeded to read out loud, *very* loud, all of my subjects and all of my grades:

"Spelling: A. Reading: A. Religion: A. French: A…" and they were all A's, all twenty grades, and at the end, she wrapped it up with:

"Gloria, you said that you *didn't* get all A's. YOU LIED!"
And with that I just put my head down on the ground and wept. I had lied. I felt so bad. It was a sin to lie.

My face had swollen and I cleaned up the blood. I sat in class for a while and remember being in this painful state of mind. I remember my seat, my place, looking out the window, the tears. The school has recently been torn down, but I remember exactly what it looked like inside and out. Sitting at my wooden desk that day so many years ago, the world was not the same for me anymore and never would be again. It had changed forever. There was no "Counselor" or "Therapist" at school in those days to mediate this kind of event; there was no resolution at that time with this mean, angry, jealous girl. I was left to deal with it alone in my seat. My mother was eventually called in even though I said I was okay and didn't want to miss school. We headed to the doctor, Dr. Jensen with the sweet face. There was only one thing that I needed: I needed to be with my Mom. It helped so much when she pulled me out of school that day. I had to be in a safe place, at least until the next day when I would have to return. My nose was fractured and couldn't be set no matter how sweet the doctor was, so I now have a nose that has a different shape than what might have been in a kinder world. That incident deeply affected my attitude about many, many things in life—competition on all levels, the quest for personal excellence, women's relationships with each other, the definitions of honesty and integrity, the educational system and the goal-oriented grading system, the value of friendship, and in general the all too real pain of growing up.

I purposely threw my grades in High School and fought for the "less than sparkling" students and their need to be respected as people of achievement in their own right. Later on I went to St. John's College—no grades given there; no Report Cards to have your face bashed-in for. One aspect of my life that runs clear through from the 3ʳᵈ grade on, is my heartfelt and intense desire to achieve the balance between competing within myself and competing with others—challenging myself to be the best I can be and helping others along the way to do the same. Not *against* each other—*with* each other.

In my business, there are situations that come up that make me wonder if we will *ever* grow up, or whether we stay as 3ʳᵈ grade Colleens internally forever, just disguised in suits and cosmetics. A few years ago, I was asked to give classes in stamping and to share the story of my business for some women. I looked forward to it. When I told a few people about it, the warnings surprised me: "Be careful, Gloria, if you teach people what you do and how you built your business, people will rip you off. They will steal your designs and take business away from you. Keep your secrets to yourself…" That sounded so foreign and so stupid to me. I simply don't think and operate like that. Partly naïve, partly idealistic, mostly adamant that it doesn't *need* to be that way, darn it! I went and taught and talked and have been doing that for years and have only gained by doing it. The networking, sharing of ideas and resource materials has benefited all of us who participate in supporting and cheering each other on.

Are there people who do rip off your ideas? Yes, there are. Why do you think there are so many of those little Copyright "c's" in the little circles all over the place, even though it is many times more of a warning-gesture than the actual fact of having the legal status? We want to protect what is original, what came from us. I didn't think about it much until someone "stole" an idea of mine once. Here is what happened:

I had been doing business with a very nice shop. The owner and my mother were friends. They sold a lot of my bookmarks/cards in the shop and would call for rush orders during the busy touristo summer months. I enjoyed their stories about international visitors buying my products. Then, for no apparent reason, the calls stopped at one point, and since I was heading to New Mexico, I decided to just drop by and see what was up. It was a business trip and I was meeting people who ordered from me that I hadn't met before, and also thanking people for their business, learning first hand if there was any way I could serve them better. I was learning a lot and one afternoon, headed to this shop.

I immediately saw the container with my bookmarks in them because I had made some unique display signs for this one store to use. As I walked closer to the display, I couldn't figure it out. It was my display sign and they were my bookmark plastic sleeves, they were handstamped bookmarks, but I didn't make them! They were not my designs, paper or stamps. Same price, same set-up except they were not mine! I stopped for a minute to gather my thoughts, and to breathe in and then out. Then I asked the girl at the counter, who was new to me and who did not know me from any other customer, if they had "any handstamped cards by Gloria Page of Impressions Hand-Stamped Originals?" "Well, we do have handstamped cards and bookmarks, but they are not by Gloria Page; *they are made by the owner's daughter*. She just finished Law School and started doing this on the side. Aren't these nice cards? The bookmarks are in that container right over there." I checked out the cards. Mine were all gone. These other ones were in *my* sleeves (almost positive because I had mine custom-made at that time and they were distinctive). The stamping was really, really sloppy. (Sorry, I just couldn't resist.)

I spent a fair amount of time in that store going through a series of emotions. I think it just ticked me off that after all the times I did rush orders for them, lost sleep, bought special images with them in mind and went out of my way to be the best vendor I could be for them, there was something so infuriating to me that these people had the nerve to:

1) Take my idea, get rid of my cards and use my display signs
2) Not communicate with me
3) Make such poor-quality cards and bookmarks and *put them in my plastic sleeves!*

As silly as it may sound, #3 was the thing that really got to me. I know that I do not have the exclusive right to be the only person in the USA and the world making cards using rubber stamps. I get inspiration and ideas by looking at what other people do and emulating certain aspects with my own flair and flavor woven in. I just didn't like the way it was done in this particular instance. And I especially don't like it when any "Art Thieves" are hanging around my friends. I get very defensive and protective on their behalf. We all know the difference between the mutual sharing of ideas and *stealing*. It's a no-brainer. It seems like somebody just getting out of Law School might have a clue as to the difference between "inspiration" and "plagiarism." They are spelled differently and it all has something to do with honor or the lack thereof. Ethics 101—good class to take.

In the end, on that lovely and uncomfortable day in New Mexico, I decided to write a note, and leave it at that. The note went something like this: "Hello. I happened to be in town visiting and dropped by to say hi. I can see that you won't need to order my cards or bookmarks anymore. Thank you for ordering from me in the past. I am grateful to everyone who helped along the way. Sincerely, Gloria Page/Impressions." Period. The end. I'm out of there. Shake the dust off my shoes from that place and leave it behind.

I was rattled and my mother was not happy. After all, this had been her friend, and how could she do that? We talked it out, and then went to a cool stamp store downtown down the street and I bought some new stamps—there's a smart way to chase away the blues. People are funny. There were other ways to go about that. Just use your own plastic sleeves, for heaven's sake. I never heard from them after that. End of that story.

There is plenty of room on the planet for more handmade cardmakers and more artists of every variety. Hallmark is the Goliath and a lot of us little Davids running around are no threat to the giant, and we certainly do not need to feel threatened by each other. I have four friends in town who also happen to have their own card businesses. We share info, help each other connect to good reps and celebrate each other's successes as well as share concerns. Who loses/who wins? We all win if we help each other out.

On another business trip, I took samples of my friends' cards along with my own new designs. I was able to make some connections for them. Was there a chance that buyers would like their cards more than mine? Sure! So what! The buyers loved the fact that I showed them a wider spectrum of products, a good use of their time, and from my perspective "a victory for one of us, is a victory for all of us." Yeah for the team! Life is too short to go around tripping people up in a conquest mode.

With generosity and kindness as the guiding forces, we can temper the ruthlessness and sharpness of competition without heart, in business relationships and personal ones as well. It's not easy sometimes, yet Competition vs. Camaraderie can be transformed into Competition *with* Camaraderie—a different world, a wonderful, wonderful world, my friend. Let's go very high and let's go really far in the Business of Life Olympics, but let's not trip each other and step on each other in the process. It doesn't have to be a race. There are better ways—how about Rivalry with Respect? It can work. That would make for an interesting, stimulating and productive world.

(Rivalry: from the Latin *rivalus*, one using the same stream as another; *rivus*, stream.)
(Respect: from the Latin *respectus*, to look back at, regard.)

As we are all in this stream together, let us look back with mutual regard for great efforts. If competition kills desire in you and scares you, find another strategy and vantage point. If competition stimulates and energizes you, use it. Whichever way you go, make sure that when you look in the mirror each morning and evening, the face looks friendly.

(As for Colleen, we must have patched things up and worked things out, because I do remember asking her to sign my 8th Grade Graduation Autograph Book. I found it in my garage recently. Her signature is there with a light, friendly message: "To a really good lookin kid. Good Luck and Much Success be yours Always…" Kids are amazing. Five years earlier she was the cause of my being introduced to painful words like "envy" and "jealousy" for the first time in my life. My nose was also re-arranged in a not very cosmetic manner. ("*Good lookin*?") And then there we were, by the end of elementary school, signing off and well-wishing each other: a good lesson in the art of moving on.)

■

There is nothing noble in being superior to some other person.
True nobility comes from being superior to your previous self.

- *Hindu* Proverb

Scars

Twenty-one years old—it was time. My cousin Sandy drove me from Connecticut to New York City ("Yew Nork City" according to my son Bryan for his first four years). It was a trip between two worlds. Sandy was my last connection with my family; I was on a journey to the land of my ancestors. I boarded the Queen Elizabeth II, the QE2, and headed for Cherbourg, France. It's a story in and of itself, but for the one at hand, we'll get ourselves to France, head down to the wine country, and reminisce about the fateful decision I made to pick grapes. It was a "must do" for someone wanting to get a feel of the land and leave a little sweat behind. Blood, however, was not in the original plan.

I hitched my way down to a small town near Marseille called Clermont L'Hérault. (Put on a beret and make it sound French in your mind.) This town did not see many Americans so I became a novelty and celebrity of sorts. Traveling alone as always, there was a freedom of movement and choice as well as a tremendous risk that I'd rather not think about too much. I'm alive to tell the story. I chose not to speak English at all while I was in France, as in *never*, which is a quaint and romantic notion totally deprived of practicality since I didn't speak anything else. Babyhood babblings and two years of rusty High School French will only get you so far. When I got off the QE2, I spoke *French*.

If an American crossed my path, I crossed the street. If a Frenchman asked me where I was from, I gave some obtuse answer like "I am a citizen of the Universe" in French, of course, and after the eyes stopped rolling, whoever asked would know for sure that indeed he or she had encountered an American and proceeded to speak to me in English. Forget it. I wasn't going there. I had my promise to keep and would not break it, no matter how lonely and foolish I felt at times. In Clermont L'Hérault this never really was much of a problem. People just didn't speak English on a daily basis, at least not around me. A fair amount of silence accompanied me and what was once uncomfortable became a comforting friend; I don't run from silence anymore.

Looking for a job in a foreign country with extremely limited language skills is a challenge, but living on very little money is even more of a challenge, so I just started talking and asking around for work. My little Larousse dictionary/phrase book was in my left hand much of the time as I feverishly flipped with my right. I could understand what was coming at me if people were kind enough to speak slowly, so I was constantly on the lookout for kind people. That particular time of year was perfect for job-hunting since it was grape harvesting time. A sweet Clairol-blond lady named Colette introduced me to the local vineyard owner named Raymond (remember your French accent, s'il vous plaît) and he hired me on the spot. He looked like he was going to enjoy this big time, having an American "picker," the only American "vendangeur" for the season. It felt like I was the only American they had ever met in the entire history of the village, which was at least 400 years that they could account for personally and accurately.

I am going to narrow my *Life in France* stories down to a particular and fateful day in the "fields." The vineyard-of-the-day was an old pick-up truck drive away from the village. It was early morning and being new to this line of work, I was in serious need of a chiropractor after a few days, but I was a trooper and didn't complain. My ancestors must have done this, who knows, maybe the same vines. My co-pickers had obviously been doing this for years, for lifetimes, for 400 years, Mon Dieu. This stone village had a name before the United States of America had one. Time was in a warp. It slowed way down. I came to understand that Americans were destined to be first on the moon. We were in a hurry to get there and landed in 1969. From what I could gather in the fields, the French could care less about it. The moon is there for romance not conquest. They look up into the night sky and sing: "Au Clair de la Lune" (By the Light of the Moon) and wonder what those crazy Americans are doing running around up there anyway. In France I always felt like I was in a rush but there was no rush around me—weird feeling.

An American in Europe on European terms and working with a European sense of time is different than an American on vacation or on a "tour." My roots are European, but we cut the umbilical cord way back there in 1776, and in 1975, I was one year shy of 200 years of Independence. But working in those fields and not knowing what the heck I was doing and everyone around me doing whatever it was very quickly, made me dependent once again. I needed to be taught, and I also needed to be paid at the end of the week.

Lesson #1: *How to Hold the Grapes*. Hold the massive, heavy, dewy cluster from the *bottom*, supporting it with your hand. In my case, my left hand was supposed to be underneath the grapes and my right hand would have the sharp cutters and do the cutting at the top of the stem. Once cut, place the clusters in an old plastic bucket, carry it from one vine to the next until the "runners" determine the bucket is full and grab it from you, leaving an empty one in its place—keep cutting! This happens quickly. One vine can have so many heavy clusters that it may take two runs with two buckets to clean it off. My co-pickers were extremely fast and steady. I had to keep pace to save face for my *country*—I could hear the razzing about lazy, pampered Americans. I knew I was the test case and that they were going to push me hard, so I pushed myself first and harder. A little contest of sorts: France vs. the USA in the Vineyard Olympics, going for the gold.

My translating ability was being stretched, especially without a dictionary in hand, and with all the questions that were being fired my way, I found myself slipping behind. And then my big mistake: I forgot Lesson #1: How to *Hold* the Grapes. In the rush of trying to catch up on my row, I grabbed the bunch of grapes *at the top* of the stem with my left hand and cut hard and fast. OWWWCH!!! *Keep going* was all that was on my mind. But all of a sudden the grapes were no longer dusty purple. They were bright red like the stripes on an American flag. I had cut the top flap of skin of my left index finger nearly off, and my middle finger got stabbed, too. By now I was seriously falling behind in my row! When my French folks saw the blood running down my arm, into the bucket, onto the grapes, and splattering French soil, they switched into a War-Effort-Rescue-Team-Mode like nothing I had ever witnessed in my life. Most of the people kept working, but the Emergency Crew was in place pronto. Before I knew what was happening, Raymond had made a mad dash back to the ancient truck and snagged a bottle of wine from the cab. Popping the cork as he ran, my two fingers, one after the other, were shoved into that bottle, mingling the lifeblood of the countryside with my own. It stung like (hell), but it was a disinfectant that I wasn't about to argue with. I couldn't swear because I didn't know any "swear words" in French and I couldn't break my code and say any in English. I was able to manage "merci beaucoup."

While my immersion was still in progress, a young French guy named Claude tore his far-from-antiseptic bandanna from his neck and ripped it into strips for my fingers. They got wrapped tight to hold the skin on. Had I been in the States, I most certainly would have been taken to the hospital for stitches. I was not stateside; I was in a distant vineyard with village townsfolk in Southern France. They asked me if I wanted to stop, to

73

see a doctor, to go *home*. I said "non," picked up my cutters and bucket and got back in my line. (This all happened much faster than it took to read here.) I worked faster than I had before, went through the pain and more importantly went through a silent rite of passage. Everything was different from that point on. The jabs about "lazy, spoiled, rich Americans" stopped. Proper bandages, aspirin and a special gift bottle of local brandy quieted the pain. At the Harvest Banquet at the end of the picking season after a hayride to an ancient lovely massive stone barn, I was toasted with autumn colors reflected in raised wine glasses: "To the American who never gave up! Salute!"

This all happened more than half my lifetime ago. Time is an interesting thing. The scars are still there, faded, but still there. When I looked at my fingers earlier today, I could smile and have proof that I did indeed live this story. The pain and blood are long gone and cleaned up. The memory is as fresh as the day it happened. I can see all the faces as if in a photo, one that I don't have, except in my mind.

There are many kinds of scars, physical and experiential. I have a business scar worth mentioning, because having an art business carries with it the very real possibility, more like probability, of experiencing rejection. Talk about getting wounded. Talk about blood on the tracks. Getting rejected hurts. Dealing with it takes time.

I was fairly new to Missouri, having just tried my first couple of art shows. They had gone well and at one of them, my booth "next door neighbor" was an art teacher from Kansas. She liked these wood magnets that were stamped that I had for sale. I liked her glazed terra cotta flowerpots and we made a trade. She suggested that I take the magnets to a store in Columbia that sold very nice craft items to see if perhaps the owners might be interested in carrying my "work," especially, she thought, the magnets for some reason. She knew someone at the shop and I thought it sounded like a good idea, so I ventured out that very same week and walked right in, wood magnets wrapped in a little box. I figured there was nothing to lose. So I thought…

I always get a little nervous when I approach a new business, but I felt bolstered by the kind lady who suggested I go and give it a try. As I walked in, I asked to speak with one of the owners and introduced myself and introduced my "product." As I was being quietly ushered to the backroom of the store, I had this sick, sinking feeling that somehow I am not the right person at the right time talking with the right person with the right thing in my hand. Oh, brother, was I ever right, and this was not the time to feel good about the fact that I was. It was politely explained to me that the quality of the finish on the wood was nowhere near "Fine Craftsman Standard." I was given a box to examine with a finish that was silk-to-the-touch as a point of comparison to my rough little primitive "blocks." I got the point; it was loud and clear even though it was whisper-mode. I agreed that my wood wasn't perfect. I just tried this out two weeks ago and knew that I didn't know what I was doing. There was truth in what was being said—there just wasn't any kindness. It was crystal clear that I did not belong there. I was in way over my head—this is the world of "*Fine* Arts and Crafts." What exactly am I doing here?

It was an uncomfortable "conversation" that I just wanted to escape from, but one last question came and I had to answer it: "…and by the way, where does your imagery come from, what is your *technique*?" (Now that we were clear about the poor quality of the wood-finish and that was all settled, let's finish this off completely and go for the imagery.) "Well, I use rubber stamps." "*Rubber stamps*? As in, *rubber stamps* like you would buy, for instance, at that little stamp store across from the mall, what is it called?

I'd Rather… something…" I finished the sentence: "*I'd Rather Be Stamping*. Yes. I buy many of my supplies from that store." "Oh, I see. Well, using rubber stamps is about as close to using clip-art as I can think of… perhaps someday you might…" and by that point *I'd Rather Be Anyplace* other than in that backroom. I didn't hear anything else because I didn't want to. It wasn't worth it to me. I turned a deep shade of red, apologized for taking up so much of her time, purchased a satin-smooth wood coaster for $4.00 plus-tax just so that I could remember what true craftsmanship feels like, and left.

Take a grape-cutter and slice right below the surface of the comments that were coming at me, and the message was loud and clear: Stamps? You, lady, are not doing real *ART*. The funny thing is that I really didn't know exactly what clip-art was at that time. I knew I should feel insulted, but it was something to look into later. (Eventually I found and love Dover Copyright-free Books. Clip-art is fun and art, by the way—so there.) Walking out the door with my little package and bruised ego was tough. The tears came within a block. I wandered around town without a Kleenex. Sniff. Sniff.

In Santa Fe, New Mexico, one of the great Art Scene Meccas of the *world*, I had never experienced rejection. Buyers and customers liked my little handstamped cards and bookmarks: simple, inexpensive, and handmade, with bold designs. On the back of each and every item it said: "Handstamped." I was honest and open about what I was doing. Along the way I did have certain feelings of insecurity because the images that I use are other people's artistic creations, "on loan" to me in a sense to design with them. I didn't *draw* that intricate Japanese koi—I *stamped* it. I chose all the papers, did the collage work and created the final product, but the image came from a stamp that I used with respect and gratitude, and see as an art tool. But I sure didn't draw it. Now my insecurities were brought straight to the surface, into the glaring light and I had to deal with the whole issue squarely. So I kept wandering around town. Thinking. Crying.

It seemed ironic to me that this was happening in Missouri, not in artsy over-the-top Santa Fe. I would have expected life to be easier and kinder here for artists. (And believe me, it is good here. This was just one tough little isolated day.) My thinking took some interesting turns. "Maybe I'd better make double-sure that all of my customers know what I am *really* doing. I wouldn't want to fool or mislead anyone. I do put it on the back of every single card but maybe people just don't get it. Then I'll probably lose accounts, especially all the Museum Gift Shops and Gallery Shops once they really know my technique and finally realize that I am not an artist at all. Who do I think I am anyway— an *artist*? Might as well be clip-art, whatever that is…" yada-yada-yada…

In my wanderings, I came upon a store called *International Gifts* or something close to that. Falling into the store with my big red eyes, it was quite dark, quiet and safe. This direct-speaking Korean woman, the owner of the shop, immediately enveloped me. Walking around the corner from her counter, she came to me and put her arm around my shoulder. What happened to me? Why the tears? I recounted the story, omitting any names and places so as to protect identities, focusing on explaining the heart of the experience. My vulnerable point had been exposed and was raw. With her wonderful accent she woke me out of my confusion and self-pity—a bowl of kimchee for the spirit.

"Gloria, from the most ancient days, Kings and royalty of many cultures have used stamps to seal great documents and proclamations. (Pointing to some hand-carved pieces on a shelf.) These stone chops were the signatures of great Oriental scholars. They are handcarved and were used with great ceremony. They are works of art themselves, not merely *stamps*. Look at how beautiful they are. Artists in history have used stamps to sign great works of art. Stamps are wonderful art tools. You *know* that. Don't ever let anyone take away what from you what you know is true. What is true is true…"

We looked closely at some of the stone chops on a glass shelf together. She translated those mysterious symbols and most had to do with Luck, Fortune, Prosperity, Double-Happiness, and other uplifting feelings and wishes that were more foreign to me in that moment than the Chinese characters themselves. Yet they were stamped in my soul that day. I will never forget that "chance" meeting. Ever.

We met again years later in the store's new location at the mall, across the street from the "famous" stamp store. This time I bought rice paper for my printmaking class, a return to "college life" for me. I re-introduced myself and didn't need to go too far into the story before she took over and told it in her way. We laughed and I thanked her most sincerely for being there for a stranger whose feelings needed to be touched by kindness.

On my "first rejection day'" years ago, I learned some good lessons. It certainly was not a really dramatic type of rejection that other artists might face, such as rejections from galleries, major art shows, exhibitions, publications and other high-level enterprises that sometimes take years of effort to even think of attempting. One shop in downtown Columbia didn't like my wood magnets; hardly the end of the world and I would handle it differently if it happened today for sure. But clocks cannot be turned back and even though I would never wish rejection on anyone and I am not begging for it to come into my life on a regular basis, it is an experience that is good for me to own. I remember my husband quietly telling me that from that point on, since I had not known rejection before, I now stood in the position of being able to understand and have compassion for other people's experiences along the same lines. It was the first time and it wasn't the last, but it was the most significant because of what it brought up in me and what it brought out in other people. My Korean friend helped me to put assertiveness in my attitude and to instill a pride in my tools. My friend Kate told me once that she learns from the difficult people in her life "exactly what she wants to *be*." That was a different take on that issue for me—I always have said that I learn from the difficult folks "exactly what *not* to be." Kate's approach is much more positive and even puts one in the position to be *grateful* to those very same people who make life much harder than "challenging." "Thank you. Because of you, I know more clearly who I want to be in this life and how I want to treat others. I am going to be enhanced and not diminished by you. I am free."

Scars are interesting things on our bodies and on our souls. Physically they fade, but they are visible just barely enough to act as a reminder of a story long ago, but not all that far away. I grew up with four brothers. There is just something about those "scar stories." They take on the aura of myth and legend. They become Badges of Honor, concrete proof of Tales of Courage and Daring (and sometimes Stupidity.) My husband's scar stories are filled with football images in later years, and of a little boy seriously hurt on his leg who wasn't ever expected to have those football stories to tell. I guess that when I got blood-and-guts original scars of my own, I felt like a bona fide member of "the club."

My fingers work fine, but they are not exactly the same as before. My nose isn't either—we've been there. We all have scars of one type or another. They can be our excuses for not getting up again or our empowerment badge depending on our perception and support system at any given time. I like my French Wine-Country scars because I like the entirety of the story, not the moment of my mistake. I own my stories of being rejected. When it happens, I am not enchanted and I don't wish them on anyone else, but they are my stories and I treasure the learning surrounding the hurt. Distance and time seem to help with getting a better vantage point. I think that when we are ready and safe enough we can share our scars. I am always amazed at the ones other people show me. I am moved by what we learn together—how to re-focus, evaluate "what's next," and get on with it. Get the Band-Aid box and ointment ready because there are more to come.

With compassion and a heightened sense of awareness, valor and humor, we'll do just fine. "Here's to *all of us*, the folks who never give up. Salute!"

Shoot that pottery!

Most times I try to save everything I make or experience from going to the trash or recycling bin. Memoir is the perfect writing-style for people like me—we save stories; we tuck quotes and memories into little boxes in our minds and hearts, whether they delight or hurt. They can be handy someday—you just never know when. As for physical things saved, I can count on two hands the number of cards that I have declared absolutely irretrievable and thrown away. And even *then* I salvage something out of the failed attempt, even if it's only the torn-up paper to pass along to a papermaker.

There are times, however, when it is a good idea to separate from things that have no hope of rejuvenation or transmutation. After all these years, I finally threw (as in flung) my first reject—a piece of clay that was so overworked, under-fired and layered with nonsense, idiotic glazes and colors that it made me negative and frustrated just to have it in the same room with me. I took my semi-circle "thing" and transformed it into a temporary Frisbee/one-way boomerang as it made its final journey to the pits of my weekly trash. It felt great. I realized that some things simply get in the way of progress.

Recounting that story to my new friend Jana a few days later as we discussed our mutual tendencies to keep everything for what we might be able to do with it "someday," she told me a story. There was a potter in her neighborhood when she was growing up who used to line up his pottery "mistakes" outside in his backyard and have a few kids over to shoot the pottery to smithereens. *Shoot it* as in "ready, aim, *fire!*" *blast* it out of existence. That totally cracked me up. I recoil around guns, but I just love the finality of that artist's plan—get that stuff *out* of my life: "*Shoot* it." *Shoot* that pottery! Let the kids have a blast, literally, then back to the wheel and on to the new. No junk just piling up eternally, cluttering the studio, my mind and vision for the future. Get it away from me!

Now, what if the thing that seems to be an impeding factor just happens to be, for example, people who are driving you nuts, attitudes and concepts (like discouragement, insecurity, etc.) dragging you down like quicksand, memories that seem determined to scar and maim you for life, or other assorted legally and practically unshootable distractions? My good-natured little son recommends punching pillows, I personally think moving out of state sounds rather inviting, and basically what needs to happen is a bit of attitudinal Tai Chi—use the force coming against us in a fluid motion to hurl it straight on past. Tai Chi it, man. Send that stuff, that major pile of a lifetime supply of accumulated junk, wrapped tight, labeled "Priority" to the nearest available black hole.

The sooner the better.

Focus on the goal and shoot for that.

Poppy on East Broadway

When one door closes, go find another one…

Having a business with 99% of the orders going far away is fine. I set things up in New York and focused my styles and energies to target New Mexican businesses. My accounts are far away and so I ship what I create. But there is something very positive to be said about setting up shop in one's own hometown, which for me at this time is Columbia, Missouri. There is a sense of belonging and connectedness that means a lot and you don't have to ship anything anywhere—just put your order in the car and deliver it personally. I enjoyed that in New York and New Mexico when I lived there. I want that wherever I live—it is a substantial experience of feeling at home.

As I began to explore possibilities along those lines, one name kept coming up: "Poppy on East Broadway." Talking with people, asking for suggestions, ideas and referrals, I would inevitably hear: "You know, Gloria, there is this wonderful gift shop downtown on Broadway between Ninth and Tenth Streets. It is called Poppy. You should check it out—they have a great selection of cards. What do you have to lose? Go and look for yourself… then meet the folks there." Sounded good to me, so I made my plan.

I would visit two places in one morning. At the first place, I would show my wood magnets; then at Poppy, I would show my cards. It seemed like a good plan.

My first stop ended up being pretty tough. I was rejected for the first time and my confidence was pretty well shot. I was rescued by a kind Korean woman, but my legs were shaky and my eyes puffy. I wasn't exactly geared up for Round Two. Going home and taking a long nap sounded great to me—one of those "mental health days" that I've heard about. (That idea made me laugh hard the first time I heard it.) Sometimes enough is enough and we should have the common sense to know when that time is upon us. That particular ability doesn't happen to be one of my strong points.

I am the type of person who used to take a snow shovel to the public tennis courts in February in Connecticut at the first sign of anything resembling *spring*. My brother David and I couldn't wait for summer and couldn't afford to play indoors. So we shoveled. At least there were no waiting lines to get a court. On one of those days, my newfangled stylish Tensor stainless steel racket got so cold that the head just snapped off and flew into the air, spinning like a coin on the court when it landed, with me left holding the handle. So I immediately switched to wood. Soon afterwards I slipped on some ice and skidded on my thumb. It was numb from the cold so that worked out fine pain-wise, but the blood was annoying, so David ran and made a snowball and stuck my thumb in it. After playing and going through several red snowballs it was holding its own. In other words, you just keep going, keep playing, damaged goods, wounded or whatever…

So I scratched the idea of a nap, figured out where Broadway was, opened the door at #914 East and walked into Poppy. I looked at the card lines and was very happy to finally see cards by Ken Logsdon. I'd read about his business in the paper, but had never seen his work "in person." As I was reading his humorous quotes and enjoying the general feel of the store, I was surprised when someone spoke directly to me. I felt alone but wasn't.

"Hello, my name is Barbara. If there is anything I can help you with, please let me know." "Thank you, I was just enjoying Ken Logsdon's cards and, and…" And I was stuck. She immediately picked up the ball.

"I noticed your tapestry briefcase. Do you by any chance have something that you would like to show me? I am one of the owners of the shop." "Oh, well, as a matter of fact, I am a cardmaker and I have some cards here that I thought you might like to look at sometime. Could I make an appointment to meet with you?" "How about right now?" "Oh, alright, thank you for taking the time." "Great! Why don't we just go to the *backroom* and we can see what you brought." The *BACKROOM*! I had just been in a *backroom* and didn't necessarily want to go to another one, but I followed her and sat down anyway. Barbara introduced me to Mary, co-owner, warm and friendly. I had the distinct feeling that this backroom was going to be just fine after all.

Now that we were face-to-face and the lighting was stronger, Barbara could see swollen eyes and the fact that I was ruffled. She had a very nice, non-intrusive but clear way of asking me if I was "all right." Well, I explained that I had just been to a shop with my wood magnets and had been rejected. I then sat up straight, cleared my throat and tried to clear my mind, getting ready to make a declaration of sorts. The point I wanted to make was this: "Before I show you my cards, I want to make this absolutely clear so that you know *exactly* what I do and how I do it. I use *rubber stamps* in my designs. The paper is handmade but I *do not* make it myself because I don't have time with all of the orders I put out. So, if you don't like rubber stamps, that's okay, but I wanted to be sure you understood how I create my images." I must have sounded and looked totally nuts! Barbara was great. She smiled and said she'd "love to see" my cards and proceeded to set aside quite a stack of cards she wanted to order—right then and there. The order turned out to be around $250.00 (15 dozen cards as I recall), which is a large first order.

After I wrote up the order, Barb looked at me and her smile broke into laughter. She quickly stepped in and said: "Please don't misunderstand me. I realize that you went through something difficult and my heart goes out to you, but I can't help but enjoy my good fortune. I think I know where you were rejected even though you discreetly didn't mention any names. (She said the name and we both smiled.) They have very nice things there and someday you may make something that will be accepted, but we have an arrangement that we don't take what the other store has. If you had sold cards there, I would have missed out. I'm so glad you came here. We are anxious to have your cards in Poppy. They are so beautiful! We love your sense of design, colors, themes, pricing, everything. Stamping—what a *great* and creative idea. We can't wait to get your order. Thank you so much…"

Thank *you*. When one door closes, wander around feeling sorry for yourself if you must, but by all means go and find another door to open. I have sold thousands of cards at Poppy and it is my hometown-connection for people who buy directly from me at shows and want to have my cards available year-round. Over the years we have done consignment of different products and this holiday season my plan is to expand what I have done there and have that be my focus. Barbara asked me to experiment with a higher-end line of cards and I sold $5.00 cards for the first time there. I am very grateful and honored to have my cards and other artwork at Poppy.

I was welcomed. That makes business a pleasure. It is a special feeling to make a delivery downtown and quietly walk to the backroom, noticing on the way that there are people picking up my cards. I make them on my drafting table and usually send them far away. Because Poppy is just down the road on East Broadway, I get to see people enjoy and buy what I have created. A few times I've walked up to customers buying my cards and quietly introduced myself. Once someone said: "I *thought* that was *you*! I've seen your picture in the paper—that's how I knew to come here to find your cards—I *love* them!" Another time: "So *you're* the one! I buy only your cards when I need something *really* special. My husband buys your cards, too. That says something to you, doesn't it?" You bet it does. I love it.

I could never quite figure out why I didn't feel totally comfortable with the saying: "When one door closes, another one will open." Sounds true but passive—it could be one very long wait. There is a certain amount of faith and hope involved and those are good things for sure, but I think I've got it—this is closer to my experience: "When one door closes, another one is just around the corner." And better yet: "When one door closes, go find another one and open the darn thing yourself!" Dry your tears, get a grip internally, get a grip on a doorknob, turn it, walk in, smile and start over again.

■

Cuando una puerta se cierra dos mil se abren.
When one door is closed, *two thousand* are opened. (Wow.)

(Every misfortune will be replaced by joy.)

- *Spanish* Dicho (Proverb)

■

Nothing in the world can take the place of persistence.
Talent will not; nothing is more common than unsuccessful men with talent.
Genius will not; unrewarded genius is almost a proverb.
Education will not; the world is full of educated derelicts.
Persistence and determination alone are omnipotent.

- *President Calvin Coolidge*

■

You grow up the day you have the first real laugh—at yourself.

- *Ethel Barrymore*
American actor (1879–1959)

Kindness

A *Japanese* Proverb says:

One kind word can warm three winter months.

Many years ago I was with a group of friends and I had this idea. I cut out a sheet of white paper for each of us and made the shape look like your basic everyday tombstone. This was the idea: first, we start with one side. Everyone writes down the epitaph on her own stone—for example: "Here lies Gloria, she was…" and then fill in the blank with what your best guess would be as to what *other people* would say about you today, should this be "your time." In other words, what is your perception of the outside world's perspective on you? This can be interesting stuff.

After everyone has finished, we turn the "stone" over, and write what we *wished* other people would say about us—even more interesting.

Some of my friends wrote lots, some a little. I wrote one word on each side. On the first side I wrote: "She was *Intense*." On the second side I wrote: "She was *Kind*."

The realization I had was that I was lucky to have some time to get from one side of the tombstone to the other. Intense is not bad; kindness is not total enlightenment. But it is closer to where I would like to be in wrapping things up when that unknown time does arrive. How about today, twenty-plus years after the last etching on typing paper stones? I wouldn't necessarily be excited about having a real "headstone" in the physical sense. As for the words, what I wish other people would write, I'd still opt for the pared down style, but this time I would enjoy something along the lines of: "She was fun, wild, "colorful," generous, one helluva friend, the genuine article, or kind, if any of these were to be true. If people smile at the sound of your name after you are gone, isn't that really enough?

(As for obituaries, I have a word to add: please, for the sake of the living, could we be a bit more creative? I promise to haunt anyone who writes a traditional snoozer for me.)

It is a good idea to spend time in reflection about kindness—when it has come to us, and when it has come from us. If, in our busy lives, we can manage to cultivate a garden of kindness and remember to remember ourselves in the process, our epitaphs and eulogies would be inscribed in memories, not on pieces of polished granite in winter.

After I wrote "Scars," sharing about my struggle with a rejection experience, a friend asked me to write about how that experience could have been different. Very simply: it seems to me that it could have been so easy to say something kind rather than derogatory. I am not asking to be coddled, but I do believe there are constructive ways to make your point and actually help a sensitive artist even as you are "rejecting" the work at that time. Rejection and other assorted hurtful experiences are going to come. It happens often enough. The way it all comes has an impact, and we pretty much have no control over the fact that it did come our way. Usually we don't have time to get prepared and secure our self-preservation defensive positions. We do, however, have total control over what the heck it is we decide to do with it after the fact, and who we become because of it.

We will be known forever
by the tracks
we leave.
- *Dakota* Proverb

"That was *Who* calling from the *What*?"

The Smithsonian Experience

Once upon a time, having been in business for about three years, there was one particular day when things turned around for me in a very big way. I was downstairs in my studio showing my new Missouri friends, Bob and Joanna, some of my tools and ongoing projects. My little guy Bryan was a toddler at the time, so he was doing his toddling things while we were talking. The phone rang. Since I had recently taken a time-management class, I knew that in order to run a home business, the First Commandment one must abide by is: "Thou shalt *not* answer the phone; thou must have an answering machine to screen all incoming calls." The phone rang twice and the answering machine kicked in, loud and clear, upstairs. I half-listened, planning to ignore anything but a call from school or a couple of other fortunate folks who might make it through the screen.

There was an unfamiliar name and then I heard: "…from the Smithsonian Institution in Washington, D.C.…." "That was *Who* calling from the *What*?" It was one of those eye-popping moments. My friends just quietly yelled "Get It! We got the baby!" and I ran to the phone. It was a time-warp experience. My mind was racing way beyond clock-time. The Smithsonian. *The Smithsonian Institution in Washington, D.C.*? This is *it*! Looking around my humble unfinished basement, thinking: "If they only knew"…my mind was in this stream-of-consciousness mode and my heart was beating fast. After what felt like an awfully long trip getting to the phone, I caught the person on the line, but not my breath. "Hello, this is Gloria Page, I'm sorry I didn't pick up right away…" gag, gasp, pant, embarrassed and flushed with excitement at the same time. In a friendly, professional, breezy kind of way I heard: "Hello, Gloria, my name is Deborah Palazzo and I am calling from The Smithsonian Institution in Washington, D.C. I was recently in New Mexico on a buying trip as the Graphics Buyer for the Museum Shops here, and I kept coming across your cards in various gift shops. The styles were unique in each place, and as I turned cards over, I was surprised to find the same business name and 800-number. So, I am calling to find out if we could possibly carry some of your cards…" and that is not an exact quote, but very, very close.

We chatted for a few minutes, and since I did not have a brochure, catalog or website at that time, the best I could offer was to send samples for Deborah to look at personally. She expressed an interest in Southwest designs so I made note of that. She would be "looking forward to seeing my samples," and we pleasantly concluded. Wow.

There I was, sitting in this area in my unfinished basement that was supposed to be a bathroom, but was commissioned for use as a little office space for my business. I had duct-taped the exposed pipelines in the floor and arranged the desk and wastebasket to cover up the evidence. At the time of this call, I hadn't even stained the concrete floor or walls in this area and no burlap was stapled to exposed studs to simulate "walls" either. I sat in this funky little space after *the* phone call. Floored. I laughed in an incredulous kind of way. The *Smithsonian*, for heaven's sake. If only she knew where I was at—in my "bathroom office," in an unfinished basement in a little sub-division smack-dab in the middle of Missouri. Thinking of the historic Smithsonian, my romanticized images of the magnificent towers and the significance of the Institution itself inspired me. I just received a call from The Smithsonian Institution in Washington, D.C. They called *me*—I did not call *them*. I never would have made a phone call to such a prestigious place at that juncture in time, that's for sure. Even now, I wonder.

Bob and Joanna were excited and I was so grateful to them for keeping my little guy entertained. I also had witnesses—this *did* happen—I wasn't making the whole thing up.

In the beginning days of my business, my Mom's good friend Toni Lawson, who has an established photo card business in New Mexico called Flying Coyote Press, passed along this advice to me: "Whatever you do (or don't do), *get an 800-number* and put it on everything you make and sell. You never know where it will go or who will dial it." I followed that good advice and look what it got me—a call "from the Smithsonian." (My use of the phrase is a bit overdone—it is as if somehow a building is giving me a call: "Hello, this is the Smithsonian calling…" No. "This is Deborah *from* the Smithsonian...") It was and is an honor to receive such an inquiry, to know there is an interest in my work.

Since I did not have either a catalog or website at that point, there was only one way to go and that was to send samples. That is an extremely time-consuming task, especially if orders are on deck, which they were. She was not specific as to which cards in my Southwest line she was interested in seeing. It was not narrowed down to certain themes or styles based on what she had seen in New Mexico, so it became my choice. Making a substantial set of individually set-up cards would take more time than I had. I know that buyers want to see what they are interested in ASAP or sooner, and my turn-around time is being watched as well. Does it take me one week, two weeks or two months to get this request together and on the road? I decided to do something that I wouldn't do again and also don't need to since I now have a scanner and a website; I sent almost sixty originals out of my Master Set. That was not very smart. What if they got lost in the mail? What if they needed to keep them for an extended period of time at the Smithsonian and I needed to use them for my incoming orders? Nevertheless, I made a written/descriptive list of all the samples for my own use and sent them out immediately. It worked out fine in the end. Thank goodness and thank you, Deborah, for getting them back to me promptly.

An interesting interchange followed. The cards were well received, but it was decided at the Smithsonian that they really didn't need to expand their line of Southwest cards after all. What else did I have? Would I be willing to do a set of cards with the theme of "spring" in mind? My mind was an absolute blank as I heard myself saying: "I would be happy to work up some ideas, handcarve the designs and get them out to you soon… thanks." And there I was, sitting and sliding into a slouch, wondering what on earth does "spring" mean and what did I get myself into? I do Southwest and Oriental. My colors are dark and earthy—I am not a flowers-butterflies-cute-sweet-happy-card kind of girl. There I went and did it: I just told "The Smithsonian" that I was going to do spring cards and I don't have any paper or ink that slightly resembles my concept of that time of year. I can't draw and just opened my big mouth and told them that I would design and carve all of the images myself. Oh, *no*.

I allowed myself one day to freak out, and then sat down in a different chair with a pencil and paper. At the top of the sheet I wrote: SPRING and underneath made a list of "spring things" from my point of view: Butterflies, Sunshine, a Heart for Love, Flowers, Creativity (a hand, since it is the logo for my business) and Dance. I just started sketching with no time allowed for thinking. Before I knew it, I had six definite images that I liked. Not bad for someone who was petrified only moments before. I carved blocks that day and set about the task of pleasing the Graphics Department of "The You Know What."

New paper, new colors, new everything. I worked for many days and finally came up with the best I could do for "spring" in the dead of winter. Off they went. The response was most interesting and deeply affected the way I did business from that day forward. A number of days after sending the submission, the phone rang and sure enough it was from Deborah. "Thank you, Gloria, for your design ideas. They are *nice* cards, but not really what we are looking for. It seems that you are trying to change what you do in order to please us. In the process, you lost what it is that drew us to your work to begin with…" Oh, great, I'm thinking. So I spoke honestly and briefly about my challenge with the idea of "spring" and Deborah opened the door and told me to think about the strengths of what I do—the layers of paper, attention to detail, unique color applications, etc. She told me to take some time, experiment with more ideas and send things along as I came up with them. I could have felt "rejected" but that is not what happened. I was re-directed back to my own instincts, and when that happens to you, it is a good idea to be deeply thankful.

It didn't happen overnight. There was no bolt of lightning. My brother Paul and his then-fiancée, now-wife Mary Jo went to the Smithsonian for me and picked up a number of books so that I could get a feel for the place long distance. *The Renwick Gallery Shop* had been mentioned as a possible destination, as well as *The U.S. Postal Museum Shop*. I bought antique postage stamps and worked with those. I was floundering. This was an opportunity that wouldn't come around again and again. Over and over in my mind I kept running this idea through, wondering what exactly *is* it that I do. I handstamp cards. They saw many examples, so the question became more like: what *new* things can I do? I felt like my time in the bottle was running out, and then I happened to discover *Somerset Studio* Magazine at a stamp club meeting, saw a technique that intrigued me and the light finally went on in my head—*this* will work for the Smithsonian—and it did.

The card line came to be known as "Scroll/Tapestry Cards." I had amassed a huge collection of fabric samples from all over the world, discontinued styles from a local design shop in town. Using handmade and recycled papers as background, I cut and fringed the "tapestry" pieces in a long scroll shape, and used a technique of melting hot glue sticks like sealing wax, imprinted my collection of stone chops into the seals and created a look that worked—the design concept was accepted and the cards were ordered, over and over again, for many years now. My Mom helps with the task of creating the "scrolls." I cut the cloth to size, ship them to her in bundles of at least one hundred, and she takes the time to pull the threads on all four sides, shipping them back to me when that major task is complete. I appreciatively take the process from there. The cards are ordered assorted, no two cards are ever the same, and there are a lot of those cards in existence on the planet. The Smithsonian truly is international in scope.

An invitation came during the course of a telephone conversation while an order was being placed for more cards: "Gloria, if you are ever in the D.C. area, please contact us and we can arrange a meeting." "I would really enjoy that." Years down that road, the time did come. My brother Paul (finally) proposed to Mary Jo, so now I could visit D.C. to celebrate with them and do a doubleheader deal, following-up on that invitation to visit. I called and made an appointment to meet June Dwyer who was directly ordering from me, and I was very happy this was all working out. After some stupid mistake of my own doing at the airport that almost left me sitting watching my plane take off without me, I flew into Dulles, ruffled and relieved. My brother was getting married to a sweetheart, we were having a special family reunion and I had an appointment at the Smithsonian: "tight" as my son would say.

My Mom and my brother Norm came with me on the subway for moral support and probably also to make sure I was safe in a big city that had overwhelmed me once before. I had gotten lost there on a field trip when I was in elementary school, so I guess they figured I needed some help, thirty-something years after that fact. Ironically enough, the place I had gotten lost was at the Washington Monument (because I insisted on *running* all the way up alone) and the place where I found my group after almost being killed running across Pennsylvania Avenue was in the lobby of the Smithsonian. This time around I was more than grateful to have friends along because I was nervous as well as excited. We were plenty early and I did a dry *run* up to the office to make sure we had the right place. They went about town and I went up the elevator once more for my meeting.

It is always interesting to observe who you are and what goes through your own mind at times like these. I had built a myth in my head about this place and the people in the hallowed halls. It was known that I made cards for the Smithsonian since it had been written about in local newspapers over the years, and that would always be a "point" to be made, say at Gallery Opening Receptions. For example: "…this is Gloria Page. She makes handmade cards as part of her business and has cards at THE SMITHSONIAN." It was a name-dropping type of thing that either happened to me or that I knowingly did myself, with a smile. Now here I was, standing at the front desk of the Graphics Department, which, by the way, was not in the main complex as I had assumed. That didn't matter—the person I was to meet—she was the key and the reason for this trip.

The kind and gracious secretary greeted me and communicated to June that I had arrived for my appointment. I was welcomed to set up any "presentation" that I had prepared in the Main Conference Room. Minor panic attack ensued. The Conference Room, which was nicely appointed and average in size, became remarkably huge and forbidding, since I did not have a professional-style presentation in tow. What was I supposed to have? All I did have was a set of a dozen cards with a slight variation to the cards we were already doing. My reason for being there was to meet June and have a little chat. That's what I understood. Now I felt under-prepared, feeling as if I were somehow shooting myself in the foot by blowing this golden opportunity to dazzle someone with all of my brilliant new ideas and business proposals—but I didn't have any, that was the only problem. It is not comfortable, feeling like a loser at a time when at least modest confidence would be handy. What can you do at a time like that? Re-group. Do anything but think too much. I walked around, looked outside, breathed in and out deeply, and pulled out my little selection of cards.

As I was spreading my twelve cards on the vast table, trying to make them look like more than what they were, my eye caught the sight of two women walking down the hallway towards my room—not one person, two. Oh my. I just had this feeling that one person was June and the other was her boss, Deborah Palazzo. That was not in the schedule, but it looked like it was happening—sure enough—I was right, and suddenly more nervous at the same time. In they came with warm smiles and extended hands.

All of the energy wasted on worry evaporated as we introduced ourselves to each other. Deborah saw that I was scheduled for a meeting and decided she'd like to be there, too, "if it was all right" with me. I was delighted. My notebook and pen were poised and I was about to learn a lot in a very concentrated period of time. Deborah shared her vision about many of the Smithsonian gift shops and described the upcoming renovations and expansions that were either in process or planned for the near future. She asked me questions about my own ideas as far as product development in my business and there was a candidness and interest that was exciting and directed to new horizons. We discussed the possibility of creating higher-end products for shops that would be moving in that direction, and then the big question came: "Gloria, I would like you to consider designing and creating a product for The Smithsonian Catalogue. It has worldwide distribution and so the numbers would have to be there. Do you have something for the catalogue?" Now, there is no way that I am going to whine and say something stupid like: "Well, I am just one person working alone in my unfinished basement, so I can't do it." Forget that. So, instead, I put my hands on the table and said: "Deborah, I would love to make something for the catalogue. Today, I am not quite set up for it, but tomorrow is a new day. I want to do it. What can I do here in Washington in a few days to get ready?" She gave me a list of Museum Shops to visit in order to understand the bigger picture. I did that, and I have yet to come up with a product prototype and proposal, but I will not give that up. It meant so much to me that the idea was even put on the table.

I was very happy to finally meet June as well. They both liked and kept the cards I had taken with me, wrote them up as an order, and we shared a few more thoughts. I said something to the effect that it was "such a great honor to have something I make in a Smithsonian gift shop, an honor that I try not to 'exaggerate or abuse' too often." They laughed and we parted company. And I just couldn't resist—I put it into the title of this book: "from 3 art stamps to *the Smithsonian*." It just happens to be a major highlight. "How did you ever manage to get into the Smithsonian?" is the most frequently asked question whenever I speak about the business of art—a favorite question to answer.

When I met my Mom and brother Norm downstairs, I was shocked to discover that the meeting had lasted only twenty minutes—it felt much, much longer. It had been packed into a concise, professional time frame where every minute counted. On the train ride back to Paul and Mary Jo's place, I quietly realized that I had gone to a new place in my own estimation. Congratulations came from family, too. We all enjoyed it together.

I do not have a piece of artwork in the Smithsonian's permanent collection—that is way out there. I have not been part of a nationally juried show there either. Those types of honors are in the big leagues of bragging rights. So what do I honestly, really have? I *do* have cards in one Smithsonian Shop that have sold continuously for years and an open invitation to create more cards for special shows, which I have done in the past and can do again. It would be a very good idea to look at the listings of upcoming special shows and challenge myself to create some new prototypes with a springtime attitude, internally.

And then there is that catalogue… Someday I am going to come up with a great idea, figure out the mass production, make a presentation and see what happens. The catalogue buyers have changed since that time, but I will try anyway. As for the card line, we experimented with a variation of the card designs. A message just came that they are "flying out the door!" An e-mail on my screen—wow—this is a big order. Just last week I sent out the "new-style" set… as always, with a distinct memory of that very first call.

Life is a succession of lessons which must be lived to be understood.

- Helen Keller

A cup of tea
...delightful sips of inspiration—drink deeply

...Springtime on a creamy white Victorian porch, my sun parasol leaning against a table, a cup of tea, silver spoon, damask and time; I stir slowly... with time... to dream...

I don't know about you, but my daily life is nothing like that. Everything seems to speed up all the time. Over the years I have come to recognize and act upon the periodic and absolute necessity to slow things down—way down. Whoa, Nelly. I need to pull back the reins and meander in lavender fields rather than constantly charge out of the gates, one after the other, on the fast track of life. I simply must find peaceful moments.

There is one mellowing, winding-down, Victorian-porch-type experience that has become a tradition for me that occurs every two months. My sense of time is altered in that I now view the course of a year as actually being six two-month intervals rather than twelve separate months. The reason: *Somerset Studio* Magazine—it is a bi-monthly publication. At least one guaranteed-evening every two months, I pull a "Whoa, Gloria" on myself, and graciously allow myself the luxury to meander, the time to dream, page by glorious page. When even the advertisements are enjoyable, it says something.

My first encounter with the magazine came about by chance and the timing couldn't have been better. Several years ago when the Smithsonian called and asked me to work up some designs for a card line, I sweated through it, trying to figure out what they wanted and missed the mark the first time around. Not wanting to miss my window of opportunity, I was floating different ideas in my head, but the synapses weren't connecting. The project was on hold and a couple of weeks had passed. I was at a loss for that "brilliant" idea. I hadn't reached panic-attack mode yet, but I was as dry as a desert, inspirationally-speaking. The pressure was on and the clock was ticking... ticking...

Right at that time, our monthly Stamp Club Meeting brought a bunch of us together for some interesting mini-event or other. At the end of the meeting, we usually tend to wander around the store, eyeing things and "toys" we'd like to buy and giving in to our desires more often than not. Some people have open-ended checkbooks, unlike me. I can, however, usually conjure up some good reason why I deserve a treat and can justify how I will make *more* money than I am spending, simply by buying whatever it is that I want. Standing at the counter, future purchases in hand, I heard for the first time the question that I myself would ask many times from that point on: "Has *Somerset Studio* Magazine come in yet?" It definitely had and the woman was clearly excited and snatched it off the shelf very quickly. I laughed at her. She laughed back. I asked what that magazine was all about anyway and all this chatter started up and I laughed again as I ran and snatched up my own copy to make sure I wasn't cut off at the pass by all these other women. No need to worry—they all had their current issues securely in the bag days ago. A few sets of eyes rolled in my general direction, the kinds that say: "Where on earth has this woman been? And *she's* the one with the stamp business? Oh, brother." Oh, well. It wasn't the first time I felt like the caboose on the train. I felt extremely lucky to get one of the last issues available in town. Whatever this was, I felt anxious to check it out. I had no idea what an eye feast and mind feast I was about to enjoy. It was going to save me, too.

And so began my ritual of buying the magazine, heading directly to the Taco Bell on Stadium Boulevard because it is the closest place to the stamp store for quiet and a bite to eat, since I never seem to manage dinner for myself before the meeting. I order two tostadas with green chile and guacamole added, and ice water. I eat and study the front and back covers only, being extremely careful with such a messy meal. Once my hands are washed, there I am, devouring the written word and visual desserts, carefully going through each page, every ad, letter-to-the-editor, every single word. I don't blink. Literally. Until my eyes hurt from the strain—then it's *quick* blinking, let me tell you. The artwork is fabulous and the photography does it justice. The artists are generous in giving out the directions on their personal techniques. I am learning as I drink in the concepts, putting my own twists on what I see, loving every second of the experience. If by some lucky chance Lynne Perrella's artwork is featured, I am stuck at Taco Bell for a *long* time. She is my favorite stamp/collage artist. I bought many Santa Claus, Southwest, and other beautiful images from her Acey Deucey Art Stamp Collection years ago. Her development as an artist is a huge inspiration to me. When she is included in an issue, it sparkles in a special way. The same holds true for Sherrill Kahn and all of her artwork.

Somerset Studio opened new doors and shed refreshing light on my stamping world. My first issue also introduced me to the idea that became my "in" at the Smithsonian. Using glue sticks to simulate sealing wax was a new concept for me—I immediately went to Michaels Arts and Crafts, picked up a few supplies and came up with the card line that became a winner, thanks to *Somerset Studio* and the artist who shared that technique. Many other product ideas were inspired as well and I went on to expand my business based on these new creations. I am very grateful. Early on, I bought every past issue that was available at the time and would pay good money for the few issues that are no longer available that I want in order to complete my collection. Every issue is saved and placed on a special shelf. Loaning them is a rarity and only extremely lucky/trustworthy people may apply for that privilege. Browsing through "old" issues always brings fresh new ideas. It never ceases to amaze me how new an old issue can be.

Being at Taco Bell is not exactly like being on a Victorian porch with an English tea-cup nestled in white-gloved hands. The atmosphere of the magazine is transporting enough to make it feel as if it is. This week the latest issue should be on the stands. Another two months have passed. I probably won't wait until Saturday's Club Meeting to get it—the stamp store will be opened during the week, of course. I can't wait.

■

I need to be filled up and energized since I am constantly in the business of creating and putting out. There are countless very valuable art books and magazines available and my very old stand-by, *Rubberstampmadness* Magazine, is always there to add another dimension to my learning process. I connected to all my original stamp sources through RSM's advertising and couldn't have done Phase One of my first years in business without it. People told me about *Vamp Stamp News* and I learned great tips from stampers willing to pass along helpful information. An ad in that publication connected me to a source for great glue sticks that I use for my Smithsonian cards. The fabulous magazine

Belle Armoire, meaning "beautiful wardrobe," takes us into the realm of Art to Wear. A new magazine has been added to the "garden" called *Expression*. This is another artistic endeavor that will reach many people. These are all "teaching" as well as artistic publications. Artists are more than willing to share techniques and supply sources. It all ties together. There is a community out there and I feel welcomed by it. I appreciate the artistic professionalism that is accompanied by warmth and humor. There are different approaches and presentations and I appreciate that fact. I sense a caring support system underlying the business aspects of publications that I respect and inherit from. Whenever artists are eager to share and there are vehicles for them to do so, the dynamics are there for creative explosions. My own writing, whether in books or magazines, is my offering and an extension of that sharing—hopefully a contribution in its own right.

Knowing first-hand how stamping books and publications helped me with my stamp business, I knew that this "writing thing" (*Holy Moly Mackeroly*) could use all the help I could get, too, as I began writing for the first time—a book no less. Was there a *Somerset Studio* for writers? I wish. My research turned up great books and I immersed myself in them. Starting with Natalie Goldberg's book *Writing Down the Bones,* I found myself compelled to buy every single book of hers, and I understand that her latest book is scheduled to come out next month. I will have it reserved and on order. Understand, please, that I am a person who loves books but is also extremely tight when it comes to buying them. The library did not have all of Natalie's books and even the ones that they did have, I still needed to have my *own* copies. Period. I ordered them without even asking how much they cost. That tells you more than you realize it's telling you. Julia Cameron followed with more mind/heart gems for this new writer's literary hope chest. More books and encouraging authors add to the entourage in a continuum and I find myself energized into action, not just impressed with their expertise.

I am wowed by lots of people and scores of books on Art, Writing, Philosophy or Whatever. I am moved when someone is willing to come close enough to my level, close enough to *me*, to put an artistic, literary, personal arm around my shoulder and show me the ropes. A person willing to help me to do battle with fears and happy to hold up the mirror to my own potential, coaxing it out with humor, kindness and skill—it could be an author, relative, friend, fellow-artist, or simply enough, another fellow human being whose path and mine crossed at some juncture on our mutual journeys. If I am tuned-in, teachers are everywhere. Inspiration is all around if I look, especially if I share my own.

Upon reflection, I have decided that I am going to graduate myself from Taco Bell and head downtown to The Lakota Café for my bi-monthly readings from now on. I will order a spot of cinnamon-cardamon tea with honey or a can of ice-cold Blue Sky orange cream soda imported from Santa Fe. It's time to crank things up a notch in the Class Act Department. It is my time after all this time: a cup of tea (or soda), *Somerset* and me…

Whether it is reading a book or magazine, taking a class and surprising yourself by learning something completely new, sharing ideas with friends, going for a walk, a solo swim, getting a massage, sinking way down in a hot tub, sailing overhead in a hot air balloon, clipping the waves in Chesapeake Bay or meditating under a maple or aspen tree (for lack of a bodhi tree), we all need to drink deeply from wells of inspiration. We can gallop in the desert for only so long. At some point, let us treat ourselves, and each other, to a honeyed cup of tea, piping hot or iced, depending on the spirit of the day.

Success and Failure

Why is it so hard to tell the difference sometimes...

Now wait a minute:
- There is big and there is small.
- There is good and there is evil.
- There is up and down, left and right, wrong and right.
- There is *success* and there is *failure*. Opposites, *right*?

My kids had this figured out before kindergarten. It's all quite simple and clear, cut-and-dry. Success is the opposite of failure and vice versa. Period. What do I mean it's "hard to tell the difference?" When something is obvious, leave it alone, why don't you. Isn't life complicated enough without purposely trying to create more confusion?

I asked myself, point blank, *quick*, Gloria, the first thing that comes to your mind when you think of "material success?" Answer: "a real bed instead of a futon on the floor and a pair of sunglasses—*not* from The Dollar Store." I was surprised by the second one—I didn't think I had a thing for sunglasses. I asked my husband Gary: "What is the first thing that comes to your mind when I say 'material success?'" Without missing a beat he said: "a car made within the decade." A bit telling about our lifestyle, I'd say.

Give me a minute or two and I would come up with a deeper, more comprehensive, intelligent, impressive, meaningful answer, but I like the honesty of the "winger" ones. When the astronomically successful author of the Harry Potter books, J.K. Rowling, was asked about her lifestyle changes since becoming "successful," she stated simply that, since she didn't drive, there was no temptation at all to have the "five cars" and all the showy trappings along those lines. The biggest impact for her was "security": freedom from monetary worries. Imagine this: before her first book she had to completely re-type the entire manuscript by hand *twice* in order to send it off (for initial rejections) because she did not have enough money to pay for copies... amazing to think of that now.

> Happiness doesn't come from having things—
> it comes from being part of things.
>> "Chris in the Morning"
>> *Northern Exposure* (TV show)

There is no doubt about one thing—personal success feels good in that fabulous moment when it hits and sinks in. We set out to achieve a goal, we do whatever work needs to be done and get there. Winning a tennis tournament and beating the #1 seed in the process is success if you entered to win. Usually that is why we play. If the goal is to lose 10 pounds and 11 pounds are miraculously shed, hey, that is success-plus. The book market is flooded with success-oriented books and the formulas, methods and mantras are all laid out. The road to success is paved with endless variations on the same basic theme. Visualization and affirmation techniques have power and get results. There are spiritual, monetary, athletic, social, educational, ad infinitum definitions of success. There is the successful person in all different arenas, and wouldn't it be the most celebrated success of all time if there actually was "Peace on this Earth" beyond the Christmas card greetings: Happy New Year, Happy Everyday, Happy Humanity and World... an answered prayer.

Don't you love all of those "Dummy" books? "Computers for Dummies," "Marriage for Dummies," all based on the premise that if you declare yourself a Dummy *first* then you will open yourself up to learning your way out of ignorance and find that success, dummy-that-you-thought-you-were. Smart move. A taste of Zen is in there, too. So you want Enlightenment, do you? The monks are going to slam the door in your face until you figure out that you don't even know your own name—a pivotal moment for sure.

I am interested in this topic of *success*. In a very real and down-to-earth way, that is what this book touches on—I am telling you stories of how I built my business. There is a certain level of success implied in the title when I say that I went "from 3 art stamps to the Smithsonian." I doubt there would be much interest if the subtitle were something along the lines of: "I started with 3 art stamps and it was all downhill from there." For anyone contemplating anything new, this is a huge issue that must be faced, not avoided.

My interest in this topic of "Success and Failure" is more involved in the gray areas, the places where things are not measurable in the everyday sense, the place where the issues get muddled—that strange and hard to understand place where money doesn't seem to be able to buy happiness and visibly successful people seem to be very visibly messed up. That odd space where we say we want success and then act as if we don't.

Let's say that I don't win the tennis tournament, but come in #2. It is the highest I've ever gone, but did I *succeed?* Is it a success to be #2 or did I simply fail to be #1? I want to lose 10 pounds and lose 5—is that a failure *or* did I succeed at losing 5 pounds, hurray, and now I have only 5 more to go. You know, the old is-the-glass-half-empty-or-half-full question. Success can be flashy and splashy and it can also be quiet, subtle, warm and cozy—very personal rather than public, a step rather than a huge leap. Success can be gradual… even deceiving. I'd like to explore a bit this foggy, blurry, gray-area realm.

If we were to slam all of our cards on the table and ask, come on, *what do you want*, success or failure, I can't see any "normal" person opting for anything but the obvious. Yet the distinction became so blurred for me at one point that I honestly found it not only hard but *impossible* to tell the difference between the two.

Over the years I have been asked at various times questions like: "Do you feel that your business is a *success*?" I always find myself kind of throwing up my hands either actually or mentally, looking at the person who asked it, wondering to myself: What the blank does that mean? Am I *rich* and *famous*—is that what you are asking? If so, then the answer is no, I am not a success by that definition at this time. Is my business a *success* in terms of growth, making a decent amount of money, and bringing a sense of happiness and satisfaction (when I am not struggling, juggling, and overwhelmed), then the answer is yes, it *is* a success. When I started writing this book, I was asked, "How would you define success in terms of publishing your first book? What is your goal? At what point do you declare victory?" What does *that* mean? Do I have fantasies of the New York Times Bestsellers' List or Oprah's Book Club—is that my personal measure of success in writing? Fantasies have no place here in this discussion. And I can tell you exactly and precisely when this book will be successful. It will be a success when the front cover is attached to the back cover and all the pages are glued in, hopefully in the right order. When *it is finished*—success, pure and simple. I had an idea and I did it—it is a done deal. An idea became a reality. It is in my hands. It is ready to be given and it is ready to be read. At that point my mother will insist on buying the first copy even though I will insist on giving it to her. And if even just one single person reads the book and tells me "because I read your book I had the encouragement I needed to go and do such-and-such that I have always wanted to try…" then success it is, full circle. Hopefully I will not lose any money by doing it and anything after that will be interesting and another story. Success can define itself in terms other than our own desires and our own definitions. It might be a pleasant surprise or a huge shock, you can't always know.

When I started this book about my business I had to set a few cards on my own table and ask myself why I was doing it and if I had enough "success" tucked under my own belt to have the gall to go ahead with the whole thing. When I thought in terms of wanting to express my gratitude through stories, it was a go. Yet I flinched and hedged big time when I thought in "resumé-mode." Let's see, let me list my credentials so I can bolster my self-confidence. I graduated from… and then I went on to do… Didn't work. Straight away I slammed into the "you know, I-never-did-finish-college" wall head-on and knocked myself out cold. I don't have that particular "success-factor" in place in my life. I am 46 and I still feel a certain level of shame, regret, and confusion over the whole issue. I fumble around when my two young children talk about college and ask me very direct questions about my own experience. I tell them the truth, but I want time to figure out some answers before they ask, not in the process of squirming. I want my sons to be proud of me when I am, at times, not proud of myself. How can I tell both of them to "go to college and finish so that you can do well in your lives" if I did not do that very thing? "Practice what you preach." Be the example—do not just act like the big advice-machine.

Listening to people and reading, I enjoy hearing about someone who is "self-taught," "self-made," all seemingly "self-assured" that their value is intact and actually enhanced because they went on some road-less-traveled and found success by "making it big" in spite of failing to complete the track of higher education. (Bill Gates has given the term "drop-out" new meaning, but it doesn't mean enough to me personally.) I am moved to tears by the stories of elderly folks in their caps and gowns graduating and getting that almighty diploma in hand, applauded by children and grandchildren in their own caps and gowns. Is it the piece of paper? That never really was the issue for me. Is the issue having a sense of completion, accomplishment, personal confidence, respect, having "expertise" in *something*, darn it! For all these years when I reflected on these things, looking in the mirror I could not stay there long without turning away and wondering what happened to me. I was always told how "bright" I was—what a "bright future" lay ahead of me…

For quite a while now I have been working with this book, which translates into working with myself and immersing myself into my own stories. One year was thinking; the rest has been writing. "Success and Failure" are issues worth examining when creating a business and a life, but I couldn't dance with this one topic like I could with most of the others. This one was different. This one was going to hurt. This was going to get sticky, rocky and rough. Let's go looking to get beat up, why don't we? Let's go looking for some deep, cold mud to get stuck in. Let's jump into the past…

At the Camp, my childhood summer dream cottage, I always hated stepping in the seaweeds in the lake. Half of our swimming area was cleared; the other half was *weeds*—yuck to the max. If an inner tube or other water toy drifted into the weeds, I braved it but it drove me crazy to have that feeling of my legs being entangled, a kind of trap that dragged me down. A touch of panic-attack ensued. This "College Thing" had become my "weeds." I always want to stay on the clear side and stay out of the weeds of this story. It's more comfortable. Lives have all kinds of tangly stories and some are best shelved.

Instead, for this particular one, I am taking a steel rake and going in to deal with it once and for all. I want a bigger swimming area—to play and let the toys drift, so I asked myself another point blank question: "Gloria, why did you leave school—what happened to you?" I went totally blank. And then ever so slowly, like waves lapping on a lakeshore, I allowed the water to wash over me. I started to see the inside story and I was shocked by what I learned. Success and failure had flip-flopped in my life and I had never seen it before. It finally was time to look and to learn. I sat down and watched—like a movie.

I am going to pull out two private scenes from this long movie—the two moments that I was convinced were the Highest and Lowest points in my life in higher education. I will rewind, visit once again, watch it blur, and then hopefully clear on the big screen.

- *Scene One*: Freshman Year, St. John's College, Santa Fe, 1972, Early Fall
  Formal Evening Seminar. Topic: Discussion of Homer's *Iliad* and *Odyssey*
  Question posed by the Tutors (Professors):
  "The Homeric Hero: the definition please."

There we were, all these young philosophers-in-the-making, with Great Books in our quaking hands, leaning on this massive solid maple table in great anticipation of the volcanic wisdom that would spew from the hearts, minds and mouths of those we were honored to be seated with. There we were in twentieth century Santa Fe, the Land of Enchantment, Nuevo Mexico, nouveau Mount Olympus, contemplating what Homer was telling us, or at least trying to tell us, centuries ago. We were to "get into his head" through his writing, go directly to the original Greek, not to literary commentaries, and certainly not our personal opinions about what our personal definitions of "Hero" would be. What did *Homer* think a Hero was—use his words—use his context—go way back there to a foreign, ancient world and figure it all out and talk about it in front of all these people who look so very smart. Pick up your fine English translations of these Greek masterpieces, delve into your Greek lexicon, wrestle with it, break it open, shake it up and put in your two drachmas worth. I was overwhelmed and humbled. Instead of talking, I listened—for a long time. I was observing and absorbing…

I thought I was as prepared as I could be for this Seminar. I had hiked up to Monte Sol and read my books. I read out loud, over and over, louder and louder, trying to feel the books come alive, hopefully making the connection to my heart, my mind, the brain inside the head with the swirling long hair and feather earrings attached, and eventually, hopefully, to my mouth and voice—and then speak—that was the main point of it all: to speak, listen to others, and engage in dialogue—a two-way street to wisdom.

The discussion was formal in that we addressed each other as "Mr. or Ms." and we spoke as if the books were center-stage, not us. The Tutors guided and engaged but did not dominate the experience. This was not a "Lecture" by any stretch of the imagination: this was a true Discussion (from the Latin roots "to break apart, shake it up"). I was fascinated and genuinely intimidated—and with all that I felt that I did *not* know and understand, I was very sure that I did know this: I am a peewee in the Major Leagues. I felt that basically I "don't know nothin' 'bout nothin' at all…" Nothing.

The discussion around me seemed at one point way beyond me. I was Dorothy sitting on her bed watching the cow and chickens flying by in the tornado, when I bounced hard and hit Oz. Something suddenly clicked in my head and the door opened—Technicolor!

I saw these threads of thought that seemed to be all over the place just come together in a clean, tight weave. It was as if I woke up from a deep sleep, seated at a word-loom. I shot up, threw the shuttle in play, entered the world of the living and faced a dead poet head-on. Plunging into the discussion, I heard myself talking about Homer and how he saw heroes and defined their qualities in his stories. I became a kid who rides her bike for the first time solo leaving the training wheels behind. I claimed the freedom to ride my thoughts. Homer and I were cruising! No brakes! I was thrown a couple of times while I was speaking because a few people snickered, but kept riding anyway, no looking back. (I found out that it was my Yankee pronunciation of "idea" that elicited the snickers. You know it's really pronounced "*idear*," right?) Anyway, when I concluded my simple and straightforward insight, I stopped talking.

And so did everyone else. I became very embarrassed and thought I must have made an absolute and total fool out of myself and sat there stunned and as red as the Zia Sun on the New Mexican state flag. I looked down at the table and the silence was breaking my head open it was so blaring and painfully long. Then finally someone spoke. One of the Tutors said, "Well, there is nothing left to say after that. Thank you and good evening." That was it. I didn't know what to do. There were all these congratulatory, sophisticated-type pats on the back, hushed awe, and highbrow-eyebrow looks aimed in my direction. My Shining Moment. My Brilliant Answer. My Deep Insight. Homer and I were tight. I had *arrived*. A star: *Success* written in lights. I was a bona fide "Johnnie" after all…

- *Scene Two*: Two months later, same place, same time in the evening, only this time it is my turn to have my Don Rag—a meeting each semester with all of my Tutors who will talk about my work in front of me. This time I get to listen.

The physical scene needs some alteration, however—the lights are dimmed because light hurts my eyes. They are affected by my illness. I am in a wheelchair and have come from the hospital to make this meeting. (Note: I *insisted* on having my Don Rag. My Tutors wanted it cancelled or at least postponed due to my condition. My style was to face it squarely, no pity, please. We were going to do this, I was going to go through it, and everyone involved was very accommodating and kind, if not also a bit exasperated by my insistence. I had one chance to meet with this group of people—only one.)

My fever is still up there and so I am seated at a distance from the people who will close in on me, significant people in my life who will describe my performance as a scholar in this rarified world that I love and am in the process of being ripped away from. I have been informed that I will need to leave school—I have severe mononucleosis that developed a form of hepatitis. I am anorexic before people called it that or knew exactly what it was. I weighed 86 pounds and was told in the hospital by a rather direct young doctor that I had better decide if I wanted a chance at growing old or wanted to opt to check-out. Serious food for thought there… So, there I was sitting in this room in the pit of personal hell with all the rugs pulled out from under me, all my aspirations to be a "true student of the universe" shriveled up in this wheelchair of despair. I felt so depressed and like an absolute failure. I picked my head up high enough to greet my professors. Then I put it back down again and listened.

Each spoke in turn and it was nice to hear compliments about my work as a student and constructive points of how I could improve. They were realistic and not playing off of my condition. I appreciated the evaluations, as much as I was able to take in under the circumstances. One after the other and then… my favorite Tutor, my Ancient Greek "professor" Mr. Ossorgin began to speak. He said very simply, quietly, without looking at me, rather looking up to the heavens in reflective thought: "When Miss Lagasse writes Ancient Greek on the blackboard, I am transported back to the time of the Ancients…" And I wept. I broke down completely. I broke and shattered all over the floor of my life.

Two Scenes from my life: One seemed so success-filled—I brought the room to silence. The other scene seemed the opposite to me at the time—all I had worked hard for my whole student-life was falling away, slipping through my tired fingers. Physically, I was broken. I was forced to leave school—it was not my choice at that point. But the funny thing is that my *heart* actually broke in Scene One, *not* in Scene Two. I hated the fact that people were carrying on about my answer. I knew that I didn't know anything. I wove some things together, but the depth wasn't there. It could easily unravel. I got lucky, touched something but was so far from grasping it, like swiping your hand through a rainbow. When I went to every class after that, I was frozen with fear that I could never measure up to my own or anyone else's expectations. I couldn't bring the room to silence every time. I didn't want to, and I wasn't trying to, but I felt the pressure. I knew I was immature, that the books were way over my head and that I wasn't ready to be there at all. The opening line in the College Catalog was "What is Truth?" That was so moving to me that it sealed my fate in terms of trying to get in. Yet once I did get in, I found myself feeling as angry as I once had been inspired. I was respected for being what I wasn't yet, and just wanted to be left alone to be ignorant, young, and naïve. I detested and would not allow phoniness and arrogance in myself and refused to pretend to be "smart," intelligent, and sophisticated. I wanted to learn, starting at ground zero. St. John's wanted us to do that very thing—I loved the Ideal of the school, still do and always will. But I knew that we all came with our baggage that wasn't easy to leave at the doorstep. I went back after a year of recuperating and started over again that next year, at age 19, and later that year left for the last time. At the end, I put poor dear Dean Neidorf through the ringer when he told me that he respected me for leaving. "What do you mean you respect me for leaving? Then what are *you* doing here?" With tears I left for the great unknown…

I, Gloria Lagasse, just wasn't ready at 18 or 19, and look forward to the day when I, Gloria Page, can go back. Will I be any more ready? I wonder. My hair is short and white now, the earrings a bit more tailored. I still "don't know nothin' 'bout nothin' at all" but at least I'm enjoying it for a change. You never know, maybe by the time my kids are ready for College, I might be, too. My internal recipe will be lightened up and chilled out, with a generous dash of humor thrown in this time around. I still have dreams about it.

In Scene Two when I broke, it was one of the most moving experiences of my life. Mr. Ossorgin's words washed over me like healing balms, and it was the highest point in my academic life ever. I broke down but it was more like breaking open—opening to the beauty of learning and touching that ethereal realm with my whole self. My teacher lifted me to the point of soaring, when externally I was imprisoned by circumstance. I loved Greek and ancient languages and he knew it. He validated my heart, not my mind. So what was Success and what was Failure? Why did I ultimately decide to leave school? Because my heart was broken, my dream floundered and I knew I had to grow up a lot more before I could honestly be "in school" in the truest sense of what that means to me. I suffered so much because I was honest with myself in leaving. If either of my children went through anything that in any way resembled my experience, I would be moved to tears and have the deepest respect for his struggle. If I could look in the mirror someday and remember what I just said I would feel for my children, perhaps I could love that young girl who wanted so much to be sincere to the bone, genuine to the core. Perhaps I could forgive her and more than that… accept her and be proud.

The Success/Failure issues in life are sometimes clear and oftentimes are not. In the blur, the fog and the distortions, I am learning. What seemed so obvious when I was a little girl watching "The Wide World of Sports" witnessing "the thrill of victory and the agony of defeat" could just as easily become "the agony of victory and the thrill of defeat." At the pinnacle, you can shatter; from the depth of a dark pit, you can soar.

In and out of "school" over the years, from psychology classes at the University of Hartford, to classical guitar lessons at Julius Hart School of Music, and also a class in the Philosophy of Religion at Columbia University in NYC, it all added up to nothing worth mentioning on paper. As far as "formal" art classes, the only things I took were a weaving class in Farmington, Connecticut from a lovely English weaver with a Swedish loom and a watercolor class at the Atheneum in Hartford. I can also add Printmaking 101 at age 45 to the short list… I believe in learning, whether picking grapes in France, sitting at Ryoan-Ji Temple in Kyoto, or listening to my children. I plan on exploring for as long as I am alive. I'll keep "check-out" time at bay for as long as possible. Life is good.

I was asked recently to give a talk at the University to a group of visiting "scholars" from around the state—high school sophomores in an honors educational program. The first thing I made sure of was that the organizers were completely aware of the fact that I did *not* have a degree—if that would be a problem, fine, they could find someone else, no harm done. As it turned out, I was still invited and was put in the segment called "The Road Less Traveled," a cool and kind way of identifying those of us who had chosen "alternative paths" and still managed to eke out some semblance of success, mine as an artist. It was a great experience, especially when this sincere young philosopher-in-the-making asked me in the Q&A period if I could please give my own "definition of Art and Beauty." I was thrown back into that old college realm, Plato popped into my mind, and this time I paused and quietly laughed. A Philosophy Professor was sitting to my right and I rambled a few examples and bumbled and explored the fact that I didn't have a definition and just said it: "I don't know yet. I *do* know that when I look into the eyes of my children and hear their laughter—*that* is Beauty to me. I *do* know that I believe that your own life is meant to be your best work of Art, but having said that, I'll leave the rest to the PhD's." The students seemed to like my presentation even if I did not have all the answers, imagine, a person as ancient as I appeared to them. Maybe it is even good for them to hear: "I don't have a clue. When *you* figure it all out, please let me know." Better yet: "Remember Socrates? Let's work on this together. We have time… yes, we do."

Perhaps we could rally and help support each other more in the "enthusiasm arena" of life rather than strapping ourselves onto the never-ending seesaw of Success-and-Failure. Now *that* would be a goal worth achieving and a road worth traveling.

"Use what talents you possess. The woods would be very silent if no birds sang there except those that sang the best."

- Henry Van Dyke
American Clergyman/Writer

"Success is going from failure to failure without losing enthusiasm."
                                                    - *Winston Churchill*

(Enthusiasm: from the Greek word *entheos* "inspired by the gods".)
"en": in / "theos": god

In all your endeavors, I wish you great *enthusiasm*. Do what you love, love what you do, and don't forget to love you, too. Believe in yourself, make a good plan and *go*. Rarely do I step on a soapbox and speak from the "Voice of Experience," so bear with me here. A quick dusting of the box, a hop on top and a few words: "If you are planning to go to college: go. If you are there: stay. If you have finished: celebrate, keep learning and move into your life. Do not minimize your fears and do not exaggerate them either. And finally, no matter what, never, ever feel that you are alone in any of this—you aren't. There will always be someone there for you, if you will only open your heart and ask."

As for the girl with the burning heart back at the New Mexican version of Mount Olympus in the '70's, what a great kid. I am proud of you. I love your idealism. Check it out in the mirror—you'll see. I won't turn my head or walk away this time... I promise.

The discussion about success and failure can be endless. It is a significant topic because no matter how much we would like to believe about ourselves that we are not in the greedy rat-race, not into "money-for-the-sake-of-money" routine, not competitive and combative within ourselves and with others, we all do battle on some level or another with these issues. Our identities get tied into definitions. It would be beneficial to all of us if our identities were more secure and at peace with feelings of contentment. It is fabulous to make great efforts and to see great results. It can also be a different variety of fabulous to make great effort, *not* get the desired result, and learn one heck of a lot in the process. "Success stories" are nice to share if I feel comfortable enough in the company of friends who do care and who won't perceive my excitement as boasting. Yet some of my favorite stories are the ones where the road was not smooth and the outcome was not peachy. Contained in those is this quiet little place of self-respect for the fact that, despite the odds and the seeming futility, I simply decided not to give up. The "successful" outcome becomes less than secondary in value. The process itself is the place to win.

This would be the perfect place for us to sing that old song from the way back years by Sam Cooke called: *(What a) Wonderful World*, especially the rendition by James Taylor, Simon and Garfunkel. You remember the one... it starts out with "Don't know much about history..." The point was that *love* is the whole point, and even if I "don't know nothin' 'bout nothin' at all" except that—then that, quite simply, is good enough.

Everyone who is successful
must have dreamed of something.
                        - Native American Proverb (*Maricopa*)

Dear George,
        Remember <u>no</u> man is a failure who has <u>friends</u>.
        Thanks for the wings! Love, Clarence
                                - (note from the angel to Jimmy Stewart)
                                It's a Wonderful Life

Regalos secretos para los santos
(Secret gifts for the saints)

Churches can sometimes feel like cavernous spaceships. Dark, candle lit corners, mysterious rooms, sky-piercing ceilings and stained glass windows that crack the sunlight into rainbows that take you straight to the heavens. A lot of emotions get stirred up in the pews—from ecstasy and fascination to sheer boredom when the sermon misses the mark, from enlightenment to confusion, from burdens of guilt to convictions that border on the saintly. *The Lives of the Saints* was a heavy, brown book with gold edges that lived in our house. The *people* who lived in the house read the book and also had it read to them. I was very involved in the stories. The idea was that you tried to emulate these great souls in your everyday life. That was a tall order. It's hard to be that good all the time.

My great-aunt was a nun at the school I went to as a child. There were great hopes and lots of pressure on me from certain quarters—not my parents, just certain quarters. I was after all, Sister Luciosa's niece. How nice and also how hard at times. She was an upper grade teacher and the Choir Director. She loved me, thank goodness. I sang in the Choir for years. She had a great laugh, all the way to heaven. I loved her, too.

Certain "privileges" come your way under such circumstances. I was allowed to work behind the scenes as a very young child now that I think about it. Lucky me got to go to the Convent and wash and polish the hallway floors, making the black border linoleum tiles sparkle. I saw the nuns *relaxing*, and *eating,* and saw that they had *bathrooms* just like regular people did. As a reward one time, a habit was put on me and I looked in the mirror and Sister Gloria was looking straight back at me. That was weird. Working in the church on a daily basis meant that I prepared water and wine for morning Masses and even played the organ for a time during the 7:30 a.m. Mass when I was about twelve years old and had a few years of piano under my belt. I loved feeling holy when those moments came. And that early in the morning, even if I made mistakes on the keyboard or foot pedals, nobody cared too much because they were basically grateful to have some, any music, even if it was flawed. There is something about organ music in church, humble, bumble, baby-level that it was.

When I first learned to write in school, I was excited and I made cards for people for every occasion. Making handmade gifts was greatly encouraged in my family because of the heart and personal effort behind the gift. At one point I put these two things together, cardmaking and "crafts" and decided that I would make a secret gift for one of the saints at church and write her a letter in one of my cards. I started pulling things together to surprise St. Thérèse. They had to be special things and everything was a big secret…

My Aunt Germaine was my father's oldest sister. She was big and had a big voice and heart and the reddest hair I had ever seen. She always reminded you that it wasn't real. She would speak on the phone in the most outrageous manner, sometimes using words that you knew you weren't supposed to use, but had no idea why not since they sounded so fun when she said them. "Hello, honey, this is your big fat Matante Germaine calling! Remember me with the fake red hair? Tell your father he'd better take you over for a visit soon—it's been too long and I have some more empty perfume bottles and jewelry surprises for you…" *Evening in Paris* bottles, smelly lotions with a little left on the bottom, golden caps, colored glass, make-up galore all sitting on her vanity that was overflowing with more glitzy "ladies' stuff" than I'd ever seen before or since. There were golden mirrors and gilded brushes, jewelry and hair accessories sparkling and begging me to try them on. She would always have something in the oven to deal with or a phone call or an animal that needed attention, so I would get the invitation to "just have fun while I'm gone…" and I would play and pretend to my heart's content—she gave me space. Then before getting picked up, I would be given a bag of treasures to take home.

I started to use those gorgeous things as the basis for my secret gifts for the saints. During the summer, my best friend Jeannie and I would pick thousands of rose petals and I tried squishing them to make my own brands of perfumes. They eventually became ghastly looking and smelly, but in the early stages they took on the appearance of new fragrances in Matante Germaine's exotic bottle collection.

My first card and perfume gift did go to St. Thérèse of Lisieux (the Little Flower). Timing for this caper was everything because I was going to hide the note and present behind the statue and you weren't supposed to go past the kneeler. It took a couple of days before I found the right time when no one was looking or praying in St. Thérèse's area. St. Ann's is a humongous church and my heart was pounding furiously as I crossed the railing, convinced that I would be caught and that this must at the very least be a venial sin even though I was giving gifts to the saint I loved the most. There were rows and rows of candles on both sides of the statue, the small 25-cent votives on the left and the tall, long-burning one-dollar donation candles on the right. My long ponytail was a worry around all these flames so I tucked it in my jacket before I snuck around. I must have been protected or something, because I wasn't caught, my pounding heart didn't echo and bang all over the stained glass windows, and my message and bottle were safely tucked behind the statue. I wanted St. Thérèse to like my present and me, too. I was a very little girl at that time, with an impressive personal collection of statues on my dresser at home. There were even some that glowed in the dark, for protection, I guess.

The contents of that and subsequent letters are lost to me now, but I think that the general tone was gratitude for all of their sacrifices and my personal promises to be a good girl even though it was hard sometimes. I knew that they couldn't write back, but believed that if I prayed hard enough, I could get a message from them in some form or another. The day after my first special delivery, I snuck back into the church to see if "she" had come to pick up my note, etc. and sure enough—it was all *gone*! I wrote more letters, some just a few words, made more cards and gifts and delivered them to many statues around the church, no matter how many attempts were necessary to keep this all between me and the saints. At times I asked for things like a Barbie doll, which I did get because I asked my Mom, too, but I decided against that style of special requests for "things" and just shared my heart and dreams. If they wanted to help me out that was fine, but I wasn't asking for anything like toys or special favors in school because I knew they had much more important matters to worry about. The whole world was asking.

After each special delivery, I knelt down and said a few words in prayer, always mindful to keep it extremely brief since I did not want to get caught. I truly and innocently believed that the saints came at night and picked up all my notes and presents. They were always gone the next day—proof. This tradition faded in time. I grew up.

On 8th Grade Graduation Day 1968, with sky blue cap and gown flying in the breeze, congratulations were everywhere for all of us, and one dapper man and his wife came to me with extended hands and kind smiles. "Foxy" Theriault put two hands around my one hand, looked me straight in the eye and asked: "Are you the little girl who used to write notes and send cards and presents to the saints behind their statues many years ago?" Blush. "Yes, Mr. Thériault, that was me all right. How did you know and remember?" "As the janitor all these years, I cleaned up everywhere and started finding things behind the statues. You never signed your name; you figured the saints would know, I guess. At night my wife and I read them together, each and every one. You made us cry, sweetie."

See. The saints did read them—I knew it—I just knew they did.

When I grew up and became a big girl, I still made cards and liked making handmade presents and even made a business out of doing it. I sign things generally, but the secret gifts are still more fun than anything else. It's a nice mix of business and pleasure.

One of the business accounts that my mother developed for me was the Santuario in Chimayo, New Mexico. It is a very old adobe structure, deeply rooted in the soil of miracles and faith. At the time, Mary ran the Gift Shop and I had made a number of card orders specifically designed for the Santuario—a whole series of saints (santos) and also images of the church itself. I did tiles and bookmarks for them, too. It has been an honor. Several years ago I was in New Mexico and wanted to meet Mary so I called ahead and made an appointment. I ended up being early, so I had time with my Mom and little son Bryan to walk around, take pictures, having a bit of quiet time before the touristos descended and started posing in front of everything.

Mary came and I loved her right away and understood why she and my Mom hit it off so well. She was warm and kind and very enthusiastic about my cards and how well they were doing in the shop. Then she completely surprised me. "Gloria, would you like to open the doors of the Santuario for me this morning? Here are the keys. After you open the front doors you will see the Santuario lit only by candles. There will be enough light for you to find all the switches in the office to light everything…if you want to, take some time there in the *real* Santuario—before all the tourists come and all the lights are on. Please." Wow. I became a little girl again—I was going to visit the saints.

I held my son's hand and he helped me to open the old wooden doors. My Mom came and the three of us had the most special experience. Only flickering candles lit our path and the ancient walls, the statues, flowers, rows of abandoned crutches, and all of the Spanish symbols of faith glowed golden before us. We put our hands in the miraculous dirt that draws pilgrims on their knees all the way from Albuquerque and beyond each year on Easter weekend. We read notes and letters pinned, tucked and taped around the statue of Santo Niño de Atocha (Holy Child) written in Spanish and English, lit by twinkling candles—most of the notes were a few words infused with great heart. Baby shoes and flowers, candles and mementos left as gifts surrounded different statues. Memories of my own secret messages and gifts came flooding over me. I didn't have any squished rose petals floating in *Evening in Paris* bottles in my pockets or cards with personal notes for these santos, but my handmade cards were in the shop across the way. Money from the sales helps support the Santuario and I felt proud of that connection. We were quiet and the saints were quiet, but I felt that they remembered me. From the huge modern stone French church in New England almost 40 years ago, to this tiny, thick-walled adobe ancient womb of faith in the heart of Spanish New Mexico, there was a continuum, a belonging. This time I didn't need to hide or be afraid of being "caught." I was given permission. Even more than that, we were given a warm invitation. In my hand, I held… the key.

It was a business trip—it had started out that way. I stamp santos on paper. I found myself in a place where the most devoted people immerse their flesh in their faith—it is not for show or good form. To touch, even from a distance, such powerful dedication, is to be changed. Then it is time to return to the secular present moment. We turned on all the electric lights, the tourists poured in, and cameras were everywhere. I returned that special key, which looked rather ordinary once we left the holiness of the Santuario.

Mary doesn't work at the shop anymore. The little, old, leathery, precious priest, Father Roca, a man I dearly love, will not be there forever either. We were chatting and joking around in the gift shop and he told me that he had written a book. I wanted to see it and bought it right there on the spot so that he could sign it for me. His book is entitled: *El Album de mis Recuerdos* (Album of my Memories). Since he wrote it in Spanish and I can't read it, I figured it was a donation to the Santuario and I just wanted to be connected to him whether I could understand it or not. He laughed when I told him that and assured me that I would be able to understand it because it was written "in the language of the heart, Spanish or English, it doesn't matter, who cares!" He signed it. As soon as I started to read the book cover, I knew he was right. The jacket said that he was born is Spain in 1918, and can you believe it? He came as a missionary to Truchas and Chimayo, New Mexico in 1954—the year I was born. The jacket said he is "jovial y vivaracho…popular y cordial." Anyone can understand that. We linked our arms together that day, posed, and Mary took a picture of us in The Santuario Gift Shop.

Originally, I went to meet my card buyer, check on my stock and write up a new card order. I accomplished all that. I also got to unlock some ancient, sacred doors, and visit my own ancient past… by candlelight.

A buen entendedor, pocas palabras bastan.
(To a good listener, a few words are enough.)

- *Spanish* Dicho (Proverb)

101

Some things are meant to be carved in stone

Words are the voice of the heart.

■

Confucius

When I first came across this saying, I wrote it down in several places. In case I misplaced one piece of paper, I'd surely find the others. It had to be front-and-center in this book, that much I knew for sure. This was the quote that caught the spirit.

Writing it down by hand, coming up with a nice computer font in English, this was fine, but not fine enough for ancient Chinese words of such purity, simplicity and depth. I needed the essence, the original, the genuine. I needed that saying to be carved in stone… by a master. I had to find a Chinese artist, as close to home as possible.

When I first came to this town in Missouri, I wondered if I was going to be able to find a place to buy *hot* Chinese and Korean food and the local Gerbes wasn't doing it for me. On a drive past another chain store one day, I was struck by the juxtaposition of a huge sign that read "Hong Kong Market," and the classic red Midwest barn-type buildings underneath the sign. A Chinese *barn*? This I've got to see, so I pulled in to check it out. My noodles and kimchee cravings were satisfied, and I was even able to buy ceremonial Joss Paper that I love for my cards—and only a ten-minute drive—perfect.

Whenever I needed a translation for a Chinese stamp or symbol that I had found, I would shop for my food supplies and then chat with the kind woman who rang me up. One day, glancing into the glass case up front, I noticed a small green brocade box with what appeared to be two tiny stone stamps with the traditional red paste in porcelain in the center. This was exciting for me and I asked to see it. Oh. The stones were blanks—they needed to be carved. "Is there anyone in Columbia who can do that for me? I would love to have my signature and business name carved into those tiny stamps." "Yes, there is a man who does that. He works here at the store and has checked out your groceries before. He is an artist from China. I will ask if he is willing to do that for you…"

There are many family connections in the Hong Kong Market business and I heard that the artist, Mr. Wang, was willing to do the carving for me and that his son Jerry, a student at the University of Missouri, would act as our translator. Two stones were carved—one for my name "Page," the other for my business name "Impressions" ("good stamp"). They were beautifully done. I finally had my own personal Chinese stone chops.

My hope was that Mr. Wang would be willing to carve the Confucian saying for this book. I left a message for him and Jerry at the store. Yes, he was willing. I was caught completely by surprise, however, when I met them at Hong Kong Market, and Mr. Wang invited me to come and see his artwork and his collection of stones so that I could choose my own. What a wonderful, learning visit. Come to find out, he is a master painter in the classical Chinese school of brush painting. His humble studio contains treasures. A glass case with stones was a little world unto itself. Mine is massive in my hand—an heirloom.

I learned from Jerry that Mr. Wang had called a Classics Professor in China to make sure that his choice of characters was historically accurate according to the original texts. He carved the stone, spoke with me in English about his work, and I am very moved and honored to have his work to share. "Work of the hands" is also the voice of the heart.

You never know who may be ringing up your ramen and handing you change…

Carolyn Birkes
and my very first art show ever

We had just moved to Columbia, Missouri, and I had met a few people and that was nice, but my whole experience was like clothes that don't quite fit for one reason or the other. I wasn't at home yet. I couldn't manage to get the right size. One day while working on organizing my makeshift basement studio, I came across a newspaper article that I had saved and taken with me from New York to New Mexico to Missouri. It meant something and that is why it kept making the moves along with me. How much it would mean manifested itself later on down the road of time. It was a local newspaper article from the *Columbia Daily Tribune*, Scene Magazine section, sometime during the summer of 1994. Gary's mother sent it as information/inspiration when the whole card business venture was new on the horizon. The Tribune article highlighted two local people, card creators, who featured postage stamps in their unique lines. One person was Ken Logsdon with a really interesting story. The other was a 15-year-old girl named Lara Birkes—I was fascinated with both stories. The article was a nice two-page spread, color photos, the works. We were all doing different things, yet we were basically all doing the same thing at the same time—handmade cards, home-business style.

Feeling pretty alone down there in the basement, I had the article in hand and decided that it would be nice to try and meet the people in the article, now that we shared the same town. I kept the folded article around on the drafting table for weeks, working my way towards making a call or some kind of a connection. I made a bigger deal out of it than necessary but being the new kid on the block comes with its own special mindset. Time-to-conquer-fear finally came. A blend of curiosity and loneliness makes for an interesting mix. I unfolded the article and re-read that if I wanted to purchase Lara's cards I could find them at The Columbia Art League on E. Walnut Street. Checking a map, it seemed easy enough to find, so I ventured out and headed downtown.

Tucked into trees, art glass sparkling in the windows, I was in the right place. A volunteer worker asked if I needed help. "Yes, please show me Lara Birkes' cards… thank you." Picking up the first one was a good feeling, like reality is in hand. Yes, this person does exist, yes there is another human being who makes handmade cards, and yes I would like to meet Lara. Glancing out the window I noticed a woman making her way to the door with her arms full of boxes and who knows what. Simultaneously the woman who had shown me to the cards said: "That is the mother of your card artist. That is Carolyn Birkes." I dashed to the door to help her get in. Boxes, artwork, books, a ton of stuff and underneath it all: a smiling Carolyn. What a ray of sunshine she brought in.

I was a little flustered and unprepared to meet one of the head honchos of the Art League since I had in mind simply to visit the gallery and quietly buy a card. Here was this person in front of me with a lovely smile, perfect black hair pulled back in a bun, sharp clothes, and that great energy that says, "I am very busy and I also have all the time in the world for you." I found out that she had just come from a local television station and had been on a morning program, advertising some event coming up for the Art League. She found out from me that I was new in town and had come to buy her daughter's cards, having carried around the newspaper article for quite some time. Her "mother's heart" was definitely warmed by that one, and after I got her to let me help her put down that load of materials, we chatted for a few minutes and made a tentative plan to meet, all three of us, for lunch—Carolyn's treat to welcome me to Columbia. This was starting to feel more like home by the minute.

In short order I received a phone call from Carolyn and Lara with an invitation to join them at the St. Louis Bread Company downtown. Ah, yes, they walked down the street together and here we are all together. This is a good day. We munched and chatted and since I knew they were both curious about my business, I had cards in my bag for "show and tell." I felt shy about the whole thing in the same kind of way that my youngest son is at his sharing time in first grade. His teacher wouldn't let him pass anymore—time to talk, little guy—show and tell time. Carolyn and Lara weren't going to give me a pass either. "Show us your stuff. Gloria... it's great!"

It is always fun for me to share information and we jammed back and forth. Papers, plastic sleeves, asking for each other's opinions and design suggestions, jotting down notes, addresses, setting in place that this was just the beginning. Carolyn, ever the friendly mentor and focused businesswoman, had some ideas even as we walked out the door. "Please consider having a booth at Art in the Park, the outdoor show. I'll send you the application. You might want to try selling your cards at gift shops like Bluestem and Poppy around the corner on East Broadway. Thank you for all of your wonderful suggestions for our business... see you soon!" With waves we parted.

I like to take the time to watch people walk or drive away until I can't see them anymore. If you are family, then you get "the wave" which means that all the folks who are staying wave to all the folks who are leaving until they are out of sight. Carolyn and Lara got "the wave" from me after our first meeting, no matter how silly that might have looked on a busy downtown street corner. It is a way of holding on, capturing and extending the experience for as long as possible. Who cares what other people think.

The ideas that Carolyn planted in my thinking needed time to take root. I carried on with business as usual, received the information and application she promised about Art in the Park, sat down and read it. What stood out for me was the seemingly endless use of the word "professional." Professional slides, *professional* as well as amateur artists... Probably the word was used only twice but I played it over and over in my head so it took on a menacing and intimidating quality. The effect was that I folded up the flyer, noted the date and planned on visiting the show in June to see what an art show in Missouri was like. Period. Out of the realm of my possibilities for sure. There are times when the obvious is just that—obvious: I am not ready. Forget it, until... the phone rang.

One evening in the middle of May 1996, I got a call that I religiously let the answering machine handle for me. "Gloria, hello, this is Carolyn Birkes..." and my kids were sufficiently engaged so I felt I could take the call and did. "Hi, Gloria. You know, the deadline for the application just passed and since we looked for yours and didn't find it, I thought I'd give you a call and see what was up. We'd love for you to have a booth at Art in the Park." Major pause on my part and then a feeble response along the lines of, "Oh, that is nice of you to think of me, but since I've missed the deadline, then it is too late. My plan is to just visit the show this year and see what it is all about. *I am not ready* for anything like that yet. I just make cards, Carolyn. Thanks, anyway."

If this were a tennis match, I would equate my response to wimpy high lobs straight into her range and advantage, and what I got back was a rapid-fire series of high-powered returns that I could barely *see* let alone get my racket on.

"Your cards are wonderful—I saw them at the restaurant. You mentioned putting them into frames—that is a good idea. You could do that, too."

"Carolyn, look, I saw the word *professional* and I am not a professional, so maybe someday I can try, and since I don't have slides and no way do I have a booth slide because I don't have a booth and anyway the show is in a little over three weeks so there is no time to do all this. I also am working on the biggest order of my life and need at least a week to finish that. At this point I am already in way over my head."

"Gloria, let me just say this: as far as the Jurying process is concerned, don't worry about it. I am the Jury and since I saw your things already, consider yourself "Juried In" as of this moment. As for the booth slide, don't worry about it. My daughter Lara is going to have a booth there, too, and she needs to get one and is planning on renting. You can work it out together and rent *two* tents and be near each other. I know the Entry Fee is a little steep if you have never done this before, so how about this? I just made you an Honorary Member of the Columbia Art League, which lowers your fee instantaneously—congratulations and welcome! What do you say?"

"Gee, Carolyn, you don't have to do all of this for me. I don't know. I just can't see how to pull it off and do a good job."

"I really believe you can do it and you will have a wonderful set-up. You will meet people in your booth over the course of those two days, people who will change your life. Your business will never be the same after that because many doors will open for you that won't open if you don't put yourself out there. This is a great way for you to learn about Missouri and feel at home here. And there is one last thing: Gloria, I really *need your help*. Please do this show—for me. As an organizer it is my responsibility to have a diversified representation of the arts and I have way too many potters this year and need to balance it out. *Can you help me by doing this???*"

What can I say at that point, especially when someone is asking for help. That gets to me every time. This may have happened about five years ago, but it is as real and present as the biting cold wind and sunshine outside my door today. I paused. In my racing mind, I played her voice and words over and over again… "…meet many people… change your life… doors will open… feel at home… I believe you can do it… *I need your help…*" and then I heard myself say it out loud:

"Okay, Carolyn, I will do it—only because you asked. I will do the best I can even though I don't have a clue as to what it all means. You can count on me. Please send me the information again and I will be in touch with Lara about the tent…" "Great! I'll let Lara know and she can do some research and get back to you soon. Take care. Talk with you soon. Goodnight!" "Goodnight and thank you, Carolyn."

Thank you. *Thank you*? What did I just do? I must be nuts. I fell into a chair and must have looked totally dazed. My husband walked in, took one look at my open-mouthed face with the shaking head attached and asked what on earth happened to me. Saying it out loud to him was the beginning of three weeks that I will never forget.

I was a cardmaker—period. Having a tent full of cards would not do. So what should I do? I guess I could make "glorified cards" which in my mind meant making them a little bit bigger in order to fit into some kind of standard-sized frame, 5x7 or 8x10. The 5x7 seemed reasonable since it meant a relatively minor step up from my 4½ x 6¼-inch world but *8x10*? That was way out there. Huge. How on earth would I work with that much surface area? Only time would tell and desperation played its part as well.

Time to explore and figure all this out was not a luxury I could afford. Everything had to work quickly, especially my head and hands. I always liked those glass clip frames so I went to a couple of stores, jotted down the name of a couple of companies and called them to see their wholesale terms and figure out if I had enough time to get them in. MCS Industries gave me the best situation and I placed an order for 72 8x10 frames and 108 5x7's. They would eventually come in the extreme final moments, but they would come. In the meantime I set about creating what would go under the glass and out to the public.

The plan was to make 250 cards, 250 bookmarks and 180 framed pieces. For the first time, I ordered "big papers" and needed more than a 12-inch paper cutter. Since the 36-inch cutter that I would eventually get cost hundreds of dollars, I opted for a quilter's self-healing mat and rotary cutter for the show at hand. I cut and glued and stamped for hours and days on end. I was learning as I was doing and the doing was most important. The tent had to be filled and that meant not only with artwork but also with the displays that would somehow showcase everything. Gary and I worked non-stop designing and making everything from basically nothing. He has a fulltime day job remember. There was no money to buy already made fixtures, so everything had to be innovated, recycled and basically dreamed-up. From burlap on pegboard to converting some old tabletop videotape holder into a card rack by cutting up plexi-glass pieces, we went nuts trying to put it all together, knowing that we were not even going to be able to test out the hanging display system in the tent beforehand, since we would be renting the tent and not even see it before the show started on Saturday morning. Crazy stuff when you think about it.

I remember my hands hurting, tears rolling down my face and some words slipping through without my kids around as I had the hardest time getting the staple gun to work properly to secure the fabric to the boards. More staples didn't work than did. I sewed a booth sign one night into the middle of the night and dozed off at the sewing machine. And in the middle of it all, my sweet little son Brandon happened to come down with the worst case of chicken pox I had ever seen and he needed a lot of care. All I could imagine was that the baby would catch it, too, but that happened later. "When it rains, it pours." Right—I was getting drenched. Aren't art shows just so much fun?

It's an interesting thing when you push through and do something you say you are going to do—everything about you and inside of you comes into play and for Gary and I, this whole fiasco/escapade became a story to use many times over. There was very little sleep during those weeks, along the lines of cramming for exams that endlessly press upon you. Finally, it was Thursday, the day before set-up. The frames had come in just a couple of days before that, I was still producing "product" and needed to work on signs, pricing, and we hadn't even started to put anything in frames, when the daily newspaper arrived and I catatonically picked it up and plopped it on the table and myself at a chair. A minor distraction that I allowed myself that day—to sort of glance at the local news, since I was pretty much out of touch with reality.

I couldn't connect with anything; I was too tired and pre-occupied until I saw a beautiful full-page picture of a cathedral somewhere with a basilica-type vaulted ceiling. It was the cover of Scene magazine, the local "what's happening around town" section and I just sat there staring at the paper. The heading spoke about "Art in the Park" and the fact that this was a watercolor done by some world-class watercolorist, Paul Jackson, who would be showing at Art in the Park, come see his booth and read all about his fabulous work on page 6, blah-bidee-blah… I was stunned, put my head on the article and sobbed like a baby. I am going to have a booth at the same show as this "real artist"? This was beyond sad; this was pathetic. Forget it. I didn't want to be part of embarrassing myself this profoundly. I'm not going—no way am I going.

Gary came home from work very shortly thereafter to find me red-eyed, babbling about what a fool I was to have said "yes" when I had absolutely no idea what I was getting us into. He listened and then proceeded to be rational, which is always annoying at times like that, but the voice of reason tends to prevail, even when emotionally distraught reactionism makes a whole lot more sense to me in moments like those. Bottom line: we've come too far, worked too hard, and spent too much money to not at least try to recoup our costs. It had nothing to do with grandiose ideas like establishing myself as an artist locally or boosting my self-esteem since I had none to begin with by that point. For the next two days we slept less hours than you have fingers on one hand, and by Saturday morning we still did not have all the pictures in frames. This was way past down-to-the-wire. I was not ready but it was show time anyway. Ready or not…

We borrowed a second small car to make less than half-a-van and got to the show grounds in the early morning hours. Lara and Carolyn Birkes greeted us with big warm smiles and helped us set up the tent. I was overwhelmed, but what are you going to do? Do it. Gary had mentally devised an ingenious hanging system for the boards and set about implementing his concept. And then, of all things, it started to rain. Rain at an outdoor show. That hadn't occurred to me really: denial. The weather had been fabulous when I got outside to notice in the past few weeks. Our tent did not have sides and every single thing I had was made with paper. We had thrown into one of the cars these rolls of blue and green parachute material that my Mom had bought at a yard sale in Santa Fe for some unknown reason and these became the makeshift sides of the white canopy E-Z Up tent. God bless the inventor of duct tape. It was raining, we had sides up, product inside, and after a few hours of setting up, I looked out onto the grounds with my mind in a fog.

The plan was that Gary would continue to put frames together in one of the cramped little cars and I would be open for business. I panicked and didn't want to be alone, but there is that point when that is exactly what has to happen—it is you, your artwork, the booth, and the rest of the world that might drop in to have a look and might just as easily or even more easily—walk on by. So, I sat down for a minute in my director's chair, and watched the rain and a few people with umbrellas, real troupers, mulling around.

From my vantage point, this was a disaster. But an interesting thing happened. I started to hear laughter. I was sure that I was mistaken, but sure enough, someone was laughing and was loud about it. One vendor was yelling to another some funny story or other about another show they had been to together, and pretty soon there was this atmosphere of "what the hell—here we are—at least we are in this together so let's make the best of it" kind of spirit, and I found myself drawn in and comforted by the attitudes around me, breaking out of their confinement in 10x10 cells, with a sense of humor. At that moment I touched something about the Midwest, a certain pioneer grip on reality and felt at home amongst the settlers. I was moved way past exhaustion and discouragement. There was some kind of crazy art family camaraderie thing going on here, fellow travelers with a nomadic lifestyle based on some notion that art is a way-of-life and I wanted in, so I laughed, too. Once you start laughing, the world looks very different.

At that moment, something amazing happened. A woman closed her umbrella and came into my tent. I thought maybe she wanted a break from the rain, but she actually wanted to see what I had for sale—and *bought* something! I cannot express in words how much that meant to me. The rain began to let up and Gary dashed to the booth to deliver more frames and I could whisper to him that, "I sold something in the rain even!" At that moment, a pretty lady popped her head into the tent and the sun established its presence for the rest of the show, rain or no rain. "Hi Gloria! How's everything going?"

Carolyn has this way of caring that has a lightness as well as depth. She apologized for the rainy day as if she had something to do with it, but she was far beyond being worried about it. The clouds were lifting and moving and so was she, from tent to tent, helping in anyway, internally and externally. I grabbed her for a minute and told her I was happy to be there after all. I relayed my story of the tears at the kitchen table after reading the article about Paul Jackson a couple of days earlier, and as I was wrapping up that little tale of woe, she had the most curious smile. She was relieved and glad to hear that I did not regret doing the show, early as it was, and then proceeded to ask if I was aware of my next-door neighbor? No, I hadn't been outside my 10x10 world since early morning. "You are right next to Paul Jackson, how about that!" "*WHAT?* Are you kidding me? Why did you do that? He is the famous person here? I am brand new, whatever! I can't be right next to Paul Jackson!" "Gloria, this is a great situation for you. Look, everybody who comes to this show finds his booth. He will probably win Best of Show (which he did) and all these people will be around this area. They will buy Paul's prints, but frankly his originals are so expensive that people will be happy to see your prices as they spill over into your tent and you will do very well..." which I couldn't even fathom or put together in my head. Guess what—it happened. What also happened is that upon her leaving my booth, I decided to march right "next door" and meet this person who scared me with his excellence that contrasted so painfully with my insecurity.

My hand extended, I recognized Paul's wife Dina from the newspaper photos and connected with her kind hand. I blithered and blathered out the story of reading the article; being exhausted and tense did not help my composure, so these tears escaped and I felt like an emotional wreck of a fool. Dina's smile was a comfort as she pointed out the fact that Paul was coming up the path and I could meet him and get rid of all this fear nonsense. That happened in less than two seconds. Friendly, down-to-earth and welcoming to me as a newcomer, they both extended themselves and I have always been grateful for that experience at the beginning of my very first art show ever. At the end of the two days, Dina came to my tent and bought a bunch of cards. It was a great wrap-up and a quiet compliment that I deeply appreciated. Sometimes I wonder if people who are thoughtful realize just how much they affect and change the world?

Carolyn's predictions did come true. As for meeting people who would change my life, become lifelong friends, customers, mentors and a host of other valuable personal connections: that all happened. Dr. Betty Scott walked in with a petroglyph design on her t-shirt and said: "You did it." "Tell me. What did I do?" I asked this friendly stranger. "You brought the spirit of the Southwest here." And then later in the conversation: "You will be teaching classes at the University, by the way." ("Ha!") Other people introduced themselves, other names were mentioned to me and business cards piled up. When a small contingent of ladies excitedly cascaded into my booth, I wondered why they seemed so enthusiastic. Come to find out, they were members of the local stamp club, and felt so happy that "a stamper" actually made it into a "juried art show." My perceived victory was something we could all share and enjoy. I was invited and joined the club.

I ended up making $1200 for that first show, which is pretty darn good when your artwork is relatively inexpensive, and went on to line up shows for the rest of that summer and kept going for years. I did eventually get those professional slides made, bought my own tent and went through the normal submission process from that point on. After my initial charmed entry into a scary realm, the fear of procedures and terminology was gone. There have been outdoor, indoor, home and gallery shows. None, however prestigious or fruitful, financially speaking, will ever be more significant to me than the first. There were layers upon layers of obstacles to overcome and they were. It got easier over time, but never better.

Carolyn effectively twisted my reluctant arm, making sure that she kept her other arm around my shoulder at the same time. She is one of those rare people who have the ability to believe in others so deeply, completely and honestly, that the confidence they impart becomes your own. They have a gift of being generous with the credit and always make sure it goes to you. They put you in the game and applaud from the sidelines.

Was I ready for that first show? Absolutely not. Was I ready to have someone else believe in me enough to make me try? Apparently yes. That is the pure and simple beauty of a mentor—and friend. Carolyn and Lara became my friends. Carolyn and I were both born in 1954, and since she beat me into the world by two months, I got to see her as my "older sister," to my great benefit. She had a teenage daughter and also a very young son, the same age as my youngest. We met at art shows over the years and she would let me know about special ones that I entered with her advice behind me. As families, we also met with our children at the pool where the Birkes family had a membership and we had an open invitation to enjoy it with them. I am glad that we went.

Our paths crossed over the years and one thing was constant—wherever you found Carolyn, you saw her giving, helping and lifting others up. She would also physically help you carry anything, set up your tent with you if you needed an extra pair of hands and this was all done despite the very obvious fact that she had a spinal condition that was beyond a challenge—it would be debilitating to anyone else. I remember telling her to "sit down right here in my tent right now so that I can give you a little shoulder rub so that you can keep going with at least a little chance to get off your feet and rest…" She would laugh and sit for a few minutes until she figured that she must be needed somewhere and couldn't just be lounging about. I would let her go with a wince of pain in my heart for her as she stood up and went on her way.

When Lara and her Dad were preparing to go to Mt. McKinley and climb to the summit, I saw Carolyn's joy and worry all rolled up in this mother's loving heart. Vicariously this woman with a lifelong spinal condition was climbing mountains with her daughter as they built a business together and then as Lara was about to climb the highest peak in North America, so young and ambitious. Mother and daughter were in these endeavors together in heart.

Before the Holidays in 1998, I got a call from Carolyn asking me if I would like to do a small indoor show at the hospital where she was working in the gift shop. Long gone were the days of needing to have my arm twisted—I jumped at the chance to do something with her. The timing was a bit difficult to manage and the financial returns on such a small show were "if-ie" at best, but experience told me to just jump in there. I headed over to do the set-up during a lunch break from teaching workshops to Girl Scout leaders from around the state of Missouri: "Beginning Stamping." (Years later I found out that one of my "students" turned out to be artist Paul Jackson's mother; small world.) Racing around trying to set up in record time so that I would not be late for my classes, I noticed Carolyn who kindly came over with a hug and offer to help in any way she could. "Don't worry about me, Carolyn. I'm fine. Just make sure you give me a holler if you need anything lifted—do not do it alone, promise?" A laugh, a few words shared and we were both going about our business. Out of the corner of my eye, I caught sight of her dashing to grab a huge box from an elderly person, Carolyn obviously in pain, wincing as she managed to get it put down before I could get to her. At that point I stopped and watched her for a minute then gave a long distance yell to "cut it out!" She waved, smiled and walked in a way that I had never seen before. Her posture was very hunched over and it hurt to look at her. I wished I had healing hands that could go over to her and help her to just stand up. Instead, she vanished into her many tasks and I dashed out the door to teach, leaving behind a little note of thanks and best wishes for the show…

It turned out to be a dismal show, financially speaking—I made about $25 and Carolyn was embarrassed to tell me that on the phone. I laughed and said something to the effect that "believe me, every penny helps" and the main point of being there was simply to have the chance to be with her, so it was "a success" after all.

Not long afterwards, I received a message that Carolyn was on her church's prayer list because she was in St. Louis to have surgery on her back. I prayed, too, with hopeful words that she would be helped to gain the strength and relief that she so needed. I tried to reach her family by phone a couple of times, leaving messages if there was anything I could do, please…

Carolyn stayed on that prayer list and in the hospital and then I received another message—Carolyn Birkes had passed away due to complications. She had just turned 45. Her life on this earth was complete. It was so hard to accept that and to let her go…

She was, is, a person who couldn't physically climb to the summit of great mountains but who completely knew how to celebrate when others did. Carolyn did her best to help many people get to the starting point of their own mountains and was more than happy to be a guide to willing climbers. The stories in the paper, the eulogies given, the memories shared among friends, all are vibrant testimonies to a woman I will always respect and love. To know Carolyn even the little that I did, was to know that she would like to say, "Come on! Let's go! Take the challenges in front of you and meet them. Be aware of the challenges others are facing and be there for them." Her spirit of generosity and support will always inspire me and guide my way. Her life sparkles.

Whenever I face something completely new, I think of her. When things get scary, I picture her smile, say her name out loud and wonder why, all of a sudden, things are a lot less scary and a heck of a lot more clear.

During that phone conversation years ago, fateful and the touch of destiny that it was, I realized that a door was being opened for me, and whether I walked through it or not was my call completely. It would never be opened the same way by the same person or any other person, ever again. And this point became absolutely clear as time went on: No matter what kind of visionary person is believing in you beyond reason, it is only going to work if you let it touch your heart and cause you to at least hope that you can begin to believe in yourself that much at some point, too.

Life contains treasure-people and hopefully we won't miss them when they enter our lives, for however long, however briefly. Treasure them.

Part Two

processing

My grandmother had the color TV downstairs, so when "Walter Disney" presented *The Wonderful World of Color*, we abandoned the black-and-white set and raced down the stairs. In the intro song, I loved hearing how it "makes no difference who you are." Everyone has the right to "wish upon a star," and it seemed pretty definite that things would work out—the song clearly said "your dreams come true."

A wish is a fabulous place to start—substantiating the wispy thoughts takes *time*. Pinocchio had a lot of processing to do before he became that "real live boy." Dorothy had to brave some hair-raising adventures before the heel-clicking routine got her back home to Kansas. It took me quite a while to get here to you.

The process itself can be a source of crushing frustration or raised to the level of art. We make that call every single moment of every single day that we wake up and decide to work towards making our dreams come true. No kidding: it is work—the best kind.

> If people only knew how hard I work to gain my mastery,
> it wouldn't seem so wonderful at all.
> - *Michelangelo*
> (1475-1564)

(The Sistine Chapel took four years to complete, mostly on his back,
from 1508-1512.
Absolutely astonishing and worth it, wouldn't you agree?)

111

Balance

Having it, losing it, getting it back

Balance, the word itself, is derived from the Latin for "having two scale pans." That is a good visual. It stimulates a vast range of imagery that is dependant upon our point of view or mood in the moment. Grab a pen and start writing about "balance." See what happens. Free float some thoughts… What got put on the paper? What came to mind? Did you get physical with images of gymnastics, ballet, circus acrobats or the complex maneuvers of figure skating? Did your pen and thought move into more metaphysical realms and reflect on the Yin-Yang aspects of the Universe, within our own psyche or relationships between people? The balance of political and economic power in a changing world? I might contemplate the balance of nature and ecological principles one day, then balancing a checkbook the next day, and in general just trying to find a balance between home and business life that would allow me the time to do things at least half as well as I would like to in any given area. When we have balance in our lives, do we understand it enough to know how to keep it? When we lose it, do we have the tools to re-group and get it back? It is always a process, and we can get better at it the more we practice.

I was a waitress at a Friendly's Restaurant in Farmington, Connecticut, during one phase of my college experience. The breakfast shift gave me a paycheck at the end of the week and time to do school work and evening classes. My pressed gray uniform with the white ruffles, white shoes and little cap were not exactly my idea of style, but the work paid some bills and after twelve years of uniforms in Catholic schools, I could adapt. One morning, more people than usual poured into the restaurant and it became too busy to be enjoyable. Everyone was in some kind of major rush and it was prickly and tense. As a waitress, I was in the position to either help them along their way or be *in* the way as far as their time pressures were concerned, so I tried my best to move quickly and efficiently. Getting water glasses in place on the counter proved that I at least acknowledged their existence and a bit of the edge was taken off. With ice water in hand, they could chill out in one form or another. "I am very busy here, and I am doing the best I can." Drink.

Three glasses in each hand, I got those out and then reached for the seventh—then it happened. My hands were wet, the icy water glass was very slippery and it just slid through my fingers through the air to the hard ground below. The weirdest thing happened—time warped and slowed way down as if in a slooowww-motion movie sequence. Falling ever so slowly, suspended in time, hitting the floor at an angle, bouncing *up* off that hard floor, *up* to my open waiting hand, I then closed my hand around it as if it was the most natural thing in the world. Not a drop was spilled, no crashing to justify all the cringed faces around me, handing it to the bemused customer I then took a bow to the applause of everyone in my bay! *That* was balance. After my little moment of glory, it was back to work as usual. It turned out to be a more fun morning than it started out to be. Juggling is a talent I had and didn't know until that very moment.

Now *losing* your balance is a different story. There was a tennis tournament that I fought hard in and won. The victory was especially sweet because I played the finals against a girl who was a member of this unbeatable Dynasty. If you heard their family name mentioned in any division, you moaned. I won. A shocker and a victory for one of the City Parks and Recreation Dept. kids (me) over the private clubs/Copper Ledges Clay Courts crowd. I was walking tall, but forgot in my moment of pride that I was actually quite short for a tennis player. I had seen this running and jumping over the net routine on TV, the winner flying into the losing opponent's court, shaking hands and that cool way of walking off the court with a towel around your neck, strutting over for the trophy and photos. So I started to run, got to the net, jumped, caught my foot on the net, lost my balance and proceeded to crash on the other side, right at my defeated opponent's feet. She had the class, composure and kindness not to laugh and I was flaming red with embarrassment, pain and blood. My knees were scraped to shreds, quite a contrast to the lovely Fred Perry whites I was sporting.

The photographer from the local newspaper was on hand and graciously let that photo-op pass, positioned all of us behind the net so that my damaged, dripping knees would be concealed. My smile was bright even under the circumstances. In the final analysis, I was more victorious than embarrassed and probably more humbled than anything else; that little showing-off scene would never be repeated again. I definitely lost my balance there in more ways than one. Keeping my feet on the ground and big head in check were better choices from that point on.

During the course of the past eight years in business, there have been countless challenges to keep things in balance. Taking the time to write a book along with maintaining the very business I am writing about is a good example. I have to learn how to strike a balance of priorities, choices and trade-offs without losing sight of details and the big picture at the same time. Not easy, but necessary. Over-extending in any one direction causes you to lose something in the middle—to get off-balance.

There are definite advantages to having a home business. Among them are things like being able to walk my children to school everyday and pick them up at the end of their day. Holding hands and chatting or just quietly strolling with "peaceful feelings" happen to be some of my life's treasured experiences. I can volunteer at school, play the guitar for the kids, attend parties, go on field trips, be home for a little sick guy and generally be a free agent, my own boss. I might even take a friend out to lunch or meet a business contact for tea—rare, but possible. Yet along with that freedom comes a certain level of confusion and struggle. The studio is downstairs, not downtown. I cannot drive to the office and leave my house and all that needs to be done there and focus on work, and I cannot leave the office at the end of the day and close the door behind me and forget it until the next day. It is hard to walk past a huge pile of laundry and it is just as hard to know that there is a big art show coming up and feel I need to work very late or maybe all through the night, for many nights in a row. I have to do it. Home and Work—the great juggling act, the life-long balance beam that I teeter on and slip from at times.

I keep this little quote on a yellowed newspaper clipping on my refrigerator. It says: "The work will wait while you show the child the rainbow, but the rainbow won't wait while you do the work." Easier said than lived, but worth the effort because it is the truth. There are certain bottom lines that I have in place, a certain level of tidiness and civilization in my upstairs world, and then I can head to work. When I caught the water glass I was present—it was a "*be here now*" moment. The little event itself was non-consequential in the cosmic balance of the universe, but the imagery works in my head. I am striving for awareness and a presence of mind that facilitates making wiser decisions for the long run. I want to allow myself the everyday pure luxury of taking the time to appreciate the double rainbows that are constantly presenting themselves. Don't keep missing the moment—grab the refreshing glass out of the air and serve it with a smile.

Rhythms find a way of working themselves into our lives and they work if we learn how to make solid, logical plans with "flex" to them. When things are going along smoothly, I don't want to get smug, complacent and arrogant and start jumping over nets to congratulate myself. Been there and done that. I try to study my own rhythms and patterns in order to remember for the off-kilter, rough times. When we slip off the beam, how do we gracefully (if possible) get back on? If graceful doesn't work, just getting back on is good enough. What do we need? A shoulder to cry on for a little while, a helping hand with the kids or the business, a walk outside and away in order to come back fresh, friendly insight and reminders of what we already know but managed to forget? Whatever the course, whatever the vehicle we decide to take, commit to it 100%.

It's all just a matter of balance.

> Those who have one foot in the canoe and one foot in the boat
> are going to fall into the river.   - Native American Proverb (*Tuscarora*)

Printmaking 101
…and speaking of "balance," going back to school at 45

I cannot remember taking even one art class in high school. It was a new school at the time and I seem to remember seeing some semblance of an art room, but I blank out at that point. When I listen to my contemporaries chatting about getting blood all over their first linoleum cut blocks and doing pinch pots during the pottery semester, I simply can't relate. I did study a bit of weaving and watercolor and took only one class in stamping—a fun and sunny afternoon in Albuquerque learning "background techniques" at the very cool China Phoenix stamp store. I needed more. At the age of 45, I decided it was time to get back into a classroom and study *art* since I do have an art business.

This is a college town and there is a healthy openness to people in my position. For an extremely reasonable price, I was able to sign up for and audit Printmaking I, after a brief interview with the professor who had to give his approval. For some odd reason(s), I got all teary-eyed and nervous. It had something to do with feeling awkward and out-of-place, old and ignorant, and just a little bit petrified of making a fool out of myself. Fortunately for me, Professor Cameron had a box of Kleenex in his office, and despite my mini-breakdown, he kindly let me take the class anyway.

It was great and scary at the same time. I love being around college kids and there I was with my white hair and old-fashioned attitudes about professors—I couldn't call him by his first name which seemed so easy for everyone else to do—and they were less than half my age. I did it, but never got used to it.

As an "audit" I didn't have the pressure that comes with grades and all that, but I still had a few recurring nightmares during that semester of the days when math tests haunted me and I woke up in cold sweats. I learned a lot about printmaking and even more about myself. It was my decision to participate in the "finals" and I'm glad I did. We displayed our work from the semester and we critiqued each other. Professor ("Ben") Cameron had me briefly share about my art business as part of my presentation and had the students look at how I took care of my tools—there was "an art" to that. It is good to be a student —again and again. I gain skills and make new friends. The more new classes, the more experiences to layer and build upon, the better. It balances out the "business" part of life.

Creative or Confused?

A few years ago, I was attending the annual Best of Missouri Hands 3-day *Art Smart Weekend*. Learning a lot, making friends, networking and just plain enjoying being immersed in the art/craft scene in this state, I was definitely "into it." There was one jam session that I decided to participate in: "Problem-solving," or something like that. The idea was that everyone would put his or her problem on the table for public display and discussion. We would then share ideas and hopefully someone would say something useful and/or insightful. When it came to my turn to go public with my dilemma, I said: "My problem is that whenever I come up with a new product idea, it sells. Everything I make sells. And I have new ideas all the time, even when I sleep, but it is driving me crazy, because I am getting blown in all different directions. I don't know what to focus on and I don't know what to do anymore. I can't figure out if I am *creative* or *confused*?" A lady directly across from me looked me straight in the eye, slowly leaned forward and said: "I don't believe this. You must be kidding, right? Are you really and truly *serious*? Your *problem* is that everything you make sells. *That* is your *problem*? We should all have such problems." She gave me this "Oi-vay" kind of look and toss of her head. Either this lady was straight from New York or she watched enough TV to get that accent down, you know, a certain kind of "Brooklyn" cadence, tone and mannerism. Folks in the group laughed, but I *was* serious. Direction in my work was what I was fielding here. I didn't know what to do. I felt all mixed-up. Was there anyone who could please help me?

I make lots of different kinds of "things." Does my work have a "signature look"? Do I have distinguishable "bodies of work"? Double "no." I can't even remember all the categories of stuff I've created, and at times have admired something, forgetting that I am the one who actually made it. When my work was recently published in a magazine I got a lot of feedback, much of it from people I had never met before. The main point of the comments: "I cannot believe how many *different kinds of things* you had in that one submission—from rocks to boxes to cards to scrolls to a tiny tile to..." whatever. My designs and materials run the gamut from the Southwest to the Far East and anything that moves my heart in general. I wondered if that was a good sign or if it was a clear sign of indecisiveness—telling symptoms of the "jack of all trades, master of none" syndrome.

There are people who find their personal art niche early on and spend a lifetime refining techniques and defining themselves in a chosen field. It is a wonder to behold. Master craftsmanship is a way of life that I deeply admire. I, on the other hand, am a latecomer and late bloomer in the artist's way of life. I do not have a particular precious jewel that I have been polishing, facet after facet, for decades. I have more of a charm bracelet that I keep adding to: Okay, let's see, how about handmade cards, that's nice, and let's try stamping on anything at all and see what the heck happens, writing a book sounds fun—charm after charm jingling on my bracelet of "things I've created over the course of a lifetime." It adds up to more than sheer volume, yet my insecurities are showing, wouldn't you agree? I don't think that I am the only one with these concerns.

Let's retro back to the conference and the group's response—I recall that right after the laughter subsided, a suggestion came that caused me to reflect. "You seem to be very much of an idea person and your instincts have proven to be right on target as far as marketability is concerned. This may be a good time to consider thinking about yourself differently—more along the lines of a designer rather than as a producer all the time. Did you ever think of hiring people to do the simple tasks to free you up for the more artistic parts of your work? Design more, create less?" Good point. I did consider that, but have chosen not to hire anyone at this time—the ideas are saved for future reference for sure, though, especially the idea of moving in the direction of becoming a "product designer." From another person came another good point: "Did you ever consider that the very fact that you do have a wide range of interests, abilities and artwork—that in and of itself *is* your signature? Who said you have to narrow down? Is there some law that says you can only do one thing as an artist? You can experiment without being chaotic. Personally, I would find that very liberating..." This kind of input proved to be very helpful.

There is more of an internal comfort zone that has developed slowly over time, yet the issue does continue to re-enter my mind, carrying with it the challenge to examine my process and direction periodically. The topic comes up in conversations, too, and I find it fascinating to hear different people's take on it. I get to hear where I'm at when I jump in and engage in those conversations, and I find that laughter is usually a part of the whole experience. There are some pretty wild characters out there.

I had the opportunity to listen to someone else put her spin on the challenge of whether creativity or confusion rules any given day, and enjoyed the encounter. It was a different conference, different year, I was also in a different position—I was now the one who had become a *juried artisan* as my fancy name tag proclaimed, and I was sought out by an aspiring artist-in-process. This woman showed me her photo album overflowing with pictures, and the range of her work was wild—even to me! "Could I ask you a question, Mrs. Page?" "Call me Gloria. Sure—go for it." "I just don't know what to do because I love doing so many things, from Victorian crafts to abstract watercolors. When you look at my photo album, what do you think? Am I *creative* or just totally *confused*? People keep telling me that I have to make a decision and I just can't do it." "Well, Virginia, let me tell you a story..." We went back and forth with anecdotes for quite some time. I was blown away by her capacity to go on these art tangents—wow.

Pulling out my own photo album for her, we laughed, and I came to the conclusion that we were not crazy—I wanted to leave her with some kind of hope even if mine was a bit on the sparse side. "Virginia, we do focus on something—we focus on *exploration*. That is good. It is very good for you and me. It is who we are right now." We smiled at each other and closed our photo albums at that point. If Virginia or I ever do find that one single great passion, the "this is *it*-thing" and dive in head first, and create whatever *it* is, happily ever after, forever and ever—amen, I say. If we don't—halleluiah—who cares?

"Say it again, please," she said, "the part about 'focusing on exploration.' I want to write it down. I liked that idea. It helped. I really needed to hear that."

So did I.

> Creativity can be described as letting go of certainties.
>
> - *Gail Sheehy*
> (American writer)

PS—Of course if you want to become famous in some art arena and you want to market yourself big time, you will need to focus and decide who you are and what you do—until then, don't worry about it too much. Some of us just need more time to play, that's all.

"Necessity is the mother of invention."

Desperation has some pretty interesting children, too.

I was at an artist's reception for a fancy show once, and I overheard a snippet of a conversation that fascinated me. That cocktail party-type atmosphere is not my style at all, so I usually avoid it or skip through quickly if I must be there. In this particular case, there was something to learn. I wasn't exactly eavesdropping—it was more like everyone was on public display along with the artwork.

A woman artist was lamenting. She had *so* much time on her hands and for *some* strange reason she was not producing art—nothing worth mentioning, showing or selling, anyway. She didn't *need* to sell, "obviously," she said. Her husband's business, as we all knew, was extremely successful; she had no need to work. Her studio was all set up—and it sounded fabulous—truly the stuff of dreams. And there they sat—her blank canvases positioned in this fairy-tale sky-lit enclosed garden environment and she "just simply could not get inspired." Oh, poor thing.

All I could see were these swirling wine glasses in hands gesturing their concern. The conversation took sympathetic turns feeling her pain. I walked out the door of that room looking for something more real to connect with. A little chit here and chat there and I finally went for a slow walk downtown before going home. I went down to my cramped, dark, unfinished, highly productive basement "studio" to think.

My art business is a business as well as a creative outlet with all the romantic connotations swirling around that. I need to make money, not for playthings, but to supplement our family's income. It is not a game and I do not have the luxury of being "uninspired" for any great length of time. I cannot afford a therapist to help me get artistically un-blocked. A stack of unpaid bills on the kitchen table will help me to get extremely creative very quickly. I do not have the luxury of not needing to work.

We all react differently when "under pressure." Sometimes we may rise to the occasion and perform, at other times we may tend to buckle and panic in the moment, but I believe that through experience and perseverance we can learn to level it off. At that precise moment, desperation can become the mother of ingenuity.

A show is coming up soon and my customers come expecting new things every time. I'll do my best to surprise them. My mind is trained to seek the amazing in the more unusual and oftentimes mundane places in order to save a dollar here and a dime there. A business mindset with an art show date on the calendar and a slim checkbook to make it all happen—these things can sure help to keep that creative edge razor sharp.

Moral of this story: "The world of idle rich artists may not be where it's at, after all." There may not be many of them floating around, but enough to cause you to reflect on your own good fortune when you hear them complain. Hang up your sleek black evening dress, forget the make-up, get on the overalls and yank up the gungo-boots. Anyone up for an evening of "dumpster-diving"? Late into the night recently, I was working at a Kinko's copier; bless them for being open 24/7. Drowsy yet still attentive, I went to throw something into the trashcan and noticed, floating on the top of a mountain of papers, a tossed copy entitled: "Chapter II: Art—a yearning for the ideal…" pages 36-37. No book title, no place to reference one, but definitely worth reading, so I sat down at Kinko's in the middle of the night to read some "trash." You can get inspired anywhere.

Necessity is the mother of "taking chances."   - *Mark Twain*

Tools of the Trade

My Dad is a toolmaker by trade. It was fascinating for me to go to our basement and see his saw-dusted ShopSmith, tool bench, and all the gadgets and gizmos galore everywhere. I can remember discussions about how the tool room needed to be cleaned and organized, and once in a while that would actually happen, but somehow I didn't care —it was a wild world and I liked it that way. It always got messed up again anyway as far as I could tell. It was so different from the "Barbie-land" I shared with my cousins Muriel and Mickey. The workshop in the basement was rougher, with metal, wood, and sharp dangerous things all over the place. You were keenly aware of your fingers and toes and how nice it was to have them and keep them attached, so you had to be careful what you did down there in the dungeon. The best part was that you *created* things—down there. Not with Crayolas and glitter and beads—with *tools*. That drew me into this other world.

As kids, our interests naturally changed over the years. At one point, my brother David had this thing for "Knights in Shining Armor." (Davy Crockett shared a similar time frame, I believe.) He needed a shield. Cardboard would never do—we were into realism in costume design. In the basement workshop, my Dad made this shield out of wood, light maple-colored paneling, and stenciled a sky blue design on the face of it. This is digging way back into the Family Archives of the Mind, but I do seem to recall a fleur-de-lis image and diagonal strip of sky blue. A leather arm strap from an old belt and metal handle for gripping made for secure holding by a proud young Knight. If all the facts are not perfectly straight, one thing remains clear—it was one very cool shield. A handmade sword came with it. Now, I might have played the Princess of the Universe in front of my brothers, but a couple of times in secret I did get into Knight-mode and practiced with that shield. It *was* a great shield—I know it from personal experience. The best part of anything that is made by hand is the fact that someone took the time to make something special because they thought you were special. Tools were part of the story.

Tools. Tools of the trade. Tools for work and tools for fun stuff. You need them for repairs and in our family they were needed so that my Dad could make a living for us. I saw the creative side of them and wanted to know names and functions all the time. My brother and I got to go on an outing once to Pop's "shop": Arthur G. Russell, Co. It was noisy, busy, huge and definitely a *"DO NOT TOUCH ANYTHING YOU SEE!"* kind of place. We snaked our way to my Dad's personal bench. He was working on a project for Kodak at the time—a machine that fed those old Instamatic flashcubes onto conveyor belts. It all appeared so Space Age and High Tech. It was the 1960's, after all, Sputnik, space races and Star Trek. My eyes rested upon my Dad's personal toolbox: old, dark, warm wood with pool table green felt lining. Our photos were tucked into the edge of the lid: a miniature portrait gallery. The box had many little drawers that held special tools and the whole thing made sense. There was order and usefulness. Sweat and oil permeated the wood in the handles so that every piece had a silent story embedded deeply in the grain. My grandfather's tools are considered family heirlooms and rightly so.

Being the only girl in a family with four brothers at that time in human history could have spelled doomsday for me in the Tool Department of Life. But it wasn't because I was as welcomed to put my hands to the tools as my brothers were. Thanks a lot, Pop. There were times when I got to go with my father to the Bristol Hardware Store for an

118

outing to pick up something we needed around the house. I learned names and functions of all kinds of weird objects. It was a world that made sense to me. A lot of other things in life don't. I still go to hardware stores and wander around wondering what things do and pushing the envelope figuring out the "art side" of all this practical stuff. I never have been intimidated, never do battle with the sense that I need someone else to take care of the project that I want done. I may have to ask a lot of questions and I may have to ask the same one a number of times before I get it, but I will get it eventually, and I will get the project done. I appreciate the fact that the seeds for that attitude, confidence and enjoyment were planted early on in my childhood. (And I do ask for help when I need it and gratefully accept it.) When my husband and I do a project together, it is fun and satisfying. I enjoy being able to hold my own and contribute to the process. He does, too.

I learned how to paint rooms, fiddle with plumbing, love drilling and bought my own scroll saw and belt sander. The drill was a Christmas present on my personal wish list, and it ended up being a gift that my husband and I gave to each other. I like useful gifts, obviously. In my studio now, I have assembled four workbenches, drilled to install the power tools and screwed up a little because I should have installed the saw on the other side of the sander, but hey, it generally works out okay, and I will think it through better the next time. The fear of losing a finger or the tops of some looms like a shadow, since I've wrapped my cut finger back together before, so I'm careful. I banged a fingernail off once when I was a kid and now that nail has ridges. I think I was angry about something. Thought for the day: Better to be happy when you are working around power tools.

"Art" is the business and yet there are times when I have to hang out on the power tool side of life, cut up the wood to mount some stamps or create a display or two. Putting together art shows, I find myself having to be a bit careful in terms of time management because I can get carried away with the set-ups and run out of time for the "art." I can't tell you how many times people have asked the price of the displays or wanted to take the display itself, figuring that it was a part of the piece. Sorry. I need that for the next show.

Love those tools. Take care of them. They are an integral part of your creative life, an extension of your body. Your mind and your hands oftentimes need help making an idea come to life. Geppetto made Pinocchio—all hand tools.

I have romantic notions of the days of old when there were Master Craftsmen and Apprentices. That kind of bond between teacher and student was forged oftentimes from one generation to another, among neighbors and village folk having ancestors who lived similar lives, working with their hands for their livelihoods and inadvertently many times, the creation of entire civilizations. I believe that the essence and heart of that way of life is being revitalized in the Arts and Crafts Movements here and in different parts of the world where "traditional folk art" and the preservation of indigenous crafts is nurtured and respected. There is commercialism, true, but there is also a surge of purity in form and function that deserves support from the culture as a whole. As artists and craftsmen in our respective genres, we are part of this pulse that, I believe, is adding important dimensions to the quality of life in the twenty-first century. Technology has a place. Art has a place. How they blend and complement each other will take wisdom on our part. I know that we can and must do it. It is part of the legacy we will want to pass on.

A stamp, hammer, drill, brayer, brush, 1940 Underwood typewriter, paper cutter, glue machine, slab roller, whatever the tool, weld the stories with respect and gratitude. They are, after all, tools of your trade. Use them, take care of them and thank them.

My very own 1940 Underwood

There is this cool stamp from the old days, originally made by Carmen's Veranda—it is a large, black, reliable-looking, vintage typewriter—Underwood, probably 1940-ish. It was one of those "must have" stamps that I ordered un-mounted so that I could save money and afford to indulge in other must-haves. The idea was to create a card that would have words coming from a tiny paper that I could cleverly insert into the typewriter roller, probably one of the first times I ever wanted to create a card line using "words" in the design *anywhere* on the card. I had always been a diehard, dyed-in-the-wool, Blank-Card-kind-of-girl. But the time had come. My collection of quotations might find a home after all. It was time to use *words*.

The Underwood Typewriter stamp got ordered, came in and eventually got mounted. I then had to figure out how to "type" the words on the little paper—no computer and no typewriter at that time in my life. Since I have a stamping business, the solution becomes obvious so I start collecting alphabet stamp sets. The letters were teeny-tiny-types and it drove me crazy to stamp out text of any length, so my quotes and phrases were extremely short, e.g. "thank you." There is only so much patience in me when it comes to thinking of doing hundreds of cards with thousands of individual letters.

On the same day that I got frustrated with the time-factor involved, I also came up with a possible brilliant solution. What if I tried to *buy* a genuine old typewriter so that I could authenticate the whole concept? To type in all of my quotes, messages and fun word-imagery—it sounded like great fun to me. Well, let's check out the Yellow Pages. I couldn't believe it—manual typewriters still exist and the store was only a 5-minute drive from my house, so I was on the road. When I got to the store, a number of models were brought out but nothing "clicked" for me. It turned into one of those "thank you for your help; I'll think about it" kind of moments and I wandered out. Then lightning struck. Gloria, go directly to The Ice Chalet Antique Mall—Do Not Pass Go. Get there as in immediately. The timing was a bit tricky, but who am I to argue with lightning? When intuition speaks, usually I obey. I was in the car and on the road again.

I plowed into the Antique Mall with this I-am-on-a-mission look and stride. Heading straight down the first aisle I glanced on the floor to my right and squinted. Tucked in with totally unrelated thing-a-ma-bobbers was this massive, black, chrome-trimmed *Underwood* typewriter: my rubber stamp in three dimensions right before my eyes.

I tried to lift this thing. It was so heavy I couldn't imagine having to carry it to the car by myself and I am not wimpy when it comes to lifting. The price tag was hanging from the side and I didn't want to look at it. It probably is ridiculous, I figured. Antique, shiny, pricey—they usually go together. Turning the tag over I thought I saw $5.00. No way. It must be a mistake; a zero or two are missing. And if it *is* correct, then it doesn't work at all and so there is a wasted $5.00 that I don't want to throw away. I went and got a piece of paper to test it. Sure enough, it didn't work. Now what? Up and down the aisles I wander, wondering what I should do. There were no other typewriters around.

Eventually I left—without the Underwood. I just drove away.

When I got home, I couldn't believe that I had gotten that close. *That close*! What a cool story except that it had a lousy ending. All I had left was an image of this perfectly non-functioning typewriter-of-my-dreams sitting on the floor in another part of the city.

A lifetime of fantasies of being a famous author, writer-type, a Lois Lane right out of the 40's pounding away on keys that make noise as well as words—all dashed to the ground. It did not type. It did not work. This whole story was out the window—worthless.

Then lightning bolt #2 struck. Maybe, just maybe, it can be *repaired*. Duh, as my son would succinctly say. I immediately called the original office store back and sure enough they are one of exactly two places in the whole state of Missouri who do the repairs as well as carry the old-style ribbons, and they are less than 5 minutes from my house. This story was starting to turn around. The deal worked this way: I bring in the typewriter. They look it over and come up with an estimate if there is any hope at all. I could expect that it would fall in the $50-$100 range. I have the option at that point to give the go-ahead or not. It sounded great to me, so I got on the phone and caught someone at Ice Chalet, asking if they could please put the typewriter aside for me. (Good luck getting it to the counter.) I had 24-hours to pick it up. In considerably less time than that, it was sitting on my table, in a place where it wouldn't topple the heavy table over. It was mine. All mine. There is always something so wonderful about getting a new tool.

I spent a long time looking at it, cleaning and polishing, reflecting on what stories it held. Who had owned it? What was written on it? Where had it traveled before landing on the floor of a Missouri Antique Mall and now on my hard-rock maple kitchen table originally from Vermont via New York? And the big question: Would it ever type again?

The repairman gave me hope and called back in a week with the good news that it could be fixed! I gave the go-ahead and sweated it out a bit because money has usually been an issue. I was hoping it would be less rather than more. Then, out of the wonderful blue, my friend Pam called and said we simply had to meet. She came over to my house and gave me an envelope. Inside there was a check, something she had received and put aside a long time ago, totally forgetting about it until re-discovering it a few days earlier. When she found it, the first thing that popped into her head was "this was meant for Gloria" and so she wrote a check out to me in that amount. It was meant for "whatever" I wanted to use it for. It just was meant for me. Pam was worried that I would think this whole thing was nutty, but I was moved to tears. And I knew exactly where the money-gift was going. The cost of the typewriter, repairs, new ribbons and paper came to within pennies of her gift. Every time I use it, I say "thank you, Pam."

I have used that 1940 Underwood for so many projects and adventures in print. All of my variations of card inserts for different lines were typed on it. All of the brochures I made over the years as well as Art Show announcements, signage for my products on store shelves, mass mailings to my accounts, as well as the original idea of the greeting cards and stamp image were done plunking and hammering away on the genuine article. At one point, we finally bought a computer. It's wonderful. It opens up worlds of high-tech possibilities. Yet I will always keep my trusty old typewriter because it opens up worlds of old-fashioned memories. It has only one "font" that is funky, a bit smudgy when magnified, and quite artsy. In our software programs we have fonts that are like old typewriters. I will confess that I started using them because it is easier, but really there is no comparison to my trusty old Underwood—that look is *real* and no two letters are ever exactly the same ever. And if the computer ever gets a little weird or we have no power, I can still type away. It takes more patience and perseverance using an old machine, but it is worth the effort. I'm sure that we have many more stories to write together.

Trash? You call that *trash*?

Just this morning, crispy autumn that it is, I heard the trash truck one street over and glanced out the window to make sure that I had indeed put our black plastic bags out on the curb my all-too-sleepy night before. I did. Fine and dandy—let's have breakfast.

But I couldn't help myself with my next step. I know that my neighbor-across-the-street is moving and so the pile is formidable over there and I just had to sneak a peek. Anything worth grabbing before the trash collectors turn the corner to our street? I spy a little old child-size school desk. I try to convince myself that it is a piece of junk if it has been relegated to the heap, but I can't resist. Straight out the door, I march across the street, no pride whatsoever. "Bag Ladies Anonymous": I am the President.

The desktop itself is in bad shape, it is pretty dusty and spider webs rule, but it is solid, the metal legs are in good shape and I see potential. A pickup truck that combs the neighborhood on Friday mornings looking for worthy trash has passed this one by—I saw him earlier doing his drive-by. Maybe he was right and just maybe he missed out. I spin internally and figure that I can replace the top; I found the screws. Spray paint the legs, put art supply bins in the opening in front and there you have it—the perfect Art Desk for my youngest son. I can park it right next to my drafting table so that we can work on projects together in my studio, each on our own surface. I pick it up and carry it to my house just in time. The trash collectors saw this I'm sure; they had just turned the corner. Neighbors may have, too, but they are probably used to it by now. Several months ago from another heap at another house I pulled out an antique vanity table (that will become a lovely writing table someday) and a Chinese birdcage that I cleaned and use for displays at my shows. Fabulous hardwood poles that I salvaged from a discarded railing became my hangers for over-sized sheets of handmade paper. This has not reached the level of obsession quite yet, but it has reached the level of shame-free enjoyment. The sport of dumpster-diving is alive and well.

I am always in search of a "treasure in the rough." Whether it is my dining room table and chairs or the next great art supply disguised as "trash," I am hunting. And I have fellow hunters, which makes it even more fun. My mother and Dr. Betty Scott team up in New Mexico and when that happens, I never know what on that enchanted earth is going to be sent to me in a box. One time I received miniature ancient-looking dried up "trees" from Betty's land in Taos. Rusted barbed wire and assorted other rusted metals, bones, rocks, Rio Grande driftwood, cholla (cactus) branches, and other natural elements of unknown origins have made it to my door. From these "things," the challenge to create "art things" is presented. Rising to the occasion is great fun. I have made and sold many such re-arranged "art pieces" after their wondrous transformations.

My Mom and our mutual friend Portia add to the collection from another angle by sending fabrics, frames, pottery of all sizes, papers, ribbons, yarn, beads, knick-knacks and do-dads—endless varieties. Mom makes the rounds of major sales and has an incredible knack for finding just what I need to experiment with just as I am in the process of figuring out that I need it. Thrift stores, yard sales, cast-offs from friends, everything has possibilities in the creative eyes and hands of those of us who can't resist.

A number of years ago I received a card in the mail. It was a stamped card and I liked it a lot, but the thing that caught my attention was the envelope—it was made from a piece of wallpaper cut from a discarded/discontinued wallpaper sample book. I had to know how that came into being so I called the woman who made it. "Oh, I just call local interior-design/furniture/decorator shops and ask if they have sample books that have been discontinued. They generally toss them out, so I pick them up instead." Genius.

Immediately I got on the phone and called around my own town. Sure enough, there were several places that had literally tons of throwaways and so I made the rounds. Over time, I have amassed and redistributed hundreds of wallpaper sample books and hundreds of pounds of fabric and tile samples as well. My sons' school has been a recipient along with the Parks and Recreation Department, an art school, my Stamp Club, and art friends.

The benefits are obvious—I get silk and brocades from Europe, India, the Far East and U.S. to play with—for free. One line of my cards called Scroll/Tapestry Cards is the choice for the Renwick Shop of the Smithsonian. The cards are created using cut pieces of this fabulous fabric. If I didn't rescue those fabrics, the rice paper, grass-cloth, glass shelf, tassels, wallpaper sample books and who-knows-what-else from the back porch of this designer shop that I have come to greatly appreciate over time, then all of this "trash" would be relegated to the dumpster. Horrors! The owner of the shop told me how much she appreciates knowing about my recycling efforts. She is paying for all of those materials and it is costly. Yet once something is discontinued or a display dismantled, it serves no business purpose and is difficult to deal with because of the sheer volume. "Please come to my back porch any evening and take whatever you would like to have." Thank you so much. I do. (See that dumpster—see the legs sticking out—guess who.) One night I took out-of-town stampers to the porch in a clandestine rescue effort—wild!

I wanted the shop owner to see some of the things I make and also to thank her, so I made some Japanese Origami boxes (Masu boxes) for her as a gift. They were made out of her silk pieces and were appreciated. That was fun to do. The only problem is the fact that you simply can't drive across town every night spying around someone's porch. It is habit-forming. One time before a major art show, I wanted to make cards using Japanese grass-cloth and my supply was very low. My "intuition" told me to head to the porch so I did, very late one night. I parked my car so the headlights would help me out and sure enough—a massive book called: "The Grass-Cloth Resource Book" was tucked under a mountain of cast-offs. Eureka—goldmine. The next day I did a drive-by—the porch was totally cleared. After making hundreds of cards from that renewed source, I still have a lot left. It can be many months of checking and oftentimes I drive away empty-handed. But the odds are with me to score on a little something for someone I know, if not for my own business. I try not to dwell on wondering what I am missing by not going *right now*.

Recycling, restoring, re-creating is beneficial. On a business level, it saves me a lot of money, allowing me to charge less and sell more. On a creative level, I get to work with beautiful materials that I otherwise could not afford, and the sheer variety keeps designs fresh and original. On an environmental level: less in the landfill and more in Museum Gift Shops. On a personal level, I get to give my friends fun things to work with, see the creative results and feel part of it. School kids and wallpaper—fabulous.

Those who are collectors already know. From hardware stores to recycling centers, from printers' shops to paint and tile stores, the creative possibilities are endless. Collage artists are famous for not being able to throw anything away. I know the feeling. Trash? Bag ladies? Pack rats? Not in my vocabulary. I believe that we are quite fashionable and politically, environmentally and artistically correct. *Dumpster-divers* UNITE!

K.I.S.S.

Keep. It. Simple. Sweetie. (*Please*)

Evolution takes time. At times it felt as if my business was an experiment in how to "do it all backwards." I need a paper cutter not scissors—make do with the scissors. I need a computer not an ancient manual typewriter. I need a glue machine not a teensy brush with globby rubber cement warping my paper and destroying my brain cells. I need to learn *how to stamp* before I can sell any of this stuff. I need a scoring tool not this bone-thing that they used in the Middle Ages. I need help. I need brochures, a website, and a million other things. I need *money*. I need—I need—I *need*... to calm down and slow down. Over time, build up the tools, build the finances, build confidence, and build the business if that is where you are headed. Don't get discouraged before getting started.

Evolution takes time, and there is just no way around, over, under or through that. The word "evolve" comes from the Latin root *evolvere*: to unroll. It is far better to unroll than to unravel. It is far better to be actively engaged in a creative process rather than a self-destructive one. Please do *not* fall apart and unravel at the seams because you can't afford something in the moment that seems like an absolute necessity. Most things are not that urgent. Contrary to popular belief at this juncture in the cosmic time continuum, most things *can wait*. It may be hard to believe, but it's true. Since the onslaught of fast food and microwaves, instant and complete communication availability, the Internet, credit cards and all of the other speed demons in our consumer/high-tech "culture," we aren't so good at waiting for anything. The fidget/aggravation-factor in grocery lines has increased exponentially in recent years. I believe that we can re-think this one. We can also help each other out in the patience department. Progress and building anything at all takes time. I am a proponent of the more classical "Keep It Simple" and "Slow Down a Little Bit" Schools of Thought. I know there are all kinds of hype and many books and compelling ads and info-mercials about *instant success*. Let me be blunt—I don't buy it. It is not the kind of success I am looking for, anyway, even if I did become suddenly "rich." There is something about building everything by hand that is so appealing to me.

I was serious about my start-up costs. I was accurate in saying that "doing it backwards" has been more the rule than the exception. I am convinced that by building up supplies according to need and the ability to gradually invest, we can meet the demand for our product if we stay in control; *keep it simple*, save money and exercise patience.

(For anyone with vast amounts of disposable income, don't waste time by reading one more word here. Go on to the next topic. For the rest of us, stick tight.)

I hate using credit cards. I use them only when absolutely necessary. Whatever it is that I buy, I want to pay it for directly out of my *Impressions* business account so that I can have a handle on the big picture by keeping it simple and clear. At first I used scissors, then after a number of months, I invested in a 12-inch paper cutter. It cost about $30 and I have used it ever since. The 36-inch paper cutter came a few years after that. It cost about $400. Could I have used it earlier? Yes, but I made due with a quilt maker's rotary cutter on a self-healing mat because that is what I could afford at the time and my volume of large papers didn't necessitate the heavy-duty cutter until later.

It is hard for me to even remember using rubber cement for cards, but I did. The fumes got to me, the paper curled and then I learned about the Daige Rollataq hand-held adhesive "machine" and bought that. It cost approximately $25. Great buy. I discovered it the day I was at a crossroads, wanting to move on to the idea of making cards with this new Chinese paper I had just found in Albuquerque and not wanting to deal with toxic fumes to adhere it to my card stock. Voilà! In comes an issue of *Rubberstampmadness* magazine and a lucky flip to the right ad put me in touch with the idea and tool that I needed. A quick call to a Santa Fe art store and I was testing it and loving it within the hour. After a couple of years of saving money and increasing sales, for time-efficiency and for the sake of mental stability, I decided to invest in the plug-in Rollataq 12-inch machine and that $400 was my single best investment as far as major tools are concerned. I wish I had a dollar for every Rollataq I inspired other people to buy.

When you make a lot of cards and your paper company does not offer the service of scoring the cards as well as cutting them, it means you have to do it. For a long time I used a contraption that I devised by taping different t-squares and rulers together with electrical tape. Every time I needed to score a batch of cards I would re-configure this thing and tape it in place on the drafting table. With a $6 scoring bone it worked—I even took a picture of it one time to show my draftsman brother, Norm. When a company called Mostly Animals came out with The Scoreboard, I bought it sooner than immediately, conveniently at the wholesale price. It is a simple tool and worth every cent and beyond even if I had paid retail: highly recommended. If something new is out there, then compare. If they are all too pricey, get some plastic t-squares and figure it out. If your paper source charges a reasonable amount to score the cards for you—pay the money! They usually do it to perfection and it saves a step or two if you need to trim your own imperfect score. Just some things to consider—creativity in the face of necessity being one of them. (I like playing the inventor and magician—something from nothing.)

One of the most useful pieces of "equipment" I own could not be simpler or cheaper. I found this piece of junk pressed fiberboard in the garage. It was going on a trip to the trash when I paused and envisioned it getting a second life—I bought a $2 utility handle, screwed it on, and use it to press my cards after they have been glued. It is used every single day in card production. Invaluable tools do not need to be "expensive."

I had a website before I had a computer or knew how to turn one on. I had a 1940 Underwood typewriter for years and wouldn't ever part with it even though I have the computer now and know how to turn it on and use it all the time.

One rubber stamp became three, then ten, fifty, hundreds and now who knows how many since I add to the collection periodically, carve my own often and never keep count. I know there are people who catalog every single image and have devised systems that would boggle my mind. Since I don't have an exact count by any stretch of the imagination, I know that certain stampers would not include me in the fold of the true stampaholics. Oh, well, that's okay. I buy and carve the images I need and as always, build slowly over time. When you think like that, you don't get depressed as often.

A woman walked into my booth at a crafts show in Jefferson City, Mo. and asked me how many stamps I had. She got very squinty-eyed and shook her head when I told her I didn't have a clue, and she proceeded to tell me that she had just spent $500 on stamps the day before and that wasn't unusual. She made a point of telling me that she also had an exact total and precise cataloguing system for all of her images, which had long ago passed the three thousand mark. Her insurance agent prepared a separate insurance policy on her collection. That was new and interesting. There was a statement tucked into the conversation about her husband being annoyed by her "habit" and his suggestion that she find a way to make money to support her insatiable appetite for new and expensive art stamps, but she clearly wasn't interested. Instead, she focused on ways of hiding her purchases and kept a separate bank account that was under lock and key. I had never met anyone like this before. She ended up not buying anything from me and I wasn't at all surprised. I sensed her nose was a bit up in the air when she walked out whispering…

That woman, "Madame Technique," definitely thought my work was absolutely beginner-level based on all the techno-babble she was exchanging with her friend. I was confused but not overly impressed. As simple as my designs are, they are out there, my husband is impressed that I make money from what was once a hobby and I don't have to engage in clandestine activities to buy supplies. Are there tools and toys out there that I would love to learn about and have? More than I even know exists, I'm sure. If anyone wanted to give me a Christmas present that was sure to please, a gift certificate to an art supply or stamp store would do the trick. But I'm not putting everything on hold waiting for that to happen. I buy what I need, use it and enjoy the explorations.

The main point here is to keep the confidence level high and the discouragement factor as low as possible. Right now I am involved in doing work in clay, especially handmade tiles. I do not have a kiln and I cannot afford to buy one. Is that the end of the story? Of course not. I have found a wonderful opportunity available at the University Craft Studio where I can take a very reasonably priced class and have access to the kilns, firings and glazes at no extra charge during the whole semester. Twenty-five pounds of clay is cheap and goes a long way. A free locker is available. For a $15 fee I can have the same privileges if I'm not signed-up for a class. The teachers are wonderfully helpful and work in the studio full-time so I am learning every time I walk in the door to work. Would it be nice to have my own set-up at home? Yes, but there are things I would miss out on, too, mainly the camaraderie, mentoring and exchange of ideas. I just happen to love clay at this time, see a future in it and feel very fortunate to have such an opportunity available. It could have been easy to not even start or to give up for lack of funds. Sometimes we do hit walls but many times they are temporary or made of tissue paper. Keep trying and keep it simple, sweetheart. I tell myself that all the time. Listening and following through—tough sometimes—do make it work.

At the beginning of the beginning, I did not envision a huge enterprise and did not get steeped in all that it might entail—things like possibly needing to hire employees or setting up a complex accounting system, for example. That was just way too many steps ahead of reality and would have been too much to digest. Why bring it on yourself? As it turned out, I decided against hiring other people and my accounting practices are as basic as they can get. It would be good to advance in this area, and I do, slowly. I just refuse to go too far, too fast, simply because it seems like I should. We know when we can handle taking on more. Then that is a good time to refine and move forward. Expertise develops. I am not advocating "unprofessional." It has been my experience that when we demand of ourselves more than we are able to deliver too early, the risk of quitting rises sharply.

One step at a time, even a very small one, is more effective than jumping and leaping haphazardly, frantically trying to "do it all today, preferably yesterday." Taking a step backwards is not such a bad idea at times either, in order to get some non-pressured perspective—looking at where I am right now and planning where I want to go—at some point down the road. There is always room to grow once things are firmly planted.

"All I want is (some) room somewhere..."
The Studio of our dreams: "...wouldn't it be loverly?"

I usually don't ask for much. All I wanted was a little space, some room to set up my business, not a *whole* room. I didn't need a very big area to begin with—one corner of the kitchen table would work just fine. I got it and that's where it all started.

The size of our entire apartment in upstate New York could be compared to a Hobbit Cottage. I loved it, but as far as *room* was concerned, there wasn't much. You walked in the front door, opened your eyes, looked around, and from that vantage point you saw pretty much just about everything you were going to see. The kitchen table was the first thing you connected with visually. I can't help it; I always smile whenever I hear tales of "kitchen-table-businesses." I know what that is all about—completely.

Our first home business, started on that particular Vermont-made hard rock maple table (which, by the way, we purchased at a yard sale for $25, five chairs included), was a miniature grapevine wreath "production company" we called "Folklands." I worked at the kitchen table and there were challenges attached to that romantic notion. Supplies for this business were numerous and tiny—product was always in process and potentially all over the floor since my son was two at the time. Brandon's character was tailor-made for this kind of thing, however. He was blessed with a natural sense of curiosity but for some unknown reason *never* put things in his mouth and just liked looking at the things I was making. I kept all potentially dangerous little things way out of reach regardless of his impeccable track record, but the wreaths were right there—miraculously untouched. At meal times everything that looked like Christmas was pushed to make room for plates—afterwards, it was business as usual—all over the table.

After the run with wreaths, and after Christmas that year, I was making handstamped bookmarks from 11 p.m.–1 a.m. In the later morning the table was lined up with dried bookmarks. They were gathered together and breakfast was put on the table. That cycle went on for many months. All of my stamping supplies could fit easily into a single plastic sweater box tucked under the table—imagine *that*.

The next major "Studio" development came when my husband built a wooden shelf unit for me that fit on the corner of a desk we had in the living room. It seemed huge to me at the time. It was wonderfully made and I have used it for my "most used stamps" ever since. I recently found a picture of me sitting at that desk one week after my second son was born, stamping bookmarks, and only one small shelf had supplies stored in it. The other seven shelves were *empty*. That seems absurd to me now and I wouldn't have believed it except for the proof of a picture. I was up to one shelf and two desk drawers to house my entire business. That was 1994.

For almost a year following that one, we lived at my Mom's home in Santa Fe as I expanded my business. I went from my table to hers, and then we discovered my old college-days drafting table in the garage and I graduated from "kitchen table" to "drafting table" business. Bookmarks and cards were still dried overnight on the kitchen table, and we cleared it off in the morning for breakfast. Some habits are hard to let go of...

The drafting table got put in the back of a Ryder truck and made its way to Missouri and a new home in a very large, very empty basement. I now had *space*. Great feeling, lots of work lay ahead and I was definitely up for it.

127

I have this black-and-white postcard of the back of Georgia O'Keeffe. It is simply entitled "Georgia O'Keeffe, 1981." Photograph by Todd Webb. Dressed in black, presumably, she is touching a large round pottery vessel, the roof is pitched, skylights, triangles and circles, a few chairs, a view to blow your mind out of windows that make me wonder if in fact they are windows—are they her canvas? Pretty much the same either way. My notion is that this is her Studio. I could be way off, but I would love it to be hers and I would love it even more if it were mine. A wide-open space with natural light, a few solid chairs and a view to drink in of a red and gold desert that soaks into your soul. The photo is black-and-white but I know those hills…

I hold this fascination for other people's workspaces. I had to know where my Dad worked inside the factory on Center Street hill, just past the railroad tracks on the left. It wasn't enough to point to the outside of the Arthur G. Russell Company building and say "There." I had to go in and hear the noise, smell the machinery and touch his wonderful old toolbox lined with green felt. Then I could visualize where he sweats to pay our bills. To see another person's art studio is a very personal experience and I don't easily enter. Looking at pictures of Mary Engelbreit's wonderfully bright St. Louis studio, a converted Orthodox Church, is one thing. Going into someone's creative space is quite another. Whenever there are Studio Tours either here in Missouri or I hear about them happening in New Mexico, I am curious and halting at the same time. I never go. Is it too sacred and I don't want to gawk? It feels something like that. Fiber artist Rebecca Bluestone of Santa Fe has an ethereal-sounding studio visited by Robert Redford who commented on the "peacefulness" there. Nice story, different league.

All of my Art Critique Group friends have places to do their artwork. I visit gently. Janet's cottage peaked-roof, sun-lighted attic, Kate's bright desk/office/gallery, Susan's power-tooled workroom on the other side of hand-painted purple-y columns, Jo's cozy upstairs in her home and University art-classrooms, Lisa's home snuggled into the woods and my basement-in-process all serve us. If you were to ask any and all of us to describe our Fantasy/Dream Studio, there would be no lack of ideas. Mine would be a separate adobe-in-the-round structure, flooded with sun streaming in from a southwest angle. It would have Frank Lloyd Wright's western tones in the spirit of the architecture and internal décor. Check out R.C. Gorman's Studio in Taos—yummy.

This morning, anticipating that I would be writing this piece, I made myself go downstairs and sit for a while in my present "Studio" for a bit of a reality-check. I hesitate with the word "studio" and generally say: "where I work downstairs." It has become cramped for me and I have reached a certain level of frustration. When you rent, you are not in total control of what and when things change. You have to wait. We are anticipating a complete renovation. Patience and gratitude will eventually win out, but until this new-and-improved space is developed, I still have "my good old space." Many thousands of things have been created in this basement. Is it my "ideal studio"? No, it isn't. I stained the concrete to look as much like adobe as possible, but the place is definitely "a room without a view." Has it worked for the last 5 years? It certainly has. I started with an unfinished basement, stained all the concrete in the working area, bought yards and yards of burlap, created panels everywhere, bulletin boards, put up metal shelves with all kinds of storage and created specific "departments." There is the Stamp Department, Card Stock Department, Handmade Paper, Envelopes-and sleeves, Fabric,

128

Ornamentation, Glue Gun, Rollataq Machine and Shipping Supplies Departments. I created a separate Office Area (which has the plumbing basics for a bathroom someday), which I did paint, with resource materials of all kinds from stamp catalogs, art/design books to magazines that range from shipping supply companies to the fine arts. My telephone, desk and director's chair and business scroll/banner allowed me to feel like the CEO of *ImpressionsArt Designs*. Some pretty wonderful people and the businesses they represent have been on the other end of the line of that phone—many times.

My Mom helped me out by buying these four massive wood workbenches that come in kits at the local hardware store. It felt good to hammer and drill these things together. I outfitted one to be the power-tool bench and decorated the front with a stamped design, of course. Everything must be functional, everything in an order that makes sense to me, everything inexpensive and strong enough to take daily use—that is my signature style. I have enjoyed, and we have worked hard for, this evolution from one shelf and two desk drawers in upstate New York to where we are now. Evolution is an active word. I look forward to the next stage, hopefully sooner than later. When it does evolve, my work area will triple in size, and all I need to do is move to another part of the same basement. Sounds easy right now. In reality, I will be tearing everything apart before it goes back together. Whether you move 20 feet, 20, 200 or 2,000 miles, moving is moving. It's good work. You get on top of organizing because you have no choice. There will be light from the outside world (so there will be plants), a family room, a computer office and storage areas. I can't wait. But I will and it will be worth it. Humble still, it is the next stage.

"All I want is (some) room somewhere…" Really, it only takes a little space to begin. I hear people say "if only" I had a place to work, "if only" my husband would clean out the basement, "if only" we had one free bedroom, etc. etc. etc., "*then* I would be able to set up a studio." Of course, but guess what? It still can be done. My conceptual adobe-in-the-round is not under construction today, but it sufficiently exists in my heart and mind's eye. I have kept pictures of the different stages of my creative spaces over the years. From time-to-time I enjoy flipping through the album. Recently, after all these years, I finally had that original dining room table and chairs professionally refinished. There is a faint trace of my very first stamp, the heart-shaped wreath that Gary bought for me, embedded in the wood with green ink. It was an accident that never happened again. I appreciate the story that is literally ingrained in my smooth old table. When I run my hand over that faint green wreath image, which probably most people wouldn't even notice, I remember beginning at the very beginning. We've come a long way—and I know with a quiet kind of confidence, that we've only just begun.

Here's a good one for the unconventional studio artists among us:

Just for a moment, we must re-visit Georgia O'Keeffe, and this time we are going to check out her favorite "mobile studio." She wrote: "I had a Model A Ford. It was the easiest car I ever had to *work* in…" This story is so wonderful. She goes on to explain that it was the best car to set up as a painting studio because the windows were so high they could let in plenty of light. I love this: she took out the passenger seat, unbolted the driver's seat and turned it around so that she could face the back. The back seat area was big enough for her to lean a canvas across, one as large as 30 x 40 inches. Then it seems that it was a great arrangement until about 4 p.m. "…bees were going home and thought it a good place to settle." After closing all the windows, it got really hot inside…

The "Model A Art Studio"—leave it to Georgia O'Keeffe to come up with that one.

It's about time
Time issues

Space and time... You and I both know that there are times when it seems that there is absolutely *no* time in any given day to do anything other than survive. If I had time to breathe with consciousness attached to it, it would be a luxury. Perhaps that is what I should ask for today since it is my 46th birthday. "Hello, everybody, special request here. For my Birthday present this year I would like time to breathe and think about it at the same time. That's all. The rest of this house and all of the inherent responsibilities connected to it and to you are not going to exist for, hmmmm, 46 minutes. Catch you later after I catch my breath." quiet..."aaaaaahhhhhh"... I don't think so—no time.

How many times have I heard myself say that I need to sleep for *three days straight*, knowing that it makes me more tired to say it out loud and that it is a stupid statement anyway. And even if I could kick my scheduled-life in the teeth, I know darn well that I would be wracked with guilt and then bored stiff. Time: a treasure and a trap. One of life's "if only's"... *If only* I had the time to work on my ideas, I could develop a business, make cards, clean the house, read a book, get some exercise, get a life, get it together, *whatever. If only* I had a year off, I could write a book. Sounds good. When I am topped-off to the max and someone dares to add one more inanity endangering my sanity, I reply that "I will certainly be available in my spare time between 2:00 and 4:00 a.m." And I don't think they always get what I just said. Taking time to eat can be exasperating.

But you know what, folks, we'd better dispense with the baloney and get right down to the bottom line of bottom lines: kid thyself and myself no longer. If I want something badly enough, there is time. Always. We always have lists of things to do. The top three are A-B and C. You have to figure out what "A" is and do it. And then B and C; if D fits into the day, great. Everything else all the way to X-Y-Z will just have to wait. A, B and C will change positions, but we can't change our commitment to figuring out how to manage our time and give ourselves a break and a life simultaneously. Setting priorities within the framework of a personal comfort zone is an art.

The ways to make an efficient time-thing happen are among life's most creative adventures, but we are in the here and now—so there is hope. Let me put it in this light: If someone offered to pay for a weekend trip to Paris for me to dine, stroll, and relax, let me ask myself: would I possibly be able to juggle my schedule and find *the time*? Could you imagine hearing yourself say out loud, "Oh, no thank you, I'll have to pass. No Paris this weekend. Housework, schedules, you know..." Forget it! *I* would make it work. No excuses. Extreme Gratitude and Superb Efficiency: that's my name, and that's my game. The smell of fresh baguettes, warm lavender fields on the breeze of Monet-country air, now *that* is catching one's breath in style. I'll be on board—no problem.

Waiting around for the round-trip tickets to Paris is, however, a major waste of that precious time that we all seem to covet so dearly. Bringing a little imagination to something we want to do is not a waste of time, however. So, you have a full-time job but would like to test the waters of trying to develop an art business. Good. Scary. Exciting. Romantic. Impractical. I want it. I don't want it. I'll give it a try. I can't lose money, too risky, *no time*, forget it... This can go on for a very *long* time, from minutes to hours to years until the end of time. And to think that all that time thinking about how little time there is anyway, the main reasoning/excuse/lie to myself, I could have been doing even a little something, ever so quietly and slowly, but moving closer to a goal, a dream, a hope. Not all the way, mind you, but a little closer.

That might translate into, perhaps, the later hours of the day, making that "my art time." I was working full-time-plus when I started to make bookmarks back there in 1993. My bookmark-making schedule was relegated to the two hours between 11:00 p.m. and 1:00 a.m. That went on for many months, over a year actually. It worked because I made it work. I wanted it more than I wanted to hang out being wiped-out. There was energy in the process, no matter how late it was. Shedding the webs of procrastination and fear disguised as "no time" leaves me feeling free. I have room to be imaginative.

I read recently in *Somerset Studio* Magazine about a woman who loves doing her artwork in her little kitchen studio area in the earliest hours of the morning before commuting to work. She found her peaceful treasure-time. It was a creative solution to the "time thing." She likes her job and doesn't want to make her art her "paying job." This plan works for her. Reading that story gave me inspiration to think of the early part of the day as possible peaceful creative time—production/orders later in the day. We all have to find our way past complaining. My friend Janet says that when she listens to her own whining for too long, there comes a point when it is *enough*. Get on with it, whatever *it* may be. If a kid is whining at the Mall, we make tracks. If I find myself doing the same thing, I'd best make the right kind of tracks, and the sooner the better.

As far as juggling time in this business over the years, I can say that it has never been smooth sailing for overly extended periods of time. As things are constantly growing and developing, the complexity factor accelerates. But all this comes with the territory called success and the challenge to go to new and more satisfying levels. Did I have time to write this chapter about "Time" on my Birthday with my two kids and their friend being "busy" around the house, a tablecloth with spilled milk needing immediate attention, Spring "Break" threatening to break me, ironing the tablecloth and all the curtains I decided to throw in just because the dust was changing the fabric colors, lunches, snacks, trip to the Mall, the bank, mailed a rush order to the Smithsonian, it is only 3:00 p.m. and I have a card order to set up before we go out to dinner and the evening seems really far away. Sure I had time to write this! Because I just read Julia Cameron carry on in her book *The Right to Write* about this very thing. I was doing that reading while I was eating something that was so non-descript I couldn't even remember what it was, five minutes after finishing. I was eating the book more than anything else.

I have time to write this now because I want to write it. Logically, it doesn't make sense; there is a resistance-factor to contend with, but hey, the topic of TIME was on my list of things-to-write-about. I laughed out loud while I was eating and reading and there was an exercise at the end of the chapter so I chose to write—to *do* my exercise. Julia Cameron said to do it—*now*. I won't argue. Just let me grab my pen. In the hierarchy of priorities I decided to put this on top—the "A" list. It has taken me a long time to get to this kind of mindset and I wonder how long I can maintain it. As I am trying not to waste time by simply eating, there is a chance to read, by gosh, and I find the joy of kindred spirits in the written word and just go with it. *Do* what I just read about instead of adding that to my list of things to be overwhelmed and befuddled by. Grab a minute. Grab the pen and paper—it's within reach. Grab a sense of accomplishment.

Inevitably in the intense conversations swirling around about the advantages and disadvantages of working at home, "time-and-task-juggling" always makes the list of issues. I have some pretty basic guidelines that I've developed that work for me. I live the "Upstairs/Downstairs" life, which translates into "the work I do for my family directly" and "the work I do for my business." I have a light mint green apron that I wear upstairs, a dark navy denim one for downstairs. Doing my best not to confuse my lives as they are lived in the same dwelling is a challenge that is worth taking on. Otherwise, I am scrambling all day never quite getting anything of substance completed for the upstairs or downstairs life. Does laundry ever stop piling up? No, but I can stop doing it during "business hours." I look down at the color of my apron and re-focus. Do orders stop coming? No, but I can close the basement door and spend the evening with my kids.

Sounds easy enough, but like everything else we want to do well, it takes practice, *time* and a certain kind of self-forgiveness that everything can't be perfect. I know myself well enough to know that all the beds have to be made in the morning, the table and counters have to be wiped down, and the living room free of toys for me to be able to go from the green apron to the blue. The dust is still there—later, another time. When 3:30 p.m. rolls around, it is time to put the inks away, wash my hands and pick up my kids. Sure the lines get fuzzy, especially during rush times for the business and I need to work at night. Or when the kids are home from school on vacation or sick. Or the house is oppressing me with its screaming to be cleaned especially when tidy visitors are coming. Time-management ideally is both solid and clear as well as flexible and forgiving. At the end of the day, it is probably a better idea to look at the list of all the things you were able to accomplish rather than that other boogey-man list of all the things that still need to be done. Go to sleep and rest. We can make a new start again in the morning.

Some of the most precious gifts in life are in very tiny boxes. Open one up: you may find… time. It is invisible and can be exceedingly elusive, but we do have it. Sometimes it is given to us and other times we need to give it to ourselves.

And before the clock strikes midnight tonight, I will find time to breathe. I promise. After letting this topic rest for a bit, I found myself re-reading, and just had to add: there are people who know how to make a spiritual experience out of daily life activities. I see these fabulously-titled New Age, Zen-style, the Organized/Meaning-filled Lifestyle books from my One Spirit Book Club, wanting me to believe that it is possible for the simplest of tasks to take on the import of ritual and the sacred. The authors would be appalled that I did not remember what I ate for lunch today, because the art of cooking a bowl of rice and eating it in the Presence of Life itself is meant to be a pure and complete act and work of art. Yes. I believe that sweeping my messy floor can be *enlightenment itself* with the right mind attached. It sounds like a lovely place and I want to go there…(someday when I have the *time*.)

Mark Twain said: "The secret to success is to make your vocation your vacation." You have a wonderful vacation, a good experience, a happy day and what comes to mind and mouth? Perhaps something like: "I had the *time* of my life!" I want to feel that way about my work, which means much more to me than a job or a way of making money. I want to embrace time, cherish it, enjoy and treasure it, not be shackled by it. I want that positive feeling and powerful energy *not* twenty years from now, looking back, not when it is too late, but right now. So here goes: "Do you know what? I love what I am doing. I really am having the time of my life." It's about time, wouldn't you say?

The whole "Rep" thing

To have or not to have, *that* is one of the questions.

A "Rep" is a person who represents a company to other businesses for the purpose of writing up orders: a representative—a middle person. I have heard many things about reps, and have participated in some interesting discussions about "the whole rep thing." I'd like to share from several different angles, mostly from my own experience. It is an important point of consideration for any business, especially in my case where *the business* means "one person." Having just one rep automatically doubles your workforce. The value of that is considerable. There is a significant time factor put into play here, definitely. If someone else is focusing on the marketing aspect, then I can focus on design and production. The business has the potential of going to a new level.

Back in *ImpressionsArt*'s prehistoric times, when bookmarks were the one and only product in approximately three shops in Santa Fe, the idea of having a rep was introduced to my Mom, who was, in actuality, my very first rep herself. We didn't think of it that way, but that's what was going on. She set up my first accounts by walking into shops with a paper bag tucked under her arm, striking up conversations with employees, managers or owners, asking them if they "would like to see what my daughter makes," these hand-stamped bookmarks that "you might be interested in carrying…" It certainly was casual and it certainly was effective. She was never turned down and hope is a nice thing that she passed on to me as orders came slowly and surely. But there were limits to this approach, and since my Mom worked in a very popular book and gift shop, she saw first-hand the procession of reps that had appointments with the owners, walking away with large orders after the meetings. A name of a rep surfaced, a man who was carrying among other things, a line of rubber stamps, images from the Maxwell Museum in Albuquerque. I was given his address and contact information. This was long before the Computer Age had entered my realm of consciousness. I did not know what e-mail was and so I wrote him a note and prepared a portfolio-of-sorts of some bookmark ideas and mailed it to him. Silence. For months. It was really starting to get to me.

This was not my idea of a booming business relationship. It was a bomb. It caused me to feel insecure and definitely silly and unprofessional at the least. After several more months, my mother decided to contact him and find out what was going on, and more specifically, why nothing was going on. His insightful answer: "Oh, yes, the bookmarks. No fish biting yet…" I was not impressed and I wasn't encouraged either. I wanted my portfolio back and so I eventually did get it. That took a long time, for some unknown reason. This guy never did get any orders for me, and come to think of it, we never talked personally—in other words, there was no connection. It just didn't work.

Fortunately for me, my mother had continued acting as my personal rep and orders kept coming from very nice places, so I kept going. Doubly fortunate for me, one day at the La Fonda Newsstand, a rep had an appointment and on her way in, happened to notice my bookmarks in the book section, asking: "Who makes these? I've never seen them before? Who is repping the line? I *love* these!" The italicized word in the previous sentence was the key point—Gini Inman, a wonderful person and my first "pro" rep, liked my product and wanted it. It turned out to be one of those proverbial "lucky days."

It just so happened that the owner of the store, Jo, was able to point to my Mom in answer to Gini's question: "There is the mother of the person who makes the bookmarks. That's how you can make the connection." Soon after that, Gini and I spoke on the phone at length—it was energizing, enlightening, and timely. Her enthusiasm for my one little product was very uplifting. We made a business connection and a personal connection. We talked money arrangements, design ideas, and all throughout the course of working together for years, I always appreciated learning from Gini, who was more than willing to teach me "the ropes." By working with her, my business expanded way beyond those initial first steps. There is nothing like having a professional *and* nice person on board.

Reps receive a commission, a percentage of the orders that they write for you. In my case, we had an arrangement that I would pay 15% of the wholesale of each order. Most reps will charge 20%, sometimes even more if it is a huge outfit that takes your product to National Level Trade Shows, but Gini said she felt comfortable with 15% because she respected the fact that all of my work was done by hand. She treated me like an Artist, long before that was a comfortable word for me to wear.

At that time, my designs were exclusively Southwest and I was living in New York, very close to one of those "George Washington Slept Here and Rode His Horse There" kinds of antiquey-towns where Southwest was not quite it. Gini lived in New Mexico and her business stomping grounds included the towns of Northern New Mexico, which was ideal for me. She had her hand on the pulse of marketing, design and color trends in the area as well as for individual shops, and carried a large line of Southwest gift items that gave her access to a wide range of shops. I needed her vantage point and expertise. She was not exclusively a "Card Rep," which none-the-less worked for me. Since she did have other card lines, there were accounts that she developed solely for cards, but I was able to get into shops riding on the tails of her wind-chime/pottery/etc. gift accounts. It made for a good mix and product exposure that proved to be successful.

Almost immediately after our initial conversation, orders started coming in the mail. First, one order, and then an envelope with several orders. The stream was continuous. A rudimentary system of numbering was devised so that we could communicate effectively in a few words on the Purchase Order forms. Over time, it was a matter of refining our system and it worked very well. We each had a master set of cards, all exactly the same, all numbered by logical codes. The biggest step that we took was going from bookmarks to cards and I detailed that at length in another story, but for here and now I will say that it created the shift that marked the biggest change in my business. That happened early on. For the past 5+ years, the ripple effect of that new direction affects and will continue to affect the thrust of my whole business. My rep said that I needed to consider *cards* rather than stay with bookmarks. It was obvious, perhaps, but not to me at that time. Gini and Kittie, the owner of Marcy Street Card Shop, guided me through that transition. The first efforts were "interesting." Having a long way to go means there is a "starting point." Getting started with support behind you helps tremendously.

Gini and I worked together for years. She was the person who wrote up my single biggest order ever: $1,660 to the Indian Pueblo Cultural Center in Albuquerque. I flipped when I saw it, and she helped me pace my thinking so that I could get it done. Over the years we met personally several times when I went to Santa Fe on business trips and that was fun as well as productive. She had a respectful way of expanding my thinking as well as my horizons. I can't imagine my business without her. I struggled a lot internally when she told me her news that she had decided to retire from her repping business in order to focus on other interests. I had floated around with other reps in other parts of the country, but nothing worked like it did with Gini.

I let three other reps "go." Part of it was "my fault" since the design-work really needed to more regionally-oriented than I was willing to invest time and money into, and mostly the reps and I just didn't "click." That certainly sounds vague and ethereal, but it is the best I can do to describe what didn't happen. And one rep ticked me off because he called me up to say that he would be coming through Columbia and wanted me to know so that I could take him out to lunch, because I "should take good care of my reps." That didn't sit so well with me. Maybe he was only kidding, but since I was not able to spend any money for anything extra, that comment and the fact that I had received so few orders from him anyway, meant that eventually I asked for my cards back from him, too.

I never signed contracts with any rep, and maybe that is bad business on my part. We had verbal-agreements and that seemed to work, but with larger agencies, I'm sure it must be more formal. I chose not to go to that level. I did not want to over-stretch my production capabilities. Two hands can do only so much. Between my Mom's accounts, one pro/effective rep and getting my own house accounts, I was always busy enough to have many late nights of work if I wanted it. It was a good experience balancing this act because I knew that my rep had a solid handle on how many orders she could write for me that I could produce in a 2-4 week time frame. I was never over-run with orders. If it did take a bit longer to get them out, either Gini or I would contact the accounts to make sure a short extension would be acceptable to them. It always worked out fine.

The question has to come up: is having a rep worth the money paid out? Wholesale is already putting you in a position where you are making only 50% of the retail value of your product. Paying out 15% more, added on top of production costs—is it worth it? My answer is that, when you have a rep like Gini or Linda Kissko, who was trained by Gini to take over her business: then yes, very definitely. My husband always said: " 85% of something is better than 100% of nothing." Retired business people in town here told me stories of how they gladly paid their good reps a lot of money, because without them—no business. If my rep writes a $200 order for me in a place that I couldn't otherwise get into, I pay her $30 and make $170. The big Cultural Center order would never had happened if she had not been there in person. That kind of order cannot be made over the phone. It was the type of order that was very hands-on with the cards and all of the visual organizing that needed to take place. The rep commission on that order was about $250 for Gini. I made a little over $1,400. It was mutually beneficial.

My best reps (including my mother) truly represented *me*. They loved what I was making and their enthusiasm mattered and made an impact. They represented me in some places better than I could myself. Because they had solid relationships with business people, I could ride in on that. Some places are not interested in meeting with the "artist." They *only* want reps—it is a more efficient use of their time. Other places want the option of meeting with the artist/manufacturer because they want the freedom to discuss new possibilities directly and want a personal and direct connection. A balance between the two approaches worked well in my business.

I learned a lot during my 1+ years of working with Linda. She inherited from Gini and added her own vision and flavor and that was to my benefit. We were moving into new territory together, and then she decided to "retire" and follow-up on a good opportunity, which ultimately was good for both of us. I wanted to write this book, and if I was overwhelmed by constant orders, I couldn't pursue this dream. It all worked out. My Mom has offered to get back in the "rep's seat" and here we are, coming full circle. There are the accounts that I personally have and all of the ones that I want to keep from my Gini/Linda years. At this time I have no plans to get any more reps lined up, although I have heard that there are reps in California interested in my work. For now, that is on hold. It is an interesting idea and I will keep it in mind.

A suggestion: pay your reps in some organized fashion. My paperwork was very organized, and my idea was to pay my reps at the beginning of every month, but sometimes I would get behind. Accounts would be late paying me, bills due, blah blah blah, but I should have been stricter with myself. I had kind and understanding reps, but I should have done a better job. I enjoyed giving them Christmas gifts such as their choice of Christmas cards that I would make for them, several dozen at least, and I did take them out when I went to Santa Fe, or had meals for them at my Mom's house. I will miss those times now that they have moved on to other things. I hope we will still stay in touch.

Stories I hear about reps are mixed. Most of the people I know who have tried working it out, have given up for one reason or another. As soon as I say that, I know I will hear another good story to counter-balance that. Recently I did hear a good story from my friend Kay about California reps and it sounds like it's working great for her. This really is a case-by-case adventure.

Since my way of "discovering" Gini was a little on the unusual side, I asked her how someone should go about trying to get a rep if they wanted one? They are not listed in the Yellow Pages as far as I can tell. Her suggestion: Go to gift shops/stores that you like a lot and feel comfortable in. Pick places where you think your product might fit in well. Ask to talk to the buyer, owner, manager—start somewhere. Explain that you have such-and-such product and you were hoping to present your product to a rep that might be interested. Would they have any recommendations based on their own experiences dealing with reps? Who knows? They might have some good suggestions and they also might want to see what you have to offer directly. You could still get rep information and possibly a house account at the same time. Ask around, look around and meet with any potential rep personally, if at all possible.

This is important to remember—reps are working for you, not the other way around. You call the shots on most levels. If the commission rate is too high, forget it. Be aware that you do need to communicate what you are able to produce and that you are not interested in being avalanched with orders beyond your ability to deliver in a reasonable time. Clarity is imperative. And let me tell you, I really think you have to "hit it off" to some extent, because this person is going to be the "face" of your business, and you need to feel confident and comfortable. Trust and mutual respect go a long way. Enthusiasm about your product is an absolute must.

As far as this whole "rep thing" is concerned, it is a very important possibility to consider. I am so grateful to two people who started out as "reps," were very good ones, and then became much more—they became friends. I have been very fortunate. Thank you, Gini and Linda. And special thanks to my Mom for getting the whole thing rolling, for being willing to jump in there first, and always once again.

Pricing
The great balancing act

Pricing products or services, whatever they might be, is a very important aspect of doing business. The word "business" itself comes from a Middle English word meaning "busy." I have been very busy during the last many years making and selling cards. I make and sell other things, too, but cards are the base of my business so far. Making money from a business, not just keeping busy and killing time is a good idea. I didn't decide to do a home business for the sheer pleasure of it or because I was bored. I decided to replace one job with another. This was a process and was done in increments over time, carefully. This is the way I work best. It is a slow-but-sure method and I am comfortable with that style. Am I rich? Not yet. There is increasingly more and more potential to increase my base looking from my present vantage point, but once again, I am taking steps with consideration. I do not have "play money." My husband and I both need to work to make ends get closer together, for necessities not for luxuries. Knowing that success is measured with many different yardsticks, I feel comfortable saying that my business at this time is a successful supplemental income.

The whole question of Money and Pricing, the decision to put a dollar amount on anything that I made, was a huge step for me. I've made "things" my whole life, but everything was in the gift-category—I gave everything away. With a business, I had to learn how to price, and with each new product and each new line I needed to re-think, get advice from artist friends, reps, and just plain test the market. For every step along the way the question has always been the same: How much is any one-thing worth? In the past, my arts-and-crafts gifts were things that I made with my hands, given from my heart and that was it. What is the monetary value? My friends and relatives placed great emotional/sentimental value on whatever I gave them. Business is different. This isn't so personal anymore. We are talking about marketing, we are dealing with outlay, overhead expenses, and we are facing competition. I had always just wanted to make people happy, not make money. With the beginning of a business at hand and with a physical handmade bookmark in my hand, I looked at it and wondered. How much should I charge for this? How much would people be willing to pay? Will they pay more in Santa Fe than in New York, Missouri, or Timbuktu? How will I know that? Do people even like and want what I make in the first place? It's one thing to have your own mother oogle and google over your efforts and quite another thing to have a card buyer from a Fine Arts Museum Shop evaluate your line. What is best: retail or wholesale? When I figure in all of the expenses, am I making enough money to make the time worth it? Should I just forget the whole thing and get a job as a waitress since I've always been good at that and the tips can be great? Money. How does it play out in this whole creative arts venture?

The first time in my stamping business when the big "How Much $?" question was popped, I wasn't there to deal with it—lucky for me, a challenge for my Mom. I had sent her 18 bookmarks made of a single piece of cardstock, 3 images stamped in a row. The size: 2¼ x 7½-inches. A hole was punched and a ribbon attached at the top, covered with a hand-cut piece of plastic. Pretty basic. When my Mom showed her boss Jo, the owner of the La Fonda Newsstand, Jo asked the big question: "How much?" My mother and I hadn't discussed it, so she didn't know and I really didn't have a clue. So, Jo stepped in and helped us out. She suggested $1.00 each wholesale and then she would charge $1.95 retail. I thought that was just great. We went with that pricing for years. The quality of the bookmarks went up, but I kept the price, especially for Jo, the same for a long time. Eventually I went up to $1.25ws/2.50 retail. And eventually after that, I let bookmarks go altogether. After taking a break from the old style, and after coming up with a new bookmark design in the middle of the night last year, I am now making them in limited quantities for $1.75ws/3.50 retail. I learned the market on these and it works really well.

"Keystoning" is the term that refers to the retail pricing of an item, which basically is doubling the wholesale cost. It works well for many products and is the most frequently used pricing system. I like balancing wholesale, retail, consignment and gallery sales. Private commissions are nice, too. Pricing is a point of discussion in each arena.

After I had been in the Bookmark/Card business for a few years, I had settled upon basic prices, changing them slightly over the years to cover my expanding expenses. After 8 years, my range is from $1.50-2.50 each or $18.00-30.00 per dozen wholesale, which translates into cards that retail for $3.00-5.00 each. I do well in that range. In time I would like to go higher-end with all my own handmade paper and push to the sky in terms of getting into Exclusive-to-the-Max Shops. Not yet. Later. But the time will come because there is also a limit as to what I can produce with two hands, and $18.00/doz. isn't always satisfying. Yet my solid base was created by not going too high too soon.

A few years ago, I attended a conference for artists and craftspeople who wanted to either start or expand their businesses. There were different topics and I attended a session addressing the issue of "Pricing Your Artwork 101," or something along those lines. A volunteer was needed to go up on stage, show artwork, and allow a discussion by the professionals and audience to center around pricing the piece. That was definitely not for me. I slumped way, way down in my seat and watched as a sweet lady volunteered. I applauded her in a relieved sort of way.

The artist sat down next to her painting. It was nice. She was new at this. When the seminar leader asked her *how much* she planned to charge for her painting, she was clearly uncomfortable, and quietly said "somewhere around $180, I don't think I could get $200." I didn't know her medium and, at the time, I didn't know art shows or the market, so that sounded okay to me. Then the avalanche of questions started: Are you sure that that is enough? Are you taking into consideration your time, material costs, electrical bills for the lights in your work area, gasoline used for getting the supplies, insurance, phone bills, and on and on ad infinitum to the point that the poor woman was told that if she wanted to make any money at all from her artwork, that she had better charge at least $800 for that painting or she was living an illusion and basically wasting her time. I got the point—of course there are many "hidden" expenses in the business of art. Of course we tend to not have enough self-confidence in our abilities and artwork to ask for the "big bucks," but my sense of the whole affair was *forget* the gas, electricity, insurance and all that. It's true enough, but I still would need to go out with the car, turn lights on and insure my family. Don't inflate cost past reason. That woman knows darn well that her painting is going to sit forever and ever at $800. What's the point of that? My "advice" would be to sell it for $180, get a customer base built up of grateful people who want to support you and appreciate a deal when they see it, and go up gradually. Have fun together, build your confidence and develop your abilities. Re-invest that $180 to keep going, not constantly hanging the same picture up with a big $800 price tag on it, only to keep taking it down, teary-eyed, as it tears your self-respect down with it.

If I had been used as the example at this conference, perhaps my cards would need to be selling for $40 apiece at the rate of valuation they were working with. That would have been a bit discouraging for me. I have been told that in the real world today there are actually handmade cards selling for $15-$20 apiece. Wow. Good for them, but that's not me. I decided a long time ago that I would rather make more sales by having lower priced items than scrambling around trying to find shops willing to buy a few pricey cards and then give you only two spaces in their card racks. Again, it's a personal choice and I may change my perspective over time, but I really do like volume sales.

Going back to the idea of putting exorbitant prices on artwork—I know people who do that, sometimes for unusual reasons. They put these huge prices on pieces that they have been very attached to for years and years. They put them out for sale, but not really. I guess that's fine as long as you don't complain about being poor along the way, and constantly reminisce about how many eons it took to create your masterpiece. I have my own style, I guess. I put my heart into everything I make, but I am not attached to any one thing forever. (I have a couple of "firsts" that I have around, but even those can get sold or given at any moment.) My artwork moves either in sales or as gifts. I am constantly trekking to new territory, keeping a record of sorts through photos, but never wanting to be stuck or overly-attached. There is room for a vision of "the new" if I haven't cluttered my world with stuff from the past. I am not saying this is better or worse than any other way of doing business—it is simply mine. "Bravo!" to the people who charge big money and get it. That happens when there is a combination of talent, marketing and customers in place—a good idea is clearly working.

When I price my cards or my "whatevers," I start out by *first* thinking of what I would like to see on the price tag if *I* were the customer. That is naturally going to be on the low side, thrift-store-loving-lady-that-I-am. Then I hit the other extreme—what would I just *love* to be able to charge, within reason. Somewhere in the middle is the answer. Being in an Art Critique Group helps so much because I can get feedback from friends who are also Art-Businesswomen. My reps know their markets and know the limits of what I can charge in their areas. And I have to know my costs and what I am willing to settle for. Put all of this in the mix, and I usually end up feeling good about my decision.

Here is a good example of a "pricing experience." In a *Somerset Studio* Magazine, I read about beautiful Japanese origami boxes called Masu (measure) boxes. I followed the directions and made a few. I thought they were great, so I gave them away and got some good feedback as in "make more." I innovated the design, used cloth that I adhered to a paper backing and test-marketed them at The Columbia Fall Festival of the Arts show. I started with varied sizes and stuck a price tag of $5.00 for each. I sold 15 out of 20 and almost everyone said they loved them and how nice that they were *so cheap*. One woman came back to my tent specifically to tell me that, and how grateful she and her friend were for the few artists like me who keep their prices so "people-friendly." "…because of you, even people like *me* can walk away from an Art Show with something in hand." I appreciated that and I enjoyed another customer that day who told me: "As soon as I pay you for *my* purchases, you have to raise your prices—your work is wonderful—and so cheap! How do you manage to keep your prices so low? I'm leaving now, so raise them."

The Masu boxes were worth more than just $5.00—I invested a lot of time in them. Listening to what people said to me at the show made that clear, and I saw something happen with other boxes in a shop in Santa Fe. Ohori's is a great coffee-bar/gift shop. I don't do coffee, so I checked out the gift shop—magic. I bought two fabulous containers that I now use to display/sell my new style bookmarks. Mom bought a set of Adinkra rubber stamps as a memento gift for me, and we both noticed these Japanese origami *paper* boxes on a shelf. Very simple, fragile and quite honestly, nothing like *my* boxes. My mother motioned for me to check out the price tag, discreetly, of course: $8.00. I couldn't believe it. "No one would pay that for *that*," I discreetly whispered and sure enough, at that very moment, a man picked one of them up, walked to the counter and bought it. I think I can charge more for mine, I thought. But I still needed to consider that the $8.00 box was bought in a different "world." That is the land of the very big spenders.

At The Golden Hippo Gallery (in Missouri), I started to sell the boxes for $12.00 and sold many. I standardized the size, they were a little larger, and the decorative elements were enhanced, but they were still basically the same. Later that year at my first Gallery Opening Reception, several artists said that I should charge even more. I asked how much. "$20.00 sounds better." My response: "I could certainly do that, but they will sit here and I would rather sell them at $12.00 than dust them off at $20.00." At my last show, I sold 15 out of 20 at the new price of $12.00, and people *still* said what great prices I have, so go figure. There are endless variations of buyers out there, from rich people who don't trust or feel comfortable with anything that is not expensive *enough*, to people on budgets that make them feel as if everything is way too expensive to even consider. There is a saying that goes around the art show circuit that goes something like this: "You can never charge too much for the rich and too little for the poor." I find and trust my own comfort zone, stick on a price tag and watch what happens.

I am learning a lot by watching my friend Janet develop her Art Quilt business. In just over a year, she has gone from the level of total beginner to Top of the Line. Her story is in this book, but for the point at hand, let me shine a light on one aspect of her experience. If Janet, one year ago, tried to sell one of her first Art Quilts, let's say, at a Crafts Fair here in Missouri locally, and she put a price tag on it of $250, it would grace the walls of her tent. Period. People would love them and they would audibly whisper to one another the most despised phrase of all artists in all booths everywhere: "Well, *I* could do that." And I must admit that I have thought that myself as I walked around shows and fairs (but would *never* say it out loud). It isn't the right market here for Janet's work, and I am not putting down Missouri, especially not in the same paragraph with Janet! Santa Fe is her market and she found her special place. I watched her being totally amazed when Thirteen Moons Gallery suggested putting $600, then $800, breaking the $1000 mark, and then recently the $2000 and close to the $3000 mark and going up to who knows where. The Gallery makes a 50% commission. It is a good arrangement since they do the work of showing and marketing in their perfectly lovely environment to customers who have money for Art and probably have little need to glance at price tags. Janet gets the prestige of being their #1 Selling Artist and putting the Gallery name on her resume. She gets to do what she loves, being the best reward of all, as well as making money in the process. What a wonderful combination. The Gallery personnel guide her in the pricing process. Their advice has led her to ever-higher levels.

As I find myself gasping at the prices her fabulous work is commanding, I am also learning to think bigger. It is inspirational and challenging. It breaks the ceiling of my smaller thinking. A meteoric rise such as hers is the exception and not the rule, but I saw it with my own eyes and it is important to know that this does happen to people. It usually takes time to "get established" and have "name recognition" in order to command top dollar in any given field, so getting started and continuing are good moves.

Pricing products involves a spectrum of considerations. I wouldn't get too many headaches over the whole thing. Keep it practical and keep yourself in check. If I spent hundreds of dollars a month on new stamp images, let's say, then my costs would be too high. I keep a rein on myself. I am very frugal and buy supplies that I can guarantee to myself will have an immediate return. I built slowly over time, going sometimes for months without buying even one stamp. Can you fathom such restraint?

Just start working with some pricing numbers, and begin. You'll find your way. I still experiment and hem-and-haw all over the place. Just last weekend, June 3-4, 2000, I had my biggest art show ever—Art in the Park 2000. It was great. At 9:40 a.m. I was pricing my frames. The cards, Masu boxes, and bookmarks had already been priced. I had 20 minutes left before the official opening time to finish pricing the frames, which was easy since I'd been there and done that. The tricky part was pricing these brand new handmade tiles that I was putting out for sale for the first time. I had 13 tiles. They were pretty small and very cool. All of a sudden it was 10:00 a.m. and a customer walked into my tent. All the pleasantries and I am flustered because right away she asks, "These tiles are so cool! HOW MUCH ARE THEY???" For weeks I had played around with the idea. I didn't have a clue, so I said, "Well, there are basically two sizes, so the smaller ones are $5.00 and the larger ones are $7.00." "*Is that all*? Then I'll take these two." And she bought something else, too. Other people came in, and even though I wasn't sure even how to display the tiles and just hung them around on my boards in not the most intelligent way, they were the first thing that people saw, and I kept selling them. And they were kind of strange designs for Missouri, or so I thought—a Pre-Colombian mask, serpent and other interesting images. The dragonflies were gone within a half hour. At 11:15 a.m., one of the out-of-town Judges for the show showed up at my booth and I usually just say hello and they go about their business and I go about mine. But this guy loved my booth and was saying that he was coming back. And he did—this time with a $100 bill in his hand and he grabbed one of the last tiles. A woman picked out two more and when he saw that, he asked how many I had left. "One left." "I'll take it, whatever it is, and now you can say that you sold out of your new tiles." That was fun. I also learned a couple of things:

1) People liked my tiles and I am going to pursue this venture.
2) Everyone commented on how cheap they were, usually right *after* they paid, so obviously I could charge more.

Do I regret that I didn't make more money because I guessed wrong at the value? No, I don't. It was more important for me this time to see that people liked them and I know they will want and watch for more. Other folks were coming to my booth over the weekend asking for more tiles because the people who did buy them were showing them off and bragging about the great bargain they discovered! By selling those tiles, I also made the money to pay for another class at the University Craft Studio where I learned to make those tiles in the first place, and I can easily afford to buy 100 lbs. of clay to make a lot more. A Raku-firing class is coming up—I'll be there.

Some reflections about Pricing:

- Whatever you can get for *free*—get it. Save money. I have a wonderful source for grass-cloth, silk, cotton, and surprises like glass shelving, for example. It is the back porch of an Interior Design business in town. The owner told me to take whatever I want from the porch in the evening before it goes out to the dumpster in the morning. It is my treasure-hunt time and I make gifts out of my "finds" to thank the owner from time to time. Free is good. It keeps your costs and prices down. You can also help other people by distributing your discoveries.

- Whatever else you need to buy, get it Wholesale if at all possible. (Get your State Tax ID# and that will take care of that.) Research sources. Once again, it saves a lot of money that can be directed in other productive, cost-effective ways.

- Know your product costs and make the pricing work for you. Pay yourself a decent hourly "wage" in the process. Don't allow yourself to feel "poor." This is not a charity operation. You need to make money. Success is good. A friend of mine says: "Poor people aren't in a really great position to help the poor."

- Prices are not set in stone—there is a flexibility factor. Keep it fair and fun for everyone, and your customers will stay with you, and they will be willing to go *up* with you, too, if the quality is excellent and your designs and products are not static. Don't be afraid to make changes thoughtfully.

- Ask questions about pricing and listen to what people say—different kinds of people in different kinds of relationships to you—acquaintances who say that they like what you make enough to want to buy from you, friends who will be honest, store owners, fellow artists, your own customers… Listen, learn and experiment.

I would like to wrap this "discussion" up with the following bottom-line analysis of my own experience—in concrete numbers. Since I have done very big orders over the years, I was able to see myself in action and document the pace on paper. Here is what I learned that I can do at this time:

Number of cards I can make in one day, on average:	6 Dozen (72) (6-hour day)
Wholesale price of the cards (to the buyers):	$18.00 per dozen / $1.50 ea.

Breakdown of card expenses:		
	Cardstock:	$ .05
	Envelope:	$ .05
	Plastic sleeve:	$ .05
	Additional paper, ink, etc.:	$ .05
(Shipping: no expense for me / customer pays)		
(Packaging supplies / free from Post Office)		
Packing supplies like tape, new stamps occasionally:		+$ .05
Cost to me per Card:		$ .25 X 72 Cards = $18.00

So, if I make 6 dozen cards in a day and charge a buyer $18.00 doz. wholesale = $108.00

minus my cost:	-18.00
my profit:	$ 90.00

Average hourly rate: $15.00 per hour

That changes if I also include a 15% commission for a Rep's fee, if that applies. 15% of $90.00 is $13.50. Profit is then $76.50; hourly is adjusted to $12.75. Realistic. Not bad.

Now, let's re-work this a bit. This time let's make my new, a bit "higher-end" cards that wholesale for $2.50 each ($30.00 a doz.). It takes the same amount of time to make 6-dozen *tall* cards as it does to make 6-dozen *standard* A-6 cards. My costs are essentially the same, but let's add on 10-cents per card for a safety net. Let's say that this order is my own account, not through a Rep. I figured it out, and it works out to be a profit of approx. $155.00, putting the hourly rate at $25.00+ per hour. That sounds pretty darn good. Am I working six hours a day, five days a week, every week of the year? No. There are times when I am working more than that—other times less. Yet I am confident that as much as I want to have work to do, I can generate it one way or another.

There are flexibility factors that need to be put into play. When I have Christmas card orders or cards with just more complex designs and layers, they are more involved in terms of detail and time, so it will take longer and my hourly rate goes down. Whenever I add embellishments, such as "leaf skeletons" that cost up to 30-cents apiece, I take a hit unless I add that on to the cost of the cards, which is what I do in order to at least absorb the difference. They are great cards. No one has complained yet.

I have been mainly describing Wholesale card orders, and my examples illustrate times when every single aspect of making the cards, from scoring, to stamping the backs, etc. is done by hand. When I do retail shows, I definitely make more money per item—it comes directly to me—no middlemen involved. I do higher-end gift items as well as cards—bigger profit there. I have to pay a booth and a jury fee, but I do local, mid-size shows so those expenses are extremely low and I have no travel expenses to tack on.

This is all real experience and real numbers for me, nothing fuzzy. I am not going to include my phone bill in here nor am I going to include the expense of taking out a customer/friend for lunch. I know enough not to depress myself. If I dissected it all down to the tiniest details, I might lose hope, so I just won't do it. I know from our annual tax returns that my expenses/personal income ratio is very commendable—I am a good shopper. I know how to do nice things with hardly any money—cheap and classy works.

Should I raise my prices? Many people say that I should. And then again, many other people say that if I did, I would price myself out of the range that works for good turnover. It is an interesting call. My designs are basic and my production system for one person, namely me, works. This is an encapsulation of what has been so far. Evolution is progress and I am more than willing to change and grow. If I move more and more into a Fine Arts realm let's say, for example with my tiles, as I learn to develop that idea, I might move away from wholesale as full-time. It will be fun to see how it all works out, doing my best to keep what I have built in a scaled-down fashion so that I might expand in other directions at the same time.

Pricing challenges are in my future, for sure. I already have some *big* tiles drying over at the University. "*How much*" will they be? We shall see. It is a balancing act, this pricing thing. You do not want to live in denial and then make the fateful discovery that you are basically not making a profit worthy of your efforts. On the other hand, if you over-inflate expenses past the point of the practical to the point of discouragement, what good is that? Keep expenses down and remember: Nickel-and-diming your way to fame, fortune, and satisfaction works if you have the patience to keep going and the creative energy to invest in getting it all to a higher level. In the final analysis, be fluid in your thinking about pricing—and laugh once in a while through the pressure. It helps.

Accounting

Keeping things straight

There is pricing and selling, and now, how to keep it all organized: accounting. This is going to be among the shortest pieces of writing in this book. Accounting is not my strong point nor is it my passion, but it is a business necessity. I hope either you love it, or love someone who loves you enough to do it for you. Or, if necessary, pay someone, whatever it takes to keep things straight.

I keep every receipt in a plastic shoebox, which is appropriately entitled: "Business Receipts." Quite professional, really now. I also keep every Invoice (yellow/2nd copy) in a three-ring binder in order of date shipped out. I found this handy-dandy three-ring hole-puncher that can be kept *in* the binder because it has holes punched into *it*. (Back-to-School Supply Section in discount stores.) I send out an order, punch my copy of the Invoice, and immediately stick it into the binder. I am on top of knowing the work that went out and the dates when money is owed to me. With my receipt box and invoice binder my business office is under control. It doesn't get any more basic than this.

Usually sometime in February or March, I take out my annual collection of Business Receipts, total them up, and get a dollar amount. Then all of my Invoices (copies) are totaled. Next, a list of all Art Shows/Retail Events is worked up and those totals get put on this report-of-sorts. Rep commission fees are worked in and I take this "Report" to my husband who then figures out what I have done money-wise in the previous year, and works up the info for the IRS. While filing the darn tax returns, Gary listens to music. *Dire Straits*, a 70's/80's group, has a few songs that work well, he says: "Money for Nothing," "Private Investigations," and "Why Worry." Hey, whatever works, I say.

I have heard that there are all kinds of useful books (ledgers, etc.) for the "number-challenged" such as myself, but I can't be bothered, and don't want to spend money on things that will give me more to do in any one given day. Should you take into consideration all of the extended expenses such as *electricity* for the lights in your studio, *gas* for runs to the Post Office, *heating* and *air-conditioning* as the seasons dictate, headache medications for stressful times, etc.? My answer for me is *no*. The lights would be on anyway, I do errands regularly, and if I didn't have my own business I'd have even bigger headaches working for someone else. We make smart enough decisions about what to claim reasonably. When I look at the figures, I can see that I do pretty darn well as far as expenditures vs. actual income. "A commendable job," my husband says.

Bottom-line: Always know how much you spent and how much you made. That will give you a clue as to whether or not it is to your advantage to keep going for another year.

Make sure you pay your reps and that your accounts pay you. They have 30 days in my system (net 30). I keep an exact list of open accounts on my drafting table and when payment comes in, I check it off, updating the list every month. If accounts are two weeks late, I send them a pleasant late notice, and less pleasant ones after that. Today I received a check for $59.00—it happens to be 7 months late. That is extremely rare in my experience, but obviously it can happen.

Presented here are the basics-of-basics. My advice to myself is: "Keep it crystal clear, simple and legal." Any fancy additions after that, and you may well be moving into the realm of "financial finesse" and I applaud you. (Good luck.)

144

Plastic sleeves, etc.

In hot pursuit of wholesale supplies

If we are going to make any money in our little businesses, we need to get all of our supplies either for free or at least at wholesale. The first one is fun and not practical, the second is practical and not always fun. It takes a lot of persistent searching to find the ultimate wholesale sources, and once you find them, you hope and pray that they stay in business so you can, too. [Hint: carry a notebook, turn things over and jot down info.]

One good example: plastic sleeves for cards. Looks simple enough—they are on millions of cards. So, you look it up in the Yellow Pages under: "Plastic Card Sleeves." Sorry, no listing. No listing for: "Wholesale Paper for the Handmade Cardmaker" either. It takes sleuthing, networking, time and sometimes sheer luck. In need of sleeves for my cards, I went to a card shop and bought several cards that had them, turned them over and called telephone numbers on the backs. One did call back and gave me a lead: a company in New York. (I loved the way they talked on the phone—reminders of *All in the Family*.)

I went with this company for years. They were doing me a big favor by taking me on and gave me minimums of (only) 3,000 of each size. They custom-cut sleeves for my cards and bookmarks. I occasionally had to wait too long, but at least I had a source. There was a seam in the back that I didn't like, but come to find out, one of their major customers was Nabisco and they made the plastic bags for Oreos, so it was a style of sorts that definitely was more suited to cookies. I know that my measly 3,000-bag order was more of a hassle than anything else. It was working in a way, but it wasn't what I wanted.

After pretty much giving up on finding anything else or anything better, I received news that my minimums were going to go astronomical on me, and I just couldn't afford that big of a layout in one hit. I ran my supply of sleeves almost to the ground, wishing that somehow they would spontaneously regenerate themselves or something.

Then, lo and behold, the Best of Missouri Hands Conference was approaching and I attended as always. I happened to meet a wonderful person, Theresa Gallup, new at that time to the organization. Her garments and accessories made out of vintage Japanese kimono cloth are exquisite. Theresa held a cozy after-hours trunk sale in her room, and my eyes immediately zeroed in on this little container that had a selection of handmade greeting cards—an experiment of hers, using remnants of her fabrics—fabulous! When I picked one up and held the plastic sleeve, I couldn't wait to ask her: "Theresa, would you mind telling me your source for the plastic card sleeves? I have been searching for 5 years for the ideal sleeve and you found it." "I'm happy to help you out, Gloria. I saw an ad in an art magazine and ordered them. I didn't know what I was doing, but I thought they looked nice." "They look *wonderful*, by the way. No seams, perfectly smooth. What are their minimums?" (cringe) "100. But if you get $40.00 worth, you get a break on the shipping. The unit price is a nickel per bag... is that good?" "Is that *good*? That's the answer I've wanted to hear for a long time. You've saved me. Thank you so much."

Needless to say, I contacted the company faster than immediately and I had my first order from Impact Images within a week of the conference. Networking plus Theresa's generosity—it is so exciting to be in a position to exchange information. As soon as I got my order in, I called Ken and Kay, two friends in town with card businesses of their own, to share the good news. Quite a few others have become Impact Images customers, too.

Some people believe in protecting their sources, and though I won't go so far as to say that I respect that, I back off. I hang out with the other fun crowd, the let's-share-and-help-each-other-out crew. I am not talking about taking another person's ideas and replicating them. I am referring to sharing information about practical, useful, general art/business supplies. Life is way too short—being generous and helpful feels great.

Track down wholesale sources. Scavenge for freebies if you have the stomach for it and don't give up on the search. Let's come up with a networking system of wholesale sources on a big scale, don't you think? Re-inventing the wheel is no fun at all.

"What if I am not the *gung-ho!* / Type-A type?"

At this conference I went to another time, several of the seminar leaders were major gung-ho/Type-*AAA* personalities. Walking into the different talks, I thought of myself as pretty confident and "together." I've had a business for many years. I'm writing a book. I'm cool. Since I always want to learn more, I took my seat, opened my notebook, pen in hand, poised and ready to learn a thing or two from the experts. Several hours later, walking out of the talks, dazed, I realized that I was utterly exhausted, totally blown away, shell-shocked by the pace, energy and sheer force of their desire to impart their insights—it felt like all of this information was being beaten into me. Other people may have loved it; I am happy for them. I got crushed and blown off the map.

The legal mumbo-jumbo, the rapid-fire graphs for behavioral modification if you planned on having any hope in managing your time effectively like "the pros" do, the long list of personal triumphs that I couldn't even begin to relate to… it was too much to take in. Could I use the information the next day? Was I empowered? (Frankly, I needed the next day to sleep and recuperate.) What could I possibly have been thinking? What was I doing there in the first place? My thinking is so small—what a lazy loser I am.

I must be a dunce, a major league incompetent, I felt. Trudging down the hall of the hotel with my head down, my friend John caught up with me and I noticed his furrowed brow immediately. He asked me: "Can you relate to these people? I don't have their manic drive. I can't work like that. Is there something wrong with me?" I laughed and felt incredibly relieved; I was not alone. John told me that his favorite moment during the entire afternoon was when I raised my hand in the final moment of the time-management seminar and timidly offered a humble example of my personal, specialized "technique." After clearing my throat, I said, "Well, in order to keep things straight, I wear two different aprons—the light green one for housework and the navy denim one for studio work. When I get confused, I look down and see which apron I am wearing and then I am not confused anymore." Laughter and applause erupted, I turned red, the seminar dismissed, and I've heard that the example proved to be helpful to people over time.

I want to be very sensitive as I write my own story. This is not toot or blare my own horn time. Who needs that? It really isn't helpful. What can be helpful are ideas and real life examples that prove beyond a shadow of a doubt that we are all in this together, and that many times it is the simplest of ideas that help the most.

The great movers and shakers that I truly admire are not always gung-ho/Type-A people—many quietly live their inspiration. They move mountains without making noise.

Angel Companies

The very first stamp I had was *not* from an "angel company." The first three southwest stamps that became the foundation of my card business were *not* from Angel Companies either. The term did not exist at that time or at least I didn't know about it. I didn't have a clue that there were any restrictions on the use of rubber stamps. The term exists now and it is important to know the definition if rubber stamps are of interest to you in your work. If your work is in other arenas, the word "Copyright" will be familiar. We are dancing around with these types of issues when we talk about Angel Companies in the art stamping world.

An Angel Company, simply stated, is a stamp manufacturing company that gives artists permission to use their designs in original hand-stamped creations that are made for re-sale. Bottom line: You can make money using their designs if you do the work by hand. They wish you luck rather than send lawyers to chase after you. Basically, there are two kinds of companies in my working vocabulary—Angel Companies and All The Rest. Personally, I only buy from the former. "All The Rest" can choose to make life pretty uncomfortable, legally speaking, for us business stampers. Who needs a cease-and-desist letter or a lawsuit? Not me.

The arguments go round and round on all sides. It is not a black-and-white issue, and the gray areas are interesting. I just tend to see things simplistically. For me, rubber stamps, art stamps, are art tools. The designs themselves come from many sources, from original drawings to reproductions of public domain art to clip art, etc. For me, if any image is *hand*stamped, I don't see the problem. If images are reproduced by printing, etc. of course you need to have restrictions, but I don't see any restrictions on what you paint with your paintbrush—it is a *tool*. Stamps are design tools. Artists' rights and royalties are involved, so the argument goes. All I know is that, if by chance, one day, a company approached me and asked if I would like to sell my handcarved designs to be reproduced as art stamps for paper or fabric (or whatever), this is what would happen:

- #1: I would be delighted!
- #2: I would ask if the company was an angel company or not—I would *only* work with an angel company.
- #3: I would find out the terms, compare, find the best arrangement with the company that most closely reflects my own style and business philosophy.
- #4: I would thoroughly enjoy seeing what creative people would do with my images and wish them the best in terms of making tons of money with their handmade work. I see it as being mutually beneficial for everyone involved.

My feeling is: Here is my design. Enjoy it. Let the image go to create happiness and beauty in the world—that's just fine with me. I can't wait to see what you come up with.

When a stamp company expects that you will send them examples of every card design that you plan on selling, frankly I can't be bothered with that. I know that the example I send is not set in stone for me, and I am not about to send a different example of every variation on every theme. I simply don't have the time or the interest.

I love it when companies advertise and say: "We are an Angel Company—use our images, make money and have a great time" or something along those lines. I know how to be respectful and I am certainly always grateful. Trust me, please, that I will use the image as a creative, artistic tool, using my hands as well as my sense of design.

My first few stamps came from a company that I will decline to mention in print. Every stamper on the face of the planet would recognize the name. Their angel policy was not exactly what I would call friendly, at least at that time. Supposedly they have eased up, but old fears are hard to shake. I only learned about this "copyright issue" down the road of experience and have been very careful ever since. After I heard that one company went after a clay artist and sued her for $10,000 for using impressions of their stamps in her pottery, I stopped in my own tracks and took stock and inventory. I don't know the details of the story, but I do know a warning when I hear one. I am not a hobbyist stamper per se. If I were, this whole discussion would be moot. I buy stamps for the purpose of adding to my working collection of designs. Almost every single stamp has a business application for me. I sold or gave away all stamps that I couldn't use freely. I contacted every stamp company whose images I do use. I believe that I am in the clear—if not, forgive me, please, and I promise I will pull the "illegal culprit" out of my collection. "I'm so sorry, really I am." The last thing I need is a lawsuit flying in my direction. I just think the entire issue needs to be lightened up.

One very good outcome of being nervous about using images that could potentially ruin rather than enhance me financially is the fact that I looked into alternative printmaking methods and found many. There are no copyright/permission worries when I make my own handcarved blocks, my own etching plates, stone chops, woodblocks, etc. The designs are free and clear. I do as I please and use rubber stamps as complements to my own creations. I am finding a good balance.

Do I advocate a boycott against non-angel companies? I do not. I still keep my original stamps in a special place for historical reasons and personal use. The same is true with a few others that have won my heart over the years. They are nice stamps.

Just in case you are contemplating a business venture with these particular "tools," these things are good to be aware of, and I do hope that over time there will be more and more "angels" around and that those companies really take off financially. There is a saying that I enjoy and feel is appropriate for this particular discussion. It goes something like: "Angels fly because they take themselves lightly." Good point.

This is as good a time and place as any to address the question of legalities in general. It is a nerve-wracking point to consider and can be overwhelming and bordering on the bizarre. There are times when you feel like you'd better have a lawyer available to get permission to work, think and breathe in your own house and/or studio. It's a good idea in such circumstances to step outside and catch some fresh air. At least that won't cost you by the hour. If I need legal advice or assistance, my inclination is to talk with my Art Critique Group friends first, following up with some reading materials—then proceed slowly from there. Being careful and wise is different than being paranoid.

From which stamps to use "legally" to the specter of bookkeeping, there is advice to be had, systems that make sense that can be put in place, and the main tool needed here is the ability and willingness to communicate. I get e-mails and calls from people asking how I handle different situations. As I share what I have learned from experience, I can hear the sighs of relief in the choice of words and tone of voice. Don't worry too much.

This is one way of doing it...
Getting a card order and getting it out the door.

Please notice that I said *one way* to do it, not the only way, the definitive way, not how you or anyone else on the planet should do it. Remember: this is not a how-to book. Over time I pulled this little plan together, and I believe there is value in looking over someone else's process, gleaning from that whatever the heck works for you. It helps to have something visual and then one can always play from there. Use *this*, forget *that*, re-work a bit here and there and then your own signature is placed on what becomes the best procedure for your needs and style.

The Purchase Order comes from my rep or I write it up personally, taking my own order. It is pretty straightforward—it is the Order form designating what the customer would like to Purchase from my business. There is a Purchase Order # (PO#): I use either the manufacturer's pre-printed #, or I use the date that the order was made as the PO#. For example: PO #33100 is designated for an order written up on March 31, 2000—easy enough. It helps in looking back in records to have actual dates rather than some meaningless list of numbers. I use the same system for the Invoices, which is the description of the contents of the order and the billing information. Since PO #33100 was sent on April 14th, I call the Invoice #41400. It makes sense. If two or more orders are shipped the same day, then an A,B,C is tacked on to the end. Orderliness and logic are the keys to the whole shebang. (Advice: I always use 8½ x 11 double or triple forms even for small orders—they don't tend to get lost in the shuffle like half-size forms do.)

As soon as a Purchase Order comes in, I always check first for the requested shipping date. It usually is ASAP meaning as soon as *you* can do it, and my expectation of myself is that I can get an order out within 2-3 weeks of receiving it. If it is quicker than that—great! If it looks like it will be beyond 4 weeks I always contact the buyer and get the okay. The general expectation for orders that are handmade is about 4-6 weeks unless you have arranged a different system with your customers. My feeling is that I want to do better than that for my customers, if at all possible. It is better for business because it is good customer service. Getting orders out within one or two weeks during peak production months is impossible when orders pile up, say, in the summer touristo months of June and July, but generally I can manage a two week turn-around. There are times when I get a whole series of orders in *April* that are to be made and sent in *October* and *November*. Many card companies place Holiday orders in the spring. I just make sure that I am doing an order at the *right* time. One time I blew it; oh, well. I now circle the shipping date so it is clear. Future orders need to be filed in order of dates—I keep them in a completely separate 3-ring binder so there is no confusion.

Okay. So, the Purchase Order is sitting on the drafting table—there is an order to do. I always write down the whole order on a separate piece of paper so that it all makes sense. I put it in order of categories of designs. I "unscramble" anything that might be confusing before I waste time with it. Every code has meaning and has a corresponding card sample in my master set. For example, FR 25 means a card with a FRamed image, so I look in that file and pull up #FR25. I line up and look at all of my cards in the order, and arrange them in a logical way so as to save time by grouping similar/same tasks together. I then take out all the cardstock to correspond to the colors that I need in the right quantities: one dozen red, two dozen gold, one dozen black, etc. (These are pre-cut to size.) When the big stack is made, the next step is to score all the cards.

There is a running theme here, and what it all boils down to is two words: "common sense." Organization is a good third word because that is the direct outcome of common sense. If all of your papers are all over your workroom, you are wasting time and mind power if you have to constantly search for what you need. I buy lots of those cheap plastic shoebox containers and have all of the cardstock stocked and stacked according to color—one color per box. The tasks are multi-layered, so I do them in an orderly fashion. If you are used to doing one card at a time from start to finish, that's great in the creativity arena of life, but when it comes to producing 24-dozen cards in something less than a decade, streamlining is a good idea. So, without boring you to tears with details, I am going to blast through the rest of this process:

- Score all the cards (get a Scoreboard or something to help you out)
- Stamp all the backs (unless you have the money/desire to have them printed)
- Line up the piles of cards and cut all papers for the surface layering
- Bring them to the glue machine (Rollataq, bless you) or glue by hand
- Press under a board with a handle that you've made for this purpose (easy)
- Do all the stamping / allow to dry
- Fold cards (I use a hard brayer) and line them up / do embellishments / dry
- Put envelopes / cards / plastic sleeves / inserts in a row and package each.
- I then wrap each dozen or 1½ dozen cards in one sheet of white tissue paper, put it into a Priority Mail video mailer, seal it, and add it to a bigger box.
- Write up the Invoice, put it in a clearly marked envelope, tape it inside on one of the internal boxes and seal the whole thing. I always indicate on the outside of a box that the Invoice is enclosed. (You will get used to the cost of shipping over time. I always guess right now, but in the beginning I took open boxes to the Post Office, and added the shipping charge to the Invoice at the counter after they were weighed—whatever works.)
- Address the packages; write legibly with permanent marker. Ship it out.
- In 30 days, receive your check, deposit it in the bank and smile… then see what's next… and do it.

Note: Thanks to the US Post Office, my shipping boxes are free. I even get them delivered by the case in assorted sizes to my door, shipping labels pre-printed, all at no charge—that's excellent service. You can get information at your local Post Office. I must say that out of all the hundreds and hundreds of orders I have shipped, the USPS has never lost one and not one has ever been returned to me because of damaged contents. The customers pay the exact shipping charges tacked on to their bills and so far everybody's happy. (I do insure huge orders.)

There are always variations on themes and the topic of production always has interesting twists and turns. Whatever it is that we are making, it just comes back to the beginning—keep it simple—and it will work. Over time I have learned how to take out the unnecessary steps: to condense and refine. And I still manage to have days when the ordinary suddenly looks monumental. Then it's back to basics and the drawing board once again.

Cranking up the volume, BIG time
Breaking through the doldrums of *production*

Getting one order out the door is one thing—big orders, infinitely more piling up on the drafting table, threatening my sanity, is another thing altogether. It's a good sign, I tell myself: business is booming. As long as I don't fall apart and "lose it" in the process, we'll be all right. Taking out a calculator, I figure out how much money I will have 30 days after I send all these orders on their merry way—that helps a bit. But they still have to be *made* before I can waltz to the bank, smiling, with a deposit slip in-hand.

I start making a plan, figuring out which order comes first, second, third, and so on. Then I can begin to grasp if there is any way to expedite the process of putting all these orders out in a timely fashion. Maybe there are a couple of orders with overlapping requests—I could save some time by doing two orders together. There are different levels of organization at play simultaneously. On the more physical level, there are infinite ideas and tools useful for setting up the ultimate systems for efficient hand-manufacturing. If you are fortunate enough to have a fortune to play with, then your Studio can be an organized state-of-the-art Heaven-on-Earth with dream shelving, containers, sky-lights, *the works* as far as efficiency and atmosphere are concerned. That would help. It would be nice. Since I don't have that kind of luxury, I make any space work with handy-dandy-cheap-solid-stuff. Efficiency with systems is one thing, but I'll tell you, organizing and galvanizing my attitude towards facing a mountain of work is another. I want to talk about the way I approach the challenge of my boggled-mindset in tackling production. This is on the more internal level. The gymnastics of production do start in the mind—mental gymnastics, so-to-speak.

I was working downstairs this morning on a project making one dozen Japanese Masu boxes out of silk, cotton, hand-tied tassels and listening at the same time to a wonderful Sounds True cassette tape of authors Natalie Goldberg and Julia Cameron sitting together, discussing *The Writing Life*. At one point they were sharing about the different places they have gone to over the years to sit down and do their writing thing. They were sharing about doing their craft in different types of atmospheres, forcing themselves to get off their backsides, out the door with a commitment to a place and a task—writing. They stand up, open the door, get out of the house, go away, and get stimulation from the environment of their choosing, whether it be on the Taos Plaza in a particular past-tense restaurant with disgusting food but a nice view, or Grand Central Station in New York, wherever. I laughed when I thought of my own situation with my business. My handy dandy tools are not exactly a notebook and a pen. Not so easy to lug a 36-inch, 60-lb. paper cutter onto the subway in a brief case en route to MOMA, or to schlep a 12-inch Rollataq glue machine in a back-pack and plunk it down on a café table in Santa Fe, asking for a seat with outlet access. I am stuck in a way, glued to the space I call my workplace, *studio*, unfinished basement, dungeon or whatever I'm calling it today, based on my mood. My stuff is here, therefore so must I be. But I'm a romantic, by gosh. I have backpacked my little heart out from the Sangre de Cristos to the French Alps, so claustrophobic-cramped is not my style of choice. A basement that needs all these lights strung everywhere with no way to grow plants? This place needs help. I need help. I determined that I would find my own ways to break the constraints.

There are different ways to "get out of the house." I needed to find creative, inexpensive ways to jump-start myself, and my attitude, into action—to simulate an inspiring atmosphere—a way to pretend I am not really where I am, with all this work to do. No matter what, I *will* find the way.

And just when I've made the leap of determination, it is absolutely incredible how many *distractions* abound at such times, for some very mysterious reason. The sheer volume of what needs to be accomplished can drive anyone to distraction, I guess. All of a sudden, I start seeing all these "other things" that *need* to be done—as in right now. For example, like spring-cleaning in October when I haven't done it for years anyway. When the mountain of laundry or alternative peak of dishes look more appealing than hiking to the studio, something needs to happen fairly quickly, because deadlines only get closer the more that I allow time to slip through my hands. One thing that has never failed me, always works *no matter what*, is to turn to music in the form of my tape player—to put in a tape or CD and *crank up the volume, big time.*

Lots of people turn to music to get started. I love to watch the Olympic skaters, especially when they start their routines. They are poised and prepared, but they do not start until the music begins. There is a most definite beginning point, and once begun, the skater keeps on going. No matter what happens: win, lose, make mistakes, fall, triumph—there is no stopping—a concerted effort to the end: until the music stops. That is the point when you can stop and take your bow—only then.

I use music to inspire myself to push past time and the sense that I am stuck in a closed-in space with too much to do. First of all, it paces me, since there is a concrete sense that yes, time is moving because I have to go over and turn the tape over, about every 15 minutes or so. I am organizing the cardstock, scoring, cutting paper, gluing, and *singing*: another key point here. But I am doing more than singing. I am wailing away, harmonizing whether it works or not, belting it out in a "singing in the shower" rock-country-opera-folk concert, performing at the Grammies right before my well-deserved Award, oblivious to the fact that perhaps people might actually be listening to all of this noise. The volume gets cranked-up for certain songs, #1 being: James Taylor's *Up on a Roof* from the old *Flag* album: "When this old world starts a-getting me down…" I am belting it out, rewinding, and going at it again, revving myself up way past the blah's, baby, and I can keep on keepin' on. My space becomes the "roof," and nobody and nothing is going to bother *me* and get me down because I really did find "a paradise that's trouble-proof." It is good to have anthems and theme songs along the way, trust me.

My tape collection is old and limited, just a few CD's, but the memory-lane aspect is fun, too. James Taylor is #1, and then I will go through phases. The most recent phase-craze is absolutely anything by Enya and before that: Anne Murray. God spare the UPS deliveryman or U.S. Postman if they must deliver something at the door and hear my overwrought rendition of "…even though we ain't got money, I'm so in love with you, honey…" and "Cheer up, sleepy Jean, oh what can it mean to a *Daydream Believer*…" There I am wailing away and laughing at myself singing my heart out, pumping myself up, and working very hard, all at the same time. In desperate moments, I will take out my guitar and allow myself ten minutes. Reflecting on how all of this may sound as you read this, I must say that 95% of the time I work in a peaceful way. I don't care for radio much, and I do like to think as I work. But when extreme measures are called for, the volume gets cranked up. And I don't care who hears. But I do wonder who does.

It is funny to watch myself walk out the front door after such sessions to check the mail or walk to pick up my kids from school. I tend to put my sunglasses on, cloudy or not, eyeing the neighborhood, wondering how loud I *really* was, and how much of a happy fool I made out of myself. At least no one has ever cited me for disturbing the peace. Maybe I have added a little spice to the quiet neighborhood. As far as my work, I am always ahead of my hopes for that day, and that means something is working.

Another little trick I use once in a while is to get myself up from being downstairs by choosing the timing carefully. If I play my cards right, when I have a highly boring, repetitive task before me, such as scoring hundreds of cards, stamping the backs of cards, pulling threads from cloth pieces, etc. I plan that task for 1 p.m. so that I can space out, work to justify my escape, and watch *Northern Exposure* re-runs, flipping around to Design Shows for a quickie cool idea or two. I laugh out loud, cry, get pointers and then get myself back downstairs for the next stage by 2 p.m. I think everyone has his or her own garden variety of jump-starts, heart-pleasers and monotony-breakers. Use them.

Today I got a nice note from a friend of mine in Illinois. She said that she was impressed that an Aries-Year-of-the-Horse person like me could actually complete anything, particularly a repetitive task, order after order, year after year. I laughed, trotted downstairs and I was simply "dancing through the Milky Way…" on the way to completing another order… One crazy "daydream believer" I am.

Note: I can't help it. I just had to include my hit parade, a song list I've called "In tune with the times." My friend who is a music professor may cringe, but this light fare has helped me to float, surf the tsunamis of too-much-to-do, sing and dance, smile and laugh at myself during the time of writing this book and working on my art business.

"When I was just a little girl" my Mom and I used to dance together stomping around, twirling in the air on Sunday mornings in the kitchen. Somehow she would find polkas on the radio. At other times she would sing, "Que sera, sera…whatever will be, will be…" To kill the boredom of long road trips, we had a hand-typed songbook on the visor in the station wagon. With memories of those careening polka mornings and all of the sing-and-dance-alongs, I developed my own traditions with my children and a solo act in my studio as well. There are many tools and tricks of the trade with no price tags attached. Find them, use them, and share them. Life is too short; you have to be nutty.

My song list follows this page. Will it be revised over time? Bob Dylan sang that the "times they are a-changin'"… Of course my hit parade will change, too, but these songs will always have a special place in my life—the encapsulation of an era.

When the heart overflows, it comes out through the mouth.

- *African* Proverb

■

Those who wish to sing
always find a song.

- *Swedish* Proverb

153

In tune with the times

Songs that carried me through…

JAMES TAYLOR
- *Up on a Roof*
- *Mexico*
- *Shower the People*
- *Never Die Young*
- *Handyman*

JONI MITCHELL
- *Free Man in Paris*
- *Both Sides Now*
- *The Circle Game*
- *You turn me on, I'm a radio*

THE BEATLES
- *I Will*

BROOKS & DUNN
- *South of Santa Fe*

BILL STAINES
- *Crossing the Water*
(performed by the Grace family)

DORIS DAY
- *Whatever Will Be, Will Be*

ANNE MURRAY
- *Greatest Hits*

SAM COOKE
- *(What a) Wonderful World*
(performed by James Taylor, Simon and Garfunkel)

BOBBY McFERRIN
- *Don't Worry, Be Happy*

ENYA
- *Pilgrim*
- *Only Time*
- *Wild Child*
- *Only if…* (my #1 personal theme song)

(Art stamp images courtesy of *Curtis' Collection*)

154

Space between the lines
Quiet times

If I need a jump-start, then I crank up the volume. I wail away and sing every line of every song whether I know the words or not—belt out the spirit of it—learn the words later. But I certainly don't want to live in that cranked-up state as a way of life. It is way too intense and pretty noisy. I am in search of..........the space between the lines.

Oriental Art acknowledges space. Look at a Zen painting of a persimmon. Ink as black as coal, one stroke, and lots of space on the rice paper. How can that black swirl look so soft and smell so sweet? There is room for me to reach into the paper and pluck it from the table that is not there. The space that is allowed does not convey "emptiness" in the negative sense as in "incomplete." It is just the opposite. To add one more stroke, one more "thing," would create clutter and imbalance—open space defines the completeness.

As I write words, one after the other, line after line, I too am searching for the space between these lines, that calm, peaceful, serene, joyful, playful, completely true point—the point of what I am trying to say. When all is said and done, when the skin of the persimmon is peeled away and the layers of words are stripped away—is the heart of the matter, the main point: is it clear, pure and simple? Is it possible to read between the lines and find simply that there is space? Not the empty kind of space, but rather the open kind —the kind of space that would allow you to run free with your own thoughts and dreams. I am not interested in being spaced-out in the least—how about being "spaced-in."

Recently, I ran myself ragged for weeks on end with seemingly no end in sight. I pushed on many different levels and this was good stuff I was working on, but I took on too much, too fast, too intensely. I subsequently wiped-out. I was engaged in new lines of products from handmade tiles to ceramic buttons, new card lines, totally new presentation for my biggest Art Show of the year, a clothing line, commissioned work, exploring professional framing, new website design and construction, putting out rush orders, restructuring my entire business, studio, house and life, writing my first book, speaking at the University, and I haven't even mentioned life at the end of the school year for my two children who also happen to have the same birthday and all the party things attached to that. Two months of too much. There was no quiet time in my mind, no space between the lines. Forget an Oriental painting; my life had become more like a Jackson Pollock painting caught on fire.

For whatever reason, it is always easier for me to crank-it-up rather than wind-it-down until I am forced flat on my back from illness, sheer exhaustion or a weird kind of suspended animation type of depression. That is rather wasteful. There has to be a better way of point-sourcing light in my life. I am seeking the balance of the intense line and the open space between the lines. I am seeking a harmonious relationship between the crashing waves and the ocean depths—knowing full well that I do love cavorting and creating in the rush of waves and pressure of time, and at the same time, I need a lounge chair, cold drink and good book on the beach of life on the other side of serious romping.

I am learning about these things, watching and listening.

I am reading about such possibilities (when I allow myself that luxury).

I could site moments of touching the hope and reality of this from the past.

Living the quiet space in daily life is my next step.

Get with the program
A Cardmaker's 12-Step Program

I am going to boil it all down to 12-Steps to Starting a Card Business.
Here it is: the bare bones—see what *you* think—that's what really counts:

- 1) Make 12 cards you like a lot and would be willing and able to make many times, over and over again—simple enough and cheap enough, too.
- 2) Make up a Company Name and logo that feels good, makes sense and looks good on paper. Call the Secretary of State's office and register the name.
- 3) Get a Tax ID# by calling the State Department of Revenue to get information, fill out the form, pay a reasonable fee and get started.
- 4) Set up a toll-free number—it is cheap, easy and necessary, so just *do* it.
- 5) Make a stamp or have one made with your new company name and logo for the back of your cards and correspondence purposes. This is good for the "confidence factor" and ego as well. Include the toll-free # on the back of all the cards, too.
- 6) Use card stock that you have purchased retail at first, but line up a wholesale source for paper and envelopes as soon as possible. You are a *business* now.
- 7) Order plastic sleeves from Impact Images. (See: CONNECTIONS)
- 8) Buy *Purchase Order* forms / carbonless / two-part
- 9) Buy *Invoice* forms / carbonless / two-part
- 10) Buy a plastic box for your card samples / give each a code #.
- 11) Find a gift shop that looks promising because you like the style of the products they carry and feel comfortable with the atmosphere. Ask to make an appointment with the card buyer and see what happens.
- 12) If the buyer likes your cards, ask, "Would you like to place an order?" If the answer is "Yes," then take out your Purchase Order form and start writing. You are in business. If the answer is "No," then say "Thank you for your time," and find someone else to ask.

The point here is that it does not have to be any more complex than this. The fussing and finessing, the refining and building will come. Getting started is the leap of faith, the biggest step of all steps. Everything else after that is a hop, skip and a jump.

If you are contemplating another business idea or just anything new at all, this idea of simplifying the steps might be useful. Put a maximum number on yourself, and stick to it. If five-steps sound reasonable and workable, then five it is. If ten works, go with ten. If it starts going into several sheets of paper, then there may be a problem. Think of an IRS Tax Return Form—and do not go there—there has to be a better, shorter style and way. You can map something out in one page or less. We are talking about beginnings here, not the re-creation of the entire universe.

"Boredom" and "Burnout"

Choose a job you love and you will never have to work a day in your life. - Confucius

In the *business* of making cards we are not talking about making a card here and a card there whenever the inspired muse descends and graces us with vision, ability and time. We are not talking about taking the entire working day to create one card with layer upon layer of the most advanced techniques that would boggle the mind of even the most avid stamping fanatic. In a card business we are talking *quantity* as well as quality. There was a time when I made up to 10,000 cards a year—year after year. We are not talking "hobby" here—we are talking "production," even "mass production," if we are on a roll of success. It always blows me away to see entries in card contests, even on a local level—I cannot even *imagine* spending 8 or 9 hours on one card. In 8 or 9 hours I would expect of myself to make at least 6-*dozen* cards, ready to ship the next morning. Production over a long period of time can lead straight into the jaws and yawns of Boredom. A case of Burnout is also a distinct possibility. From personal experience, I know. Since being bored to tears and tired are hardly inspiring states of mind to be in as an artist, I'd like to examine the topic because it is not an unusual problem. There is hope.

Let us sketch out a scenario here: A Purchase Order comes in and you look at it. Several orders are included in the packet, let's say. That's normal. As you start looking over the "requests," it can sometimes be exhausting even before beginning. Going back a number of years, I can remember clearly—an order came from my rep. Most orders at that time were in the $100-$200 range, taking about 2-3 days to finish. This order in my hand had a different feel to it. I glanced at it quickly and it seemed like I saw the number $166, had to run to do an errand, and came back later to check on that packet from Gini. It was incredibly detailed and *long*. As it turned out, I had misread the amount: the order was actually $1,660—and that was wholesale, the single largest card order that I have ever had—to this day, anyway.

I needed to sit down. I couldn't even imagine how to begin. We are talking about 84 dozen cards and 400 bookmarks to *one place*. The list of the code numbers was scary to say the least. The place was The Indian Pueblo Cultural Center in Albuquerque. I called my rep so we could chat about this and I could find out how this happened. In our phone conversation she could sense, without being a mind reader, that I was overwhelmed, blown away, and basically at a total loss as to how to begin, let alone get a grip and produce that order. She calmed me down first, and I will never forget the simplicity of the lessons I learned through her words: "Gloria, just take your time and break it down into workable parts. Split it in two, if you want. This is not a rush order, and in doing it, you will learn a lot about your production capabilities and you will be able to refine your methods by figuring out how to organize this one big order. You are in business, you know! This is good news! Right?" Use this as a "learning opportunity." It took 15 days to pace and complete the order. (During the same time I was also preparing for my first art show.) It took one whole day just to pack everything. At the end of wrapping it up to ship in two large boxes, I felt satisfied and smiled on the way to the Post Office, and smiled even more when I got to deposit a big check 30 days later. Along the road of those 2+ weeks, I hit bumps of sheer boredom and exhaustion. Where do you go with that? And we are talking year-after-year here, not one little isolated incident with one order…

People who take many hours to make one card using all kinds of mysterious techniques and supplies experience a distinct kind of pure satisfaction from that accomplishment—and that is something perhaps I will dive into and revel in someday, but I frankly can't imagine it right now. And many people have told me that they cannot fathom how I can stand to make 3-dozen of the same card for an order and then hundreds, even thousands of the very same cards over time. It sounds so monotonous and boring.

What is your "cringe factor"? What makes me cringe? Here's an example: some of the designs from my sets are more labor-intensive than others. That is a nice way of saying that some cards I designed and was foolish enough to put out in the public domain for consumption, are a big pain-in-the-backside to produce in any quantity greater than one—my whole Holiday Line, for example. I see on a Purchase Order the code letter "H" for "Holiday" and then I hear myself moan—audibly. There are so many details in these cards and I have to do layers of work on them. Score all the cards, stamp the backs (3 separate images), cut all the papers, glue, stamp, let it dry, do the coloring, spray, glitter glue, dry *again*, fold, etc… and I just want to get it over with, carve a new simple Southwest image, whack it out in black ink and be finished in 1/10 the time; same money/less time-consuming. But Christmas does come every year. What are my options when faced with the boredom and frustration that are inherent in this business? For starters, here are some of the choices before me:

1) Quit making cards all together
2) Omit the cards from the line that are particularly "painful" to do
3) Take a hot bath every 2 hours during production
4) Figure out how to change my perception of the task at hand

For me, #1 is not an option or a choice that I would make at this time. #2 is a good idea—then you get to freshen things up with new designs that are more creator-friendly, and your *buyers* are not bored looking at the same cards year-after-year. If, however, they flip-out because you have cut out a fabulous seller for them, consider making an exception. I have done that, and not only do you make a customer beam with gratitude but you go back to your old nemesis-card and do happy-battle once again, knowing that it is just one dozen, no big deal—there *is* an end to this. #3 needs to be re-negotiated to perhaps every evening *with* scented candles and #4 is the key to victory. Everyone has his or her own set of keys, and I will share some of mine.

The task at hand is repetitious—this is true. The number one key is to start by admitting and accepting that as fact. Do not fight it; it *is* a fact. Designing a card is interesting—making a dozen and seeing them lined-up for the first time is rewarding. Getting orders for the card is encouraging. Producing the same card for dozens of orders over years can be a drag. It is a task rather on the mindless side of life in a way, and that can be *relaxing*, how about that? I do not have to create something from scratch when I get an order and stress out over it. I pull Card # GL 27 from my master set, put it up on my little display shelf above my drafting table and make one dozen of them. That's all. Simple. Listen to music. Sing. Don't bother to over-think the work and just do it. If you are into "thinking," then channel it and make it productive. If you meditate, this kind of time can be a variation: "Zen and the Art of Making Zillions of Cards." Find a rhythm in some music and in your mind that works. James Taylor never fails me. A good audio book or program is stimulating. Run outside for a minute and drink in the sun or rain, make a snowball, throw it as far as you can, go back inside, sit down and keep going.

I don't like being "bored." I do enjoy what we call in our family "peaceful feelings." These may very well be two sides of one of my many business coins. It is a toss that I am in control of in any given moment: "Boredom" or "Peaceful Feelings?" It's an easy call as to which I would prefer. I also gently remind myself of the following, in varying order depending on my mood and needs in the moment:

- I started this business to make money for my family and if I have orders it means that that is still happening—this is good news.
- A surprise along the way was the fact that I found that I was also doing it because I love the creativity and independence and don't want to give it up. Card orders are my bread-and-butter—thank goodness for bread-and-butter. It affords me the opportunity to experiment with other art mediums on the side.
- The challenge is to keep the repetition aspect in mind but not let it dominate my thinking. Keep moving with new ideas internally and act on them. My friend, artist Paul Jackson, told me that this exercise is a must-do: Take time each week, even if it is only for one hour, to do creative stuff just for *fun*, not for "the business," not for any other reason other than to play with new ideas and new tools. It took me a long time to *do* that instead of *thinking* how nice it would be if I did. I started to find different outlets of refreshment over time playing junior art explorer and consequently my horizons, business and attitude expanded.
- And sometimes, when I am just sick and tired of the whole thing, there is one thought that pulls me through every single time, bar none. I sit down, sit back in my chair, push it away from the drafting table and reminisce… it's the stories, those wonderful stories over the years that make it all worth it. The times with customers and the special times with my kids that could not have happened if I were not working at home. As for the customers, meet a few here:

I heard that a teacher from Germany bought 40 bookmarks once to take back to her students as her souvenirs from Santa Fe… that was a great feeling. I have to wonder where on earth are all of those countless cards, Masu boxes, tiles, jewelry pieces, framed pieces, etc. Many of my cards have been purchased by Japanese tourists in New Mexico and were taken back to Japan. I love the thought that my designs are in different parts of the world and are valued. My Mom's friend Toni, who became my friend, too, told me early on to "get an 800-number, no matter what, and put it on the back of every card." Okay, I did that. I have received calls from an Englishwoman in Hawaii, an artist in Vermont, a bookmark collector in Texas and the Smithsonian Institution in Washington, D.C. because of Toni's sage and welcomed advice. These are connections—connections to people and their own stories. When I hear that my cards were bought for that "most special Birthday," or because "I could only give your card to my wife for Valentine's Day," I am moved to tears. At one show, a woman came up to me and introduced herself—she was a former mayor of Columbia and told me that she had wanted to buy a special card for the mayor of Jefferson City for quite some time. Finally, she "discovered" my cards and found the perfect one—mayor to mayor. I love these stories and I cherish them. They are a kind of sustenance, a lifeline, when times are a little challenging and especially when times are very hard.

When you hear many times over and over that people "frame your cards" or "just can't toss them out" because they are "definite keepers," it is rewarding. When I heard from a Gallery owner that Matthew, a very nice person and collector of my creations, came in to buy a piece of mine to celebrate his new job, a congratulatory gift to himself, I celebrated with him and felt so honored that my artwork was his meaningful gift choice.

Recently I gave a talk at the University and at the end of my presentation, Missy McCormick, Philosophy Professor and totally "sparkling person," raised her hand and wanted to tell a story of her own: One day she spoke with three friends on the phone—all in different places—all were going through major things in their lives. After receiving their "news," she had an idea—she got up, walked to Poppy downtown in order to buy three of my cards to send to each of those special people. Putting her heart onto the blank page, they were addressed, stamped and sent. Calculating when they would be received by each of her friends, sure enough, they all called her. She had sent "the perfect message in the perfect card…" I cried when I heard that one, too. How wonderful. There I am in my basement in the middle of nowhere really, dinking around with rubber stamps, inks and papers, making cards and sometimes having a hard time cranking out one more, just one more, and then I realize that this very card may be destined for a special moment in someone's life… I can keep going for a very long time with that thought in mind.

Boredom and burnout are treatable conditions and they also may be gentle warning signs if we listen and don't panic. It is good to examine the direction we are going in and take the time to reflect. Perhaps a time for change is presenting itself. We don't have to lose everything we worked hard for if we stand on the foundation and build up and out. I love Frank Lloyd Wright's design of the home that became known as "Fallingwater." Its organic natural structure grew from the land loved by the owners. The design wrapped itself around the sounds of water, nestled in trees, an architectural statement in its understatement. The house was built up and out of the landscape. I want my business to be similarly built—around my natural creativity, curiosity and ability to be flexible and adaptable. I want what I do on the outside to be an extension of who I am internally. A solid foundation allows me the freedom to experiment, the confidence to make new statements. I can figure out in time the way to hang on to some things and let others go. At that very moment, boredom and burnout are non-existent. I can work through it.

And trust me here, for an Aries woman born in the Chinese Year of the Horse, to have persevered for many years in a row with basically the same task at hand—to not have torched the whole thing and galloped away—if there is hope for me, there is hope for most people.

Are all of these points just a series of mental gymnastics to keep myself pumped up? Sure they are. I am trying to inspire myself to push past momentary doldrums and get to a new starting line. When people say to me "thank you for creating those wonderful cards," I say "you're welcome and thank you for buying them and appreciating them." When people asked me "what new things are you working on now?" I usually have an interesting answer. There is always something new, at least in the idea stage.

I love this: Picasso was asked which was his favorite painting out of all of his prolific work. His answer: "The next one."

I'm sure no Picasso, but where's that next order—I'm ready.

Therapy:

American Heritage Dictionary definition:

1) Treatment of illness or disability   2) Psychotherapy   3) Healing power or quality.
   (*ouch!*)   (cringe)   (…ah, yes…)

There is the 50-minute hour for the price of $90.00, worth every penny, I say. You can always squeeze in a few extra minutes, walking out the door and down the hall. That is certainly one form of therapy. There are others. I like asking people to chat about their personal healing balms, and I especially like having the time to sit and listen to their answers. The range is vast, from doing artwork in the middle of the night to writing in journals, acting, spending lots of money, secretly binging on chocolate, you name it. Getting hugs from my husband, being in the presence of my two kids when they are thoroughly enjoying each other and phone calls from my Mom are high on my own list.

For two months now, I have been experiencing the most intense period of time in my business life ever. Nearing the completion of this book, I can't even begin to describe the intensity of what was coming at me and expected of me. Most of it is great, wonderful, inspiring, hopeful stuff. My friend Janet asked me if I had made a list of all the projects I am involved in, and I couldn't muster the energy to add the making of a list to all the rest, even at the risk of forgetting something important. My plate is overflowing, potential is screaming in living color on my personal horizon, and here I am—catatonic.

I choose that word rather than depressed because it is a better fit—I am more "tired" than "out of it." A professional would have a heyday with me, and also some tidy, nifty label to stick on my forehead, but I can't afford the luxury of making an appointment for clarification purposes—this will have to do. In reality, I have never been this high up as far as acclaim goes. Yet there have been many days recently when I wake up and all I want to do is bury my head in my pillow and pretend it is not really as late as those darn little blinding, buzzing red neon numbers on the clock tell me it is. I buy a little more time. Then, after feeding my kids and making the beds in order to prove that I am still somewhat "together," loving my kids and honoring civilization, I head to the shower and hide out there so that I don't have to make any decisions about planning the day any sooner than absolutely necessary. Success is oppressive? What is the deal with me?

I partially cloistered myself at the risk of certain friendships becoming endangered, knowing that the genuine ones would endure. The other side of me sought out advice in the form of a few people, books, a movie: *Finding Forrester*, and several in-your-face sessions looking in the mirror. (Sean Connery's character, by the way, is an author in seclusion. He meets the world and himself again through Jamal, a black kid from the Bronx. Great, great stuff in there, including a fabulous rendition of "Over the Rainbow / What a Wonderful World.")

I was helped by all these "medications," and even though I wasn't able to pinpoint everything, some themes seemed to surface on a regular basis. Things like the fact that even though I keep hearing: "*that* idea will make you a *fortune*" to whatever I put my hands to, at the same time I see the checks being written endlessly and the ones to be cashed few and far between. "This is *planting the seeds* time," I tell myself over and over again. "Read your own book for inspiration," other people tell me over and over again: "you already have the answers." Thank you. I do appreciate that. I know what chapters you are referring to. I wrote it, but I just can't *do* it right now. Here's what I would like to know: what about *harvest time?* I'm curious. Does it ever come? Is it here and I'm missing it entirely? And what if my confidence is shredded even though I have proof all around me that that stance is unnecessary and basically a bunch of nonsense? Looking directly in front of me, I notice that I have two hands and way too much to do. All this business of chasing horizons and rainbows can go on for only so long without arriving. My husband compares this kind of time to a nice, humble, sweet little worm on a rainy street trying desperately to get to the lush green lawn… just…… right…… over…… there…………… The *last* thing she needs is a sunny day or traffic… She may just need a little more time.

As I commiserate here, I am in the thick of it, about an inch past the halfway mark out of the fog en route to the lawn. I am looking for substance, not a spotlight, and most definitely I want to be immersed in and baptized by the humor of it all. The minute you can laugh at yourself and the entirety of your circumstances, it starts to turn around. I want a sense of success, not flashy and self-aggrandizing, no need for statuettes or speeches at podiums: "success" more along the lines of receiving the gift of a tiny little box, simply wrapped, tied with a ribbon of peace with a touch and scent of quiet satisfaction inside. Fits in the palm of your hand, slips easily into a pocket—call it …fulfillment.

Can this actually happen? Can the whole picture get so completely out of focus that the vision feels lost? Even though you want to be the one to paint it rosy and clear for everyone else—can you admit that it gets so painful and lonely sometimes that crying hard and taking a long nap are the only things that feel comforting? It's okay. I just did.

On the other side of a two-and-a-half hour, "only seven-cents-a-minute" talk with my Mom on the phone, I received this e-mail:

"Gloria—I think that this is what therapy is all about. When we get lost, blocked, immobilized, sucked down into the black hole, sometimes what we need is a person guide to help us find our way back to "our own answers"—the answers that we own—our own truths—the answers that we have forgotten—the answers that we haven't found / heard in our own selves yet. Sometimes guides (and guides can be books also) give us some of "their" answers (as a help, a stepping stone) and when that resonates in us, it's because the words they choose are different than ours, but the meaning of their answer is like our own answer, within us. And in that way, the "real spirit" of our "true answers" connect us all, in a very deep way.   Love you, Ma" (Love you, too, Gloria)

■

> The soul would have no rainbow
> if the eyes had no tears.
> - Native American Proverb (*Minquass*)

> Rain beats a leopard's skin, but it does not wash out the spots.
> - African Proverb (*Ashanti*)

162

When two hands are not enough...

...what do you do at that point?

Growing a third hand is not an option. Extending the day and the week past the 24/7 limit will not work either. What do you do when you are a success-of-sorts and have orders that surpass your ability to produce them in a timely fashion? I slammed against the wall of great expectations, cried, blew my nose and figured out that I had a limit that was reached. It is an interesting point to arrive at. I didn't expect or anticipate it in time to have a plan in place. I had built a business that became bigger than me.

I will skip way ahead of that moment and say in retrospect that I have always remained a one-person operation. It's my style. When my style got cramped, I learned ways to strategize time and refine my systems. I also learned how to receive help from friends to get me through rush times that required temporary bailing-out: putting large quantities of cards in plastic sleeves, for example. My mother helps tremendously by taking on time-consuming tasks for me such as pulling threads from tapestry fabrics for particular card designs and doing the tinwork for another line. We mail supplies/finished products back-and-forth to each other and my workload is significantly lightened. Last week she broke her right arm so I am losing *my* "right arm" for this holiday season. So much for hiking in the mountains to see aspen in the fall just before your 70th birthday. She's going to be fine, and so will I.

It is a big question for every small-business person to face and to answer: Should I hire someone to work for me? There are many angles to consider, personally and legally. Do you like working alone or do you enjoy other people's energy and input around you? Will there be a creative-friction-factor to consider if you share your studio? How much are you willing to pay per hour? What is fair and how much are you able to let go of and still make it work? Do you have to set up all kinds of legal structures to cover yourself and your employee(s)? Taxes, insurance, "independent contractor status," ouch! I get lost and confused by all the issues, so I just go downstairs and work all through the night. So much for big solutions from me.

My friend Ken who makes (many) thousands of cards each year, decided at one point to hire a high school student to work with and for him. It worked well for quite some time. After seeing my Rollataq adhesive system machine and ordering one the very same day, he found that his production time was reduced enough for him to be able to reconsider the need for paying another person to work. The student was moving on to other things, so it was a good time to rearrange. Ken works solo once again.

As far as the legal issues are concerned in hiring other people to work for you, that is not my forte, so I will just say that it is very important to look into it and make a decision with your eyes wide open. An "independent contractor" working for you gets paid as an employee but works supposedly "away" from your workplace—not very convenient in many cases, convenient in others. Insurance and taxes aside, my biggest issue was always that I needed to make as much money as possible on every order, since I was mostly wholesaling and that already puts a crimp on profit percentages. Paying a rep 15% is in a sense paying an "employee" already. My desire to pay a helper "well" would mean that I would not be making enough to make it worth it with the quantity of business I was taking in. So, I ended up working longer hours and figuring out with my rep what was the

163

best way to space orders based on my production rate. It all has worked out. But I have a ceiling over my head by working with "two hands only."

A woman in Missouri who started out needing to repair a damaged screen on her screen door, ended up creating an angel with a piece of that screen and a huge business followed from those humble beginnings. Dodi Eisenhower of Village Crafts employs *many* people and ships internationally. It is important to explore options such as hers. It did not happen overnight—it was a process over time that did become very successful.

Another way of getting help is also a way of giving help at the same time. My friend Janet makes art quilts and a student at the University Fine Arts Department, Beth, is her apprentice. It is a fabulous arrangement for both of them: Beth gets college credit for working with Janet five hours a week, and Janet gets help with sometimes mundane, oftentimes very creative tasks and doesn't have to pay money for having the help. It is mutually beneficial. Listening to them each talk about the other is a treat. It turned out to be a good "match" arranged by Jo Stealey, the University professor who made it happen. A student connected to a local working artist—they are learning a lot from each other and having a great time in the process. Now they have four hands and more than double their energy generated. If it is the right combination of personalities and art styles, it works.

There is a possibility that I could also connect to such an arrangement. Several students that I met in a Creative Process Class at the University have expressed an interest to work with me in my studio. Now that the studio is set up in a way that can definitely accommodate two people easily, I am considering it. Perhaps a student from the Art Department would be interested in an apprenticeship with me as a cardmaker or tilemaker. Once again, as with Janet and Beth's working-relationship, I believe it could be mutually beneficial—and fun. Whatever happens, the idea deserves to be planted and developed when the timing is right.

There are times when I have "part time help" that makes a big difference in the way things operate. My husband and I are a good team. When I have a design idea, for example, hanging display boards for my booth, I come up with the plan and the basic structural components, and Gary will take it from there. He is very creative at the hardware store and comes back with handy-dandy innovative supplies; then the idea becomes reality. He devised an ingeniously simple way to hang boards in an outdoor booth, and now other vendors have gone from admiring his concept to using it on their own boards. When we put up the tent, our son Brandon joins in to help, and I thoroughly enjoy and appreciate this "team effort" aspect of my business that finds me usually alone.

On the other side of happy stories, there are stories that have not-so-happy endings and it is important to consider that not all "partnerships" were made in heaven, to last "until death do us part." A friend of mine was in a silk-screening business with a partner for years. It appeared that all was well and successful until it was discovered that the partner was less than honest about the reality of money matters, and without knowing more than that, I can say that a disaster followed that caused great financial hardship to my friend's family. Disillusionment, betrayal, depression, and fear—these are all very real possibilities in life in general. I have always felt cautious, particularly in my business, and step slowly and carefully. Having a business partner can be a successful venture or not. I would give a lot of serious thought to the idea before doing it.

Another cautionary note, not for the sake of discouragement, but for the sake of using experiences to learn from… Another friend of mine started out making handmade cards using stamps. At one point she designed a whole line based on her watercolor paintings and decided to get into "printing." It would save so much of that precious and rare commodity we call *time*. It was a good idea, but the problem became this: In order to get the price breaks on printing that make it all worth it, the quantities are usually quite large. The bottom-line is that she over-extended herself and had a huge printing bill that turned into a debt. She couldn't predict which of her cards would be the bestsellers and since she probably had too many styles to begin with anyway, and did not go deep enough with what eventually would become bestsellers, she was stuck with thousands of cards sitting on shelves, making her miserable instead of making her money. She was able to surface, but it is a story worth considering and learning from. Research and experimentation with reasonable risks are probably good ideas.

One person working alone can accomplish a lot. In my case, with the additional help I have described, it works just fine for me. As for increasing the amount of money I can make working with just my own two hands, I have options. I am in the process of developing more expensive card lines that actually take almost exactly the same amount of time to produce as the standard cards, with slightly higher supply costs, but have a significantly higher profit margin. I can make more money in the same amount of time *or* I can make the same amount of money in less time. This helps when you have a family to love and take care of at the same time you are trying to do a home business. The design and licensing arena is wide open and that is a fabulous way to expand the business— design once, let others manufacture from your originals and receive the royalty checks as you design more new ideas. Then there is also more "free time" for the purely creative side of art and your spirit is nourished. The beginning stages of this are in motion at this time. I am also in the process of moving into totally new areas of art all the time.

Janet's friend Beth just happened to write a book recently for a school project in graphic design. I just happen to be at a juncture with this book where I need graphic design help, so I called Beth and we are going to team up to see this through. I can learn from her and she can benefit from working on a project that goes beyond the classroom. Some teams are just meant to be.

As it turned out, Beth took my original cover artwork and basic concept and designed the cover of this book. I am so happy with it and grateful to her. We were a good team because the ideas could flow between us and there were no ego issues to get in the way. She wanted to connect with the spirit of my own vision for the book, and I respected her and trusted that she could get us there. I could not do it alone. "Cover artwork by Gloria Page. Cover design by Elizabeth Howard." That is very satisfying to both of us.

In terms of expanding your business by hiring people to work for you, there are a number of good books available that cover topics such as these in detail. Check them out in the Crafts or Business sections of your local bookstore. Check out books from the library. They are a valuable resource, especially if there are legal questions involved. The best idea is to be informed rather than be intimidated and in the dark.

As always for me, the best resources of all are people close by and in the art world who have been there and done that, and are willing to share their stories, good and bad. Those lessons are invaluable, a practical, usable inheritance—if I am listening. Growing a business has different challenges, even in the middle of success. One of the things that grows with the business is your own self-confidence, a key ingredient to that "success." With confidence, you can make decisions that direct the ever-expanding next stage.

A BIGGER *company isn't necessarily* better
When "getting somewhere" might find you in the same seat…

There can be so much hype about building a *big* business, a *big* bank account, really *getting somewhere* in life and proving it, that it can become very easy to lose sight of a simple fact: bigger is not always better. High quality things can come in tiny packages. Huge hearts can exist in compact people—Mother Theresa comes to mind.

It's a wild time with all the excitement and drive to make it in the big world of e-commerce and the dot-com universe. There are stories of farmers' wives in the middle of the countryside in rural, basically Middle Ages Ireland, raking in big bucks from their websites, with these major advertising agencies sending their push people into sheep-country to try and talk these entrepreneurs into going "big time." Some do and some don't—there is a risk either way. Go too big too fast and it is slip/slide down the slippery slope. On the other hand, miss the big wave when it is cresting and you just might find yourself in low tide sitting on a surfboard in the muck, stuck and going nowhere fast.

I met a woman who sold just two cards—one for ten dollars and the other for twenty dollars. That may well be it for her "card business." That may be enough satisfaction and affirmation of her talent or need for extra cash and so that may be it for whatever reason. Another woman I know has one account only. That is her "business" and it is the perfect size—that cozy place of knowing that you can produce very lovely, time-consuming cards at a pace that works after a long day working at the Red Cross under stress—two accounts would be too much right now. It is very important to know that about yourself and wear it like a comfortable sweater—snuggly warm and a good fit for the season.

Rather than push my own business to get bigger and bigger by hiring people, etc., I actually went in the opposite direction and made it smaller in order to redefine it. That's a little scary, but I felt resilient and sure enough of my footing to surf the distance to a new shore. The names of the business over time tell part of the story. From the original:
- *Folklands* and then on to:
- *Impressions Handstamped Cards*
- *Impressions Handstamped Originals*
- *ImpressionsArt Cards*
- *ImpressionsArt*
- *ImpressionsArt Designs*… where we are today.

I can see other developments in the future, and name changes, subtle as they may be, will reflect those changes. *Designs* is the biggest single word statement in the above list. That signifies a major shift from production to designing, a dream for many years and now a reality-in-the-making. My business is still small in that it means my two hands, but the scope is changing, moving now into the world of printing. I have been knitting this particular sweater for eight years and it is almost ready to try on. It feels right.

We have the power to decide, to take detours, race in the fast lane or hike solo on foot. Getting a little stepladder view of my own situation, I am thoroughly enjoying the fact that the stories that at times seemed so isolated and unrelated, are now weaving together. There is a big picture composed of many smaller ones. My take on the whole experience is that the key ingredient has been one over-riding theme: just keep going. My drafting table has been with me for thirty years—the work being done on the surface has changed a lot. I am still short, yet my ideas get bigger all the time.

Mistakes and Accidents
Crisis or Opportunity?

Making mistakes and having things go wrong are not my favorite activities. I like it when life is fairly smooth sailing with interesting twists and turns but not a whole lot of turbulence: so much for wishful thinking.

When I was a really little girl I had this wonderful place to play in our basement. It was behind an old bar and there were shelves to set up toys. My mother had given me this wonderfully delicate tea set that had been hers when she was a child. This was in the treasure category since it was "My Mom's" and she gave it to *me*. It was so special.

I dusted each piece, washed and carefully lined them up. Tea parties for my dolls were an occasion, a private affair. I never let another "regular" person touch them in case they would break something. So I did it instead. I broke the fragile handle off of one of the teacups. It was an accident, a mistake, a heartbreak, and I cried for a very long time. The glue I had didn't work and I was afraid to make it even worse. It was a major bind to be in—I needed help to learn what I could use to fix it, but to talk would be to give the secret away. After asking a couple of adults some very oblique questions and getting nowhere kinds of answers, I gave up. I hid the cup by wrapping it in Kleenex, tucking it way back in a corner, hoping my mother wouldn't come downstairs and count them up and find out that one was missing. For days I cried myself to sleep.

Were those tears of fear? No, they weren't. I just couldn't believe that I had broken something so special to my mother and I couldn't bear to tell her. About twenty years later on a plane flight with my family when everyone got into this "let's confess all our secrets, why don't we?" mood, I finally told my mother that I broke her teacup. She couldn't believe that I had held onto that for so long and I couldn't either. It felt great to smile together, let it go, and know that everything was all right now. Neither one of us is sure where the set is, but we are absolutely sure that it isn't the best idea around to hold onto something like that for so many, many years…

A list of mistakes and accidents would be profoundly and perhaps disturbingly long, so I would like to make the point here in a straightforward way: Mistakes and Accidents can be opportunities and, as much as possible, I try to handle them that way. When my little boy Bryan was about two, he took an inked brayer and rolled it across 24 newly made bookmarks destined for the Case Trading Post at the Wheelwright Museum. He was playing and I was tired. Luckily for him and for me, I had just learned how to do a simple technique of sponging ink with torn paper that made a nice textured look. The bookmarks, when renovated, were better than my original design and from that point on, I often used "the Bryan effect" to add some character and color.

Trying to employ a positive approach to mess-ups can be rewarding and also a stretch at times. Recently I spent a lot of time on handmade tiles that are going to be part of collaborative pieces with my friend Janet. I took the tiles home to expedite the drying time and in the process noticed that the St. Francis tile was a tiny bit warped. Being very new to the clay world, I then proceeded to make a mistake, pressed down on it, and accidentally broke the tile. I felt almost as sick about this as I did about my mother's teacup, but I didn't cry, just got upset. Did I call Janet and tell her? No, not yet, but I suspect that I will get to it before too many years slip away.

We have a deadline for an entry to *Somerset Studio* Magazine in about two weeks. There is not enough time to make a new tile. After trying unsuccessfully to mend it with clay, I walked away wondering what to do. I have rarely thrown anything away that I have messed up and almost always come up with a rescue plan that improves the original concept. This time I felt more stuck because someone else was involved—this was not a solo blunder. Janet's beautiful quilt was supposed to be attached to this tile. Wandering around the house, I finally decided to look at a magazine to clear my mind. It just so happened that I picked up a *Somerset Studio* and turned to the article on artist Nick Bantock. And there it was, right in front of my face, a quote from Nick Bantock himself:

"It's the nasty and the accidents that form the foundation for elegance that comes later."

After laughing and thanking Nick, I went and looked at the tile again, playing with the possibilities. It is going to be very cool and definitely strong and probably stronger than it would be if I hadn't broken it. It was damaged but not destroyed. I learned about a glue that will work. It can be more than fixed—it can be re-created. The potential is staring me in the face. It will be more multi-dimensional than what I have done before, and I have wanted to make that leap. Apparently, it's time. I left a note at the Craft Studio where it will be fired that went something like this:

"Hi—thanks for doing the tiles. I AM THE ONE WHO BROKE THE TILE and I am determined to save it… so fire away!………….thanks…"

Several months ago, someone other than me broke a finger off of a "hand" tile I had made—the little finger was separated from the rest of the hand. I must say it looked pretty weird. It got fired and glazed anyway—it could be saved, or least I could try. I found the kind of epoxy that would work, re-attached the pinky, took a real piece of turquoise and fashioned a striking Southwest pinky ring to cover up the crack. That was not part of the original plan. It improved the design significantly. Who knows? It might even make it into a magazine someday. It is being saved as a possibility. (PS: Guess what? That very tile made it into a *book*, mind you! Sharilyn Miller's second book, entitled: *The Stamp Artist's Project Book: 85 projects to make and decorate*. Rockport Publishers. Check out page 125 and the Contents page. Some mistakes get a second life.)

I do not want to appear to be living in a state of suspended animation where life's trials and problems do not affect me—I am trying to even the keel for the long haul. Personally, I have a hard time with the concept that "everything happens for a reason." Sometimes that fits and helps and is amazingly accurate, but at other times it just misses the mark completely. I can use that way of thinking to manipulate my own thinking, if I'm honest enough to admit it. For example: "I got lost driving to Iowa. I probably avoided a car accident by ending up in Milwaukee instead, so I got lost for a reason…" Yeah, sure, but another way of looking at it could be along these lines: "Man, I got lost big time. I listened to verbal directions and figured I could wing it without looking at a map. That was a waste of time and gas: stupid me. Next time I will look at the map and learn something about this part of the country in the process. Milwaukee is not on the way to Iowa City when you start out in Chicago." It is far better to own it than to make excuses or conjure up cosmic reasons of how it was "meant to be" or must certainly be *someone else's fault.* My kids have heard this before in various forms from me, for sure: "I own my mistakes. It's up to me what I do with them. So, own yours." That, in fact, is extremely liberating. It is a waste of energy to manufacture excuses and accusations.

Mistakes and accidents with "things" and "places" are a lot less volatile and critical than blunders made with people. If a handmade card is really, truly bad, just rip it up and throw it into the recycling bin—it will become handmade paper at least. On the other hand, throwing people away isn't an option, and some relationships can be extremely hard to save, recycle or repair; others need only a few minor adjustments. In respect to interpersonal problems, whatever creative efforts we may make, gluing pieces of turquoise on top of rifts won't help, and sweeping things under carpets only creates huge mounds to trip over. In a realistic/optimistic way, I will always hold tight to the belief that there is hope on the other side of mistakes and accidents. How to *get* to the other side is one of the reasons for the existence of things like religion, philosophy, therapists, punching pillows, and "Tension Tamer Tea" by Celestial Seasonings.

Note: I called Janet one day after writing this. She laughed and said that mistakes on her art quilts are "the starting point for something new and better." I was given a vote of confidence from the only person whose vote counts when it comes to the St. Francis tile fiasco. I later ended up making a completely new tile since I wanted it wider and with no cracks—visible or invisible—and added real turquoise chips to the design. We went on to complete the project together. The finished piece was just right. It went on to Espiritu Gallery in Colorado and was sold during the holiday season. It has a home now.

When written in Chinese, the word 'crisis' is composed of two characters—
one represents danger and the other represents opportunity.

— President John F. Kennedy—
▪

I am not discouraged,
because every wrong attempt discarded
is another step forward.

—Thomas Edison—
▪

Jump into the middle of things, get your hands dirty, fall flat on your face,
and then reach for the stars.

—Joan L. Curcio—
(American Educator)
▪

Learn from the mistakes of others—you can't live long enough
to make them all yourself.

—Martin Vanbee—

"Gloria, get back up on your horse—make three more tiles."

There can be a point when you have just had it—enough is enough. You work on something for hours, days, weeks on end, there is a deadline that you are crunching and even though the artwork objectively speaking is beautiful, you are sick to death of it. I did a collaborative piece with my friend Janet—we called it "Autumn Fairy." There is a lovely quilted fairy dancing in the leaves and I made a big leaf tile to be the header for the piece. I sketched, drew, transferred the design to a carving block, carved, prepared the clay and stamped it out. It was then carefully dried for weeks, bisque-fired for two days and gingerly transported to a big farm to be Raku-fired. We had all kinds of challenges with the size of the piece, so after I glazed it, I had to dig a special pit in the ground so it could be "smoked" in the pit separately. There were so many steps and potential pitfalls with this that it is beyond my patience to write it all down. The first firing was a less than thrilling color—it was precariously fired again—and it was just beautiful.

I treated this tile like it was made of paper-thin glass. The color of the glaze was perfect with the fairy and after I had made the secure attachment between quilt and tile, I wrapped it with bubble wrap and towels, layers of protection. I had one morning, one window of an opportunity to have it professionally photographed before I sent it out to California for my first to-be-published article I had written myself. It was the culmination of months of work and preparation and a team effort—I picked up the box to bring it to the studio to be photographed and heard "ping." I felt sick as I lifted the towel and there it was—cracked, straight across the tile—gone. Forever.

These tears just flew out of my eyes. I could not wish or will the tile back together. I tried gluing it with epoxy, but it showed. Even though at that seam it would last until the end of time itself—it *showed*—you can't have glue and cracks showing. That was it. Gone. And there was no time; not enough anyway to go through that all over again…

The sick feeling stuck in my gut. I got into the car and did this zombie-drive to the university to get other tiles for the article. My internal plan was to say nothing. I did not want to make a fool out of myself by crying over a broken tile since I had by that time reasoned with myself that there were tragedies worthy of the level of emotions I was feeling, and a cracked tile was not high up on that list. Still, it represented a lot of work and was tied into my friend's work, too—bummer to the max.

A very quiet "good morning" to the folks at the Studio, shuffle around, get the other tiles together, and then my Raku teacher happens to show up. Oh, no. I do my greeting thing, shuffle around some more, and ask if he would like to see other slides I had before sending them off to California as part of the submission. Regular nice chitchat, so I thought, and then I just came out with it: "I broke the leaf tile this morning." "I wondered what was up with you. Gloria, get back up on your horse—make three more tiles—now." "But, Joe, there isn't time. The studio is closed for vacation tomorrow, the tiles won't have time to dry, and then all the firings; it will never work." "We can work around all that. I'll roll out the slab for you. I'll take my kids with me here to the Studio on Sunday and show you how to dry them quickly. The firings will happen—don't worry—other people's pottery can go in together with yours. We can pull this off—it is going to work."

170

It did. And it was crazy. Out of three new tiles, one cracked as it was drying—goodbye. Two made it to the Raku firing, but it had rained so much for too many days that it took five hours just to dry out the kiln and took two more hours to fire two tiles after that, pushing it way past midnight. It was a dark, starry night, and with a flashlight in hand, we edited the article for *Somerset Studio* that would be entitled "The Tile Project" and appear in the November/December 2001 issue. The next tile came out a strange color of teal blue—not exactly "Autumn Fairy." The last that came out in the middle of the night was… perfect. I sent the submission; it made it in time. And can you believe this? It never made it to the publication—other pieces were chosen—*not* that one! Months later, I re-glazed the strange blue leaves, risking it, and it was beautiful. It came out of the kiln in the morning and sold that same evening at a local home-studio show. The "Autumn Fairy" is hanging in a gallery in Colorado Springs—we'll see. What I learned through this experience was the obvious—sometimes all that grit and determination we thought we had needs some help—a boost into the stirrup. Whether that particular tile got into the magazine or not, whether it gets sold or not, in the big picture, it simply doesn't matter. Not giving up—that does matter.

Altogether there were four big leaf tiles; their fates are as follows:
- #1) now lives, repaired with epoxy strong enough to last forever, on Janet and George's garage. It catches the sunlight and looks lovely.
- #2) That tile got recycled into the clay abyss at the Craft Studio and is now probably part of a pot somewhere.
- #3) was re-glazed, transformed into stoneware, and found a home in my friend Alan's collection of "Leaf Things."
- #4) did not sell at the gallery in Colorado, smashed to bits in the box shipped back to me, and caused me to pause and wonder. After all this big production over creating this tile that not only did not make it into the magazine, it did not sell at the gallery and now is a pile of shards with no apparent historical significance—now what? I laughed. Let's see, how can we make some good ending to this story out of all of this. How about this? Janet, whose lovely "Autumn Fairy" art quilt is connected to the smashed leaves said: "I think this piece just was not meant to be." Laughing again, I took another path in thought. Janet and I have a mutual friend, Barbara, who creates mosaics all over her house in an organic, never-ending creative exercise in home design. She would love Raku shards and if I am lucky, maybe these can find a home near some of the real ancient shards I gave her from New Mexico. Then I had a flash of an idea—galleries insure their return shipments, right (?), so why not claim the damage and get some compensation for the "loss." So I did—I got the money and recycled it right back into the business in the form of some tools and stamps that I otherwise would not have been able to afford—good idea? Defeat is not my favorite word, and I could not imagine that any Raku tile could ever be officially declared "trash." Janet took it even further, re-stitched the "Autumn Fairy," and without a tile, entered it in a contest, winning a place on the cover of a Calendar of Art Quilt Artists—great ending after all.

Morale is when your hands and feet keep on working
when your head says it can't be done.   - *Benjamin Morrell*

171

"...sorry, I don't do logos..."

Now *that* was a dumb thing to say.

The phone rang, and as usual, I let it go on the answering machine. Once I realized that it was some "State of Missouri Department of This or That" asking me about my business, I picked up, introduced myself and listened.

It was interesting. In a recent *Best of Missouri Hands Newsletter*, a few of my handcarved images had been featured as decorative elements. They were designs of "hands." I was pleased with them—they were simple and that-was-that as far as I was concerned—in a newsletter, over and out. The person on the phone had noticed those images and wondered if I would be interested in working up some similar designs for her department—some statewide art type organization—they needed a logo and wanted me to submit some ideas. As soon as I had a basic grasp of what she was talking about, I basically interrupted her and said: "Sorry, I don't do logos. I know of some professional graphic designers in town, and if you would like, I'd be happy to get names and numbers for you." There was a pause as she re-grouped and attempted to get me back into the conversation rather than letting me escape front and center. "There are plenty of graphic designers here in Jefferson City, Gloria, but we are not interested in pursuing that avenue. We have seen your work and we want *you*." "Oh, I see."

I carried on a bit about how I was honored and all that, but I had to be perfectly straight and honest—I have never done that kind of work before, and they really needed to understand that, but I was willing to listen to the format and give it a try. Which is what happened. It took a bit of time and wrangling to get me to that point.

Sure, I had done a cover design for a wonderful booklet called "Opening the window of your soul" for my friend, Gwen Ratermann. If you stretched the idea a bit, you could see it as a kind of logo. I had also designed a set of cards for Coyote Cafe in Santa Fe based on their logo—but I had not designed the logo itself—so that one didn't count. I had carved many hands, since that was my theme element for my business, but this was to be printed on 85,000 books and to be used as stationary letterhead, etc. I don't know about this—it's pretty much way over my head. I sat down, drew a sketch, carved away and the whole project, including going to Kinko's and making prototype examples of possible uses of color, added up to ten working hours. After consulting some friends in-the-know who advised me to charge between $25-$50 an hour for my "designer's fee," I chose $30, wrapped the stamp carefully and sent the nice package I had prepared along with a bill for $300, which was promptly paid. I guess I do logos now.

At a conference not long after that, I did see what they had in mind in print and I loved the variation on my idea. It inspired me to see how someone could take my work and add a personal artistic twist to it. I have no idea if it ever made it to the big time as far as mass production is concerned, and at one point it didn't even matter. I used the experience over and over in my thinking and in my daily business relationships. When something new comes along, I do not brush it away simply because I haven't done it before. I am still honest, but I am much more open and will say something along these lines: "This is new and it sounds exciting. I want to try it, and then you can see what you think. We'll go from there." I am not so quick to send the business elsewhere due to lack of confidence or experience. There is only one way to get and build both of those—try.

Brochures

It is inevitable. You have this business started and people always ask you for two things: your business card *and* a brochure. Of course it is better if they don't have to ask and you offer them ahead of time, but who is *that* together from the get-go? Not me.

With all the new-fangled computer jazz around these days, really anybody can either make or have a business card made cheaply at Kinko's. Being a handmade card person meant that I have had almost an obligation to make my business cards by hand, which I still do. Some people became collectors and dropped by my booth at shows just to pick up the latest business card whether they made a purchase or not—fine with me. The *brochure* thing, though, kept me intimidated for way too long because I did not want to put out a lot of money for fancy four-color printing, knowing darn well that I was going to be making many changes and didn't want to be stuck with thousands of irrelevant pieces of pricey paper. Solution: I made my own using my 1940 Underwood Typewriter since that was during my B.C. era (Before Computer). I simply had run out of excuses as to why I didn't have a brochure or catalog of some sort.

With the old typewriter keys as a retro font, handcarved images throughout, and a photo of me walking towards a doorway in Santa Fe, my simple brochure was a hit. I received many compliments and was told that it was a "keeper" since it had "character," vs. a slick, generic, Madison Avenue look. Slick can be good and it can be effective, even crucial in some circles, but if you can't afford it like I couldn't, then there is no point whimpering about it and squirming with embarrassment every single time someone asks you for one. It is so easy and cheap to photocopy my own that I had a number of different ones for different occasions or points of emphasis.

Crank this thing up a notch and raise the bar if you have a computer and color printer/scanner, etc. Brochures are set up on 8½ x 11 paper divided into thirds. Create a front and back panel and put your jazzy artwork out there in color with all the fun fonts you want and print them out yourself. Not as cheap as using ancient typewriters and photocopiers, but still a whole lot cheaper than having them done professionally. One step at a time gets us to new places and a new look to match. Madison Avenue doesn't need to be all that far away if that is the destination. As for me, I'm more of a Center Street, Downtown, USA kinda girl.

Buy your own paper at Staples, Office Depot or some nice paper store if you want to, change the text whenever you feel like it, keep a running theme and color-scheme and *presto*. You are in business and you even look like it. It feels good to have no excuses.

We all have a desire to show what we have made. "Look at me, Mom!" It's the very same thing only a tad more sophisticated. Advertising, whether it is a brochure, pamphlet, website, postcard, flyer, invitation to an Opening, whatever form of communication—is a visual voice to wanting to share our creations, and we should find a means to that end. It is natural to want to show what we do, and invite others to enjoy it along with us.

Work is love made visible.

- Kahlil Gibran
The Prophet

Fine Arts, Fine Crafts, okay, fine:

- let's do an art show!
- and while we're at it, let's put our hearts on the line…

With all of the different shows around, indoor/outdoor, Fine-This and Fine-That, Art Here and Craft There, a certain type of delineation and (excuse me) a certain air of elitism, dare I say snobbery, hovers over part of the scene. What's the point I ask myself? Personally, I try to shake it off because I love it all. I would like a friendlier atmosphere and more mutual respect amongst all "branches" of the art tree.

I would like to reflect here on some of my own "show" experiences…

The first art show I "juried into," more honestly "skated into," happened to be a Fine Arts Show. I didn't realize it until it was too late, which turned out for the best in the long run. I was definitely more "crafts" as far as technique and experience at that time from my point of view, yet I sold well even though I felt rather out of place in a Fine Arts environment. Thanks to my first customers, I gained the confidence to keep going.

Having a fair amount of artwork left after the first show, I looked into and got into another Fine Art Show just two weeks later. It was in another town, Fulton, and they just happened to have one opening, and waived the jury process (whew!) because, well, "if you were in Art in the Park in Columbia last week, you certainly also belong here—no problem." A lucky break once again, since I had no slides to send them anyway. "Art by the Lake" went well, too, for the size of the turnout and all factors considered. At the first show, I made $1200 in retail sales; at the second I made a little over $600—not bad for two shows in two weeks, being the new kid on the block and all.

Two weeks after *that* another outdoor show possibility came up, this one in Boonville, Missouri, and it definitely had more of a country crafts feeling to it. Let's just say that I covered the booth fee and swallowed a lot of white chalky dust in the process. I made about $120 and learned a few things:

- #1: never do that show again because it wasn't a good fit for me and my artwork
- #2: research if at all possible *before* signing up in order to find the "good fits"
- #3: no matter how much of a bomb it is financially, there is always something(s) good that comes out of every major effort like that. In the case of the Boonville show, it was meeting a fellow vendor, Melynda Lotven, the "Gourd Lady" of Just Gourds, who became a good friend from that point on. It was worth going for the things I learned, especially for the person I met. Jefferson City was another disaster when I made only $150, but I was with my Mom visiting from New Mexico and the experience was going to be fabulous no matter *what* because we did it together, the preparation as well as the actual show. But I sure wouldn't do that one again. The distance and the time factors were not worth the money.

For the past five years I have done local shows, the largest being Art in the Park, which is the biggest outdoor art show in mid-Missouri. The best I have done in terms of sales was this past spring when I made over $1600 for the two days, not bad when my prices are low and pieces are small. Every year I consistently increased my sales and customer base. I am *not* the showgirl-in-the-know, however, as thousands of people are all over the country. It is a vast community, a traveling troupe of dedicated and extremely hard-working artists and craftsmen who make a living creating with their hearts and hands, getting on the road to offer the fruits of their labors to collectors and art enthusiasts all over the country. The range, caliber and unreal scheduling of these events are mind-boggling. The competition to jury into top-level National Shows is intense, and the monetary expenditures are substantial when you take booth fees, travel, overnight accommodations and product expenses into account. But it is all part of the "Art Scene" at this time, and the making and enhancing of reputations and status is all tied into the process. It is fascinating, exhausting, and lucrative enough for enough people to keep the cogs in this machine moving. I worry sometimes that the calendar is too packed with events and that the whole business will suffer on account of that. I believe that artists are also flexible and market-smart, able to handle the fluxes and shifts that naturally occur over time. The shows will get more creative and more specialized; the best will endure.

I have friends who do two shows a year. I have other friends who do more than twenty. For some, it has evolved into a complete life-style choice. There are "down months" as far as shows go, and that means premium production time. Building a stock is crucial if you are on the road long-distance for weeks on end once art/craft show season begins. There are folks who love to travel in large RV's, which include mini-workshops internally for on-the-road production to replenish stock as needed. That I can't imagine doing myself, but then again, when I saw couples parked at shows doing quilt-work and whittling side-by-side in lawn chairs chatting with us "customers," I was drawn in by the rhythm of their stories of life on the road.

There is a whole lot of sensitivity and controversy surrounding the creative arts as I alluded to in the first paragraph. I don't want to pick fights with anyone over the whole matter because there is enough combustion and friction to keep the fire going for a long time. When people ask me: "And what do you do?" I have squirmed for years and now have settled for the time being on: "I have an art business." Then comes: "What kind of art?" "I started with handmade cards and have been learning a lot of other things along the way." I find that in this way I am free to talk about the "things I enjoy creating" rather than defining and defending myself. My position is eternally "the beginner," which means I never have to be "the expert" at anything, and it is perfectly natural for me to say "I don't know" more often than not. The beauty of the whole approach is that I am squarely in a great position to learn *all the time*. When I do know something and have some valuable information to pass on, I am more than happy to share ideas and sources. The courtesy is returned and we all gain in the process.

Today I may be more in the craftsman mode, tomorrow in the artisan mode in the morning, artist in the afternoon and burnt-out by evening. I respect titles that have been earned by tremendous effort and blood on the tracks of the artist's Way , the artist's path. I will call *you* anything that you want to be called, that's fine with me. I just take issue with the attitude of superiority that relegates value to some and demeans others. I have seen my friends rejected from shows because they were "craft" and not "art." It can be true and it can even be helpful. But it can also hurt.

When I went through my own little rejection experience and my rubber stamp tools were looked down upon as "something akin to clip art," I didn't even know what clip art was at the time. Talk about ignorance. Here I was being insulted and I wasn't even well versed enough to understand the reference that was being made. As it turns out, I like certain kinds of clip art, now that I know a little bit more about it. I'm a big fan of the Dover Books Copyright-free Art Series. The heart of the point that was being made was loud and clear, though—you, Gloria, are a cut well below the realm of Art or Fine Craft. "Thank you for your deep insight," as we say in our house.

Shortly after that episode, I went to visit the largest indoor Crafts Show in this part of the state. It is HUGE. The Hearnes Center in Columbia in the fall is geared up for thousands of visitors. The crowds sweep you down the aisles—you might have to turn a corner and re-try an "exit" to a booth that you got swept past the first time around. I lived in New York City years ago—this Hearnes Center event is the closest thing to Grand Central Station at rush hour that I've experienced in the Midwest. The Hearnes Show is very "country" in style—I had never experienced anything like it before that first time. Here I am with this Southwest/Oriental thing going on in my brain waves and all of a sudden I am surrounded by bears, ducks, yard and door ornaments, all manner of cute and local-humor signage, and I am amazed as I watch people carrying tons of purchases to their cars, walkie-talkies in hand connecting with spouses to make pick-up arrangements for the rest of the haul! Incredible to watch; fascinating to be stampeded.

I had two friends with booths there and I love what they do with wool and with gourds—whimsical, comical, and I saw that they were doing well. Other than those two booths and a couple of others, I was in a foreign land in a way. This is not my style, but not because it is below me. I'm just not into "Country," though I do appreciate the skills involved. I was caught completely off-guard as an unexpected event began to unfold...

I was being shoved around the hall. I had just been through my own put-down about stamps and the cut was still stinging. It was not as a customer that I was taking in the experience of the Hearnes show—it was as a fellow crafter this time. As I was looking at each artist's face in that hall, each booth filled with endless hours of work to produce what would fill a 10x10 space to overflowing, I was moved. I saw so much hope in those faces that customers would buy and not just look and comment on how they "could easily make the same thing at home." My heart was completely open. I pulled away from the main crowd at one point and went to the out-of-the-way booths, probably newcomers or late entries. I glanced to my left and all I saw was lace, billows of it, and these little plastic doll heads sticking out. If I had distanced myself, I would have thought "hokey," and moved on. But I refused to be distant and a snob and I moved right in on this table. I looked at all of the work involved in sewing layer upon layer of lace tiers to create these dolls' skirts. Then I glanced up and saw the folks who made them. It was a farming family. They spoke quiet words with pleasant country accents for my New England ears. There was a shyness about all of them. I complimented the quality of the workmanship involved and the time-consuming nature of the design. "Why, thank you, Ma'am, it sure is kind of you to notice..." and all of a sudden the tears just started rolling down my face, a veritable fountain of warm tears. I double-swiped my cheeks several times, nodded a smile, reciprocated a quiet "thank *you* and good luck to you" and moved on.

Why the emotion? I had not been in the presence of an original Monet, Picasso, or O'Keeffe. I had not been awed by an Ansel Adams photograph in the Yosemite studio or excited by seeing R.C. Gorman walking down the street in Taos. I saw a Missouri farm family sitting behind their lacy dolls, the sincerity of their effort, and their hope that I would buy, that anyone, *someone* would buy. It just blew my heart to bits. Were they doing Fine Art, Fine Crafts, Country Crafts, craftsy-crafts not deserving any capital letters? It didn't matter, and to me it just doesn't matter ever. It was a home business and I felt a kinship far beyond the product. We all work very hard at this and put our hearts on

176

the line every single time, every single minute of every single show. Some people buy and more people walk by. Achieving the balance between sensitivity and stamina is all part of the experience. After that particular experience, I will never attend a show, either as an artist or customer, in the same way…

As for the practical aspects of *getting into* a show, I'd like to share some basics that may be helpful:

- If at all possible, visit shows under consideration first as a visitor, customer, and *potential* vendor and ask questions (without being nosey or annoying). Don't ever ask someone how much they make, but ask artists of similar taste and technique as yours if this is a good show for them and why? Do not monopolize time by chatting—spend time mostly *observing*. Is this an active selling show or are people interested only in looking at everything? Buy something yourself if you can.

- Find the Information Booth and get basic information—have your name put on a mailing list for the next show if it looks promising.

- Mark your calendar and do not miss the deadlines. There is very little space at shows and there is a lot of competition for those spaces. Out-of-town and out-of-state entries are likely. You won't get better treatment if you are local. If you are late with your entry, you may pay a late fee or forfeit the chance all together. In some cases you might get put on a waiting list, but I wouldn't count on it. That is not a good position to be in.

- If the process calls for a Jury and you are expected to submit slides, do *not* send your own attempts—get the slides done professionally. Ask around. It can be very costly or very reasonable. Good slides always make a difference with your acceptance possibilities. Always have your photos shot with only *one* featured art piece, not a collection. Four to six shots are standard. It can be more or less than that, but always follow the entry directions exactly. It is not the time to be creative. Do that later in your booth if you are accepted.

- If a booth slide is expected and you never did a show before—say that! Explain that you will be renting or buying a white Easy-Up tent or whatever and verbally explain in a few words what your set-up will look like. If it is a high fallutin' show, you probably won't get in, but get realistic and start smaller locally. You will get in somewhere and make steps from there.

- When you do your first show and every one after that, my suggestion is to take *both* color slides and color prints—either have two cameras, do one film one day and switch the next or co-ordinate with a friend who can help out as photographer. You will then have booth slides for upcoming applications that are current, and you will have visual documentation of your progress over time. I can't believe I made everything I see in my old photos. It is inspiring, and when I get blocked and need ideas, I go back and look at photos—very stimulating for getting new ideas rolling.

- This is not in any Rule Book, but it is my personal standard: when I am accepted, I immediately send a brief thank you note saying that "I sincerely look forward to participating in the upcoming show and will do my best to make a good showing in my booth." If rejected, my friend Susan says: "Just think, okay, what's next? And get on with it." She looks at the bigger picture, tries to learn something from the experience and sometimes (without malice) may contact someone in the Jury process to try to understand what happened and see if she can improve her next submission. If getting into that particular show is an important goal to shoot for and attain, it is worth following up.

- Pay everything on schedule.
- Hope for the best, do your best, and...
- If it is an outdoor show, pray it doesn't rain too much.

As for the practical aspects of how to *be there* in a show once you get in, a few points for consideration:

- Make your booth harmonious with your work—it is an extension of your art and the expression of your taste. It does not need to cost a lot of money. Creatively re-working "junk" from yard sales, etc. makes for interesting discussions in the booth. The props, however, shouldn't overpower the work.
- Set your artwork up *high* enough and don't make people bend down to look at things. The use of pedestals and different types of levels make for points of interest and allow you to showcase special pieces. Do not overcrowd, yet have backups available.
- Lighting is a key point, especially indoors.
- When you are in the booth, *be in the booth*! Customers love meeting the artist. It adds to the experience and entertainment value of the show. It is the main ingredient of a wonderful recipe—it goes way beyond "vendor and customer." People want a connection. Do *not* hide out in the back reading a book, even if it is related to your craft. Be available without being pushy. *Be there* is the point. Your personality needs to glow, not glare. If you are quiet, expressive, whatever, the most important thing is to be genuine and respectful of your customers' natures.
- This is one piece of advice that I have the hardest time with, so I will tape this to my forehead before the next show: "Do not get so over-stressed by working such insane hours for the two weeks before, that by the time the show comes, you are in the Twilight Zone." Exhausted artists may inspire some people, but if your speech slurs, your eyes squint in a vain attempt to engage in the simplest conversation, and you are worried that you will give the wrong change because your brain is on hold, it is time to re-assess. I can push to get ready, but adrenalin goes only so far for so long. Pace things down to realistic levels. Sounds great. We'll see if I can ever pull this one off.
- Price everything clearly and fairly. People don't like to ask how much something costs. They want to see the price, think about it, and then make the decision on their own.
- Always have business cards available and any printed matter like brochures that can be taken home. It adds to the feeling of connectedness and future possibilities. Have them on a little table or special place designated for an official "check writing area."
- Remember to have bags/boxes to pack purchases.

178

- Be yourself, love your own story, embrace your art, put a price on it, sell it and let it go. People are buying a piece of you; a piece of your story goes home with them. Appreciate your customers deeply in heart. Sales techniques that require manipulation or mind games are out of my book and are not my style. We can, however, learn skills of selling that can make our customers more comfortable and ourselves more relaxed, confident, and successful in a natural way.
- Make friendships with the other artists, help each other out and add positive energy to the atmosphere. Above all else, have fun and *enjoy* the show.
- When it is over, pack up, go home and rest. If counting your money makes you feel good, start counting. Congratulations, by the way. Some people feel comfortable talking about how much they make—others don't. Good thought to keep in mind: do not ask other artists how much money they made, only tell people if you feel comfortable, and if anyone ever says, "Is that all?" then just smile, pick your tired little self up off the ground, and head to the bank.

There are hundreds of points to be made beyond what I have made here, but I have gleaned those that stand out for me. Once again, there is always "another book" to take you deeper and higher, yet I find that if I get the heart of the matter first, good form and the right supplementary information will follow. I would highly, *highly* recommend an audiocassette: "Be a Dynamic Craft Seller: A Motivational Tape for Craftspeople" by Bruce Baker, and any tape by Bruce—he is currently working on several more. If you have the chance to go to a workshop with him—do it. (See CONNECTIONS)

I would also like to voice a word of friendly, compassionate caution: be careful not to get burned out. Whenever I attend shows as a customer, I see that and it is painful. Sometimes it is just too much; too many years of too much of the same thing. Perhaps there are times that require refreshment and renewal. I do not do many shows, but I have skipped a couple of my usual and successful shows because I needed the break. I met this couple, jewelers, who were my booth neighbors. They had been potters for seventeen years. They got exhausted and *old*. Their hands were tired and backs broken from lugging crates of pottery all over creation. Pottery is physical. They wanted to continue with the show circuit; it had become their life. So, they took classes, developed a fabulous jewelry line and started anew. They are so happy and it is contagious when you are with them.

As for praying that it doesn't rain at outdoor shows, you might want to re-consider. Of course that is usually a type of disaster, but once again my concept was shattered recently. A big two-day show got rained on for two days. I felt so bad for my five participating friends and everyone else involved. And I will admit that I was relieved that I wasn't sitting under my own tent at this one. I accidentally missed the entry deadline: boo-hoo. (Whew.) Visiting on the second day I came across a great story from my friend Yueying Zhong, a painter. He had a very good weekend in the rain. How could that be?

- #1: People that come to outdoor shows in the rain are serious buyers. The volume and percentage of browsers is way down.
- #2: In his case, there was a couple that had been interested in his work for a long time, but his booth was always too crowded for their taste and comfort level. A rainy day was perfect for them. They had the artist "all to themselves," and

bought $800 worth of paintings after having an opportunity to make a personal connection with him. With just a few other sales after that, it was a good show. You just never know… (I still pray that it doesn't rain.)

We are all creating something all the time, whether it is our own breath, in and out, a thought in our minds, words on paper, dinner, a conversation, something with our hands, squishing grapes with our feet or whatever appendage works for the creative project at hand. As human beings, we are creators. It is a joy come full circle when we share our creativity with others and it is appreciated and valued enough to be purchased. Knowing that my work, the things I have created with my hands, mind and heart are now part of people's homes and their lives in some way, is very rewarding. The art show experience is one way to make that connection. And you get to see it unfold in person.

I myself tried doing the Hearnes Spring Show the year after meeting the farm family with the lace dolls. Friends hounded me to "at least *try*." I shared a booth with my friend Gail Shen and we both bombed big time. I made $57, and if I remember correctly, the booth fee was $50. I doubt if anyone walked away from my booth with tears streaming down—mostly we got strange looks in the spirit of: "What on earth *is* that stuff and what are you doing here anyway?" That's okay. Gail and I had a long-wished-for chance to talk and see what our artwork looked like together—we thought we were outstanding. We never went back to that show, not because it is below us but because we didn't quite fit in. It wasn't our show. We do better at art shows than craft shows. I learned.

It is good that I developed my business here in Missouri, particularly the show aspect. If I had stayed in Santa Fe and tried it there, it would have been very difficult for a beginner to get into, let's say, one of the Craft Shows downtown on the Plaza. Those shows are juried to a very high standard and I would not have made it in, at least in the beginning. I could possibly have found a way to break in somehow later, but I am grateful for the steps I was able to make here: more gradual and less "nationally" competitive. Originality and perseverance are good combinations for success in the Art Show scene wherever the locale, whatever the level. If we know that more people are going to walk by than walk in and buy, we might not take it so personally. If I focus on the people who enter my world and welcome them, good things are bound to happen.

Here is a last practical suggestion: all of those checks that people write? Before you deposit them, ask the bank teller to make copies of the checks so that you have the names and addresses showing. That, combined with a sign-is guest book available in your booth, becomes the foundation for your customer mailing list for future shows and events.

A reflection on the variety of arts and artists…

If the *only* flowers on earth were fine black orchids, they would become ordinary, garden-variety. If only one single daisy was left on the entire earth, how priceless, rather than commonplace, it would become. Creativity is the garden of the human experience. The greater the variety and contrast, the lovelier our garden will forever be. What flowers do you love the most? If I could plant the "garden of my dreams" today, it would include 12-foot sunflowers with heads that weigh ten pounds each, cosmos, daisies, and fields of hardy, profusely fragrant French lavender that would invite you to walk right on through. I want to see creative people as fellow gardeners on a shared path, each tending unique gardens, from the formal elegance of Versailles to a tumble-weeded yard with wild desert sage, chamisa and piñon trees scattered about. We are all in this together.

Juries and Judges

Juries decide whether or not you get into an art show. Generally you pay a non-refundable Jury Fee when you apply for a show, which in essence means you may be paying money for someone (or some group) to summarily reject you from a show and make you feel bad in some form or another. The Jury may also send you the sparkling news that you have been *accepted* so that you can feel good in some form or another.

Judges, on the other hand, are people who attend shows and decide who should win the prizes, money awards, etc. Some volunteer their services, while others have been paid by the show sponsors. In my experience, Judges walk around with notebooks, pencils or pens and a bit of an aloof air about them—detached, shall we say. It is a little comical to me when I happen to know the Judges personally and see them in their "judgment mode." I tend to go about my business and they tend to go about theirs.

There are all kinds of politically correct and incorrect things to say about this whole topic and process and I am simply not getting into it. I have heard high praises and some very choice words to describe "disappointment" over not being selected or awarded. It can be fairly emotional and get pretty personal. My ambitions are not so tied into the process that I get all worked-up; I tend to distance myself and observe. The shows that I try for are within my range and a Jury has not rejected me—so far. Figuring that I am not in contention for any major awards, I keep my booth closed until show time and let the Judges peek in if they want to. Honestly speaking, from the get go, I cringe whenever I see either of the above two words, and after I get a grip, I usually also have a learning experience. After all, the Jurors and Judges are selected because they do have expertise.

Hearing through the grapevine or asking a Juror or Judge directly to critique your work to you personally after they have seen your slides and/or presentation can be enlightening. They may even say nice, encouraging things. Constructive criticism can be good, too, of course. My favorite experience with a Judge was during an outdoor show. You remember. Realizing that I was being analyzed, I gave him a little nod, smile and mental dismissal. About an hour later, coming back without the dreaded little tally sheet, he's the one who handed me a $100 bill and wanted any tiles I had left. Come to find out, he is an artist from St. Louis, thought my booth and tiles were very cool, and even though it was my first time showing tiles—he bought the last ones. A Judge who became a customer—how nice and shocking is that. My stereotyping was happily challenged.

Years ago, I was fortunate to become a Juried Artisan Member of *The Best of Missouri Hands*, an organization created to support arts and crafts people of this state. Thank God for the Jury at that time. My marks were higher than my work deserved, so I worked very hard to become worthy as soon as possible. I am still working on that, grateful at the same time for the opportunities available by being part of a network of good people and a variety of artists. It feels good to use my gold BOMH stickers.

If the challenge of high-level events is attractive to you, go in with your eyes open and heart a bit protected, especially in the beginning. Read my friend Susan's piece called "Zen and the Art of Art" in this book, and try not to take it all too personally. Jurors and Judges are people with their own tastes and preferences. They may be able to be somewhat objective if that is at all humanly possible when it comes to responding to art. I was asked once to be on a Jury for a show. "No thank you," I said. I had friends entering.

Galleries

You've been to art galleries before. There are the major leagues as well as the minor leagues. There are museum galleries where nothing is for sale and everything is revered; at least by someone. There are fun galleries where everything is for sale, if only you had the money. I used to imagine when I was a kid what it would be like to have something that I made hanging up on a gallery wall. I could stand in a corner watching the people looking at my artwork. That always sounded like fun. Would I be proud, nervous and twitchy to the point of having to leave the room, or would it just be exciting? In my later-life experiences, all guesses applied based on a couple of minor league, good experiences.

Once again, you can get all in a tizzy about "what it means to get into a gallery" and do all kinds of research, but please, only to the extent that you don't lose your nerve. Start small and cozy, don't overshoot to the moon when you just need to get to first base, and you will have a learning experience if nothing else.

I had absolutely no interest in being in a gallery myself for many years, when all of a sudden, an opportunity presented itself and caused me to stop and re-think my position.

My "position" included facts like:
- I am not ready.
- No gallery would be interested in craft-level items.
- 50% of the retail is okay in a gallery, but I am getting 60% for consignment in a nice shop, so why bother—stick with consignment.
- The thought of doing Artist Receptions and getting all dressed-up for "the show" basically is not my style.
- …and other thoughts along those lines…

The person who designed my first website had an idea—she would create a gallery that would double as her downtown office. All artists who were on the website network could pay a minimal fee in a co-op type atmosphere and we would give it a whirl. And whirl it was. "The Golden Hippo Gallery" only lasted downtown for one year, but it was a great experience for me. The nature of the business worked for my needs and I was comfortable in what had once seemed like foreign territory. I sold small things, met some good folks, shattered a few concepts, and sadly saw the sign come down because there wasn't the customer base needed to really take off. They liked looking but didn't buy big.

I have participated in small gallery shows and can generally last through the receptions because I can always find a moment to escape outdoors and think. Finding a powerhouse gallery situation can be a great catalyst for many artists. It may be a treasure hunt experience for you—look at a map of the United States and pick an area that you love. Explore the area on foot personally (if possible) or on the Internet. Talk with people who know you and your work and get suggestions from them about places they know and love that might be interested in carrying your artwork. Read trade magazines in your field of expertise and get ideas of destinations in the realm of reality as well as in your dreams. A friend of mine keeps going with her gallery search, has work in some fine ones and has a ten-year goal to be at the top in her field—and she will do that. It is a career path and personal goal. It takes focus, connections, and tenacity, sometimes luck and always work.

There are artists who have made an active choice *not* to go the gallery route. I met such a person in an interesting situation. My Mom and I were walking around the grounds of The Santa Fe Flea Market—what a place. It is a drive out of town and right next to The Santa Fe Opera. One windy, sunny place… Booth after booth of the most interesting wares, from African trade beads to Guatemalan hand-woven clothes, old woodblocks from India to Japanese temple bells. The jewelry—fabulous selection, of course—silver and turquoise, gold, you name it. As we wandered and spent a few dollars here and there, we came upon a very "gallery" type booth that stood out. The artist was a photographer—black-and-white exclusively. The tent was outstanding in the way it was designed and furnished. The artist shared a bit of his experience.

I asked him *why* he was at The Flea Market and not in a fancy gallery on Canyon Road. Not a very subtle approach on my part, but he was up for it and gave me a good laugh to begin with. It boiled down to these basic facts—he had tried some galleries and had been approached by others. He was unable to find the right situation and financial arrangement that suited him, since there were galleries that put prices of his work higher than he felt comfortable with. He wanted his work to be accessible to the general public, not just to the rich folks. There were other galleries that set the prices more reasonably and then put great pressure on him to "produce-produce-produce" because his pieces "moved." This restricted his time outdoors traveling and shooting pictures, cramping his lifestyle into the darkroom and forcing a mindset of mass production. That will never do for a Santa Fe artist. One possible solution? Set up a semi-permanent booth at the Flea Market after being on a waiting list for a few years, get a solid customer base, control the prices and your schedule. Downside? It's so darn dusty up there, but you learn how to deal with it and you become well known in your own way, on your own terms.

It is quite something when people look at your work, whether in a gallery, booth or store and *buy* it, especially if you happen to be there. If that is an experience you want—then get it. It will take time and you will have interesting stories if nothing else.

When we think of Galleries, of course the big names pop into our minds. The "Big Names" for you may be quite different from the "Big Names" for me, so I will mention one of my favorite "biggies" and an interesting gallery experience she described. Georgia O'Keeffe had this unbelievably direct, no-nonsense way of seeing herself and everything else around her. She spoke of the "wise men" of Art of her day and the fact that some saw her paintings as "Art;" others as "not Art—they disagree. Some of them do not care." *Do not care*? Can you imagine that?

She sent some of her first drawings to a girl friend and asked her not to show anyone, so of course she did. Alfred Stieglitz was the lucky one who saw them, and he insisted on showing the work in his Gallery "291" in New York City. In the Exhibition Catalogue, she flatly states that she does "not want to have this exhibition because, among other reasons, there are so many exhibitions that it seems ridiculous for me to add to the mess." That is not the typical fare in an "Artist's Statement." She goes on to say that, "…I guess I'm lying. I probably want to see my things hang on a wall… And I presume, if I must be honest, that I am also interested in what anybody else has to say about them and also in what they don't say because that means something to me, too."

- *Georgia O'Keeffe*
(Excerpts from the Exhibition Catalogue,
Anderson Galleries, 1923)

"My team"

There is something to be said for the "doing it all by myself" kind of thinking. I like playing singles in tennis and I like building my own worktables in my studio—fine and dandy. There is also something wonderful to be said for "team spirit" and I am extremely grateful for all of the teams I have been part of over the years. My old high school girls' basketball, field hockey, and tennis team days—those were girls' locker room, sweat-together, win-and-lose-together times. Teams of friends and family, the neighborhood, classmates and clubs… life is full of teams if we choose to jump in and join.

What about now? At this time in my life they are my family, friends in the arts and friends at school, business buddies, my customers and my mentors. My neighbors are great, too. It is always amazing to me how many wonderful groups and clusters form around friendships—bouquets of people that matter most.

Speaking of teams, football is becoming a big deal in our family for our kids—yay, Dad. We recently rented the movie *Remember the Titans* and watched it together. It catches your heart and the chant grips your mind and won't let go. We keep going around the house singing: "We are the Titans, mighty, mighty Titans…" And of course we are going to play with that a bit and came up with: "We are the Pages, mighty, mighty Pages!" This, above all others, is "my main team."

Part, if not most, of my business is an "alone" thing. Of course there are contacts and relationships, but for the most part, a working day for me means that I am by myself putting out orders. Togetherness is a good contrast. There is something very special and uplifting that happens when Gary and I work on a project together, whether it is figuring out display boards for a booth or jamming ideas for changes on the websites. One day I came home to find this fabulous graphic design on the computer screen. The closer I got, the more I squinted—that looks like some artwork of mine—but where did he get it and how on earth did he get those special effects? Come to find out, the original was my old journal cover that was dusted off before finding a new life in Gary's hands. My work plus his work equals a whole new dimension. It becomes "our art."

Preparing for and setting up an art show is a major project. My favorite activity is setting up with Gary and our oldest son, Brandon, on the evening before. We get into this "team mode" and it is my rally and my calm before the opening in the morning. The judges, the customers, the lookers, the passersby, the blur of motion is continuous and then my favorite single moment comes on the second day—Gary takes Brandon and Bryan to see "Mom's booth." That precious moment when I see their sweet faces and beaming smiles, so proud of Mom, is my moment of secret glory. I get hugs and a few moments to quietly be "the mighty, mighty, Pages." I am busy, and my children are absorbing and learning things through the experience that I hope will serve as inspiration for them in the future. On the surface, I am just chatting and wrapping up purchases…

My husband makes sure all is secure with the tent stakes, I let him know how it is going, and then they are on their way until I finish up the show, all sun-drenched, exhausted, relieved and grateful. Gary and I break everything down, share stories and head home. We unload the cars together and I will make more sense out of the mountain of stuff tomorrow. I missed everybody and just need to get cozy and be home.

No matter what I do or build on my own, whatever the accomplishment, the most meaningful things I do, as simple as they may be, are with my family. I love "my team."

It's **SHOW BIZ** *Time!*

Being a movie star or an actress was never high on my list of wanna-be's and do's. A fantasy here or there perhaps, but I was always too nervous about forgetting lines and knew that I didn't have "the look." I did practice signing my name in secret many times just in case I became famous in some way and developed my own way of writing "G" that was cool-looking in contrast to the capital G's one did in perfect penmanship class— I wanted to be ready just in case.

Having your own business in a relatively quiet, small city (compared to Hollywood or New York) has its advantages. It isn't that difficult to become "known" around town. Having given classes at the University of Missouri every semester for five years with students from the well-known School of Journalism as a portion of my listeners gave me some unique opportunities. They saw me as a potential class project. I was asked to do interviews for special assignments and always went along with the idea even though at times I didn't want to tell my story *one more time* and then one more time again. I did it primarily to be friendly and to help the students out, but I started to learn that I was actually benefiting by doing this over and over. The stories weren't getting old, they were getting clearer. The nature of the questions put to me showed me what people found particularly interesting about my business and life. The whole experience was another major catalyst for the book you have in your hands.

From class assignments, we went on to newspaper articles. A unique feature of this J-School is the fact that the school produces a local daily newspaper called *The Missourian*, with students as staff writers, photographers, etc. My basement became a bit crowded several times when I was interviewed and photos were shot using professional equipment. It is quite something when a two-page spread comes out about *you*. Thousands of people see it, whether they read it or not, and in my experience a lot do because I hear about it later on. Perhaps at an art show someone will approach me and ask about the article. A good reporter will get your name spelled correctly and put in some gentle advertising and this does have a ripple effect. I know that I have card customers who learned from the paper that I sell cards at Poppy downtown.

One newspaper picks you up—the other paper in town might, too. The major paper, *The Columbia Daily Tribune*, called and asked if they could do a special feature in a "Senior Section" and I was a little put off. After explaining that I was only 44-years-old, the white hair has been part of the look for as long as I can remember, and what exactly did they have in mind, I learned it had to do with crafts. The writer had heard that I worked with rubber stamps and wondered if I would be willing to share about the hobby as a possible craft for seniors. The article was done in conjunction with our local stamping store and I was featured sitting at my drafting table, dinking away. Nice small black-and-white photo and all the facts were basically straight.

Over time there have been other articles, and I highly recommend being open to the possibility, and even pursuing it if you have the inclination. The word is "exposure," and it is good for business and isn't bad for your self-esteem either. Except, however, when some stupid mistake is made in print and there is no way you can either control it or take it back. I was interviewed at the end of 1999 for a special "Arts in the New Millennium" feature article. A certain amount of the focus would be on selling art through the Internet and my first webmaster (and friend) Jennifer and her business were to be included. It was to be a big two-page color spread, several artists featured, the camera crew came to my house, shot a lot of photos, and then... you wait.

The day the article came out, I drove to a newspaper stand early so that I wouldn't have to wait any longer than necessary. Flipping, flipping, found it: I can't be*lieve* it. First of all, after all those camera/tripod/flash set-ups, not one picture from my studio. The layout was a little strange and then I see my name is the leadoff... Reading down the column I couldn't believe how stupid my business sounded. I can't quote it exactly because I threw this thing out within minutes of reading it, but it went something along the lines of "she has a home-business in her unfinished basement lined with plastic shoe boxes and after 17 years..." *Seventeen years*? In the interview I told them seven years. I said that several times as a matter of fact. The whole tone of the article was screwy and I was embarrassed to be part of it. After "seventeen years in business," what kind of loser still works in an unfinished basement with cheap plastic everywhere? Worded one way, it might work and you sound adventurous and creative; worded the way it was, it didn't. What can you do at that point? Get mad for as long as you want to be in that bad space, switch to a liberating laugh, find the nearest trashcan and throw it away I guess. That's what I did anyway. (I can always find one redeeming word or something in there, and I do thank them for that. Don't burn media bridges too quickly—you just never know...)

You can say the most profound, clever, humorous, insightful, honest, truly brilliant things in an interview and read the article, see your name spelled wrong and wonder how on earth anyone could quote you for saying the silly, incomplete, incoherent thoughts attributed to you. Or you can have a nice quiet interview and meet with a writer who catches the essence and details of what you are saying and gets it across in style, first class. It might be accompanied by a photo that is perfect and you sigh, smile and make a phone call to thank everyone involved for their professional and personal ability to get into your story and get it right in print. That happened for me once at the University paper. I bought the rights to the photo—thank you, David Vargas. To Nora Bresnahan, a promising writer, I wish you the best of luck. I was honored to be featured in that article and it has become an identifying piece for my business. Two students did what "the pros" botched at the big-time paper.

I am not a razz-ma-tazz type who likes photos taken and all that jazz, but when Show Biz means connections, it does have value and I can go through the hoops. How about television? I always thought it was wild that certain old TV shows were taped in front of live studio audiences and I liked the energy. *I Love Lucy* was, and is, brilliant. My friend Dennis, who is a regular guest for a stamping-techniques segment on a local TV show, asked me to join him. I was to show how I handcarve my own blocks and print them. The thought unnerved me and I had these visions of getting rattled as I talked and saying "...um...um...um." I hate that. The worst fear I had was that my hands would start shaking. Here comes the camera for a close-up shot zooming in on my trembling hands, I slip with the lino-cutter and there is blood all over the place—on *live* TV. I've cut my hands before—it wouldn't be the first time. It is messy and painful. I eventually agreed to do the show mostly because I was scared to death and knew that if I did go through with it, I would come out of the whole experience having put the hardest thing in that particular moment behind me. Another time would be easier or I would choose never do it again, but at least I tried TV. And my sons would have a good laugh, guaranteed.

It was a great experience, it really was. Paul Pepper and James Mouser are the hosts of *Pepper & Friends* and they put me totally at ease. Dennis was with me, there were no medical emergencies, and my voice and hands were under control. It was conversational and comfortable. The Show Biz bug bit me! Paul and James became friends beyond the title of the show, and I was asked to come on a number of times, both solo for stamping techniques, and with my two children and some of their friends to demonstrate some fun crafts in the *Kids' Corner* segment. Each time I was more relaxed and came to enjoy it. Apparently, I even picked up a famous gesture and inserted it into my presentation—Paul complimented me on my "Vanna White hand sweep" and asked me to do it one more time—on *live* TV. I knew what he meant, but I had never seen an entire *Wheel of Fortune* show. I did repeat my little "sweep" over my kids' crafts, and as soon as possible, I gave him a hard time when the lights told me we were OFF-THE-AIR… "How *could* you???"

An extension of the adventure came about when Paul and James connected with my sons Brandon and Bryan and did TV shows on location live from their classrooms. Brandon's second grade and Bryan's pre-school friends and teachers learned a lot about television by being on it, and you never know how that affected the children and their future aspirations. I learned that I am not afraid of the cameras or the experience.

There is a wonderful rippling effect that takes place as we venture out into new territories. Speaking in classrooms led to speaking on TV. TV shows led to teaching techniques at the local stamp store as well as to large groups of Girl Scout counselors at a conference and getting paid to do these classes. Another offshoot ripple was being asked to be a guest speaker for a special program at the University and actually getting paid to do that. It was a nice moment to open an envelope and see a check written out to me with the notation: "Speaker's Fee." I had expressed that I was happy to do it "for free." It was gratifying to receive compensation or monetary gratitude along with the heartfelt words. My story had some kind of perceived value and I appreciated knowing that.

I did a radio piece one time, too, that wasn't live but was interesting to tape. My favorite music of the moment was inserted in the background and snippets of my business experience as well as working philosophy were included. I heard it came off well—I personally missed it because I was volunteering at school at the time it aired.

There was a point when I had my first experience of having artwork published in a major publication and that was exciting. *Somerset Studio* Magazine accepted a number of my pieces and that became another series of layers of experiences built one on top of the other. I enjoy the process and enjoy it most when other people are along for the ride, too.

One story, one chapter leads into another. Did I set out to be on TV and all the rest? No. My nature is more internal in many ways. But I learned that there is a part of me that enjoys being out there with people in new and interesting environments and what I learn and gain along the way opens more avenues in business and friendship arenas. Stripping down fears and insecurities always serves us well and I know that in a very real way, this affects my children who get to ride on the waves of good fortune with me. We have studio videotapes of all the times we were on TV together. It is an interesting variation on the "home movies" concept. You never know what tools and skills will make themselves available, and I try as hard as I can to make myself available to whatever's coming next.

"Only those who risk going too far can possibly find out how far we can go."
- *T. S. Eliot*

PS: It Figures! Of course it would happen. Write about a newspaper experience that went bad and sure enough, they will retaliate—they'll write a *good* article just to get back at you. Thank you, *Tribune*.

On November 1st I gave a talk that was sponsored by FARC (Fine Arts Residential College) at the University. Seated in the audience, unbeknownst (I like that word) to me, sat a journalist with the local paper. He blended in like a student. When I received a phone call a few days later and found out who "Mr. Unbeknownst" was, I was not really excited about doing an article at that particular time. Internally, my inter-personal dialogue went along the lines of: "How about another time, like when I am finished with my (this) book, for example? The publicity will be nice and I will feel more razz-ma-tazzy instead of blitzed. How about when my torn-apart-basement-used-to-be-studio is usable and photograph-able *later*? Thanksgiving and Christmas are pressing in on me, rush orders are piling up, I still have only two hands after all these years and well… you know." The list was impressively much longer, but you get the idea.

In the evening my husband Gary listened to my litany of reasonable excuses why this is the worst possible time in my personal history to do even a small newspaper article and then during the next day I found myself playing telephone tag with a reporter who was as determined to write my story as I was to avoid it. Me, the person writing and talking all the time, wants to sit tight and shut up? Interesting. Gary was taking sides with the reporter—that takes guts when I am ranting. His rational, haunting comment was simple:

"You never know all the good that may come from *just doing it*."

The basic philosophy of that statement didn't sound all that unfamiliar since it *is* the main point of everything I've written, but it wasn't particularly supportive of my desire to posture myself in this staunch isolationist stance. Everybody stay away. I'm not ready.

I was sure of one thing. The telephone interviews were okay—I can be a nice person. But let me be very clear: "*no one is coming to my house* for interviews, *no one,* do you understand? So, Mr. Tim Higgins, Mr. Good Guy Journalist with the Big Time Paper in a medium-sized town, you will have to figure out what to do for pictures, but they sure as *h---* are not being taken in my basement mess, don't cross that line, don't mess with me, young man…" I think I made myself quite clear in a bit gentler yet still obstinate manner.

We made Plan B. I needed to push myself to get a lot of work done, so I made a verbal commitment to have a delivery made by the next day to Poppy, my main store in Columbia. The pictures could be taken there. This so happened to be the day before Thanksgiving—not too busy or anything. 2:00 p.m. it is, and I did have things ready even though I was flustery. Tim, the writer, and Don, the photographer—I liked them both right away—a lot. Now this I cannot believe—in the matter of an extremely short period of time, I actually gave in and let them come to my house for a photo-shoot directly after photos at Poppy. Amazing. They pushed a little and I actually gave the okay.

I became temporarily insane: either that or I liked them a whole lot and trusted them, or some combination of those. I think I messed up directions to my house and forgot to tell them about one significant right-hand turn, but hey, it did buy me a few minutes so I could put on a bracelet that my son gave me years ago. (They got directions from a sheriff or policeman or someone in that line of work.)

Then the doorbell rang and I was letting people into my inner sanctum sanctorum mess. There were stamps on the drafting table that had not been cleaned for weeks if not

188

months. No time to clean anything—there is this camera roaming around, hungry for something to shoot. I push things aside and scramble to think of what I could do for these "close-up" shots. I whip out a piece of deep maroon banana leaf paper from Thailand and grab for some handcarved blocks to print with. Camera: click—click—click. I am telling myself to calm down and stay focused. Then Don asks if he can take a picture of *me*, portrait-style, sitting in my black director's chair. Oh, why not at this point. A quick scan of my surroundings makes me cringe. If I had time, I would completely re-do everything the camera would pick up on. Too late—the natural state of affairs is recorded. It is a done deal. We shake hands and I can't believe I just did what I did. Hopefully this was going to be tucked away in some invisible part of the paper.

Thanksgiving came and went and then Saturday came soon enough. The article was slated for that paper. I slept in and then remembered that I shouldn't forget to look at the paper and prayed one last quick one for invisibility. Oh, no. The top left hand corner of the front page announced that I was the feature lead article for the weekly Business section. I didn't have a clue that that was going to happen. I never asked a fairly basic question like, "Excuse me, where in the paper is this little article going to be tucked away?" A full three-page spread with four very good color photos is what greeted me Saturday morning.

Wrapping up this story goes as follows—many people called and congratulated me on the article. It was written based on a talk followed by interviews, so the tone was more personal, internal and *emotional*. My first reading through, I was very pleased. I called Tim and thanked him and Don for the gift of a job well done. (They were welcomed to come back when my act and studio were more together someday.) My second reading, I got worried. I asked a number of people if I sounded like an emotional basket case because it seemed that I cried a lot according to the article. My friend Janet told me to "forget it and don't worry about it. It is good to cry. People like to know that other people cry and it's okay to be moved by things in life." Big, wonderful discussions started to happen. I learned what made Janet cry and I laughed in whole-hearted agreement. My Mom called with her congrats and I asked her the same thing and she laughed and told me I wasn't nuts, that I was giving a gift to people by being open-hearted. We shared countless stories of what makes both of us cry—meeting people coming in on trains, saying good-byes at airports, the movie *Strangers in Good Company* and of course *It's a Wonderful Life* and all kinds of wonderful things.

Books do me in. I cry watching TV shows and even commercials if you can believe that. Hallmark Holiday commercials are the worst (the best). Here I am, a miniscule competitor of the colossal cardmaker, and instead of turning the TV off in protest to their mega-monopoly over my business, I get all teary-eyed at their commercials and go out and buy from the nearest Hallmark store. I could never boycott or bad-mouth a company that makes tear-jerking commercials like that. I know it's Madison Avenue slick, but I fall for it every single time and offer no resistance, no excuses whatsoever. I have cried listening to the announcements at the elementary school because the children are so sincere. When my son tells me what makes him "nervousy" in first grade, I listen, hug him, smile and hold it back so that he can get a better grip, and then I cry for him later on. If I see a really old couple holding hands at the mall, I find the nearest bench so that I can sit down, watch and grab a Kleenex. A baby's face, someone hurting on the inside or the outside, a quiet compliment coming my way… It doesn't stop, but I will here.

What I have learned in the past few days since the article came out is that there is a kind of secret club out there. I have been on TV and other articles have been written, but this time it is different. I think people want to hear honest-to-goodness stories of people who cry and allow that to actually be written in the newspaper. I didn't exactly *allow* it or give my permission, but it happened and it is okay—I went past the embarrassment. Today I was downtown making a card delivery and a perfect stranger walked up to me, wanted to shake my hand, to connect, and say nice things about the article in the paper. It had touched her deeply and she wanted to thank me. I was blown away. I was moved to tears—is that any great surprise? Who knows? Maybe a fair number of people rolled their eyes reading the article or seeing me on Broadway with a stranger in good company, talking in the middle of the road. It's okay. I want to be a member of the Ladies Who Love to Be Totally Free to Cry Club. I am already a member of the Ladies Who Love to Laugh and Do Crazy Things Club—I'm coming out of the closet on the other one. It is time to celebrate that trait rather than hide and question my sanity all the time.

This was good timing after all. I had to trust people around me rather than dwell on my embarrassment that things and me are not as together as I would like them to be before "going public."

Tomorrow I will go and give my fanciest signature at the University so that they can cut me a check for a speaker's fee from the FARC presentation mentioned earlier. That is very nice and will help tremendously with Christmas gifts.

This is how it all grew: I did Art in the Park five years ago and met Dr. Betty Scott. She connected me to FARC. FARC connected me to Tim and the *Daily Tribune* article. The article connected me to a kindly stranger on the street and a darling little boy this morning at school who looked up at me with his eyes opened very wide because I was "the famous lady he saw in the newspaper!" One thing leads to another if I am willing to take the next step, to take a brisk hike up whatever mountain presents itself, or a bungee-jump off the bridge of my current fears—whatever it takes to keep going.

"You never know all the good that may come from just doing it." I appreciate that a lot. Thanks, Gary. After all, "the show must go on."

> Those who don't know how to weep with their whole heart
> don't know how to laugh either.
>
> *- Golda Meir*

> Give me a *Northern Exposure* episode during lunch and I will show you how
> to cry and laugh seamlessly even *simultaneously* any day of the year.
>
> *- Gloria Page*

> The shell must break
> before the bird can fly.
>
> *- Alfred Tennyson*

Having a Website
Is it necessary? Is it worth it?

In the afternoon of the second day of an autumn art show, I was busy and trying to keep myself awake at the same time. The second day of any show, after weeks of preparation, has its challenges. For a moment, the tent was empty and I found myself drinking in the sunlight, soaking in some warmth and hopefully some renewed energy to make it to the grand finale—only four more hours to go. I want this to be a good show. All of a sudden, two young women breezed into the tent, and I could tell they had a plan other than buying my artwork, so I let them beam their smiles and I listened.

The apparent "CEO" of this new business venture was carrying a wicker basket with packets neatly arranged, and one of them was in my hand as introductions were being made. I came to quickly understand that these two entrepreneurs were in the business of designing websites and wondered if I was interested. I laughed. We did not even own a computer and our eight-year-old son was the resident expert since we knew nothing at all. It seemed like a waste of time to talk with me about computers, but we talked anyway.

As it turned out, I got an incredible deal because she was starting out and wanting to learn how to design Art Sites. I was game to try since we had an arrangement that e-mail messages (which I had never seen or experienced before) and potential orders would be forwarded to me by phone until we entered the High Tech Age, scraped enough money together to buy a computer, and figured out how to turn it on. It cost me only $250 to set up a Wholesale/Retail site with a display of 48 cards. There was no "shopping cart" and I was not set up with credit cards. It was a simple and effective site—in less than two weeks, with the orders I received, I had more than paid for the site and that felt great.

From the outset it is extremely important to make it perfectly clear that having a website is not a leap into some magical realm of instant fame and fortune. I just finished saying that my site was paid for within two weeks—that happened because I used the site as a point of communication for clients I already had, and one new one that I directed there, not because someone in a foreign country was doing a search and found me in cyberspace. That kind of thing came later, but for a good long time, it was pretty basic—I advertised my site on all correspondence and on all products. My original site was connected to a group site and that was okay for a beginning, but it is much better to have your own domain name. We also advanced to getting our own wonderful computer and my husband took off to levels unimaginable to me and taught himself how to take over, re-design and manage these sites. Believe me, that is invaluable and a lot cheaper than paying someone for every change. We are co-designers and in complete control of our "look" and the pace we want to set. It has been a "bonding" type experience and has added a creative dimension to our marriage as well. (impressionsart, holymolymackeroly, and mesapointpublishing: all dot-coms, are the bases for our businesses at this time.)

Over the years I know that many people have gone to the sites. I have received orders from different parts of the country from people surfing and finding my card lines, tiles, etc. Mostly I've used the sites as a form of communication to put new products online for my already existing customers. I've watched enough shows on TV about the potential of e-commerce to know that everyone wants to hear that absolutely fabulous "you will never believe how my business expanded and flew off into the outer reaches of space" kind of tale, so I knew that before this went into print I'd darn well better have one, too, and so the Universe cooperated nicely and in a timely fashion. I got the e-mail of my dreams, not exactly from a foreign country, but Burbank is pretty way out there for me.

A music company was looking for a handmade cardmaker for a very big, new concept in card design—a beautifully produced CD with ten Christmas songs would be included along with a high-quality holiday card that would be printed based on the original artwork. The retail price would essentially be so reasonable as to render the CD a "free gift." I was intrigued by the whole idea, very excited by the potential as I listened to the marketing plans and wanted the contract very much. There was a long process of submissions and finally I got the word—I was chosen to be the card designer for the line. I signed my first contract for licensing of designs and everything has changed for me. I created 100 Christmas cards—48 were selected for the inaugural line. I am so impressed with the professionalism, enthusiasm, respect and hard work that have surrounded this project and me. There were points when I was overwhelmed by the realization that there were serious investors putting a lot of money behind this project and the designs were my responsibility. But I was eased through that time with humor and trust… we will see what happens. We are at the beginning of the adventure and I am up for the ride. I celebrated by officially adding the word "Designs" to my business name.

The numbers that are being tossed around blow my mind—240,000 cards for the initial print run which translates into 5,000 each of the 48 cards. Even before that happens, this is already the biggest job I have completed in eight years. After working for one month at a snail's pace rate of 5-6 cards per day due to the detail and individual design factors, I was paid as much for that one month as I have sometimes made in a year (in the earlier years). Other contracts for design work and licensing agreements are also pending, in large part due to the fact that I have websites as points of confirmation that I do have a viable, visible business and a means of communicating ideas.

Would I say that having a website is a good idea? Yes, and I would be quick to add that it is important to know that it takes time, a lot of advertising to get people pointed in the direction of your site, and an attitude of "working and using the site," not just sitting around once you are online, waiting for the orders and money to miraculously roll in. There is a lot to learn and you need a good webmaster/web-designer who knows how to work the search engines to your advantage. It is an investment that needs to be considered. The volume that you are able to produce once you get online and potentially have that avalanche of orders—that needs to be considered, too. Take steps that make sense financially and personally. It can be approached as an experiment that evolves rather than an "all or nothing" gamble. Talk to people who have websites, talk to people who create them and ask all of your questions, especially the ones you think are dumb ones. As you listen and learn, you will find out if it is the right thing and the right timing.

My husband Gary works very hard at developing his skills on the computer and enjoys it. He is self-taught, willing to teach me as much as I am able to handle, and has created his own stylized and exceptional works of "tech art." I am grateful and fortunate. There's something special and economical about being married to a web designer. My feeling is that we are on track to something good for both of us.

Gabby Marques, the Marketing Director in Burbank, who "discovered" and chose me for the Holiday card opportunity, shared with me what his father always said—this is good: "The harder I work, the luckier I get." Practically and cosmically speaking, that is right on the money. A website is work, it is worth it, and you just might get lucky, too.

On Fire or Ice-berged?

Okay, so now you've heard and read some stories and are getting warmed up to the idea that, Hey, maybe I could try this business thing after all. Yes, maybe even *me*! You get that tingly feeling and the creative juices start flowing, the adrenaline burns things up inside your head and that heart of yours beats faster. The day looks sunny and even feels hot and ripe and who the heck cares if it is the dead of winter anyway. I can do this. I think I can. *I know I can.* I AM ON *FIRE*! The world looks different from the passion of this moment—I like the way it looks. Just a moment ago my disorganized pseudo-studio depressed me. Then, all of a sudden, talk about Transcendence and Spontaneous Transformations—*look* at this place! There is potential here. Can't you see it: "l'atelier:" The Artist's Studio. I feel it and see it and I can touch it. You hear yourself making declarations of independence from the tyranny of the corporate world and the strictures of life in general, knowing that finally the dream is within your grasp, and this just feels like your lucky day! You are more than ready for something new. And *then*...you sit down...
...way

   ▪

   ▪

   ▪

down, to think about it, you know, honestly. Realistically. Practically. Deadly.

And the passion of possibilities, that scorching of the seat of your pants, starts cooling down—way down. Misty. Foggy. Messy. Like a drizzle at first...dribble, dribble, then drivel, drivel. "The Artist's *Studio*," now really. Take one good look around, you mumble in your own ear—what a disaster. Even if I had all the tools that I would need, I would never find them in this place. I'm nowhere near ready; get real. The drizzle becomes freezing rain—can you feel it in your bones? The brain numbs out, the heart goes into a cardiac arrest-of-desire, and the excuse list of the century takes shape right before your very own myopic eyes. The list of impediments, if placed vertically, would dwarf Everest—it was conquerable and enticingly friendly just moments before. The snow front moves in like an avalanche, oh, it is winter, after all, even though it may be the scorchingest day in meteorological history. In the end, there you are, immobilized in that chair, a veritable iceberg of self-doubt and excuses disguised as reasons, frozen solid.

Right here, let me ask you a few questions: Who said that you have to quit your job, the one that makes money and has all the benefits you would be freaked out to lose? Who said it's an all-or-nothing proposition? Why can't you just play around with the idea of having an Art Business and try those ideas out as a hobby, a petty-cash operation, part-time additional bucks for big-time pleasure? Test the warm waters without danger or fear. There is nothing to lose if you choose to not let the tide of the moment sweep you away.

If you find yourself *frozen*: then what. Take a blowtorch to that part of your thinking, free it up, burn it up, and take one step—one—no matter how much of a teetering, tiny, itsy-bitsy baby step it is. Just *do* something. Call someone or throw something if it helps. *Anything* but staying ice-berged.

Nobody's going to rain on my parade, including me.
- *Hallie Beachem Brooks* (Am. Librarian)

Submissions for Publication

- Putting out the best of your best for review, crossing your fingers, hoping…
- Jumping hurdles that peak into mountains
- Breaking through the glass ceiling I put in place myself

No one knows what it is that he can do until he tries. - *Syrus*

A sub-topic generally jumps out at me if one is called for, but I was bombarded this time and settled on the three above. Making a submission definitely brought out the best and stretched the most in me, far beyond any show or speaking presentation to date. I've heard of writer's block and haven't gone there yet, but I squarely faced "artist's block" and it knocked me around pretty hard. It all looked so fun and easy in the beginning. I had a vision and the sun was shining. Why the barriers all of a sudden? What happened?

Seven years in business, seven years of admiring and learning from other people's work, a few years of devouring every issue of *Somerset Studio* Magazine and countless books and publications, and then I wondered—what would it be like to see my own work published? Was my best good enough yet? Would I be accepted if I gave it a try?

Early in 2000, I noticed a "call for entries" for various upcoming issues of *Somerset Studio* with themes in place for each issue. Going down the column, I stopped wide-eyed at the deadline date for the *Asian Arts* issue: August 25, 2000. I love Asian arts. It's been a life-long passion. My very first tiny rental house was a study in how to blend Southwest and Oriental and it was a success—from my viewpoint anyway. I have wonderful art stamp images from the Curtis Uyeda Collection, as well as many of my own handcarved images. The wheels of my thinking were spinning and I saw this as my big chance to breakthrough my reluctance to send anything as a submission. All of my work is very place-specific. These particular cards are for that particular order going to The Museum of International Folk Art; these tiles are for the Chimayo order, these scrolls for The Festival of the Arts Show. I make gifts for people, but I do not make things just "for the sake of making them" very often. Always a destination, a purpose—usually for sale. The idea of creating artwork purely for the sake of creating the best of what I do to show others in print was foreign thinking-territory for me. I was excited to contemplate what might come out of the whole experience.

I kind of tilted my head and squinted my eyes when I heard from a friend that she spent *nine hours* making *one* card to enter in a card contest. I entered a couple of times as well, but there was really no point since she almost always won. I wasn't about to start taking nine hours per card, but I was beginning to taste that level of engagement with my work. August 25th was *many* months away—no problem. You know how that goes. On December 26th you collapse and revel in the knowledge that there are at least 364 days until the *next* Christmas, and *next* time I will surely be more ready when that one comes. Needless to say, there is this time-tornado that does a number on your calendar, whipping those months off the face of the planet and "Jingle Bells" is being Muzakked in your local grocery store as soon as they get rid of the pumpkins. I felt like I had plenty of time to make a great plan and the best presentation I ever made—plenty of time…

Whatever show or order came up along the way, I put it through the sieve of "could I also use this for the *Asian Arts* submission?" I carved many images for my big show in June with that in mind. I had lists that were often revised of what I was planning to make, and purchased things along the way in order to have the raw materials handy for when the muse would alight. A nice pile of supply-stuff was accumulating. A nice list of "to do's" was taped to my drafting table. There was absolutely no lack of ideas or enthusiasm for months. The only trouble was, that at one point, I froze—as in solid. But time was not freezing and standing still with me. It was running wild, galloping away from me.

After my show in June, I wiped-out and got sick. It had been a huge effort and a major departure for me. I had handcarved almost all of the images for the show, greatly changing my look and it was a risk. I put myself out on a limb largely for three reasons:

1) I wanted to make the step from designing only with commercial stamps to going exclusively with my own handcarved images—to explore bigger and bolder looks.

2) I needed to try this out if I was going to make the submission to *Somerset Studio*, which I decided was a necessary next step for me to take because it was something I was afraid of doing.

3) Unless I was a "Published *Artist*" in terms of my work, I felt I had no business and no foundation at all to stand on to become a "Published *Author*" of an art-related book. If my name and work were not "out there" in the public arena of art, then "Holy Moly…" *what*? *Who* wrote that? …Who would care? That was my thinking, right or wrong.

Needless to say, the pressure was on, cranked-up by yours truly on herself. After recuperating somewhat after an extremely successful show, both acceptance-wise and financially, I became preoccupied with the upcoming presentation. Pressure cooker situations usually bring out the best in me, so I don't run from them, but being frozen and blocked was not a familiar state to be in. My mind was telling me millions of fabulous suggestions. I had fantasies of "blowing them away," "knocking their socks off," and maybe, just maybe, making it to the *cover*, and then I couldn't make my hand commit to inking up one single block. It had become so huge and the ramifications were wildly out of proportion. If I don't make it in, then I have wasted a year and more on this book… I'm not a real "artist"… who am I to think… things along those lines. It wasn't helping.

In July, I took a Mexican river rock and wrapped a piece of copper foil tape around it, added strands of silver Japanese mizuhiki paper cord, topped it off with sealing wax and a stone chop and it looked pretty cool. It was my own proof to myself that I had begun. Something existed outside of the realm of my imagination. This rock was on my table. But it sat there, all alone, for weeks collecting dust. I put it in a plastic bag so I didn't have to keep dusting it off. I made one card in July, too. One simple card—not a nine-hour card. Now I had two things. This was clearly not "blow them away" material.

I was mad when August 1st came around—how dare Time move that fast. Going nuts trying to give my kids a good summer vacation with swimming and tennis lessons and practicing both as much as possible and everything else that never seems to let up in life, how could it be August already and I only have one rock and one short $3.00 card, not even one of those tall cards that I sell for $5.00? This was not looking good, and since I had opened my big mouth and told quite a few people out loud that I was committed to doing this, there was no way out—I did it purposely that way, but I did have second and third thoughts. I wanted so much to do the best of my best. Knowing that I would face hurdles, I felt that after seven years of self-training, I could handle it, not knowing that the hurdles would morph into mountains before my very eyes. "The sky's the limit and doesn't need to be" has come out of my mouth many times before. Why the glass ceiling now? Who's putting the barrier there? Certainly not the magazine. My perception did.

My internal critic was dynamiting my self-confidence and obliterating my creative sensibilities. The *real* artists get published—not wanna-be's like me. The likes of us merely look, sigh, and pay our subscriptions. Insecurity can reign supreme.

The beginning of August meant that on the first Tuesday of the month we would have our Art Critique Group meeting. I was flustered by the thought of it. I should be showing my finished products by now. I am going to take one rock and one card to this meeting? I don't think so. I pulled together some raw materials hoping that they would look more impressive than they actually were, just to make it appear that I had some semblance of a plan in place. I had started several fabric Masu boxes that were not quite finished but had potential, pulled those out, packed my box up and went to the meeting.

Five out of six of us were there, and it was upbeat around me, but not in me. Figuring I could soak up some energy and inspiration from being around productive, successful people, I might come away with some hope. I was hanging back as far as making my own presentation to the group, and wanted more than anything else to just pass this one time, but I wasn't going to be allowed to get away with that this time, thank you very much. "So, Gloria, how is your preparation going for your submission to *Somerset Studio*?" "Well, I brought a few things I'm working on, like this piece of red cloth that I want to make into a scroll. (Show the blank cloth.) I have a few unfinished Masu boxes and I have a lot of ideas…" Fizzle, fizzle, fffzzzzt, like a candle at the very end of its existence, light's out in a puddle of melted wax.

Some nice comments came my way, but we all silently knew that I had an incredibly long way to go and not much time to get there. We were at Susan's house, and I knew she had a houseful of family en route, arriving the next day and had lots to do. Still, I hung around at the end and asked if she could give me a few minutes—so that I could cry and get advice. I cried as quickly as I could and asked if she could encapsulate in a few words how she had become so peaceful and even-keel recently. She was handling ups and downs, acceptances and rejections as an artist differently these days. Her answer was her advice: "I ask myself, and I suggest you ask yourself this simple question: 'What's next?' and then do exactly that. Don't go all over the place emotionally, project, look back, procrastinate, daydream and waste time and energy. Just decide 'What's next?' and do it with all of your attention. Then ask again 'What's next?' and do that. You'll get this done. You have all the ideas, you have all the supplies, just take one thing at a time, finish it, put it aside and go to the next piece. You'll knock their socks off, I know you." Hug and out the door. Now I was on my own again, this time armed with a real tool to work on my freeze-framed mind, and the support of everyone in my group. One last good cry in the car—put that behind me, and I would start the morning with "What's next?"

The scrambly pieces started to line up. I started with the large red hand-dyed cloth scroll. I ironed it first. (This was my most scary piece because there was only one piece of this fabric and if I botched it, no getting it back.) What's next? Make the seams. What's next? Ink up the wonderful carved Chinese paper-cut fish that I made for this very purpose and commit it to the cloth. Do not over-think. Do not worry. I do know how to stamp. I've been doing this for seven *years*. If I slip, I'll fix it, so what. For the next three weeks it went just like that. When thoughts of rejection or time constraints or whatever worries tried to creep in, I came back to "What's next?" and put a torch to the negative thought and just kept going. Piece after piece, day after day, piling up a nice, very nice, my *best* presentation ever. It was quite a journey getting to that point.

196

I have experienced this before—the problem of running the gamut from being inspired to frozen: "On Fire or Ice-Berged." I read it, and re-read it, and felt frustrated that I seemed to know what I was talking about then, and wondered what had happened since. It reminded me of the years of reading books about raising children, attending parenting classes, endless mutual advice chats with friends, TV specials and documentaries, feeling like I am "basically a good person," and then one of my children stands right in front of me and says in a loud voice "NO!" and all that knowledge and comfortable psychology goes right down the tubes. "You said *what*?" Breathe, count to ten at least, and try to remember one canned-response from some wise author or other so that you can keep it together. It is the same when you write something yourself and then have to actually *live it* and act upon your own fabulous wisdom that you so confidently impart to others. Okay. I made myself repeat after me who said: "…take one step. One. Just *do* something. *Anything* but staying ice-berged." That one step was asking my friend for help, listening to the help she gave and acting on it. All the helpful advice in the world isn't worth anything if we write it down for future reference. It is in the "doing" that we make the changes and get the power needed to breakthrough and maintain momentum.

The following is a list of what I did eventually send on to California for my very first submission to a major publication:

- 10 Cloth Scrolls (various sizes)
- 9 Cloth-covered Masu Boxes (Origami-style)
- 5 Framed Pieces (Glass / Assorted Art Stamps and Blockprints)
- 15 Cards: 10 Tall cards (#10) / 5 Standard-size (A-6)
- 5 Bookmarks (Split Bamboo Style)
- 1 Scarf (hand-dyed fabric / stamped images)
- 5 Decorated River Stones
- 1 Tiny Tile (thrown in at the final moment) (approx. 1 ½-inch square)

That was my submission. As you can see, I made quite a few things in those weeks—51 stamped items to be exact. What you can't see is the amount of time, effort and design that went into every layer of this "box" that actually took three whole working days just to *pack*. My goal was to have every layer of opening this package to be an "Ooo, aah," experience. This was for *Asian Arts*. I spent enough time in Japan to absorb and observe that the art of packaging is as essential as the art of the gift enclosed. I had to find the perfect shipping box—it was a guess that worked. Decorating the inside and outside was a lot of fun. Not too over-the-top, it had to reflect the contents and feel like getting closer to the treasure with each layer peeled away.

I e-mailed ahead and asked if someone would kindly send me a short message that the box had arrived safely and met the deadline. I would appreciate it. "When you get a large box wrapped in Japanese grass-cloth from Missouri, that will probably be mine…" Natural grass-cloth, black cloth tape, decorated label, tailored and exotic at the same time. I don't know if I could have taken a blade to that to tear into it, but I'm glad somebody did. Each time you opened the next layer, there was stamping, from a large gold Chinese character for "Gratitude," to the next signature layer of stamps and fish designs. Once the whole box was opened, there was a natural muslin cloth to wrap the entire contents, block-printed with giant Chinese fish, tied with black and gold ribbon.

Inside, each and every piece was carefully wrapped in tissue paper, tied with raffia or ribbon and labeled with printed descriptions, using my favorite fonts. At the Post Office, the Postmaster was impressed and "honored" to affix the postage, including, of course, the Chinese Year of the Dragon stamps. It was flying off to California.

The best of me was in there as far as my work over the past seven years was concerned. I put as much, if not more, effort into that one box (which I could easily carry by myself) as I put into a 10x10 booth at a show. Was I going to make any money from these "products?" Not directly, although I might sell them later on when they are shipped back to me eventually. Money isn't the point—creativity is. I saw what I can do now. Now the question became what would *they* think? I had to wait a few days to find out…

The package was shipped on August 17th. On August 21st an e-mail arrived from the advertising manager of *Somerset Studio*. Here are a few excerpts: it started out with: "Oh Gloria, you are such a talented artist! We've all had such fun opening your box of submissions for the *Asian Arts* issue! Thank you so much for sending such top quality material…you can be certain that some of it will appear in the magazine!"

What a way to start. And it kept going… "I was sitting in my office this afternoon working along like usual and heard the excited voices of Kellene (the publisher) and Sharilyn (the managing editor) calling my name. I went into the conference room where they were gazing in rapture at your huge box—it was like Christmas! By the time we all had opened everything, there were several staff members in the conference room looking at all your items. There were a lot of ooooohhhh's and aaaaahhh's intermingled with comments like, 'wow, look at this, it's awesome'…Best regards to an excellent artist (you!)"!!!… After reading that, I sat there stunned. Is that wonderful or *what*?

My simple request was for a two-word confirmation that the package had arrived. "It's here," would have been fine. Instead, I received a wonderful description that kindly and joyously allowed me to be part of the whole experience to the point of connection. E-mailing back, I asked that each person please celebrate "Christmas-in-August" with me and choose *whatever* each person would like from the box and enjoy it—a small way to say thank you and to celebrate this event for me that was bigger than I initially wanted to admit. Can you believe this—out of everything in the box, two people had their eyes on the "tiny tile," the one thing that I almost did not send because it was so small and the only one I had, so it looked a bit stranded and out of place—that tiny tile led to big things. (They can work it out in California as to who gets what. I hope it's fun.)

I have 21 pages of computer printouts from the e-mails that flew back and forth during the course of that three-week sprint of time. Some were just a few sentences, others longer, all a totally new level of experience for me. The warmth, friendliness, support, gratitude and professionalism coming from those offices over there blew me away and continue to do so.

It was a little after midnight which would have made it August 23rd and I was folding laundry in the living room watching some *A&E* show to keep me going, when I heard my husband call me into our room to check on something. "One of the kids?" "No, did you know that there was an e-mail from Sharilyn Miller at *Somerset Studio*?" "*Sharilyn Miller* the *person*, not the office?" "Of course the person, here read this, you did it! You did what you set out to do—she says it right here…" This was going to be good, I could tell by the introduction I had just been given. Don't you love e-mail when it is inspiring?

I sat down at the computer and read:

"Dear Gloria,

Hi, this is Sharilyn Miller at *Somerset Studio*. We have all been drooling over your gorgeous artwork submission. I just know that some of it will appear in the *Asian Arts* issue, and we are planning on doing an extra issue of *Asian Arts* to publish all the overflow… so you never know, some of your work may appear in that issue as well! We have been, well, blessed lately with an absolute ton of artwork for *Asian Arts*, so it's become rather a challenge to impress us, if you know what I mean. Your submission just *knocked our socks off…*" And at that point I was moved to tears and my husband enjoyed it thoroughly, especially that he could be there in the moment, having brought me to the seat at the computer in the middle of the night.

Sharilyn's letter continued, and she opened the door to many possibilities including a special article in *Somerset Studio* about some aspect of my work someday and she encouraged me to consider creating wearable art for the upcoming *Belle Armoire* magazine. She then proceeded to knock *my* socks off by asking if there was anything that I could submit to her on very short notice for consideration to be included in her second book to be published and available in the spring. She was not talking about using anything in the box I had just sent, and in that box was everything I had, and the best of everything I had ever done. There was nothing left in my studio. The deadline was September 5th—about 10 days away—all the artwork had to be in her hands by then. I racked my brain that night and an idea went on like a light. I e-mailed the next morning.

I remembered that over the course of the summer I had made some stamped clay tiles at The University Craft Studio and missed the time to have them fired so they were still on a shelf. This was nutty short notice, however, and I was going to be asking for major help because it would likely entail a special firing and out-of-the-schedule trips to the Studio for staff members who already go way beyond the call of duty all the time. I asked and was kindly and completely taken care of. Chris gave the okay, Joe gave all the extra time I needed, and after I spent 10 hours in two days doing the prep work and glazing, they took over the firing. The glaze color itself was beginner's luck: a happy, ecstatic accident. I was trying for a teal wash kind of look and ended up with a green that took on the appearance of liquid, crystallized jade—it was beautiful! The labeling, packaging, etc. was not as fancy as it was safe—just get them to California *ASAP* with no damage. It all worked out. It took a major team effort in order for that to happen. I am grateful.

It appears that the tiles will be published in the book. We will see when it actually happens. But whatever happens, I feel that I have made new friends and I am so very moved by the entire experience. This went so far beyond my expectation of a business-type, legalistic "transaction." I was expecting something more along the lines of: I send my artwork to a Jury, I get a return letter of Acceptance or Rejection and a whole litany of copyright this-and-that's and We Are Not Responsible For Damage To Your Property blah-bidee-blah-bidee-blahs… It was so completely different than that—what actually happened was special. A wonderful supportive community exists, and we are fortunate to be invited to be part of it, and add our own unique flavor to the mix.

I mentioned to Sharilyn that I was planning on taking a Raku Class, which I am doing right now. Immediately she responded and wants to know everything about the process. She asked about the possibility of Raku-fired jewelry tiles, so guess what I am working on? They should turn out great and I just might be making a submission to *Belle Armoire* in the near future. You should have read what Sharilyn said about my other tiles.

I am not going to include it because I will just appear to be boasting. The names *Somerset Studio*, Sharilyn Miller and that whole crew and world seemed so lofty and distant to me. In reality, they are inspiring, close and supportive. I'm not afraid of making submissions anymore. I don't expect every experience in other forums to be the same, but it really doesn't matter to me at this point. I made copies of all of our e-mails during that concentrated wonderland time and when I freeze up, I take out that folder and get warm once again. Confidence is developed over time—it is a gift when others help us build it.

Do I have to blow people away or knock people's socks off every single time I make a submission? I sure hope not. I am sure that if my work does get selected, it won't be everything I sent. If something does make it: what a great honor. If nothing this time— perhaps another. The point is that I did battle with my fear and insecurities about even attempting such a venture and went past the blocks. The next thing I am going to do is to send one solitary card or a couple of Raku buttons, something small, so I can break the expectation in myself that it has to be a "big huge deal" every time. Later, maybe a little jewelry and then I'll want to do a "big splash" again at some point later on.

Eventually I will attempt submissions to other publications, galleries, shows and whatever just to see what happens. I shot extremely high on the first shot and was blessed to connect to people of great heart. We have yet to "meet," but from the very first call and initial correspondence, I felt that I had known these special people all my life. I can't wait until the day comes when I can extend my hands and heart in a grateful hug.

...a few more words from Sharilyn:

Hi Gloria!

...Never fear, many of your pieces will appear in *Return to Asia*. I've already seen them... Don't worry about your insecurities. That's actually a good sign... Just be true to yourself, and to your talent. Everything else follows from there...

Sharilyn

It turned out that 25 individual pieces of mine were selected and published in the special issue, *Return to Asia*. I was thrilled and honored. The "tiny tile," which I literally threw in at the final moment, became the focal point and launched big adventures. My tiles were included in Sharilyn's beautiful second book *The Stamp Artist's Project Book* and I went on to write extensive articles for both *Somerset Studio* (Nov/Dec 2001 issue: "The Tile Project") and *Belle Armoire* (Spring issue 2002: "The Button Project.") I was actually paid for the honor of writing the articles, and that launched a new confidence level. In 2003, I will have tile work in *The Complete Guide to Rubber Stamped Jewelry*, also by Sharilyn Miller. There will be more submissions from me, both artwork as well as creative ideas for possible art project articles in the future. I have had pieces published in the beautiful *St. Louis Homes and Lifestyles* magazine. Susan Fadem, Editor-in-Chief, is a fabulous person and avid supporter of the arts. To be included in such a first-class publication is a thrill, and opens up new opportunities... What once seemed like an insurmountable challenge has become comfortable and natural, due in great part to people who welcomed me to an exciting world. It also helped to want it—very much.

Just don't give up trying to do what you really want to do.
Where there is love and inspiration,
I don't think you can go wrong.   – *Ella Fitzgerald*

What is *luck*, anyway?

Are you *lucky*? I've heard time and time again that I am. "Gloria, you are so *lucky* that:

- Carolyn Birkes squeezed you into your First Art Show: no jury, no slides, no pain, and a reduced fee to boot—you lucked out.
- your mother jumped in as your first rep and sends you such fabulous surprise art supplies from New Mexico all the time.
- your husband doesn't stand in the way of your art business telling you to get a 'real job,' and actually helps and supports you along the way.
- you have two beautiful children, you got published in *Somerset Studio*, etc…"

"You are just *so lucky* that the Smithsonian buyer just happened to be in Santa Fe and just happened to turn your cards over and just happened to see your 800-number and called you." It was lucky that I was home at the time to get the call personally, and that my "beautiful child" was quiet, too. Lucky that someone found my website… lucky.

I agree that I am very fortunate for many things in my life. But what exactly is luck?

Words like fate, fortune, and "chance," come to mind. There is good luck and there is also bad luck, or we may just be down-on-our-luck for a time. Some would say that there is no luck at all smiling down upon them—luck always seems to smile upon "the other guy." It all seems so arbitrary and ethereal. Is it? Or is it more "earthy" than that?

My friend Lisa recently gave me this t-shirt emblazoned with the saying and emblem for: "The Luckiest Girls in the World Club!" with great graphics, color and spirit infused into every fiber. The gift was accompanied by a business-card-size Membership Card to the Club, and I just love the whole concept and story behind it. I want to quote a couple of things from The Luckiest Girls Club philosophy:
- "Luck is not a trait, it is a State of Mind."
- "Declare yourself Lucky, don't wait for it to happen 'someday'."

This is good stuff. It puts us in the realm of self-empowerment and affirmation. I am not overly fond of the state of melancholic wishful thinking. A whole different reality is within reach if we define the terms and act progressively. I can *wish* that I could go to a new level in my business, or I can get up off my backside, take classes, educate myself, use my hands and head and make that happen. I can do whatever it is that I set my mind to, luck or no luck, good luck or bad luck, if I *own* it. No excuses, no wiggle room, no blaming everyone and everything else. Whenever someone declares *me* lucky, I reflect on it. I cringe a little because it usually sounds like somehow, in some passive state of charmed existence on my part, the sun decided to shine specifically on me. But I know differently—there is a lot of work behind the scenes of that seemingly "blessed moment."

Jealousy plays a part in the whole experience. When I hear myself say to someone, "Man, you are so lucky!" I know what I am thinking: "I wish I was that fortunate, too. I wish I had what you had, went where you went…" I think I am pretty safe in saying that a few of us have visited that mental plane once or twice before. On the other hand, whenever I declare *myself* lucky, I follow it up with action and do my best to set more good things in motion. At that point I always say out loud: "Thank You, *Thank You*." You give out—the Universe gives back. What is luck really? I think *blessing* is a better definition than merely "chance." And always remember: "The harder I work…"

201

Everyone has to start somewhere

I recently read a piece written about home businesses and found myself drawn in, as the topic just happened to be about a handmade card business. Just a few words in, I became uneasy. The more I read, the more upset I became. My husband got an earful later in the day, as I "tiraded" against what I felt was a totally unfair assessment of the life I am living and have lived for the past eight years. The computer keys heated up later that same night as I fired off a rebuttal piece that got my late '60's/early '70's blood boiling in protest to such corporate arrogance and artistic elitism. Several days after cooling the anger down, I hit the Delete button. I'll start over here.

The bottom line of the author's comments went along these lines:

If you are considering starting a handmade card business:

#1: You are wasting your time because you will never make any *real* money.
#2: This is a process with one conclusion: you will wake up eventually and get out.

What is wrong with this picture? I would start with the following:

#1: Everyone has to start somewhere and getting rich may not be part of Stage One.
#2: This is a process with a huge range of possibilities, including things like product development, success, setbacks, re-adjustments, confidence-building, the most amazing, expanding array of friendships, and a host of other potential outcomes and benefits. A pre-destined "failure" is not set in stone here—a very real "process" has begun.

Of course I could get out of the handmade card business. I am in the process of doing just that right now. Is it because it has been a failure, because I finally realized what a loser-lifestyle I have been living? Hardly. It is because I am moving to new levels of a business that I love. Without the foundation that I've worked hard to develop, no *way* would I be heading in this new direction at this time. A lot more money is possible now. That's great and I'll believe it when I see it, but that wasn't the point to begin with.

Do I want to go head-to-head with the author and debate the issue? Not really. When I looked at what it was that got me so riled up, I realized that it was a matter of the very powerful nature of words. Reading the article at this time in my life did not dissuade me from my choices—it actually galvanized my resolve. On the other hand, if I had read that article a number of years ago, say when I felt like a "starving artist" or during a slow business season, or after a bomb of a show, it would have pounded me to the ground in humiliation. And if, by some unlucky turn of events, I had read that *before* I had ever started—I shudder at the thought. It bothers me a lot that people may read and lose heart. Words are very powerful. We need to think, say, write and read them very carefully.

Speaking of words and the punch they can pack, once you say out loud that you are going to follow your dream and do whatever eccentric, brave, exciting thing it is that you feel destined to do, you can absolutely count on three things:

#1) Some people are definitely going to think, and possibly even say, that you are: totally nuts, irresponsible, not thinking of your future, going to regret it, eventually going to get over it, etc. You can count on it. Don't waste your energy being shocked by it.

#2) Some other people are going to think, and possibly say, "how brave you are" and "good luck to you" (sounds like double meanings to me). These guys will generally be hanging around watching, curious about how things will turn out for you, not exactly committed to your success, just curious. Whether you do well or totally bomb, these guys will most likely say "I told you." Just smile and wave in their general direction.

#3) If you are extremely fortunate like I have been, there will be this cozy little select group of folks who will be cheering you on with support on many levels, acting like a net when you lose your balance and engaging in that most wonderful of all activities: believing in you.

As for the first group, it figures. As for the second, what else is new? As for the third, count your lucky stars and remember every single one of those loving, kind faces.

In the end, and in order to make a solid beginning, the only thing that really matters is if you believe in yourself. Whatever is written, said or thought by others, whatever experience anyone else has had or is having, simply does not need to be a major determining factor on what your personal carousel ride is going to be like. Maybe you will go round and round in circles and get absolutely nowhere fast. Maybe you'll stop the ride and get off. And just maybe you will pull a Mary Poppins maneuver and your carousel pony will take off from the traditional, redundant, "overly sweet," boring ride in the park and win the race on the fast track. Mary Poppins knew how to be real in a cartoon world and got a kick out of the dynamics. We are the ones who give people permission to discourage us or not. There will not always be a private cheering section. That must come from within.

Famous people had to start somewhere, too. Mary Engelbreit wanted to write books that no one wanted to publish—hard to imagine that now. One person suggested that her designs might lend themselves to greeting cards. I guess in one way that could have been considered a put down, but in another way, it simply was a way to get one foot in the door and get started. Now she is the queen of a designing and publishing kingdom of artwork that has delighted millions. Making cards wasn't such a dumb move after all. Now she has books and licensed art products that could cover the face of the planet.

We make a living by what we get.
We make a life by what we give.

- Sir Winston Churchill

Anger helps straighten out a problem
like a fan helps straighten out a pile of papers.

- Susan Marcot
(American writer)

Bartering
.... beyond money

Part of the thrust of this book is the discussion of various ways of making money through the development of a personal art business. One way of "making" money is "not spending it." That is called saving, but that's no fun when there are things you would like to buy, so let's talk about bartering. This is an old and oftentimes overlooked method of exchange. There are things or services I would like to procure, but don't necessarily have the money to easily fork out in that direction. It is handy to know that there are artists who are willing to make bartering arrangements with their work, and with ingenuity and willing friends, this works very well. Here are a few examples from my own experience:

- At art shows, I have neighbors in surrounding booths who have lovely things for sale. At every single art show I have ever done, I always come home with some treat, either for our home, a gift, or for me, because I traded with another artist. I meet someone, we hit it off, I love the work and would love to have something, but simply won't spend the money. Someone may feel the same way about my work, one of us breaks the ice and starts asking if "a trade" would be a fun thing to do—I always say "yes!" and then the fun begins. The easiest way I find is to simply go "retail-for-retail" as far as the exchange rate is concerned, and I can't help myself: I always give a "friendly artist's discount and a little bonus gift" to go along with the deal. I have beautiful things around my house and have been able to give handmade gifts to family and friends. This bartering "saves" money and connects me to many styles of artwork. We both have time and materials invested, but it still is mutually beneficial. (I may even get a treat for me!)
- Nancy Burdick does fabulous framing and matting—her own business. The scraps of mat board are valuable to me, and something in the way for her, so I ended up inheriting them a number of times. Since I knew for a fact that Nancy liked my Japanese cloth Masu boxes (she bought them at a gallery where I sold them), I made some for her as a type of bartering/trade/thank you gesture. I feel more comfortable receiving when I am giving as well. We both have enjoyed this informal "bartering" arrangement.
- Here's a different twist: My youngest son was in part-time day care, and at one point I needed to have a little more concentrated work time, so I bartered with my friend Julie, the director of the school. I created some specially handstamped "monopoly money" called "Impressions bucks" that were made on heavy paper with various monetary denominations on them: $5, $10, $25. I paid her the extra hours in childcare with bartering money, which she could redeem at shows or with special personal orders. She may still have some left, I'd better check.
- I have bartered Christmas cards for homemade beauty products, fish and dragonfly tiles for handmade gourds and *lots* of cards for an oil painting of a Southwest *Santuario*, framed pieces for dichroic glass jewelry, and on and on.

Bartering is a smart, fun, viable way of extending the way you see your artwork and offers another twist on how to "make money" or reshuffle money in a people-friendly way. You may have absolutely no interest in starting a business, but the idea of bartering could be a nice add-on to a hobby. Let's leave this as something to consider. It is fun.

Teaching classes

Another way to make money from your art or craft is to teach what you know. If you are an expert in your field, congratulations. You can charge more because you are a big deal. If you are not an expert, like me, for example, you can still teach a particular aspect of your work, especially on a beginner-level if that feels more comfortable for starters. I teach Beginning Stamping to groups from time to time and I enjoy it. It is always fun to watch people's faces light up when they see heat embossing for the first time. I also give classes in Beginning Carving. I gave a (free) fifteen-minute impromptu "class" to a friend in a university hallway—I love his work in pottery. He understood every word. I set him up with a few supplies and he has taken off to new levels of the art. To be a part of that process with someone is very rewarding. I look forward to carving together—I will learn a lot because David understands the clay application better than I do. We like to share.

Beyond the obvious advantage of making some money for your efforts when you are teaching more formally than in hallways, there are definite benefits: connecting with people who may become friends, honing skills that you do have, and also learning to articulate those skills in words. Preparing for classes is a good exercise because I always want to give my students *more* than what I already know, so I end up doing research on one level or other and come to my class with new things for them as well as for me.

Several times I've had students who were clearly more advanced in my technique than I was—that was a bit disconcerting. There you are at the beginning of your class and this student pulls out work to show "the teacher," and you are standing there with your mouth open wide, in awe, wishing that you could reverse rolls immediately. Flustered or not, I *am* the teacher, and rise to the occasion. The beauty of it is that those talented students and I always give something to each other. One woman in particular stands out for me. Her carving is superb—she didn't need a *Beginning* Carving Class. When I told Diana at the end of the class that I wished she had been the teacher and I could have been her student, she said: "Oh, no, Gloria. I really needed to be here. There were things that you said that helped me so much—practical, usable ideas that helped me with problems and glitches that I have dealt with and couldn't solve for years. In a few sentences, you blew the problems away! You gave me new ways to think about carving. I'm so glad that I came. It was exactly what I needed…" We learned from each other. Teacher and Student/Student and Teacher: lines don't need to be drawn in the sand. When your students surpass you in expertise—that is a moment to enjoy. Sign up for their classes.

Sure, it is nice to get paid for teaching what you know. It is also nice to know that by sharing, I am giving part of myself and I get so excited to see what another person comes up with, based on what I "taught." There is something very heart-warming and special about hearing someone say: "That person over there is Gloria Page—she was my teacher. It was a great class!" or "You know that willow chair stamp I carved in your class years ago? I still use the original one on all my correspondence." Consider the many values of teaching, from classes of school children to one person who would love a new hobby; the rewards are there. Seeing yourself as a teacher is a reward in itself: share what you know.

To teach is to learn.

- *Japanese* Proverb

Part Three

the path

The phrase "off the beaten path" has always resonated with me. I am drawn to things, places and people that are a bit "offbeat" in the sense of being engagingly fascinating, non-conformist and warm in their provocative take on life. At the same time, I love and am comforted by the absolutely normal, everyday aspects of life and people who are totally down-to-earth, genuine to the core "regular" folks. I dance around wanting to trek both paths—a little offbeat, a little "normal." I would like to believe about myself that I have a pretty wide tolerance-spectrum, but there are things that I detest, e.g. I just hate it when I am *boring*! I dyed my hair purple by accident one time, and then decided to let it go white once and for all. (Natural, yes. Boring, yes again.) I have a friend who did the purple thing—florescent—on purpose. That was a statement a bit out of the ordinary.

When I was traveling alone in Europe eons ago, I had this huge map that I carried in my backpack. My whole trip was penned in, highlights of all the criss-crossing and zig-zagging I had managed in a number of months, a visual navigational chart of my journey. Yet there were various levels of paths all being hiked at the same time, visual as well as invisible. The French map with the blue-inked lines was clearly a record of my footpath; the significant ones were the head and heart paths etched into my soul—no visible trace of those except for the stories I remember and the person I became.

As far as my art business life is concerned, there is a course, a path as well. There are some parts along the way that are predictable and normal, while my favorite parts are of the "off the beaten path" variety. There are fellow travelers and teachers encountered on this long and winding road—we head to the unknown, finding each other and ourselves.

Starving Artist
Fact or fiction?

"No es desgracia ser pobre pero es muy inconveniente."
(It is no disgrace to be poor, but it is very inconvenient.)

- *Spanish* Dicho (Proverb)

Of all the topics to cover in a book about an "art" business, talk about "touchy." Who really wants to deal with this one? Another time, another book, another author... please. But no matter how much I'd like to, I can't avoid it any longer. Let's just jump in there. "Poverty" is a powerful fear issue. Let's deal with it once and for all.

From an inspiring book cover to the exciting challenge on the back cover and all the pages in between, I am clearly and unabashedly in the "inspiration business." When I tell a story, I like a happy ending. When I asked my friends to contribute pieces for the book, I wasn't too specific, but I sure wasn't hoping for a series of "war stories from the trenches of hell" or "tales of pain on the path to poverty." We tend to want the upbeat, hopeful stuff—and I tend to want to write that, too. And then there is reality... oh *that*.

There are concepts that can seem part of the fabric of cultural lore, e.g. "writers" are miserable souls who drink too much and are bottom feeders of the angst of the world for sustenance. Another stereotypical portrayal is of the "*starving artist*," the visionary who creates with a passion and ends up dying a pauper only to have his work worth megamillions after the fact that he is dead, and the world finally "gets it." Hemingway and van Gogh come to mind. The starving artist syndrome: real? Temporary condition? Destiny?

We all know that there are great writers who have agonized moments as well as happy ones, embrace them, and know how to transform personal struggle and joy into word-visuals that speak to all of us. There are countless artists who never give up, believe in their own creativity, and finally become successful; not always rich, but that's just one definition of success, right? I would like to talk a little bit about the roller coaster that we experience when we do get on the home-business-in-art ride—the "starving artist" periods of time that take us from way up there to careening downhill at full speed— usually temporary; always disconcerting.

I can say that I have never lost money in my business. I can also say that for quite a few years there was a steady growth rate to the point that I did reach my physical limit of how much I could produce in a given month. There were times when I was in way over my head with orders and that was quite stressful until the checks came in and then it was all of a sudden very rewarding—kind of like being sick—you can't remember exactly how bad it was after you start feeling better. And then, very honestly, there are these "dry periods," weeks that can sometimes turn into months when the orders are not flowing in like a river and the money is flowing out in a torrent of bills. It feels like you are flushing it straight down the drain, funneling every red cent into the big black hole of expenses—a one-way street into the gutter leading directly to Skid Row. It is depressing. Is there a light at the end of this unbelievably long tunnel? Let's sketch out a common scenario:

You need stock—paper and envelopes, for example. The minimum order is $250. Then you check your supply of plastic card sleeves—sh(oo)t. I need those, too and it isn't worth buying less than $50 worth of those. Oh, *great*—I need to have professional photos

207

taken for that show coming up and the booth fee is due if I don't want a $25 late fee tacked onto that. In order to do the show, I need a minimum order of frames and that will eat up $250 more, so I will try to get someone to go in on the order with me. Whew—Kay needs frames, too, so we will help each other out just in the nick of time. Preparing submissions is exciting but it costs money. The value is tremendous in the long run, yet a lot of supplies and outside services are necessary to pull all of these projects together.

A gallery may have sold a lot of things for a solid period of time, and then suddenly the tourists are not buying for some mysterious reason. What seemed consistent and promising looks bleak for a season and the dream gets a bit shaky. Hidden expenses are making themselves more than visible and some questions and worries come to the surface: How can I manage? Can I make it through this period of time? How can I make this work? I do not want to become the proverbial, neon-lit, poor, pathetic starving artist.

When I decided to write this book, I altered my existence and business. I have not been miserable and I did not start to drink, but the money was not coming in like it used to. My husband worked more and I had to hang on to some things and let others go. It was a good move that I do not regret, but it stretched us pretty far and thin.

I really appreciated it when my friend Nancy gave me the "starving artist rate" on the framing mats I needed to have cut for my upcoming show. She has a home business herself—she knows. One of her pleasures in owning her own business is the fact that she can do exactly as she pleases—charge whatever the heck she wants. I know what she means—I do it, too, and I am grateful for help when I need it. We all hope for each other that the hard times are trials that will pass.

Let's examine those unnerving questions one at a time, briefly:

- *How can I manage*? It takes a plan that is steady with short-term and long-term objectives. Stagger the outgoing money with interim moneymaking projects. Accept the fact that we must spend (invest) money in order to make money and do it with wisdom and hope attached. Set priorities—in logical order. I manage best when I realize that I am not alone and seek out the assurance of friends.
- *Can I make it through this period of time*? Yes, especially as I learn the rhythms of my own business over time. Spring is always crazy for me with orders pouring in; winter is dead—no big surprise after two or three years of the same pattern. I find ways to make money during the winter by doing indoor holiday shows and using the down time to organize, carve more images, and get ready for the onslaught ahead. Take a class or two—invest in learning new techniques that will pay off in the life enrichment portion of life as well as in the future development of the business. Slow times can be very productive and refreshing—if I don't panic. I developed fabric and clay techniques during such times—a good use of time that eventually took my business much higher than staying with cards only.
- *How can I make this work*? By being innovative, focused and not giving up. The biggest obstacle to doing anything new at all usually has something to do with the very powerful four-letter word: Fear. If we run like crazy, it still chases us. This may sound a little on the nutty side, but I'll say it anyway: Shake hands with Fear and treat it like an old friend rather than a mortal enemy. "Hello. So, we meet again. How are you? I am a lot stronger than when we last met." Do not run away. Stand your ground, and walk with your "old friend" until you can part company.

I don't know anyone who looks forward to struggling. But I know a lot of people who love to tell the stories of how they did struggle, overcame fear, and eventually won. The victories take many forms and they take time. There is a deep sense of satisfaction that comes from persevering and putting the best of ourselves into action, giving it the best shot we can. When things get tight, keep the vision and "keep the faith." This book has helped me out more than once under those tight circumstances—I go back and re-read my own story and remember once again what a treasure of a life I have right now. "The Starving Artist?" Once in a while it feels that way, but mostly my plate is full and there is a banquet of possibilities—that is a fact. What kind of "rich" are we really after?

In wrapping up this discussion about "starving artists," I am going to say this loud and perfectly clear: if, in the final analysis, your business idea simply cannot work out, there is absolutely no way that it is working financially, emotionally, or for whatever reason under the sun—it just ain't gonna fly—then I say, *"Bravo!"* for the effort. You don't have to starve; you don't have to be miserable or feel defeated. Get another job. Pull up a chair and have a seat at a new table. Celebrate. Eat and enjoy it. We will all raise our glasses to honor you. *"Cheers!"* to all dreamers who try. No regrets there.

> The greater part of our happiness or misery depends on our dispositions and not on our circumstances.   - *Martha Washington*

> Why not go out on a limb? Isn't that where the fruit is?
> - *Frank Scully*

Sticking one toe in the water…

Forget those guys who jump into insanely cold Arctic holes in the ice—that is my idea of a swimming pool from hell without the heat. I am a toe-dipper most of the time. I'll work my way into the pool, thank you very much, in my own sweet time, in my own way. I prefer testing the waters before making the really big plunges. I'll get there…

That's why I started trying to sell cards by dropping them off *very* late at night on a cafeteria table where my husband was taking classes. I was toying with the idea of a "card business." I left purchasing instructions on a pleasant enough little card next to the basket of first-tries, a tin can for the cash. There was a certain level of safety in the anonymity of the whole "approach." I could handle that much at that time. Luckily for me, and my ego, there was money in the tin can and the card basket was empty at the end of the week as I retrieved them—very, very late at night. Twenty-four dollars for twelve Mother's Day cards: not bad for a first "dip." I was now ready to go ankle-deep.

I do want to say this: if you decide to stick your toe in or neck out in a similar fashion, and happen to find no money and all your cards still sitting there, please do not assume that your test-marketing was a failure and "a sign" that you might as well forget the whole thing. If you really like what you are doing, simply assume that the people who frequent that particular cafeteria have no taste or class whatsoever and try another place.

Sink or swim; dip or dive. There are as many outcomes and styles as there are people. The valuable point to consider here is simply the importance of making a commitment.

> No one tests the depth of a river with both feet.   - African Proverb (*Ashanti*)

Eagle Dance at San Felipe Pueblo

Cold. Biting cold. Several days after Christmas and the snowstorm that blanketed Santa Fe, we received a call from my Mom's friend, Dolores. She was at home at Santo Domingo Pueblo and knew that there were going to be dances at San Felipe that morning: Buffalo, Eagle and a Community Dance. We were welcomed to go—would we like to…?

As soon as my Mom hung up the phone, she was in high gear and I knew that this was good. We had missed the Christmas Day dances, and this would be our last chance for this visit. We were definitely not going to miss it. Jackets and car keys started flying.

My family had gathered for the Holidays—a re-union, a joyous celebration, and a grab-life-and-live-it-to-the-max-while-you-can kind of time. It was the end of 2000. It was a time of intense contrast for us, as if winter and summer collided on the very same day. My husband's Dad had just passed away. We had been there with him. The spirit his wife Flo showed and taught us made each moment more alive. "Life is for the living!" she said in her most amazing way of knowing the fine balance between deep sorrow and celebration. How could we possibly leave Missouri in tears, take the train to New Mexico and laugh, enjoying life? "That's *exactly* what your Dad would have wanted," she said. We received her warm blessing to remember, to cherish and to travel on… with love.

There was family from Maryland, Denver, Los Angeles, my family from Missouri and of course the welcoming crew, the folks at home base, Casa Rajotte/Lagasse in Santa Fe. We were *all* invited to attend the dances. Phone calls buzzed and a good part of the whole contingent was able to be part of the roundup. It had to happen quickly or not at all. "Indian time" has its own unique relationship to the universe and not necessarily to clocks and watches. Dolores knows. When she says: "It's best to go as soon as possible," then you do just that. Two cars were filled and we were on the way.

Heading south to Albuquerque, we would take an exit and follow the magical views. When chamisa and piñon trees are laden with snow, the vistas wide, the destination unknown, never having been there before, there is this wild west, wide-open feeling that takes over your eyes and your mind. I had never been to dances that were not public performances: those are nice, colorful, and staged for outsiders. It is generous, but not the real thing. This time it would be different. These dances were at the pueblo for the people living there. We had been invited to the inside world. I don't easily say yes and go into other people's sacred places as a spectator… We followed the signs, made the turns, slowed down, and took a left at the adobe houses, listening for the sound of the drums. It seemed like the right direction. It was. Rolling down our windows, the drums told us so.

I wanted to express my excitement, but my mother helped me to remember this was a more internal time. Like going inside a church, we were entering an outdoor holy ground. The drums seemed as if they were pounding from inside the earth, and then all of a sudden, they were coming around the corner, right where we were standing—I was stunned. The powerful Buffalo Dancers were making their way down a narrow dirt road. That dance had just concluded. It was time for the Eagle Dance at San Felipe Pueblo.

We found our way to the central plaza, a wide-open space surrounded by homes made of adobe. The tones are all of the earth. Patches of snow and ice were scattered on the packed dirt. People are the colors in New Mexico embraced by turquoise skies. It was so interesting to walk in and look around. We were the only white people there. All around the square, people of the pueblo sat with their Wal-Mart folding chairs lined up, others on benches, porches and verandas, wrapped in colorful blankets, all silent, all waiting for the Eagle Dance to begin. The drummers and chanters returned. The Eagles came to the center and the earth shook from deep inside. The eagles would soar. They would begin on earth with us and transform themselves before our eyes. My sons were very quiet. They watched intently and my youngest son sat on my lap as I sat on the frozen ground. We didn't bring lawn chairs. We stood or we sat so we could feel the beat with as much of ourselves as possible. At one point I felt self-conscious and out of place. I never wanted to gawk. I didn't want people pushing me away in their minds because of the color or lack of color of my skin. Could I be there without belonging there? I know that I do not understand the significance of what I am seeing and hearing and I know even more deeply that I long to at least touch the outside of beginning to understand. One thought alone turned it all around—we had been invited. Dolores and her daughter Maria wanted our family there. That was enough belonging for me that day.

The Eagle Dance begins. A group of men with beautiful feathered costumes start moving to the rhythm of the drums played by men and boys in the left-hand corner of the plaza. The beat intensifies, mesmerizes your senses and moves into the core of your soul. It breaks up your thinking patterns and grinds out nonsense and trivial thoughts if you surrender to it. The earth opens up and swallows you in blankets of pounding. The chants are the human cry and the Eagles prepare. There is a point when the men are gone and only Eagles remain. They speak in the tongue of nature itself and tell their story. There were moments when I was away with them. Most moments I was sitting on the hard ground with my son tapping his feet to the rhythm of Time itself.

The dance ended. There was no applause. Just silence. The Eagles became men again and they left the plaza with the drummers as the Buffalo had done. I held the cry of the eagles in the center of my mind. Then before our eyes, a large circle of dancers formed.

What struck me about the final dance was the number of participants and the tiny, tiny steps that were made throughout the entire dance. Perhaps fifty or more people circled—men, women and children of all ages in various costumes. They barely moved; their feet barely lifted off the ground as they moved together. If you have ever been in Grand Central Station during rush hour, take that experience and create in your mind the cosmic polar opposite and multiply it by a thousand—*that* was the community dance.

Different world, different sense of time and meaning… On our way out, we stopped to buy some roasted piñon nuts. I had to laugh because I realized that in order to eat these you had to take off the tiny shells, one at a time. I am so used to everything being instant. If I wanted these tasty nuts, I was going to have to be patient and work for them.

The Eagle Dance touched on many things for me. It is perhaps the closest physical expression of the spiritual experience of art and life that I have ever seen. We start on the earth in our costumes. We find a certain rhythm and go with it. If we are true to our heart and pursue the dream, we dance with our muses and become transformed as we seek to transform raw materials into new creations. We take flight and soar high in the purest moments, our internal voices shrill with delight. There is this sense that we can be all and whatever we want to be, create whatever is in our mind's eye. The time comes when it is finished. The earth closes up once again, our feet sense the snow and packed mud and we all fold our lawn chairs and go home. The drums are quiet now—I am alone in silence. Heaven was touched. Warmly wrapped all snug in bright blankets—I know… it was real.

A bamboo day

Anyone who knows me, or my artwork, knows that I have this "thing" for bamboo. It has just gone to a new level today. For whatever reason, I am completely surrounded by a virtual and subliminal forest of the stuff. There is no escape. It all started when my Mom called and asked how many bamboo placemats I would like from Pier One. There is this substantial *Sale* going on, and we would never pass one of *those* by, now would we. I could possibly use these mats to highlight my Japanese Masu boxes in my booth at art shows. "One bamboo placemat would be great, thank you so much, Ma." I then jump into my little red chile car to dash around and get some things done. At JoAnn's Fabrics, I pick up what I need and then pick up a few fab-house-decorator magazines, flipping quickly-and-quietly, inhaling the images so I don't have to buy *all* of them, just one today, and sure enough, bamboo shades and bamboo furniture are highlighted. Fabulous look, and I get to thinking about my studio and house and how to re-decorate with shades like those with my own innovations, of course, and how to make creative furniture—cheap. I run over to the Mall and a book jumps out at me—bamboo on the cover. I decided not to open the book because I wanted to reflect on this subject on my own this time, without the help of an author who did all the research for me. So, I make a conscious decision to become actively involved in this whole bamboo-obsession-thing and to participate with enthusiasm and curiosity for the whole day: a bamboo day.

I start thinking about all the cool things I can make using the two types of bamboo shades that I bought specifically for the purpose of pulling them apart to cut up and use on cards—flat bamboo slats and the long-spaghetti style rolled ones. Maybe I'll make some more tall votive lights with my 48-inch bamboo poles and handmade paper. New card designs and fabric scroll ideas come to mind. Display concepts start to gel. I see flying thing-a-ma-bobbers and bamboo stakes in the ground with Tibetan Prayer Flags fluttering. It's fun to take a one-thing-topic like "bamboo," something on the ordinary, take-it-for-granted side of life, push it and run with it. These thought waves of mine have become mental tidal waves during the course of doing a few practical errands.

Back at home, I tried to find my Sumi-e painting book that talks about bamboo notches. There are something like 80 or so different basic types of notches that you need to learn how to paint in order to have a basic working knowledge of bamboo, from the quick swish of a brush to the result on paper. Can't find the book, but that causes me to think harder to re-capture it without holding it in my hands. I glance at my Haiku books and Chinese philosophy books that have bamboo all over them. Doing laundry, I notice these bags of natural bamboo leaves that I bought from the Chinese food store, not to roll and steam rice in, but for some art thing or other, yet to materialize. Perhaps my own hand-made bamboo paper? As I sit here at the computer, I glance behind me: above my bed, for years and years, I have had this wonderful hand-painted scroll, longer than I am tall, of classic blowing bamboo done in traditional jet black ink with red signature chops in the corner. It was done in Korea many years ago on rice paper and silk, a gift from my friend in Chappaqua, NY. Then there are these wonderful stamps that I got years ago from Lynette, the original owner of Guadalupe's #1 A-OK Rubber Stamp Store just off the Plaza in Santa Fe—bamboo in a set of 4 stamps—create your own instant-gratification, Sumi-e style, no-need-to-know-the-notches kind of class act stamps. Stamp with these, and you feel like you are a master calligrapher in a Shinto Temple. And just when I thought I had had enough of this bamboo-obsession for the day and decided to have a late lunch, I sat down and couldn't believe it—turning on the TV, there was Lynette Jennings walking around this man's house in San Diego, in his personal *bamboo grove* no less, chatting it up about the strength and versatility of this amazing plant.

I have always loved the look, the feel, grace, color and spirit of bamboo. It has incredible strength, enough to build structures like houses and scaffolding 20 stories high. On the other hand, it is such an airy, blissful, delicate subject for painting, ancient and modern. It is a design element that transcends convention—it is not strictly Oriental—try Art Nouveau or Deco bamboo. Feng Shui delights in it, and practically mandates using bamboo to balance elements in interior design strategies. There is an inherent power concealed in the hollow chambers, in the fibers, and in the long, slender leaves. There are endless applications and creative uses for bamboo in its different forms. From the Fine Arts to the Home Arts, it is very utilitarian and elegant. You can make furniture and countless household objects from it, from drinking glasses to those placemats my mother is probably buying right now, to chopsticks, garden stakes, vases, writing instruments, and paint brushes for starters. There is a simplicity and a purity, a closeness to earth and sky in the same instant. I come from New England, the land of "hard rock maple." Solid, massive, heavy, and oh-so-sweet when the sap runs into your maple syrup dreams. Bamboo also is resilient and strong, yet, in contrast to Western hardwoods, it is hollow and light. You won't get maple sap running off, but you can eat the tender little shoots in the earliest stages of growth. When you put it to your mouth in another form, as a flute, such lovely sounds from different cultures float on the air. Peruvian, Japanese, East Indian—transporting melodies, evoking the exotic in our hearts. Anyone can play a bamboo flute, your own wind-breath whispering through the chambers. Try it sometime.

Today, I think what I found I love most about bamboo is not so much what I or anyone else can make with it, how it "looks," sounds, feels or tastes. The point is not what we can do with it—mostly just what it is without us. Flexible, graceful and tough, it has integrity and a simplicity of presentation. It is not dark and gnarly, twisted, rough and complex. Bamboo has a light, smooth, pared-down beauty—classic lines. In meeting strikingly clear and delightful people, I will sometimes say: "Can I be like you when I grow up?" I intend to learn some secret of life that they seem to possess. In meeting this natural substance in a fresh new way today, I know that I need to learn something very basic about and from bamboo, an object that is usually only an "art supply" for me. What is that secret? What can I learn from bamboo?

It is very, very simple: I have observed that bamboo *bends with the wind*. It can take extremely harsh winds as well as butterfly breezes. It has stamina and fortitude. Standing there, in place, it takes whatever comes, moves with it, and is not blown away. And as much as we can get buffeted around in life, and as rigid as we might become, that is a good thing to reflect upon. "As I grow up, I'd like to be like bamboo. It is flexible and it is strong. It bends with the wind." It endures with grace and style. There is intense beauty in its simplicity. One of my traveling goals in life is to visit a bamboo forest, to see it from a distance and then get closer and closer, finally entering. What a different world, to be surrounded and enveloped by such a marvelous creation. I would go in deep and then take out a little cloth, spread it out, then sit… and listen… to the leaves and the silence.

Lao-tzu, founder of Taoism, described bamboo as "yielding but triumphant." That's it!

The simple life

Couldn't life just be simpler? Does it always have to get so complicated all the time? I want to prune the complexities, anxieties and inanities right off the tree of my existence, from the roots up. I want to simply live a clear life, to love the people I love, to do what I love doing and make a living from it, if that is at all possible. I want *out* from the rat race and I pray for the pure joy of knowing that what I am doing everyday has meaning beyond making money and keeping the house and people living in it relatively together. In search of new direction and change, I want to explore options. This is not a mid-life crisis and I am not in need of crisis management or therapy for this particular point. I just need to understand how I can pare things down in order to put things and me in order.

I have been hearing such thoughts spoken out loud around me, from friends and acquaintances, and from inside of myself, too. In an interesting twist, as we constantly seem to be building upon our past, there is this counter-point desire to seek and find the Simpler Life, a way of almost pulling it all apart and "un-building." I am not advocating a retreat from "civilization," though at times that sounds pretty inviting, I must admit. I am proposing an attitude shift.

On the most basic material level, *simplifying* has to do with nitty-gritty things like cleaning out basements and closets, garages, and dusty boxes. There is a movement in this country that borders on the religious that speaks of the value of re-evaluating our cluttered lives and getting out from under the heap. This is good. We can click into this gung-ho attitude that translates into major garage sales, buying plastic organizer boxes and shelving units, making donations to the Salvation Army, all in hopes of attaining a certain level of salvation and sanity for ourselves. Save me, please, from being buried alive by *stuff*. I don't need all of this. I lived for months in a tent in France—you literally can carry on your back what you really "need." A fair amount of the rest of it is fluff. Comedian George Carlin does this great routine about the cycles of acquiring "stuff" and later trying to unload it in order to make room so that we can get even more. My personal goal is basic when it comes to "the material world": I would like to know what I have and where I put it. I want to label and protect what is archival and valuable. I would like to know that what I don't need could find a useful home somewhere else or deep-six it and be done with it. Order and purpose—period.

When I gaze at photos of the rooms in classic Japanese homes, a predominant feature is *space*. What an odd and wonderful idea that is: space, pure and simple. I'm not all that sure that what I am seeing in those photographs is all that practical—there must be a Fine Art of Storage—but I do know that I am on a quest for the kind of simplicity that such pictures evoke. The challenge then becomes finding the applications to different aspects of my own life in stages.

Buying a ticket to Tokyo first thing in the morning to see a Room With Space isn't the answer. Reading up on Feng Shui and organizing my house and studio is part of the answer that I need to work on, and another part of the answer is something that I have been working on for a number of years now. In seeking to define a Simpler Life, I decided that working from my home was a significant part of that quest. That was many years ago. I sincerely felt that by having a home-based business my life could be more my own for me and my family. There have been interesting twists and turns in the time since. Some things became simpler, others complicated—everything more meaningful.

Today I met with several people and was listening at one point to a friend talking about her job and how burnt-out she is. Years and years in a profession, feeling tired, frustrated and a list of other emotions that spelled: drained. Her story brought out other people's stories, and in the course of an extended conversation, we all reflected on this need we are feeling to express ourselves in our work in meaningful ways—to get to the essence of who we are and find the simple lifestyle that would most genuinely express that. A lawyer goes the whole distance from grinding through Law School to passing the bar to realizing he just doesn't want to be a Lawyer after all. Where do you go with that? A nurse finds that the world of medicine is a different world today than when she entered the profession, and wants out. She also happens to be an emerging artist—where does she go from here? A full-time artist friend is wondering if she should just give in and get a job at McDonald's, or keep going and not give up. So, working at home isn't always the easy way out and the great cure-all miracle answer either. Are there any simple answers in the pursuit of simplicity and fulfillment?

There are plenty of folks who are satisfied with their lifestyle choices. That's great. The rest of us need to be there for each other, to be creative, gentle, and determined to take steps, one after the other. To have a dream and vision grounded in reality—to be a personal conduit between heaven and earth. To remain open and hopeful enough to see possibilities when they present themselves, with enough good, clean energy and common sense to act upon them. One of my friends today was addressing the issue of people believing that if they do pursue their passion in life, somehow, automatically, magically, they will be showered with money and success—this attitude that, for some reason, they are entitled to it, *expecting* it because it is due to them after all of their pain and suffering. That is for the info-mercials and all power to them if dedication and the $49.95 packet can make that happen. That is the world of defining your passion usually in terms of money. In the creative arts world, on the other hand, a simpler life is possible, but there may also be sacrifices involved, some small and others substantial.

Speaking of my own situation, I don't have to spend my days working for someone else, have a boss directing my every thought and move, deal with stressful work-related problems and relationships in the workplace, doing work that means nothing to me as a person. My life is much simpler in many ways. On the other hand, things are not always easy and cushy and clear. I have to make decisions everyday by myself. Some days I make better decisions than on other days. I have also chosen to make sacrifices, too. In my house, what we consider luxuries are basic necessities to a lot of people we know and to Middle America in general. We have made certain trade-offs for many years now, and I have no regrets. I do have ambitions and pursue them. And without my husband's support and his willingness to put up with the nonsense of his job that has security benefits for all of us, I probably wouldn't be sitting here writing this book talking about my pursuit of the simpler life and a personal-passion lifestyle. I am very grateful. I hope our children will look back on our lives with happy memories and a secure sense of values, confident to pursue their own dreams and willing to work hard to get there.

One of my many personal goals is to go on all of my children's field trips—simple enough. I watched my son Brandon wading in a stream yesterday and saw a part of him that was new and glorious for me to see. Hearing *about* "the trip" later could never give me what I was given by being there. He saw *me* going after bugs with a butterfly net, proudly catching a damsel fly for him, which he proudly sketched, sitting with friends by the bubbling, cool stream at the dawn of summer. We were there, learning and romping together. A photo could never re-create or give me what we shared. It was a simple kind of day, and because of my lifestyle, humble as it is, this day was possible.

From time to time in my life, people have said that I probably would have fit into life better at an earlier time in human history, before things got too high speed and high tech. I think I know what they mean, and tend to agree with the heart of the insight. Yet the fact of the matter is that here we are, together on this planet at this time-juncture, as crazy and complicated as it is, with choices spread out before us. I believe that success, satisfaction, and simplicity are compatible and attainable. It's worth a whole-hearted try, no matter where we're coming from or where we're headed. A simpler life begins in our minds. How that translates into a lifestyle from that point on is our choice.

Life is what we make it, always has been, always will be.
- *Grandma Moses*

The "Neutral Zone"

Transitions: from complicated to simple, from one place to another—transitions can take many forms. It is good to take note of the stages and recognize that we also need a little space and time. Does everything have to be in such a rush? I don't think it does.

There are times when we are in high gear. Life is fabulous; the job is a dream. There are other times when everything seems to be in reverse and the emergency brake is good for absolutely nothing. Cruising along smoothly is a preferred state of affairs, and when that happens, we hope it lasts for as long as possible. Then there is "The Neutral Zone."

My friend Janet is the first one to coin that phrase for me and I adopted it and worked it around in my own head. Being in the neutral zone is not exactly stalling, but we aren't going forward or backward either. It isn't negative in its essence, it's not really depression (reverse), more of a kind of funk of indecisiveness—my motor is humming, but I'm not moving in any direction quite yet. Things and life in general are on hold for the time being—everything in me and around me is in neutral.

At first I get nervous when I feel like that. I have "neutral-zoned" a number of times in the past year, so I am getting a little used to it and can find first gear sooner and easier now. What I would like to say about the neutral zone is that I have found it to be a very good place if I embrace it rather than panic. (Panicking is not a productive state of mind, I tell myself.) The neutral zone is a place of observation and reflection once we kick fear and embarrassment out of the picture. I tend to get a lot of little things done in the neutral zone because I have chosen to contemplate the bigger picture and tend to hover around home base. One thought—it can be lonely there, so it is good to remember that friends exist and to reach out during the process. Getting to a new place means that we might visit the neutral zone first. Don't worry—it isn't The Twilight Zone or The Twinkie Zone. It doesn't need to be scary or crazy. We have time to think, and might as well make it "interesting" and memorable while we're here. Look around. Check out the scenery and visit with fellow travelers. This is simply a visit—we won't stay here forever.

Hanging on and *Letting go*
When you want to advance to new things and not lose your foundation
and your mind in the process…

It had been a number of years since doing a "bookmark order." The telephone rang and it was a nice woman from Texas with a special request: "A couple of years ago I was in New Mexico and bought several of your bookmarks—I love them and wondered if you could make more for me. I will order at least ten or twenty. Would you do that for me? Please? *Please*?" I paused. I'm basically a nice person, so I've been told. I want to make my customers happy, so I said, "Yes, just for you." The order turned out to be twenty assorted bookmarks. It took me too long to get to it, so I included several freebies as apologies and learned something in the process—I really don't want to do wholesale bookmarks anymore. I let that go.

Several weeks ago a man called from Kansas. Someone in New Mexico bought and sent him a St. Francis card that I made years ago and wondered if he could order a dozen for himself. (Sigh.) I said, "Yes, just for you." If I don't make that order *today* I will not let myself sleep. It should have gone out two days ago. I might as well send a few extra cards to accompany my apologies in there, too. I dragged my feet both times because I really didn't want to do that type of order *one more time*. In the moment I wasn't able to admit it to myself or communicate my position in a way that was acceptable to me.

There are times when it is probably an excellent idea to let things go even though people may want you to hang on and you may question your own wisdom and sanity in wanting to pursue new avenues when the secure foundation seems to be firmly in place. I just don't want to get stuck or feel trapped—I want to build upon foundations—to feel the freedom to expand without stretching it all (and myself) too thin in the process.

I love making cards and have a plan in place as to how I can reduce and expand simultaneously—let certain accounts go and focus on the ones that allow me to experiment with higher-end products. Grab my paper tools and push them into clay, lay them out on fabric and write about the whole process as it is happening. I am hanging on and letting go. It is working. It is also a lot easier said than done.

I am happy to do "special favor orders" for people from time to time, but I also need to free it up internally to be able to say: "Thank you for the compliment. I am doing other things at this time. You are welcomed to check out my websites to see what's new!"… Then let it go at that, right then and there. It is time to move on—to grab something new.

This is a trapeze act and you are the artist. The safety net is a contingency plan and friends—you'd better have a few of them on stand-by. Swinging in the air, hanging on for dear life—a moment of release—*right there*—you suspend reality and defy gravity. You let go…….aaaaaahhhhhhhh! You are flying!

The only courage that matters
is the kind that gets you from one minute to the next.
- *Mignon McLaughlin*
(American writer)

You should always know when you are shifting gears in life.
- *Leontyne Price* (American Opera Singer)

217

Change is the only given

"One cannot step twice into the same river."   - *Herakleitos*

Find a mountain, sit down and look at it. Do not move. If you don't have the Rockies in your backyard, just pretend. With a camera, take a picture of what you see, then take another picture right after the first one. When they are developed, put them side-by-side. They look exactly the same, right? But are they?

What looked static to the eye and then appeared to be the very same in print is deceiving—tremendous change took place, unseen by the camera lens or naked eye. Let's say the season happens to be fall. Thousands of leaves fell in the time it took to take the two photos. The rush of water from earth through roots nourishing all the living cells of the trees, the insects and earth critters scampering, burrowing, eating, dying, reproducing —the sheer forces of nature and life itself are pulsing and vibrating in what we perceive as a peaceful "still" shot—not to mention the fact that the moon is trucking around the earth, the earth is spinning like a top as it simultaneously cruises at 66,600 mph around the sun… So much dizzying, stimulating motion and change. And I am just sitting here.

Let's narrow the focus and turn the camera on ourselves: self-portraits. Take two quick back-to-back photos. Pretty much the same, wouldn't you say, and yet even in a split-second of time such as that, great changes can take place. I can break a fear that has gripped me forever. I can make a choice that will alter my course in life. I can say "yes" (when my comfort zone tells me "no") to change. A frown became a smile. Everything in life, from the sub-atomic to cosmic levels, is in constant motion and change. There is a certain point when I get sick and tired of not actively engaging and participating. It is time to get out of my chair and dance to a new tune. Sometimes it is just time to *change*.

Is it time to sell the tent and outdoor art show "stuff?" Then sell it at a fair price to help another artist along on his or her path—and move on. Is it time to get a part-time job to supplement the artist's life, which is not as predictable as we would sometimes like it to be? Then find one and feel grateful for it. Change can be as liberating as it can be frightening. I decided to take my entire master set of cards, over 300 designs organized in many different lines, pull them out of their carefully labeled sleeves—and chop them up. It was a bit on the traumatic and dramatic side of things when I pulled the first card out, knowing that once I did that I could no longer identify that card with a rep or customer. A system developed over eight years became completely defunct in no time at all. I actually stuck it back in the plastic sleeve for one panic-ridden second, got a grip, pulled it back out and kept going. Faster and faster, free from what had been and on to what could be.

A substantial pile of sleeves got trashed. To my right were hundreds of cards that meant a lot to me, so I started chopping them up—in order to save them for one last journey to one outdoor show and also one wonderful bookstore. I cut and glued, creating a beautiful one-of-a-kind set of cards that I will never make again. For the show, I made many more new cards, did a great blowout sale of ten cards for $20 and sold a lot. There were 156 cards left, 13-dozen exactly. St. John's College Bookstore in Santa Fe wanted every single one of them. My samples were all gone—even the Christmas ones in June.

Immediately following that, I received an e-mail that set a whole new pace for me— enter the "age of design" instead of production. One-two-three major jobs lined up which made such a major impact that I decided to change the name of my business. I breathe differently when contemplating major decisions, knowing that change is the only given.

In honor of passion

I touch the future. I teach. – *Christa McAuliffe*

I was a college freshman who was into natural foods and was openly "anti-smoking." This was a long time ago, so there were no "no smoking" rules that prevailed in the classrooms. I was subjected to smoke occasionally and generally resented it. It was a "No Tolerance Zone" for me, except in this one-and-only case. Somehow I had room in my strongly held belief system to allow one person on the planet the freedom from my judgment on smoking. *Only* one—his name: Mr. Michael Ossorgin, my Ancient Greek professor at St. John's College in Santa Fe.

I loved this man, my tutor. I loved his stories and his presence. His accent was laced with a Russian spirit, his hair a thick shock of white, those penetrating eyes blue enough to make Poseidon, Greek god of the sea, envious. He was solid, massive and warm-hearted. I think I've mythologized his tale over the years, but I don't really care. Some people deserve to be Myths. It seems he was the descendant of the Mayor of Moscow at the time of the Russian Revolution and had to flee to Paris. He became a Russian Orthodox priest and had a chapel on his land in Santa Fe, near St. John's. I loved the way he taught Greek because I knew he loved the language personally, not just academically. He knew I did, too. We met on that hallowed ground. Mount Olympus U. had a branch in Santa Fe. It was tucked into the hills of Monte Sol and Monte Luna.

One day in class, he started teaching and lit up one cigarette. I hardly noticed. I was intent on the translations and discussion. Another was lit—he was transported by some story he was telling us. The first two were still going and then as he meandered around the room and history, two more were lit, all four cigarettes going at the same time! He paused to make a point and asked a question: "Where is my cigarette?" We couldn't believe it! "Which *one*, Mr. Ossorgin? You have four cigarettes going at the same time!" His face became bright red and he laughed heartily as we all joined in. He put out three, picked up the last one, looked to the heavens and transported us back in time to the land of the Ancients, a mere wisp of smoke away…

To see people carried away by their passions… it is an honor and a trust. I was in the presence of a genius heart and mind that were shamelessly impassioned and I wanted to immerse myself in the ether of the whole atmosphere. It isn't everyday that one encounters a True Teacher. It isn't everyday that I have the opportunity to engage and be elevated in the process—to be set free and know myself as a True Student.

Whenever I listen to or read a biography, I listen very closely for the references to "the teacher in my life" stories. Whatever grade, whatever subject, it doesn't matter. For all of us, I believe, there was at least one teacher whose life touched ours for the good, and I believe in holding on to that. Whenever I give presentations at schools, whether it be a Creative Process Class at the University or a 5th Grade Career Fair talk or wherever, I always ask myself a question in preparation before entering a classroom: "If I could leave this class having imparted just one helpful, good, wise word, what would it be?" After all of these years and all the different ages and events, three words always come to mind: Inheritance, Generosity and Gratitude. Those are big words for 5th graders and they are big life lessons at any age. Leaving a word to think about is one thing—living the example is the main point. I am always in search of people who actually do what they say. They are our teachers and they come in all shapes, sizes, ages and times in our lives.

Here is a most special person: my high school English teacher, Mr. Dale Wagner. Before meeting him, I had been driven to learn. I crammed information in and more was pushed in than I could sometimes assimilate. Mr. Wagner revealed the world of *loving* to learn and the universe and my mind opened up. He believed I could *write* and so here I am, writing. He believed I was "the most thoughtful person ever to graduate from St. Paul." (That was written in a note sent to me in 1997.) It is a personal daily goal to live up to that compliment. We were both *old* by that time in 1997, both with white hair I presume, although I can't imagine his red hair becoming anything but more red. The warmth of memories and mutual gratitude burn bright, despite the passage of time.

I remember our class was invited once to his home. This was so novel and absolutely the wildest thing I could imagine. For eight years my experience had been that teachers were nuns who lived in convents. My freshman English teacher was a man who had a wife and a regular life that he invited students to share. We were ready and starving for that kind of reality, a new depth of commitment and connection; we were welcomed into his world. Certain boundaries and fears were gently opened and cleared. He was always "the teacher." We, as students, maintained a sincere level of respect and appropriate distance, yet he allowed and fostered a closeness to what we were learning and to each other that showed us that wonderful experiential world of learning as a community.

Way back when, Mr. Wagner gave me the highest grade in English you can get. Twenty or so years later, when we met again in the high school hallway because I decided to drop in when I was visiting family in Connecticut, he remembered me, and remembered the fact that he had given me that grade. He said that he later questioned doing that and had never before or since given the "perfect" grade to anyone else—we all know that no one is perfect. I have to say that I didn't feel from the look on his face or the tone of the story that he regretted having given it to me, and I can honestly and quietly say that I wouldn't give it back, not because I think I deserved the perfect grade, but because I know that my experience with our teacher did. It was perfectly wonderful.

There are other teachers and friends who have been, are, and will be in the active position of "teacher" in my life if I am open and willing enough to inherit from them. Their generosity is a point of deep gratitude for me. My son Brandon has a piano teacher, Brad Johnston. He is my teacher, too. I make him an omelet every Sunday morning before the lesson for several reasons, the main one being that I thoroughly enjoy his company, humor, wisdom and insights. My piano playing has vastly improved by osmosis as well. Sitting quietly at the kitchen table, I don't miss a word.

Inheritance, generosity and gratitude—in my business, too, those three words have played a significant role. Positioning myself as a student time and again, giving what I have to offer to others in the best ways I know how, and being grateful for the whole process is a lot of what this book is about. I want to know that place of being so completely involved, so completely in love with whatever it is that I am doing, with living itself, with my special people, that I ignite in spontaneous emotional/spiritual combustion and "light up!"

Mr. Ossorgin passed away many years ago. His daughter Lydia told my Mom that he always kept an embroidered velvet bookmark I had made for him decades ago in his cherished old Bible on the altar in his chapel. It was such a little gift, that bookmark. I do remember making it for him, all the careful, tiny stitches… I love the fact that it was used, not just admired—so wonderful to have a place in the pages of a loved book…

…I am going to make a copy of this and send it along to Avon, Connecticut and hope that Mr. Wagner is still at the last address I have for him. Perhaps he will take out a red pen once again—he's more than welcomed—I need all the "English" help I can get. I don't know if I can pull "A's" anymore and it certainly doesn't matter. I do know that the most important thing to consider is the fact that, in the big picture, you never know how many times you will have the opportunity to say "thank you," those two truly "magical words." Write them down and send them, Gloria. Don't wait. Better yet, call information and get his home number. I did. St. Paul Catholic High got the next call, and sure enough, he is still teaching there. I left a message for him that I would be trying to reach him, and tonight we spoke on the phone. It was so great to laugh together, reminisce and say "thank you" …to each other. I sent a bit of this book along and later this e-mail came:

…"Thirty years later I am still in awe of how well you write and how much feeling you can infuse into a simple sentence. You have the power to charm. There is something naïve and unaffected in these personal reminiscences. Nothing appeals to me more! I remember the young Gloria of promise, hope, and undaunted nature. The one who believed there were "sermons in stones and good in everything." It is good to meet her again in these pages. Dale"

The teacher/student relationship—two models have moved me most profoundly—two models of "learning" that I enjoy the most. Here is a little sketch of both:

Journey to ancient Greece, find Socrates and walk with him. Listen to his questions, engage in a dialogue, watch him write in the sand. Whatever you thought you knew, however confident you were to define the greatest and the most common of ideas, will be humbly and completely challenged. Go ahead—tell Socrates how you would define "virtue." You will go on a mind quest that will test and twist the core of your being. You are not playing a philosophical game of bending words. You are searching for: the Truth.

Now, trek to Japan dressed in the humble robes of a novitiate covering your body and hiding your arrogance. Go ahead—knock at the gate of the monastery and wait. After a good long time, a monk will come eventually (and slowly) and ask you a question like, "Who are you and what do you want?" Not exactly subtle. You answer (since you were asked) and after all your politeness and hierarchical correctness, stand there and find the door slammed in your face. Hang on a minute. You said your name. You said you wanted to be a *student*. You also found out that until you could give up your name and realize that you had no clue as to what it is, you were not going to get past the gate, and once in: good luck. Go ahead—sit down with the master and tell him, ever so humbly that you are here to be his student. As he silently pours tea into your cup, and keeps pouring until it is all over the table and your lap, it might mean back to the gate for you until you can next figure out that you had better empty your "cup" before sitting with the teacher. I love it!

There is a passion in the heart of the teacher. There is a passion in the heart of the student. Teacher and student—when they meet, there, right there—no matter what time, place, style of words or no words at all—*that* is the sacred place of learning.

The most useful piece of learning for the uses of life is to unlearn what is untrue.
                                                              - *Antisthenes* (Greek Philosopher)

Creative Process Class

Wait a second: Who's the teacher and who's the student here?

Ever since meeting Dr. Betty Scott at my first Art in the Park outdoor show, I have been teaching one class each semester in her Creative Process Class at the University of Missouri. I can still hear her declaration in my tent years ago that "…you will be teaching classes at the University" and my reaction to that, which was to laugh hard and long… wondering. I was also told to *write this down*: Natalie Goldberg/*Writing Down the Bones*. I wrote it down. It was five years later when I finally bought it—and read it.

I still laugh when she makes big declarations, but I listen harder now because I am serious at the same time. Some doors are being shown to me, some are being opened and others require forced entry if I want what's on the other side badly enough. Betty brings out the experimental artist in me. This is good.

Betty has been a Music Professor at the University for 25 years—trumpet is her specialty, the students are her "kids," and the CP Class her creation. I have been fortunate to tag along. Each semester, year after year, different seasons, different moods, I found myself skinnier one time, a bit heavier the next, the same question was mine to address to a new set of faces: "How did I start my art business and where am I at today?" I talked about the process from there to here from "today's" vantage point. "Self-illuminating" is a good expression to nail down the experience. It is a unique opportunity to be able to do that year after year. It took a few years to sink that into conscious awareness. Oh my, look at me. How interesting: this presentation is *very* different than last time, which is a complete metamorphosis from the very first. One time I took quite a bizarre turn into a tangential plane that led us into "life in the sixties and hippies," as I tried, I guess, to reminisce my way back into feeling what it was like to be the same age as the students before me. Betty kindly brought me back to the present tense and the topic at hand, thank you very much. She left me on my own after the first couple of classes. Sometimes I was bubbly, at other times reflective, a few times wiped-out or scared. I stood there, right in front, no matter *what* was going on inside of me and started talking. Speaking is good training for living. The foundation for this book was being written by being spoken first.

It became crystal clear that even though I was the person in front of the class with the responsibility to keep on talking for most of the 1½ hours, I clearly was a student of my own story as much as anyone sitting in the "listeners' seats." I was asked to "teach" the class, but I have really been a student in the Creative Process Class for many years. "Did I pass? Do I get to graduate, Dr. Betty?" (Her answer: "That takes a lifetime, my dear.")

While I was sitting on the floor in the hallway today waiting for one class to clear out, I reflected on past years and decided to read a little before going to the head of the class. I pulled out Natalie Goldberg's *Wild Mind* and found myself reading the chapter on "Enlightenment." The "Try This" section directed me to confidently proclaim in public: "I am a writer!" whenever people asked me what I do. Here I am, sitting on the floor, the students start filing in, I watch, read, get myself up and stand in front of the class. With my finger positioned in the book, I open it, read out loud what I just had finished reading, and did exactly what I was told to do. *Say it*. "I am a writer! I am writing a book about my art business and that is what I am going to talk about today. I am an artist. I am Gloria Page and I am happy to be here." Period. That was a fairly big leap from earlier classes— believe me. (This was in February of 2000. I had started writing the month before.)

The very first class, I didn't have a clue as to how big the University was and how insane parking can be. Balancing two big display/materials boxes, I ran to the classroom and barely made it in time. As I was clearly flustered, Betty calmly took the pressure off by doing a few things with the students so that I could set up and settle down. I brought many pieces, many glass-framed, and my back was killing me. I held my notes and found my way. I got through it anyway. After the class, Betty and I were chatting and she put me through a delightfully painful little exercise called "Who Are You?" (Remember?) Despite my nervousness and insecurities, it was the beginning of giving "talks." There were students who laughed, cried, reflected; some asked interesting questions. One (tired?/*bored*?) student snored (disconcerting!). A few students apologized for him—that was nice. Others started their own card businesses, inspired to try. That felt very good.

Over time, I carried less "stuff" to the talks since I think I didn't need to physically prove that I indeed did what I said I was doing—I brought photos and cards instead; from a long speech written out, to one page of notes, to one 3x5 index card with these same "book stories." I sometimes gave artwork away as treats. Offering to teach stamp classes at my house to interested students turned into a big deal when they actually took me up on the offer. A couple of times we had to make two classes because so many students wanted to come to my small space. My husband was very helpful—he took our kids for Sunday afternoon outings and the students had my attention and all of my supplies to play with. I just loved watching the creative energy flowing around my studio and the ingenious ways of using my tools. Once again, I was the "teacher" I suppose, but why do I always come away feeling that I have learned a heck of a lot more than I've taught? That is an excellent position to be in, I must say. Many of their artistic creations became part of mid-term projects, and I felt proud of their work and the fact that I was part of it.

Quite a few MU students in the Creative Process Class are J-School students (School of Journalism). I have been part of many interviews, class papers, newspaper articles, even a radio show, by connecting with people in the class. I make myself available as much as possible. This evening I will be meeting at the Lakota Café downtown for an interview. Lauren sees me as a good "school project" apparently. Even though I've been there before as the "interview-ee," each time is fresh and new. It will be interesting to see where we go with the story. It is now October and so much has changed since sitting on the floor way back there in February.

It is never "the same old story," no matter how many times I tell it. I knew at one point that this opportunity was a limited time offer. My hesitation to give more classes had turned into my requesting to do them. Betty has retired. She *is* the Creative Process Class, so wherever she goes from this point on, the "class" goes with her. A loss for the university for sure, but I am lucky. She is my friend. And as we know, everything in life is a process. Betty, thank you for the Creative Process Class—a gift that keeps on giving.

While driving to the campus, I would always ask myself what I wanted to give them, and came up with lists of stories and three words: Inheritance, Generosity and Gratitude. If I put myself in the "beginner's mind" mode, I stand to *inherit* from young and old and from circumstances that might otherwise have whooshed right on past or caused me to stumble. If I am *generous* with what has been given to me, and express *gratitude* along the way, life is rich, filled with gifts. Why not three other words like happiness, goodness and love? And what about all of the other powerfully good words? I believe that if we practice, breathe and live the first three, the result will be a life filled with all the rest.

Fifth Grade Career Fair

My son Brandon came home with a paper. You know how *that* goes—there are millions of papers—with two kids it means there are billions. I am pretty careful because I have responsibilities attached to the info. One whole side of my refrigerator is dedicated to "Derby Ridge Elementary Notes and Calendars." Good luck keeping that straight.

A Fifth Grade Career Fair was coming up and volunteers were needed to represent different occupations. Okay. I have been writing for the last ten months about my business—it is a good time to talk once again, so I signed up. But I didn't hear anything back, so I figured they were set for artists and let it go. Then the day before, I got a message from the Elementary Career Counselor, Alice, asking if I had any questions before the event and *my presentation*? Hmmm—interesting question and timing.

Brandon is con*vinced* that he gave the papers to me and I am convinced that the same culprit who eats socks in the laundry is responsible for the disappearance of these three mysterious papers. No problem—we'll wing it. What else is new? Alice and I connect the afternoon before; I get those three papers in hand and don't let go. I stay up until way after midnight (no big deal), making 40 very cool bookmarks for my potential booth visitors. School colors: purple and green. Mascot: Dragon. Combining a Chinese dragon stamp, handmade paper from India, all color-coordinated and sparkled with holographic embossing powder, I am destined to have happy smiles on the children surrounding me.

Little did I know what kind of impact this was going to have on me personally…

Sixteen adults showed up to make presentations. I was told that as the "Artist" I had the biggest sign up—that was interesting to me. My son signed up to hear me, but he was re-routed to other presentations—he knows my story already, I guess. The idea was that within the confines of one hour, each of us was to give our talk four times to up to ten children each rotation. With traveling to different trailers and a two-minute Q&A period at the end, realistically we are talking ten minutes at the max. *Ten minutes* to address the following guideline questions:

- Describe what a day is like at your job?
- What kinds of things do you do?
- Where do you work?
- With whom do you work?

Tell why you chose your career path and specific career.
Describe the training or education needed for the job.

Which school subjects do you need most in your career? (We are trying to show students how all of these subjects are relevant to them, so please emphasize the specific subjects and clearly illustrate the significance of each in your profession:)

Reading	Social Studies	Computer	Science
Math	Spelling	Language	Writing
Fine Arts	Phys-Ed		

- When you were a child, which subjects were your best or favorites?
- What do you like about your job?
- What do you *dis*like about your job?
- What advice do you have for someone thinking about this job as a career?

There you go. Answer all of those questions in *ten minutes or less*, show your visual aids, take questions, give answers and hope that it makes sense and leaves some kind of good impression so that the students will be left with inspiration and not total confusion.

This was a very good thing for me to do at this time. I have been writing a lot and there are scores of papers, thousands of words. Now throw it all in the dryer on high and shrink it down in major ways. Condense all these words, stories and examples and tell the basic bare bones of it all. I did it. I actually dealt with every single topic. Writing this book has helped my thinking and honed my speaking. I even managed to give a reason as to why PE played into my profession: you need muscles and stamina to set up art shows and good arm strength for the amount of stamping I do on a daily basis—creative answer. At the end of the hour I was stretched, exhausted, smiling, reflective and very moved by the whole experience of being with the kids and my fellow adults, quite a diverse and caring group. It took me a few minutes longer than most to pick up my display materials, so I got to hear a direct compliment about me from one of the students reporting to her teacher and classmates about her experience. That makes it more than worth the effort.

When I opened the door of the school to leave, a fifth-grader from another class who had attended my presentation, Shane, ran over and asked if he could meet me by the water cooler in the morning so that I could *sign* his bookmark! Isn't that just the best? The value of the artist's signature—Shane knew. We met in the morning. I was ready with three different pens so that he could choose the color and the place for me to sign—superb taste he has—he knew the best color and the perfect spot. As I wrote my name, I watched his beaming face. Proudly displaying his bookmark to a Special Ed Teacher who happened to be walking by, I suddenly realized that she also happened to be Shane's Mom—nice timing and connection. He wants so much to an artist when he grows up…

A couple of tears made their way down my cheeks, and as I walked home, I slowed things way down. I crammed and jammed a lot of stuff the day before. Why do I do what I do? What do I like and what do I dislike? I said that I liked the entrepreneurial life, the creativity and freedom to make my business as big or small as I wanted. Being my own boss was a big plus because it meant that I could make choices to be with my kids and not be pulled away. I could be at the Career Fair if I wanted to be. I said that I disliked two things: Getting bored sometimes if the work was too repetitive and working alone and at times feeling lonely. Other than that, I was more than happy.

The "advice" question was the same one that a junior high student asked me last year in a telephone interview, and I answered in the same basic way: "Learn everything that you can about many subjects and don't limit yourself to what you think you might need. The 'life of an artist' sounds so nice—all you have to do is sit under a tree painting or drawing, right? Wrong. Making money at it is another matter. It is work and it brings into play a lot more of yourself and life skills than a brush in your hand. My advice: *Just Do It* if this is your heart's desire. Give whatever you try your very best effort and stay open to the road ahead." It only takes a few seconds to say that. Living it… well…

Looking at their sincere faces, some serious, others bubbly, silly, indifferent, curious, tired, respectful, honest, and on and on, I couldn't help but think of how much I would have loved and appreciated such an opportunity when I was so young. These are fifth graders and they have classes challenging them to learn about and consider "what they might want to be when they grow up." They are not just having that question thrust at them, but they are being given opportunities to engage in conversations with adults from divergent backgrounds who willing to share encouragement and enthusiasm, one-on-one.

The day after the Fifth Grade Career Fair, after my long slow walk, I spoke at the University to the Creative Process Class once again, probably for the last time, since Dr. Betty Scott is retiring. Here they were, back-to-back experiences of the same basic idea, laced with slightly different vocabularies—from 10-year-olds to 20-something-year-olds. This time I had an hour-and-a-half for one class instead of ten minutes and I decided to use the fifth grade outline as a loose guide. It was very gratifying and revealing. As certain things are being wrapped up in my business life experience to date, others are opening up and I am in transition to the new. I was teaching and learning, once again.

 Signing that bookmark at Derby Ridge Elementary was a circle completed for me. I started with bookmarks at the very beginning of the business in 1993. I made some once again for the Career Fair and I'm sure there will be more to come still, yet that is not "the business" any longer. Wrapping up five years of presentations at the University Creative Process Class, semester after semester, now that is finished, completed, too. The next chapter is in the process of being written even as I write about the wrap-ups.

In a follow-up questionnaire to Career Fair participants, we were asked if we would be willing to speak at other schools if the need should arise for volunteers in our respective fields. Would I jump at another chance to make rapid-fire presentations to ten-year-olds? You bet. It would be an honor and my heartfelt pleasure.

The honor did come—a new year, a new school and a new me to give the presentation. I take these things seriously and joyfully. I learn a lot by seeing that what could be "the same old thing" just isn't that at all. My approach and what I feel I'd like to offer develops over time. Each child is a whole world to the future. All you need to do to know that is to look into their eyes and listen to their questions. When a bright-faced fifth grader raises his hand and respectfully asks: "Can I ask you if you feel that doing creative work is a spiritual experience for you?" it takes your breath away and makes you acutely aware of the beauty and power of words. I paused and breathed deeply before venturing an answer, because I knew it was going straight to his heart. I said, "…yes, it most definitely is, and I am so moved that you would ask that question. What is your experience? Is it spiritual for you?" "It's hard to put it into words. Something happens as if it is coming from outside of you, a kind of feeling and idea that you didn't know you had until it comes to you… something like that. Do you know what I mean?" "In my best moments, yes, I do know what you mean." Time was up and the kids were out the door and I just had to sit down and reflect for just a second until the next group arrived. I didn't want to feel stuck in regret that my answer was nothing compared to what it might have been, so I started my talk once again and knew I was changed by that little boy with the very big question.

 Around the same time as this experience, I found myself sitting with friends at the lovely candlelit dining table at Kate's home for our first Art Critique Group meeting of this New Year. My friend Jo, an art professor at the University, leaned over and told me that several students in her class told her that the single most significant presentation for them in the semester happened to be the presentation that I made as a "visiting artist" in her class. The reason—they had been struggling, each in his or her own way, with the idea of being an artist and what that meant in their lives, and points in my story helped them go to a new place internally. That is so moving to me. These are college students.

The opportunity to plant seeds of hope and challenge in their hearts as well as in the hearts of fifth graders or any person is so rewarding because I know that a word, a phrase, a look, a smile of encouragement from someone along the way can go very far and very deep no matter how old or young we are.

Here is a sampling of letters I received from the children at one of the elementary schools after the Career Fair presentation on "A Profession in the Arts":

Dear Ms. Page,
    Thank you for taking the time to come and talk about art. I learned that art doesn't always have to be about drawing.   Thank you, *Stephanie*

Dear Gloria Page,
    Thank you for everything you showed us all. I learned that I can make and do anything I want. My favorite part was when you showed us the newspaper and the things you made. Thank you for taking time away from your job to talk to us about your job.
                                    Sincerely, *Jessie*

Dear Gloria Page,
    …I'm surprised that you can make stamps and also carve wood! You can do everything you set your mind to!   Thanks again, *Katherine*
(P.S. This summer I'm going to try one of those Art camps!)

Shane has created beautiful artwork for me to see over the years. I added a few art supplies to his personal collection, and now that he is older and has moved on to another school, I say "hello" to his mother when I see her, wishing them both well.

K-Mart trees

    One generation plants the trees; another gets the shade. – *Chinese* Proverb

My oldest son had just finished kindergarten. I was headed to K-Mart to drop off the photos from the end of the school year and noticed a big SALE sign. The garden area was getting rid of all the stragglers at the end of the season, so I moseyed over to check out the deals. This little evergreen just "spoke to me." It was so cute in an odd, Charlie Brown Christmas tree kind of way. The tag said: $2.39. I kept wondering why I had to have it, but the price tag convinced me that I could buy it now and figure it out later. On the way home, the idea of the "Kindergarten Tree" was born.

I grabbed my son, we planted the tiny tree together and I took a picture of him dwarfing the tree. On the first day of school, every year without fail, we have a picture in front of the Kindergarten Tree. Little brother grew up, graduated from Kindergarten, there was another sale at K-Mart and he got to plant his own evergreen—a different variety, and also a little unusual—too symmetrical would be boring.

Two trees, two brothers: all growing. Brandon's tree got up to his knees, then his head and now it towers over us. Bryan's tree is solid and sage-y, destined for his waist in no time. Observing and caring for something living and growing over time—this is good. Maple trees from seeds, tiny pines from Kentucky… we have a miniature story forest.

"Mr. Tamotzu, would you like some apple pie?"

I was 20 years old and the first manager of The Haven Restaurant on Canyon Road. It was a newly renovated place then, and I was new in terms of managing. The space used to be a funky hippy-style pizza joint that I would frequent when I was at St. John's College. I almost always ate there alone—I thought it was so cool to do that for some reason. Something along the lines of I "didn't need to wait for a date to eat out and I am in college now so I can do what I want when I want." There was a nice plant shop attached to The Haven and I bought many plants for my apartment there. The background is a bigger story to me than this, but this covers the bases for now. The year was 1974.

In the afternoons I would work at The Haven (now called Celebrations) doing prep work for dinner. It was peaceful work—I liked being there. One afternoon, the door opened way before opening time while I was working on salads and desserts. The hours were posted, so whoever opened the door wasn't the least bit put off by the CLOSED sign. The sign was pleasantly designed, so apparently it was more welcoming than deterring. I stretched over the butcher-block kitchen counter to catch a glimpse of the person entering my space, and was a bit stunned, in a most fascinated way.

In walked a very old, very compact, very Japanese man. He chose a table and sat down as I walked over to him, wiping my hands on my apron as I approached him. We exchanged smiles and observed each other. It was quiet. Then he said: "You have an Oriental Spirit." I bowed and smiled bigger. I was not wearing a kimono or anything close. I was sporting a denim patchwork jumper and clogs, hair clipped back in a bun. There was this wonderful person with hands poised on his walking stick, checking me out—I *loved* it. We chatted a bit and I learned that his name was Mr. Tamotzu, an artist out for a walk on a beautiful Santa Fe day, needing a place to rest and a piece of apple pie if we had any. We did. I asked if à la mode was to his satisfaction, it was, and I got it for him… and so began my quiet times with Mr. Chuzo Tamotzu.

From time to time the door of The Haven would open, and I would offer greetings, asking each time: "Mr. Tamotzu, would you like some apple pie?" He always did and one day he asked me if I ever did *art*. I hesitated and fumbled around and he cut through that quickly and asked if I would like to come and visit his studio sometime, a simple way to thank me for my kindness, since I never would charge him for his dessert treats. I was excited, curious and grateful, so I accepted. One day when I had the afternoon off from work, I strolled down Canyon Road and found his place tucked into this old adobe neighborhood. I can't remember much of the architecture or layout at all. I focused on this person entirely. I was mesmerized by his story. This happened more than a quarter of a century ago, so the details are internalized, though some do come to the surface. I do recall that his story was so intriguing, and I kept wanting to ask for more, but stopped myself. Here was this ancient Japanese man reminiscing about his formal studies in classical Oriental painting and calligraphy in his youth, something about his father and a rebellion against tradition that led him to Europe and the whole French art scene. It seemed like he said that he knew Picasso and he explained that his own evolution as an artist involved the convergence of the old classical Far Eastern style and the modern movements. His work, the little that I saw, was wonderful. There was a point when the story ended and he took out rice paper, laid it before me, and showed me how to start making my own ink with an old ink stone and ink stick. It was a quiet time.

I rubbed the ink stick for a long, long time. When the ink was ready, he spoke quietly about releasing my fears and thoughts, letting a painting come, rather than pushing it down on the paper. It all sounded very Zen and extremely foreign, not in the geographical sense, in the artistic sense. "I can't draw" was the basic mantra I was working off of at the time, and there I was sitting with this incredible Master looking at my blank piece of Sumi-e paper and bamboo brush saturated with jet black ink, waiting… "Just begin." Hmmm. Okay. So, I touched the tip of the brush onto the paper and began. I did not think. I wasn't on the brink of enlightenment or anything close to that—I was simply scared stiff. Then all of a sudden I saw a tree coming on to the paper—a tall pine tree. That was all—pretty simple and childish from my point of view. "Good. Keep going…" Then I did some other things that weren't getting the "good" rating, but now *I* wanted to keep going. My last piece that day was of a little humble cottage tucked into the woods and Mr. Tamotzu said: "This one is your best piece. You were free when you did this. You weren't thinking." It was true. The ink, paper and I did not struggle—we were fluid—it seemed as if the brush never even lifted off the paper—we surfed the surface.

In time, I moved away and I missed him. Trying to find him many years after my lesson, I heard that he had passed away (1888-1975). The time for apple pie and art lessons was past, but I still needed a connection so I decided to find his home. My mother and I drove to 314½ Garcia St. and knocked on the door, hoping perhaps his wife Louise might open it, and I could touch him through her hand, a smile, a word. But there was no answer—only silence. It was a good day, the right time, for a long, quiet walk…

Way back then, during the same Apple Pie Summer, another person touched my life, and these two stories are intertwined in my mind and inseparable. I was hiking up Canyon Road on my way to the mountains for one of these strenuous alone-hikes I often took, and a woman and I crossed paths. Friendly greetings turned into a conversation. We sat down, and I remember feeling that I had known her for a very long time, yet her name never stayed with me. I was 20 and my new friend was 46, my age today as I write. I remember that because she said that 25 years earlier she had taken a journey and she had been 21 at the time, close to my age, that perfect Southwest sage-in-the-air day long ago. It came time to part ways and we made a meeting time the next day. She said that she wanted to show me something that was very special to her, and I was the one person who could understand. I wondered and wondered what this something could be. The time went slowly from one day to the next. The mountain and I were in a haze that day.

I hiked to her home. It was adobe, small and dark in that musty earthy kind of way. We sat on the wood plank floor and she opened a very old trunk. She gently removed a piece of perfectly folded purple cloth, stood up and with two hands outstretched, bowed to me and presented me with the cloth. I was overwhelmed as I listened to the story…

Twenty-five years earlier, the young woman this woman had been, went to Japan and embarked on a one-year journey. Beginning at a Temple, instructed by Zen monks, she made preparations and set out, walking completely around an island in Japan as a humble, head-shaven monk with a Western woman's face. Her food would come only from the kindness of strangers in the traditional way. Upon completion of her pilgrimage, she would return to the Temple of origin and sit with the Master there. After one year she did that. The Master then presented her with a prayer cloth, purple with a white Zen circle surrounding ancient Kanji. He did not translate it for her. She never found anyone confident to translate the script. It had become a mystery that now was mine to unravel.

I sat there with tears, knowing that I did not have any idea as to why I had inherited this extremely meaningful treasure from a total stranger's past. She said that when we met the day before, she knew that I had to have this cloth; that it belonged to me. That was all. It was happily clear in her *kokoro* (heart/mind) that it was simply mine to receive. I can't explain why I never saw her again. I went for a visit bringing a gift not long after our encounter and no one lived there anymore. She faded from my life, but the story and heart we shared never did. We weren't strangers at all.

I had the cloth framed by a professional in Santa Fe. I didn't have money to do things like that, but there was no question in my mind—it had to be done. It is a fairly large frame and wherever I went, it went with me. At one point, I felt compelled to give it to a very special friend and that was a mistake. In a family move from one house to another, the Purple Cloth was lost—for nine years. It had been carefully packed and stored and slipped into oblivion. It surfaced and when I saw it again, I did what I had never done before in my life—I asked for it back. It was a happy reunion all the way around. One other time I entertained the thought of giving it once again, but pulled back, knowing finally that there was a special destiny connected to me and I needed to respect that, not run from it. I had felt so unworthy for so long to have received such a gift—it took years to learn that I had to allow the gift to be mine.

During these many years I have asked people to translate the Kanji for me. I would always hear how there was "a very good spirit" about the piece, but the characters were from the old school and were difficult to translate today. Finally, *finally*, about ten years ago, a Japanese woman said she would do her best. She said that the piece had a lovely and powerful spirit. The white circle meant Eternity/Forever and she thought that the calligraphy translated "On the Road to Happy Mountain." How wonderful. How perfect.

Apple pie and a purple cloth… I never eat apple pie without thinking of Mr. Tamotzu and the Happy Mountain cloth is on the wall behind me as I write this for you. The red frame is old now, and the cloth is faded a bit. Now I am the one who is 46, still hiking on. Long ago I was deeply affected by these two people who touched my life like a warm evening breeze, only to vanish in the morning of time. Glancing back over a lifetime, how many people have I seated at restaurant tables and how many have I hiked on past. I am so glad that the door was unlocked and that we had apple pie at The Haven that day. I am so glad that I wasn't in my usual mode of flurry-and-hurry to dash up into the Sangre de Cristo Mountains that other day. I sat down both times… and listened…

I heard a number of years ago that a book was being written about Mr. Tamotzu. Every year I ask and wait for it. Someday I will meet him again through the book that I do hope gets written. And I will always wonder if there is a kind old woman somewhere in the world who remembers a young girl on Canyon Road, one who didn't give up and finally found her translation. It would be so nice to go for a slow stroll together, maybe not around an entire island—perhaps arm-in-arm around the block somewhere. I would lean over and whisper in her ear: "I know the translation: on the road to happy mountain—*forever*." We would both smile and surely laugh—together.

(Mrs. Louise Tamotzu passed away at the age of 99 in Santa Fe, early 2002. In a 1987 interview, she expressed a wish that her husband would not be forgotten. He won't be…)

Portia

When my son Brandon was 6 years old, I asked him a question: "Brandon, who is the most interesting person you have ever met in your life?" He was quiet for a while and then he said: "There are three people: "Mémère (my mother), Portia, and Dr. Betty." I asked him to explain why he chose each of them. This is what he said about Portia: "Mom, how many people do *you* know who have a trapeze bar over their bed and have a coyote fence in their backyard because real coyotes come and visit? How many people do you know who have swings for chairs that are hanging from their ceilings?" Good questions. When I asked him why I wasn't on his list yet, he looked at me and said: "You're working on it."... I loved it.

Years ago, my Mom did housecleaning work for people in Santa Fe as a side-job to her job at the La Fonda Newsstand. I would hear stories from time-to-time of some of her adventures, such as the time she jumped off a counter after cleaning something and broke her leg, or nice experiences she had meeting and getting to know the people she was working for. I would hear the name "Portia," and so I met her first through stories. She was the kind of person, it sounded like, who would get woven into sentences while you were talking about Georgia O'Keeffe. For example, I can remember hearing things like... "You should see the *wonder*-full artifacts that Portia collects and has around her house. Bones and skulls right out of Georgia O'Keeffe's paintings, no kidding!"... I would hear about her sense of design, fabric, and yarn in colors that would make your eyes zing and make you feel like doing a Mexican hat dance on the spot. I would hear stories about this mysterious "Studio," stacked and bulging with bones, rocks, cholla branches, Rio Grande driftwood, tinwork supplies, and tools—all kinds of tools—a Southwestern personal excavation warehouse of elements, treasure-finds from countless hikes to the lands of the Ancient Ones. She lived in a creative artist's dream-playground—not all pretty and fussy with *commercial* written all over it—more like a chunk of land brought inside.

So many times I would hear things like: "You should see what Portia did. It's fabulous. You would love it!" And then always: "Someday you two will have to meet."

That happened down the arroyo of time. I don't remember how many years ago that was. I do remember being pretty nervous beforehand. We drove a ways to get there. Her home is nestled into the land, this cozy, earthy adobe-nest with decorations that seem more organic than "placed" or "designed." It was hard not to appear to be gawking as we approached the massive wood door, because I *was* gawking with my mouth opened, wanting to take it all in and it took time. Wherever your eyes rested, oh, something so intriguing. We did manage to get from the car to the door eventually and there was something even to the way you knocked on the door—again it is a fuzzy thought but I remember a sense of delight! ... Back to being nervous—that was certainly a waste of energy, but I did go with that feeling until Portia opened the door and smiled. I shook her hand, which quickly became a hug, and felt that I had known her for a very long time. She made me feel that much at home *standing in the doorway*—imagine that.

Portia's home is her element—it isn't something that she is "in," it is more like something that she wraps around herself like a hand-woven serape. It fits and it flows. It is an extension of her creative being, more of a process than an over-designed finished product. It is so personal; you wouldn't want to do a photo-shoot and include it in a book

231

of *The Ultimate Santa Fe Homes*. In a way it is one of those types of homes, but in most ways it is more like a sanctuary that needs protection. I have been honored over the years to have a few opportunities to do an internal/emotional/personal photo-shoot of memories. On my first visit, she gave me a little tour with stories attached to what I was seeing. *Her* stories of the things I was seeing, not some extravagantly paid designer's interpretation of her taste. We chatted, munched some tasty goodies, and so began what would become a special relationship for me.

Probably I sent her a little thank you note after the visit. Over time I would discover that every card, note, or photo that I have ever sent has been kept. That blows me away. When I have new design ideas, I think of Portia—what would she think of this. She has kept up with the news of my developing business and has been very supportive. We have different ways of keeping in touch over time and distance. I don't get to Santa Fe as often as I would like, and I cannot begin to tell you how much fun it is to receive a box from Portia with the most interesting things inside. I use these "treasure-things" in real life. My pencil holders are handmade pottery she sent. A little Mexican bowl is by my kitchen phone and has loose change in it for school lunches and downtown parking—daily stuff. To-be-*used* and enjoyed not gazed-upon with an invisible "Do Not Touch" sign scorching your hand should you get too close—functional fun stuff is so much better.

When I was a little girl, my mother emphasized gratitude as an attitude, a mind-set vs. a formality. She would say things like: "You know, Gloria, your father had to work hard for three hours in the noisy factory so you could have that blouse… that lamp was a gift from Mon Oncle Marcel, your Cinderella dress came from cousin June, the billows of pouffant slips from cousin Carol…" etc. It was not done in the spirit of making me feel guilty for the hours in the factory—it was done in the spirit of learning concretely that things did not just "appear" in your life. There was a person, love, work, thought, intention, caring, and stories all infused into these possessions. There was *Meaning* with a capital-M. Don't forget the big picture and focus on the material side only. Therefore, throughout my whole life, I have always maintained that perspective on the material world. I know who gave me everything I have, and I always have this internal thing going on where I am saying: "Thank you, Portia, for the sweet punched-tin flower holder… thank you for the pottery cup with the tree design that is perfect for paint brushes… for the Georgia O'Keeffe book…" and on and on like that. Needless to say, Portia is part of every day in my "thank you's," even though our direct meeting times have been so rare.

I have told Portia this personally, so I want to say it here, too. Over the years, when I have gotten stuck artistically, bogged-down, dry like an arroyo in August, I take a journey in my mind. I go back to Portia's home and sit with her for a while. She lets me look around all I want so that I can fill up again, not taking from her space, but rather entering her atmosphere. I can "see" how natural it is to be creative as a lifestyle not as a job. An image will come to mind and I am empowered by it: one of her wild little rock-people, for instance. This is hard to explain but I hope I have touched it enough with words so you can touch it for yourself. In a way I am "beaming myself up and out" of my world of being void of inspiration, feeling invited for a visit and a treat at Portia's. The rejuvenation experience translates into new ideas, and once again I find myself saying "thank you" out loud. Just the thought of being with her brings a radiance to my day.

Those kinds of reflections cause me to want to go to new places in my work. Once in a while she will directly ask me to try something—when I was first starting with cards, one of her first comments was about "framing" these things. "How about that, Gloria?" That thought had never even entered my mind. The cards that I was making at that time didn't even seem worth sending, let alone *framing*. But she planted that idea and I did go out to Hobby Lobby, bought my first clip-frame, did a very simple stamped image of Georgia O'Keeffe on orange Chinese Joss Paper, and timidly presented this first attempt to her. The next time I visited, tears came to my eyes when I saw it hanging on a wall in her house. It was there for a long time and may still be around. That is extremely moving to me. Portia has Real Art pieces in her home. Hmmm… a point of reflection for me. Years later, I bought hundreds of those clip-frames and sold the pieces that I made at art shows. The seed had taken hold. If Portia hung one up in *her* house, someone else might, too. Sure enough. It has happened—a lot.

My Mom had mentioned that Portia really appreciated hearing from me and saved my notes. I knew that, and felt moved and also a little challenged to send things that were worth being saved. Even though I knew she saved things, I was not prepared for the effect that would have on me a few years ago when I went for a visit. Greetings at the door, happy, fun, I believe I brought fresh flowers and then Wham! In the living room I saw a whole display, a Gallery-style presentation of every single card, note and photo I had ever sent her. There they were—all arranged on poster boards, rows of my own hand work, treasured. The dam broke. I cried those good warm tears. Portia took me over, arm in arm, to see the displays. "Remember when you made this card for my 20th Anniversary of being in my home? …remember when you sent these pictures of the boys?…" Remember when—how wonderful to remember when. I honestly did *not* remember sending all the things I saw there, and was so moved that she had kept them over the years. We laughed in enjoyment of seeing some semblance of artistic progress over time.

The next year Portia hand-wove many gorgeous long "belts" of colorful wool yarns and natural cotton chords. She used these to display my cards by attaching them in long rows, color-grouped, in different rooms. They looked wonderful, and right now as I am sitting here writing, I have this strong urge to go and make another card to surprise her. I don't always, however, send the "show" stuff, what would make me look good in her estimation. Sometimes I will send a new, as yet unpolished, concept in the earliest stages because I know she values the pioneer aspect of my learning process. One time I took my soft-cut blocks and lino-cutting tools for our visit—she loved seeing how they were done. Portia made many of those wonderful hand-woven hanging belts for me and I used them in my last Art Show and received many compliments on them. They helped me sell the scrolls on bamboo that were hanging from them, fluttering in the autumn breeze.

She is a designer/artist lady. The necklaces she fashions out of the most beautiful and unique "beads" blow me away. Her ability to add a piece of turquoise to cloth, paint her bathroom door with a dramatic graphic design, drape a piece of mustard-gold cloth over a table, make door knobs out of East Indian woodblocks… the stories go on even as I write, I'm sure of it. And the materials she uses are not necessarily pricey, out-of-my-league supplies. The bolt of mustard-gold cloth was very cheap and she made it go very far. I got a cut from it—lucky me! I do stamps. Portia instinctively puts her "stamp" on everything. Whether it is adding a button, or sewing different pieces of clothing together to make something entirely new, it has her signature. She gave my mother an informal "class" in traditional Mexican tinwork one time. They made the coolest things. I was the lucky recipient of several of their creations. Where did she learn how to do this and everything else that I've mentioned and haven't mentioned? Did she graduate from some big time school, qualifying her for the jobs she would later get in design work in Chicago? No, she is self-taught and got those first design jobs from the sheer force of her personality projection of confidence that she could do it. I thought it was fascinating that she told my mother that she never wanted to be "too trained" in tinwork because it would lose the flavor of being genuine folk art. That's a good point to keep in mind.

My sons spent one afternoon with Portia years ago. They were very little. I was very nervous taking them into a home with museum quality Native American pottery and art everywhere. Mom told me to let Portia handle it and we all had a blast. She put them onto these fabulous swing-chairs suspended from the vigas with chains, pushing them and swirling them around—this was in her bedroom. Also in her bedroom, she stunned all of us when she got up on her bed, pointed to the trapeze-type bar overhead, got her legs through and proceeded to do these gymnastic moves while explaining the benefits for the spinal column and general health and well-being. I couldn't believe it. We went to the large picture window in the room and heard stories of the coyote visits. Brandon was fixated as he absorbed the stories and also inherited the New Mexican way of saying "coyote" from listening so intently. We piled into her (Calistoga) station wagon, in the spirit of the Old Santa Fe Trailblazers and probably on the Old Santa Fe Trail itself, heading for an outing to the Rio Grande, a holy ground for her. It was a very special time. We were singing, I think, on the way back and Bryan, who was still a baby, was making some kind of funny noises, and the more Portia laughed, the more he gave her.

That all happened in a handful of hours. It impacted my son Brandon so much that he named Portia as that most interesting person and to this day, both of my kids tell stories about that time. How much the little guy actually remembers and how much is memory from having heard his brother is anybody's guess, but it doesn't matter anyway. The point is that there is this person in our lives who touches us all.

Just this morning, April 18, 2000, my mother called and said she was so happy to have gotten a call from Portia. It had been a while. We reminisced nice stories and it came up that Portia is now 75. Which means that when she was swinging from the rafters for our enjoyment and hers, she was over 70. She is quite some lady.

Well, I think it's time to make another card for her and send this story along with it. It is a very good time.

Curtis Uyeda

A person I never met, but then again, I did…

Early on in my stamping experience, having collected Southwestern images almost exclusively, the time came to venture out in new directions. I had gone to the Museum of International Folk Art in Santa Fe and saw playful, sacred, bold, ancient images and started to gather information about what designs were available for me to buy to design cards for that particular shop. And at that same time, my brother Norm, who had a membership at Ten Thousand Waves, the Japanese Health Spa in Santa Fe, mentioned to me that there was a small yet impressive gift shop at the resort—perhaps I could sell cards there? Ah, yes—Japanese designs. From the Southwest to Folk Art to the Far East, this was most definitely the next step. The search for design ideas began immediately.

I needed art stamps first of all, or at least a catalog so that I could have something in hand to show the retail buyer at Ten Thousand Waves. Then we could talk. I bought the current issue of "Rubberstampmadness" for the purpose of reading the advertisements— the art articles were secondary this time around. Browsing page after page, I noticed a very simple ad—Curtis Uyeda. Clearly an Oriental collection by the graphics—totally understated in style. I knew this was it—no need to go any further. I sent for my first Curtis Uyeda catalog, which was #2 in his series, copyright 1993. Little did I know…

An envelope arrived in the mail. No, correction: a *work of art* arrived in the mail. There was a U.S. postage stamp and that was familiar territory, but receiving Mail Art for the first time was a heart-warmer and mind-opener. But we are not talking ornate or lavish here. We are talking First Class in every good sense of the phrase. The funny thing is that at first I didn't have a clue who this was for and what on earth it could be! Here was this #10 manila envelope with a Japanese teapot stamped on it. Stamping perfection: clean, exact, placed. There was a touch of white pencil highlight. An extremely fine red line formed a fluid design out of the teapot's spout—oh, my, it's… *my name*! I had never seen my name handwritten so beautifully and creatively. I was stunned and sat there for a long time with my envelope. How can you tear into something like that? Not easily. I used a knife to get the straightest edge I could, and it all slowly started to come together. Curtis Uyeda, Palo Alto, the stamp catalog I ordered, this must be it. The size did not fit my expectation. The personal touch didn't either. Receiving this in the mail made my day. Welcome to Curtis' world.

I heard over the years that people would buy Curtis' catalogs even if they had no interest in rubber stamps or ordering from his line—they collected his catalogs for the sheer beauty of the layout and I think everyone loves to see his or her own name written by an artist. Curtis would always include an added element, whether it was a folded white origami bird attached to the cover, a hand-colored stamped image—something to say that this piece was prepared for you personally, not just "off the press" and packaged.

All of the images that I buy from Curtis' company are unmounted. They do not come mounted even if you want to pay the money for the convenience. This introduced me to learning to mount my own stamps and I much prefer this method even though it means more effort on my part. Originally I liked it because of the savings. Eventually I liked it because I bought the simple power tools to do it and the stamps are more personalized with my own chunky, primitive style vs. the slick commercial standard. This is not a put-down to pretty and convenient stamps. I just do not want people deterred from mounting. Curtis' art stamps are always trimmed to perfection and the red rubber is superior quality. These stamps ink up, in all their glorious detail, like no others.

Corresponding with Curtis was beyond the norm as far as business is concerned. Always the professional, always timely and precise, you could also expect a little surprise in each order along with his wonderful handwriting. Money was tight for me, so my orders were generally small but regular. My address changed over the years and Curtis kept up with them as I moved my business from New York to New Mexico to Missouri. His address stayed constant in Palo Alto, California—I could always count on him.

At one point I realized that I had been using his images in one account and wasn't completely aware of the copyright issues with stamps. I got very nervous when I thought I might be in trouble using Curtis' stamps without his permission, so I wrote him a letter. His response was very interesting. He didn't say that I could use them and he didn't say that I couldn't, at first. He said that he wanted people to use his stamps for "personal enjoyment" and "fine artists" could use them in their work… He challenged me to go higher, and when I was juried into Best of Missouri Hands using several of his images in my major submissions, I then had his permission. It felt good—I was arriving.

One time several years ago, my Mom attended the Rubberama Stamp Convention in Albuquerque and found herself in this new world alone and for the first time. I had never attended a major convention myself, and I was the one with the business. It was close to the end of the day when she came upon a booth that was outstanding and drew her in. Sure enough, it was Curtis' booth. She introduced herself and then mentioned that her daughter, Gloria, loved his stamps and he took it from there. He knew my whole name and gently joked that I did "tend to move around the country" a bit. They chatted and he sent his greetings to me. It was the highlight of the show for her; I heard all about it.

I let him know in my next order how much my Mom appreciated meeting him and enjoyed the atmosphere in and around his booth. Someday I sure would like to meet him personally… it was my hope, and as far as I was concerned, it was a plan; it was destiny.

Time passed and I just had to have some more of Curtis' images, whether in fact I "needed" them or not. Since I had every catalog starting with #2, I also ordered the latest. The correspondence was always refreshing and using the images always creatively inspiring. I sent the order… and nothing came. It was a long period of waiting that never happened before. I followed up with a note, asking him if he had received my check—if it was lost in the mail, I would be happy to send another…

A friend of mine called. Had I heard? Curtis Uyeda passed away quietly in his sleep. No one knows why—he lived such a natural and healthy life. He was only 37 years old. It was a quiet, reflective time—October of 1997.

We wondered, selfishly, I guess, if we would be able to ever order "from him" again. Would someone else buy and take over the company? Would we have to lose the connection that so many people had come to love and appreciate? Many of those people sent cards to his family, using Curtis' images in loving tribute to him and what he gave to us. He had a business; I ordered stamps from him. But it was much more than that…

After a time, customers, "friends," received a warm and consoling message from Curtis' family, in his tradition. I know so many people were happy to hear that the business was given a new life with a new name: "Curtis' Collection" and Midory Uyeda, his mother, is now the person to connect with. The catalog is wonderful, and now a note from Midory warms my day. Her decorated envelopes are sweet reminders of her son and we can enjoy her stamping and appreciate her heart at the same time.

I never met Curtis Uyeda—not face-to-face, anyway. But I did meet him in other ways and for that I will always be grateful. I never send an envelope to anyone for any reason without thinking of Curtis. Even a bill payment might get a bit of embellishment or a more careful handwriting style, because, after all, a person is receiving this at the other end. It may be "just business," but it also just might make someone's day special.

…The blending of the Business of Art and the Art of Life…

We thank you, Curtis.

"Thank you, James."

Being in Santa Fe with my family during this one particular year meant that you never quite knew what would or could happen next. We were, after all, in The Land of Enchantment, specifically in "The City Different." We went with the notion that this transitional year between New York and Missouri was a creative time to develop my business on my favorite turf on planet Earth. It was an open-ended kind of time. It was a *Ride 'em, cowgirl!* life and I was up for it.

We were staying at my mother's house and she was out for the evening. The phone rang and so I got it. It was for me and it was my Mom on the other end. "Gloria, I'm at Wild Oats, the new health food store. Guess who is here? *Guess*." I didn't have a clue. "*James Taylor* is here eating at the salad bar. Get over here quick so you can see him. Do you know where Wild Oats is…? Good. You'd better hurry or you'll miss him. Bye."

Okay. So here I am, 41 years old, a wife and mother of two little children, all of a sudden rushing around like a wacky-woman, telling my husband as I fly out the door: "Please take care of the kids. See you later. I'm going to see James Taylor. Right now. He's eating a salad at Wild Oats. Bye." I am out of there.

I never screamed for the Beatles and never went dreamy over the Monkees—that kind of nonsense drove me nuts. So here is middle-aged wacky-woman acting like a groupie, en route to a local health food franchise so I can look at a man eating greens. What can I say? I loved James Taylor half my lifetime ago, and have listened to his music ever since. While I am working and choose to have music in the background, it is more often than not his. As I am driving to Wild Oats, a bit on the fast side, I am reminiscing, humming, singing "Up on a Roof," "Shower the People," "Fire and Rain," and trying hard to remember which ones he actually wrote, which were Carole King's, as if that really mattered under the circumstances. I guess I didn't want to say anything stupid like thanking him for writing a song that he didn't write, something like that.

My mother was waiting at the door, very excited that I had made it. He was "still here!" I had run in, so I was out of breath. She pointed out the Salad Bar area towards the far side of the store. This was not a time to over-think. If I thought about this too much, the whole thing would get stranger than it already was, I would hesitate, falter, talk myself out of making a fool of myself, as well as interrupting a man's nice meal and conversation, and basically just get the hell out of there. So what *am* I supposed to do here? Pretend like I am shopping after jogging and that is why I am all out of breath? Do you just look at this famous person and say to yourself: Wow, I just saw James Taylor eating a salad? That was about the length and depth of my thinking as I walked up the aisles, went right up to the high-table with two stools where he was sitting with a friend and profoundly said: "James Taylor?"

There I stood, this white-haired, dishevelly-looking housewife, nervous in a school-girl kind of way, looking for words in front of a man whose words meant so much to me throughout a lifetime. He has the best smile and I got one of them. "Yes." "I'm sorry to interrupt you, but I would just like to thank you for the music you gave to all of us. You gave us words and music to help us through difficult times, and I would like to personally say how much I appreciate you." He wasn't eating his salad while I was trying to speak from my heart, he was looking at my teary face, listening to my shaky voice, and quietly said something along the lines of: "Thank you. I really appreciate that." That was about it. Then I turned around and zombied my way back to the front of the store.

Stunned and a little bumbly, I found myself not knowing quite what to do with what I had just done. My mother hugged me and now she was the one all teary-eyed, so happy that she had made this happen for me. It was truly a once-in-a-lifetime type moment. We wandered around the store a bit, looking at their greeting card selection and trying to figure out how I could get my cards in there, too. Always the business team we are. I bought a card, a reproduction of an old Edward S. Curtis photograph of Hopi women up on a roof, looking down at the scene below, the men dancing. I dated the card, titled it "Up on a Roof," and framed it, then took it to Missouri with me later that year. An autograph would have been nice, but I didn't want to push things too far and overdo it.

It is interesting to reflect on experiences. Would James Taylor remember that little incident? I doubt it. But I will always remember having that chance that doesn't come often, the opportunity to say "thank you" face-to-face to a famous face whose work and art have touched your life in some significant way. I did not want to take anything from this person; I had already received so much. And the only thing I had to give was my gratitude and I gave it. And upon further reflection, the Not-So-Rich and Famous in our daily lives could use a loving heap of thanks, too. If you "shower the people you love with love" we are all much happier because we did something. It was not just a thought. We actually followed through. It doesn't take a lot to give something. We all smile.

My mother has probably gone to more James Taylor concerts than I have since I only went to one in Chicago light-years ago. She has tapes of his music, too. One day when I wasn't around her neck of the woods, she went to Souper Salad for lunch with her friend Grace and as she opened the door, someone behind her thoughtfully held the door for her. She turned around, realized who this kind person was, smiled and simply said with an amused-gratitude: "Thank you, James." How cool is that.

> "Shower the people you love with love,
> …show them the way that you feel…
> things are gonna work out fine if you only will."

> *- James Taylor*
> "Shower the People"

The Reading List

These made a difference while writing…

NATALIE GOLDBERG
- *Writing Down the Bones*
- *Wild Mind*
- *Long Quiet Highway*
- *Living Color*
- *Thunder and Lightning*

JULIA CAMERON
- *The Right to Write*

ANNE LAMOTT
- *Bird by Bird*

GAIL SHER
- *One Continuous Mistake*

NANCY DAVIDOFF KELTON
- *Writing From Personal Experience*

CANFIELD/HANSEN/GARDNER
- *Chicken Soup for the Writer's Soul*

DAN POYNTER
- *The Self-Publishing Manual*

ADELINE YEN MAH
- *Watching the Tree*

don MIGUEL RUIZ
- *The Four Agreements*

GARY THORP
- *Sweeping Changes*

SOMERSET STUDIO MAGAZINE

LIDDELL and SCOTT: *Greek-English Lexicon*

AMERICAN HERITAGE DICTIONARY

LAROUSSE DICTIONNAIRE MODERNE

(Art Stamp Images Courtesy of *Curtis' Collection*)

Part Four

other people's stories

Throughout this book, many people are mentioned, some woven in again and again. Throughout my whole life, there are many more people who have touched me and given in countless ways. It would be very gratifying for me to express my ongoing appreciation in print here between the front and back covers. But logistically speaking, I simply cannot do that and keep this thing under 1,000 pages! What I am trying to say is that I don't want anyone that I care about to feel left out… you know who you are. On the other side of this coin, I purposely left out some names of people and names of places as a courtesy, with a desire to extract the value from a particular story, and then to simply move on. You might know who you are, too.

"Holy Moly…" is primarily about my art business, so the people included are connected to the "art aspect" of my life. My experience has been that this adventure and stage we call "life" is not a solo performance. We grow and thrive as many leaves on the tree together… I asked friends to write their own stories and they generously agreed.

Highlighted in this section:
- The story of my Art Critique Group—how we came together
- A Creative Contribution shared by each of the six of us in the original Group
- Five Friends telling stories about their own Businesses in the Arts

For me, these people and what they chose to share are all treasures.
I am so happy to introduce you to some very special friends...

241

My Art Critique Group
My personal oasis with a view

How did it all start? It started at the beginning… years ago.

Once upon a time I was dropping off some cards at the Columbia Art League downtown and the director came over and whispered: "Have you seen the work by Susan Taylor Glasgow? It's wonderful and so is she. You two just have to meet…" I smiled, nodded, and found myself smiling even more as I spent time looking at her art. At the time, she was creating these wonderful fun-furniture-type, whimsically painted pieces. Her artist statement and photo told part of her story, though I did feel distant from the professional aspects of her training and career. I figured we would meet someday in some casual way. She made that happen. Susan makes a lot of things happen.

It was set-up time for the Artisan Showcase at my first Best of Missouri Hands Conference. I was nervous, not yet a Juried Artist Member, and feeling rather awkward and definitely out of my element. My little display of hand-stamped cards was tucked in amongst beautiful jewelry, weaving, woodwork pieces with the texture of silk, folk art, pewter, and much more. This artist-lady, "Susan Taylor Glasgow," around the corner from me, was putting the finishing touches on her lovely booth with her candlesticks and boxes. Her swirls of purples and greens with touches of gold created this lush world on a three-foot table. Susan came up to me and we introduced ourselves to each other. I told her that she had an amazing ability to make magical environments anywhere…

Over time we would see each other once in a while and she was always so kind and enthusiastic about the "new things" I was coming up with. I was constantly blown away by her range of experimentation; her art has this quality of being serious art and yet playful at the same time. Susan would oftentimes say things like "we should get together for coffee" and I would agree on the outside and feel intimidated on the inside. I knew she meant what she said, and I knew that I wanted to be her friend, but my insecurity built up over time as Susan became more recognized. Finally, she put an end to all of that nonsense and made me commit to a date to meet for tea, coffee or whatever. She *would* pick this fancy place: Trattoria Strada Nova: very cool and artsy. We sat in the back and one of her college-age friends was the waitress, so we got special treatment. This was a chitchat meeting—with a purpose. Susan had this idea; I listened.

"Wouldn't it be great to have a group of artists who could come together on a regular basis as a kind of "critique group" to help each other advance their work? We could have different specialties, not all the same art background, so that we could benefit from a different perspective on our work, not in a competitive sense. When we are stuck, or need help with pricing, things like that, we would have a place to go to, friends to turn to. What do you think, Gloria? Do you want to do that with me?"

"That sounds like a great idea, Susan. I'm sure you could round up a dynamite group here in town. You have lots of connections—go for it!"

That's what I said with my mouth. In my head it went more like this: "*Critique*" group? That word makes me nervous. I don't want to sit around with a bunch of professional artists drinking wine and listening to them criticizing my little stamped stuff. I'm sure Susan will find the right people who can handle that kind of atmosphere and who can measure up, etc. etc…" I thanked her for even considering me, but pretty much brushed the idea gently aside. She wasn't, however, going to let me get away with it, I could tell. We said our good-byes and left the restaurant with friendly waves and promises to get together soon after thinking things over. Dragging me in kicking and screaming wouldn't be her style, and reluctance with such notions would definitely be mine—for a while. Part of me felt like hiding; the better part would not let me run away.

At another juncture we chatted again. She invited a few people to her house and I couldn't go for some reason that I did not fabricate, it was legitimate, so I missed the first get-together. In my mind it had passed me by and I wished her well. Forget that. Susan called with the next invitation and if memory serves me, the next phase went through the Art League. I showed up late and since there were only three of us there and only one of us had artwork to share, we disbanded for that evening. What a dismal story, wouldn't you say? There is this idealistic artist-soldier-girl Susan valiantly trying to pull these troops together all by herself and what do I do to help? I support her with my constant driveling of insecurities! Some friend I was. I wanted to feel connected. I longed to be an artist. I wished I could get over my fear. She must have sensed all those things somehow, because for her own bewildering-to-me reasons, she kept on calling. Bless her sincere and unrelenting heart and indefatigable telephone-dialing finger.

Susan set up another meeting and asked me to invite a friend if I would like to. I called her back and told her that I had met a woman who had started making art quilts. We met at a Best of Missouri Hands Conference. I thought of inviting her—Susan said "great!" so I called. Janet was enthusiastic (how nice) and it was the three of us. It was so nice to be together. We shared, we did not get *critical*, we enjoyed nice food treats and each other's company. Janet then invited Lisa, her friend, a jewelry maker at the time, and next Susan invited Kate, a watercolor artist and graphic designer, just moved here from Albuquerque. It was getting more and more captivating. Each person adds a dimension, a special kind of laughter, a perspective, her own personal taste and expertise. Each person brings chips, fruit, a bottle of wine, cheese or something and an opinion offered from an open, honest, encouraging heart; it doesn't get any better than this. We care about each other, where we are now and where we are headed. It's called "support."

I believe we have been together for well over three years now. We meet the first Wednesday of each month, starting at 7:00 p.m. and go for a few hours. There have been times when we have invited other people to join us, but it feels more like in the visitor capacity. When Janet invited her friend Jo, who is an Associate Professor of Art at the University specializing in fiber arts and handmade paper, she went way past the "visitor" status immediately. We are a family of friends, the six of us—*The Art Critique Group*.

To each meeting we bring a number of things: ourselves, minds and emotions, new artwork and/or prototypes of ideas in process, questions, a commitment to be there for each other, some kind of snack treat and *time*. Yes, we come with time to give to each other. We bring a willingness to open up and speak about what is going on in our art business lives and we bring the desire to listen. We take turns and that happens naturally, though at times we thought maybe we would draw straws or pick numbers.

The tone of our meetings varies from month to month. We have no idea what people are bringing to the meeting for "show and tell" and we don't know all the details of what life has been like for everyone since meeting last. There is an excitement in the air as we approach these unknowns. The location varies somewhat, though we tend to gravitate towards Susan's home and butterfly around from time to time. I am the one with young children, so I escape. When my new studio is completed, I think I'll offer the invitation. Wherever we are, it always feels like the perfect place for that night… a safe place.

We laugh, cry once in a while, and we even sang together once. When the artwork comes out of boxes, duffel bags, portfolios or plastic bags, we pay attention. This is our purpose and we are dedicated. Recently, Janet and I began doing collaborative pieces: her art quilts and my handmade tiles. We showed the group and got some very useful feedback. The next morning Janet went to work adding glass beads based on the suggestions we heard the night before—fabulous. Ideas are offered and may or may not be employed, but the give-and-take always results in more solid pieces of work.

Each person's work is so uniquely an expression of the essence within…

Goddesses alight and find their true identities revealed in Janet's hands. The fabric takes on qualities that transcend two dimensions. The detail of the countless stitches and the intricacy of the beads, gentleness of the faces… you have seen loveliness.

To hold an exquisite necklace of freshwater pearls is to sense Lisa's love of beauty and ornamentation—just watch her put that sparkler around her neck—such style!

Watch Kate's hands as she takes out her watercolors and splashes you with her laughter, at the same time touching your mind with her ability to capture the sunlight.

A sacred altar shrine in Jo's earthtones and natural elements—to run your hands over the textures of the handmade paper and tiny, smooth vessels is to embrace Mother Earth.

Take flight into the world of the fanciful when Susan unwraps story boxes with angel wings, starlet faces behind glass and words that break up your thinking so that you can think straight into a new frame of mind—she calls herself: "the poster child of diversity."

Opening my box this month, tonight actually, you will find a gift folder that I prepared for each of my friends with pieces, including this one, from my book. I want to say: "Thank you" and "Look at us! Aren't we just the best all together?"

My early life was spent without having sisters. Now I have five. The composition of the group will naturally change over the years, and we have experienced transitions, yet I know that wherever we end up, we will always be together. This is the original group represented here; our new group is great, too. I have tried to employ a visual to describe what this whole group means to me. I thought of a multi-faceted prism, a precious gem, a room with six sides including the ceiling and the floor and lots of windows. I worked with those images and they all work in some way, yet the one that stands out for me at this time is "oasis." My Art Critique Group is my personal oasis with a spectacular view. We are a safe, cozy, fun place, a fertile, yummy, green place when we find ourselves at times surrounded by desert. Set up the lawn chairs, girlfriends, put on your straw hats, take a refreshing sip of inspiration and watch that sun rise, watch it set, and in all that we do, keep the vision. And more than anything else, when we are together, I feel at home.

One person did have a vision and she didn't give up on it. So here we are.

When I set out to write this book, there was one thought that came early and never quit—I needed each of the six of us to take one 8½ x 11 sheet of paper and use it as a canvas to say something. I wanted a verbal piece of art—do your individual thing—no rules except please do it. This is our offering, our small way of sharing who we are as individuals and as "The Art Critique Group." This group changes my life for the best.

Pull up your own lawn chair, sit back and join us… you're in for a treat.

The capacity to care is the thing that gives life its deepest meaning… *- Pablo Casals*

> I am an artist.
> I work in a studio.
> I create beautiful items that people admire.
> I make my living as an artist.

This is an affirmation that I wrote several years ago while working my way through "The Artist's Way" by Julia Cameron. Did I believe these words when I first wrote them on a 3x5 index card? Did I believe them as I faithfully read them every morning when I got up and every night before I went to bed? Did I believe this could ever happen to me? *No way!* But I do believe that we have the power to create our reality by the words and thoughts we write and say. At first I read these words silently to myself. Each time I read them that little critic in my mind reared its ugly head and whispered "imposter" in my ear. But I persevered. Soon, I began tentatively saying the words out loud—I practiced them in safety—only my family, my dog and my closest friends could hear me say: "I am an artist." And very slowly, the affirmations combined with the support of good friends and hard work helped me to begin to believe in myself and to make the affirmations become a reality. Today I can say these words loudly and with conviction. The following are my suggestions on "how to be an ARTIST":

A   Act as if… Call yourself an artist. It is awkward at first, but the more you say it and believe it, the easier it becomes.

R   Rename your working space. Artists work in studios. I resisted this for the longest time—it was my "art room." But I noticed that the "real" artists all had studios and to my great surprise they weren't always as grand as I had imagined. They were basements and attics and corners of rooms. If you think of yourself going to your *studio,* you will be surprised at how much more professional you will feel and how much more like an artist.

T   Treat yourself. Subscribe to lavishly illustrated art magazines that inspire you. Go to the library and ramble through the many fine art and craft books that are available. Glean ideas from artists working in mediums different than yours. Go to museums and art openings in your area. Buy yourself a yummy quarter yard of material, a small vial of sparkly seed beads, a new notebook for your ideas—whatever small item you can afford that feeds your spirit.

I   Imagine the possibilities. Visualize your ideal scenario. Write it down. If you want to show or sell your work in a particular store or gallery, take a photo of the front of that place and hang it in your studio. Find out what it would take to have your work shown there.

S   Surround yourself. Choose friends who will support you, encourage you and give you good constructive feedback in a kind and gentle way. Be part of a group that shares your same interests—you can learn valuable skills and techniques from them. Also, try to form a critique group with artists from different disciplines since they will look at your work from a different perspective and have ideas that your peer group might not have.

T   Test the waters. Give yourself plenty of time to develop your confidence, but once you have artwork that you feel might have possibilities, take a deep breath and put it out there. Maybe you don't feel you are ready for that "ideal scenario" yet, but take small steps towards it. You might be surprised when someone says "yes!"

Janet Ghio

Trust

There is nothing like the synergy and power of a group with a common focus.
For me, finding that group was the answer to an unspoken prayer.

Even though I had never been trained as an artist and my background was in the corporate world, I found myself drawn to creating art through jewelry design. It was very humble beginnings. I wasn't even sure anyone else would like what I was creating.

Yet, as fate (or Spirit) would have it, I was invited to be part of a group that was forming. This small group of women artists agreed to meet once a month to give each other help and support. Some of them I barely knew and others I did not know at all. The group members offered each other honest opinions, advice, and encouragement. Most of all, they offered a safe place to try out new ideas.

Even before I was ready to call myself an artist, they were doing it. Yet, these women taught me more by their actions than by anything they said.

Over time, I witnessed each of us refine our work and grow in unexpected ways as people and as artists. Those that were already accomplished artists expanded their territory or honed their craft. Others branched out and tried new modalities. I started with the basics of how to market my wares.

Little did I know in the beginning how much I needed this group of women to come along when they did. No gauge could measure the difference they made in my life. It is funny how the universe conspired to put me right where I needed to be. It has been a privilege to be a part of this group. They are my champions.

Whether you are a beginner or a celebrated artist, may you trust in the universe to provide you with what (or whom) you need as you take the next big step into the unknown and find it (or them) as the sturdy ground rising up to meet your foot.

Lisa Christian

It is my world
and my journey

To live it with a soul that is centered and
a heart that is patience

To see with more than just my eyes

To have and give love
that is full and unconditional

These are my choices
and wherever they
take me that is where
I will go and be

As I learn and grow
I know I have no choice
but to paint and draw
it is in my being
it is my soul

Thank you for viewing my dear friend's book
I wish you blessings on your own journey

STATS:
Painting since the age of 8, Degree in Advertising Art,
18 plus years of design experience....

Born in Texas; where I was raised,
13 years in New Mexico; where I learned to see and
3 years in Missouri; where I have learned to believe

Decalogo del artista
Decalogue of the Artist

By: *Gabriela Mistral*
Chilean Poet / 1889-1957

I. You shall love beauty, which is the shadow of God over the Universe.

II. There is no godless art. Although you love not the Creator, you shall bear witness to Him creating His likeness.

III. You shall create beauty not to excite the senses but to give sustenance to the soul.

IV. You shall never use beauty as a pretext for luxury and vanity but as a spiritual devotion.

V. You shall not seek beauty at carnival or fair or offer your work there, for beauty is virginal and is not to be found at carnival or fair.

VI. Beauty shall rise from your heart in song, and you shall be the first to be purified.

VII. The beauty you create shall be known as compassion and shall console the hearts of men.

VIII. You shall bring forth your work as a mother brings forth her child: out of the blood of your heart.

IX. Beauty shall not be an opiate that puts you to sleep but a strong wine that fires you to action, for if you fail to be a true man or a true woman, you will fail to be an artist.

X. Each act of creation shall leave you humble, for it is never as great as your dream and always inferior to that most marvelous dream of God which is Nature.

Translated by Doris Dana

(Contributed by *Josephine Stealey*)

Zen and the Art of Art

"What's next?" It's the question asked after
you've asked yourself: "Where do I start?"
But you know the answer to that one:
You start in the beginning. You've started.
And then: "What's next?"
I ask it when I'm confused.
I ask it when I'm so happy I can't think straight.
It's the question that is savior after crushing defeat.
It's the ground after soaring success.
It's the same question that keeps you from mourning too hard,
celebrating too long,
or being fearful of taking the next step.
Because all of these things keep you from your task,
your purpose
of
Art.

■

"What's next?"

Susan Taylor Glasgow

Your very own Masterpiece

If our own lives are meant to be our ultimate *Works of Art*, our personal Masterpieces, what does that really mean? Is it romance or reality? I freely admit that I simply do not live days and years that translate into a Rembrandt, do you? A Rembrandt moment here or there perhaps, but a whole *day*? Many times my head feels disjointed resembling a Picasso with a mind boxed-in like a Mondrian. The comforting thing is that these are all masters, so the company is entertaining.

"Life is a tapestry, life is a work of art, life is a path, a journey…" Yes, but… Life can also be a tangled-up mess, a slab of rock hard clay, or a direct flight over handlebars to the concrete below. We might as well not set ourselves up for major disappointments by thinking that it all has to be Michelangelo, Leonardo or Monet. They had their own issues, too, let us not forget, and we all have a problem figuring out what Mona Lisa's enigmatic smile is really all about.

I have fun toying with the idea of finding an artist whose work matches my day or mood. There are so many artists whose work I love. A class in Art History beckons at some point so that I can explore more. On my current "favorite artists Rolodex," you will find Georgia O'Keeffe, R.C. Gorman, Andrew Wyeth (and anyone related to him), Alexander Calder who happened to have designed and fashioned Georgia's highly-photographed brooch, Mary Jane Colter—the amazing architect of Southwest treasures—Frank Lloyd Wright, of course, the people who vision-painted the Lascaux caves, petroglyph shamans, Japanese woodblock printmakers and Chinese calligraphers. I can't leave out Celtic carvers, Greek sculptors, Mexican tilemakers, Norman Rockwell, Matisse (especially his paper cuts) and Charles Schultz (especially his Lucy). We haven't even touched the surface. This wasn't in any particular order—I was flipping around.

When my ideas are bigger than the canvas of my practical brain, I am a Georgia O'Keeffe flower existing beyond the borders of the frame. When I am holding my hurt young son, who just flew off his new bicycle, trying desperately to take away the pain, I am a Gorman madonna soothing her precious one in folds of comfort. In wistful moments, when reminiscing and daydreams are the plane of my consciousness, I line up the seashells of my memories on a windowsill with Wyeth's lace curtains blowing the warm earth breezes into my soul. A Calder mobile is massive and graceful—that kind of day hangs together and things are working with other people on the planet—we are moving harmoniously and not banging into each other.

Primitive earth-longings bring me to caves and among rocks; a search for simplicity and directness—the Oriental brush. When I think I am tired and *my* back is breaking because of stress, there is always the Sistine Chapel to reflect upon. When frustration rules the day, go ahead, play a CD of Beethoven's "Ninth Symphony" and pretend you wrote it and can't hear a single note.

When life is tidy and straight like a weaving, this is good. When it is more along the lines of graffiti on a New York subway or a chunk of clay on the wheel spinning out of control, it is good to remember that some people call that art, too. I want my life to add up to something—something worth living and giving. It may be a cartoon at times, it may be funny, sad, fulfilling, frustrating or any spectrum of descriptions, but in the end it all has to add up. I am learning. I am creating. I am moving and not waiting. Glancing past my own sphere, I notice so many people are dealing with major issues and they are handling them with huge hearts that have room for vision. I am observing and deeply moved. Their work in life is truly in the Masterpiece category.

As the Artists of our Destiny, we stand in the position to create a living, vibrant museum of our moments, visiting and appreciating others in theirs. The definition of Masterpiece is wide open. My entry: Life Collage: Mixed Media/Multi-Dimensional… my door to creative joy…

Gloria Page

HOLY COW!!!
...look what *they* did!...

Five friends tell their own Home Business Stories

You think you know your friends, therefore you think you know their stories—sometimes true, but not always. This became crystal clear to me when I asked five of my friends who have their own home businesses to "please write your story for my book. Write it your way, your style. Anywhere from one to four pages would be great—thanks so much." Over time the pages started trickling in and it was a most wonderful experience for me to get the encapsulated, historical and personal version in print. It's different when you chat together over the years. When a person commits pen to paper, pauses to reflect, decides what is most relevant and most meaningful, the tone is altered and the details are added that give a more complete picture. I love every word.

Kay, Ken, Janet, BJ, and Lara—how did I meet each of you?

Kay, one day I received a telephone call from you. Your kind voice told me that you were considering starting a handmade card business and had some questions. We chatted, cleared up the "glue problem," and got together at Lakota for shared inspirations. Thanks.

Ken, I read an article about you and found your cards in town before we met. I expected your cards to be rather on the serious, historical side. Instead, I found that they were on the intellectual, hysterical side. You called me and we both connected with Kay.

Janet, it was at The Best of Missouri Hands Annual Conference: lunch time. I was walking past your table and I heard this question directed to me: "Excuse me, are you the person who makes the Southwest greeting cards with the petroglyphs?" "Yes, I am." "Great! I wanted to meet you. Would you like to sit at my table?" "I sure would."

BJ, I was new to Columbia and had wandered around looking for a stamp store. The phone book was no help, so I asked and asked. Finally, someone said: "You know, I think there is a new store… let me tell you where." Sure enough—a stamp store *was* in town!

Lara, we met because I wanted to follow up on a newspaper article about your business when you were just 15 years old at the time. At the Columbia Art League I bumped into your Mom, she invited me to tea with you at the St. Louis Bread Company…special time.

I cannot remember *not* knowing these five great people. There is a connection that runs deep. All of us get very busy, we may not meet often, but when we do in some form or other, it is always refreshing. Their stories mean so much to me personally, that I decided that my "second book" begins right here: "other people's stories."

None of us are rich because of our life choices—not yet, anyway. But we have pockets full of stories and all feel richly blessed to have them. We are not alone and remind each other of that. Stories are good. It is my privilege to pass theirs on to you.

A dreamer of dreams

Kay Foley
Ampersand Cards

I have a file folder on my computer desktop labeled "Dream Life." My dream has always been to make my way in the world as a writer and an artist. I wrote little stories as a young girl, made cards and books for people's birthdays, kept diaries and journals, and wrote scads of letters, but nothing as long as a good-sized short story.

As an adult, I changed directions every few years. I taught piano for awhile, co-owned a crafts store where I sold "country crafts" of my own design, worked as a secretary, and finally earned a degree in psychology and a Master's in counseling, while working full-time and raising my three sons. Even when I was in school, though, I routinely considered switching to creative writing. I preferred reading novels to psychology journals, poetry to case histories. Many of my friends were writers. I had always loved the arts. But I had gone so far in psychology that it seemed too difficult to make the change. And since I was, by then, a single mother, I could not afford the luxury of changing majors and starting over.

Then, three years ago, my sister and I were both working in jobs that didn't suit us. I was an underpaid, overworked and very stressed therapist, working with drug-addicted and alcoholic women in a residential treatment center. My sister and I lived about 1500 miles away from each other, and we lamented the fact that our employers dictated how much time we were able to spend with each other and with other members of our far-flung family. Each of us was thinking about making a life change. I had bought the book *The Artist's Way* by Julia Cameron a couple of years earlier and I asked my sister if she wanted to work through the book with me. The book is a "spiritual guide to higher creativity," an antidote to creative blocks, and it is laid out in 12 one-week segments. We read the chapters, did the exercises, and checked in with each other by phone every Sunday evening. It was a wonderful, enriching experience. We both grew creatively, and we learned all sorts of things about each other.

By the time we had reached the end of the book, we were both thinking about ways to incorporate creativity more fully into our lives. I swallowed hard and quit my counseling job, knowing that I had a variety of skills I could draw upon to pay the bills. I could always teach piano again. I had taught for years before I had children and on and off since then as well. A friend suggested proofreading and editing. I am a fast typist, too, and I thought that, if worse came to worst, I could do temp work or be a secretary again. But I had in mind a lifestyle that included many of the things I love to do—some writing, some art, some music—a lifestyle that I had pictured for myself when I was 17, and one that resurfaced as a possible dream again during the course of working through *The Artist's Way.*

One day my sister said to me, "Why don't we make cards?" I thought it sounded like a good idea, and we agreed to give it a try. I had been collecting great quotes for a long time and had used them in calendars I made for family and friends as well as in a newsletter I had written in a former job. I also loved playing with fonts and layout on the computer, but I didn't know much about copyright privileges, and I am someone who does not like legal things and little details. So, in a little side step maneuver, one beautiful

252

spring afternoon I went out to the backyard with an old spiral notebook and a pen and started writing things down, little bits of writing, little observations and thoughts, whatever came into my head. I probably wrote down 50 of them and today many of those little writings appear on my cards. It came so easily! And thankfully, it still does. It is by far the most fun part of cardmaking for me. I seem to have found my genre—(Gloria calls them "the shortest short stories ever written")—although I still aspire to publish little books and to write at least one novel before I die.

It was much harder for me to design the artwork on the cards. And it was harder still to figure out things like suppliers, printers, licenses, sales reps, etc. Glue was a huge obstacle! Paper, envelopes, finding a printer who would work with me, learning about the printing process and things like "letter press scoring"—all that was difficult and time consuming (and not fun!). I did work out basic graphic deigns by stamping with sponges and doodling with glitter glue and they were coming together. Finally I got up the nerve to call two local card artists—Ken Logsdon and Gloria Page. I picked up tips and ideas from them (solved the glue problem), but I continued working mostly in isolation since my sister ended up doing something else completely. Incredibly, I did not even look at magazines or books, go to workshops or take classes in anything back then.

A friend of a friend happened to be a sales rep for greeting cards and I sent a bunch of my cards to him. He was somewhat discouraging and didn't think he could sell them. But he did offer lots of constructive criticism and suggested I show them to Barbara McCormick at Poppy. It took me about two months to get up the nerve to call her, and when I did, she said, "I was wondering when you'd call!" She was very welcoming and encouraged me to come in that same day.

Barbara loved my writing but was tentative about the cards. Many of them were not geared to any specific type of occasion, and they did not have inside greetings. Some of the writing was pretty quirky. Barbara suggested writing for occasions and including a simple inside greeting like "Happy Birthday!" I thought I could tie some of the ones I had already written to an occasion and turn them into occasion cards. She agreed to try them out in the store on consignment and see how they did; the first "order" was 6 each of 12 designs. Barbara also took me through the store, talking about this or that line of cards, basically teaching me the wholesale card business from a retailer's point of view. My cards sold well enough at Poppy that Barbara decided to buy them outright. Now the store carries at least 30 different designs from my line at any given time. It seems that my quirky writing says the things that people cannot quite say for themselves, and I have discovered that I have a small, dedicated following!

I have two sales reps in California who have placed my cards in 35 shops there. I have a local sales rep and three new ones in the Pacific Northwest. I also started making larger, more complex pieces as well as accordion fold books, and my work has been accepted at some big art/craft shows. I pretty much have the lifestyle that I dreamed about when I was 17. There is an aspect to it, though, that I didn't think about back then. When you work at home, you work alone. I am a social person and have found that it is very important for me to see people throughout the week. Even though I teach piano in the late afternoons, I make sure to have lunch or coffee with friends a couple of times a week.

Gloria and I stay in touch, though we're both busy. The first time she called, she just wanted to help me in any way she could. We met for coffee, conversation, and from my point of view, inspiration. At the end of that first meeting, I remember her asking me, "Is there anything else I can do for you?" I was pretty flabbergasted. Over the past two years she has been a source of encouragement and support, and she has given practical advice, resources, *stuff*, and most importantly, friendship.

I'm still creating my Dream Life, and I think that's as it should be. After all, isn't the real excitement and energy more in the *creation* of the thing you love rather than already having finished it? I think so.

Here are some of my favorite card sayings…

I resolved to surround myself with EXPLORERS who are not afraid to wander the backroads of their minds. Luckily for me, I enjoy small, intimate parties.

She fed the birds every day, but a fat grey squirrel came along and ate everything before they got much. She decided to change her way of thinking. "I'm feeding that grey squirrel & I hope to God the birds don't get to it first." It made her very happy.

She daydreamed about being a hot air balloon pilot or a hatmaker. One day she up & walked out of the factory and took off down the road. I never saw her again, but one time she sent me a photograph of herself riding on the back of an elephant.

She ate chocolate truffles while pondering the bigger questions of life. It didn't help her thought process, but it did make the whole enterprise more enjoyable.

As a child, I did not like school and even now, I am tempted, when passing a schoolyard, to throw open the gates and call out, "You're free! Go! GO! You're free!!!" and watch, smiling, as all the children run gaily off to play their own games, no bell or buzzer telling them when to STOP.

"You are not a real dog," she would often remind him, "only a French poodle." But she kissed the top of his curly little head and gave him a small artificial bone, which he buried thoughtfully under her bed pillow.

I decided that the world of work
is not conducive to joy ---
and so I became a dreamer of dreams that come true.
I'm much happier
NOW.

"Less is more, more or less..."

Ken Logsdon
Post-a-Quote Cards

In the summer of 1990, or close to that year, my family and I went to an arts festival in Steamboat Springs, Colorado. Little did I know that it would be a life-changing event or I might have remembered the specific date. I met Edie Dismuke, a Denver artist who created jewelry from postage stamps. Being a big fan of Winston Churchill, I special ordered a piece from her. I picked it up later at her Denver studio. My wife and I were very taken with her talent and made several trips to her studio to buy gifts. A friendship developed. On one occasion Edie, knowing my love of Churchill, gave me some greeting cards decorated with Churchill stamps. I suggested, quote collector that I am, that there needed to be quotes on the cards. Edie graciously invited me to do just that and *Post-a-Quote* was born.

At the time I was self-employed and well paid. I had no intention of leaving the partnership I was in. I was satisfied—mostly. Other than dabbling in writing, I had never been involved in any creative endeavor. I had no formal art training but Edie gave me a friendly critique of my initial efforts and spurred my creativity. (Looking back at those first efforts, I now realize how kind she was!) I began doing more and more of the cards for my own enjoyment and for friends and relatives.

Eventually I got up the courage to arrange an appointment with the card buyer for Denver's Tattered Cover Book Store, a huge, wonderful place dedicated to books—not just a seller of them—that I referred to then and now as my secular temple. Anne Marie Martin ordered 150 cards, which at that time was a *ton* of those initial efforts. (She, too, was most kind about my shaky artistic abilities.) Anne Marie's boldness rubbed off. I decided that if the Tattered Cover, one of the country's premier bookstores bought my cards, others would too. The Tattered Cover opened many doors for Post-a-Quote. Appropriately, their logo is of open doors...

Laura Benton, also integral to my success and a friend of my sister, took the cards to a bookstore in Scottsdale, Arizona. They ended up ordering and I was pushed further into the world of wholesale/retail sales. From that account I ended up with my first sales rep and an order from The Smithsonian—which still orders my cards. I built the business from those first starts. I hadn't planned any of this but it did take work on my part to make it happen.

As I got more involved and satisfied with Post-a-Quote, I found myself less enamored with my "real" job. I recall someone, I don't remember who it was, suggesting that I quit my job and do Post-a-Quote fulltime. My response was "I'm not that stupid." As it turned out, I wasn't that stupid, then. In 1993, after two years of doing the cards in my spare time, I quit my partnership, moved east to Columbia, Missouri, and began making greeting cards as a career.

When people ask me about that move—thinking that they might do something as bold—I always make sure that they have a few facts in place:

#1: My wife Lynnette, an R.N., had a "real" job in place with health benefits for the entire family.

2: I had some money put away from the partnership for retirement.

255

#3: I moved from Denver where the cost of living was comparatively high, to the Midwest where it was moderate. We used the equity from the sale of our home in Denver to "buy down" our house payment and live more modestly.

4: Even after ten years, with many accounts and tens of thousands of cards sold, I still do not clear enough to support a family of four.

As to point #1: At the risk of making this sound like an Academy Award acceptance speech, I would be remiss if I did not mention my wife's role in all of this. Essentially, the fact is that Lynnette gave her blessing to this enterprise and did it by giving up a job she loved, a lifestyle that she found most satisfactory, a beautiful state she had lived in most of her life, and moving away from family and friends. #1 indeed.

I am now in my tenth year and still shipping orders all over the United States and to Canada. I continue to average 13,000 handwritten cards per year. Ironically, one of my oldest accounts is the Winston Churchill Memorial in Fulton, Missouri, home of the famous "Iron Curtain Speech." I had no idea there was any such memorial in the U.S. until I discovered it in the Columbia telephone directory while investigating our move to Missouri.

I recently opened my website at www.postaquote.com and look forward to reaching those people who haven't yet seen my cards.

Post-a-Quote is a story of more or less: more fulfillment, less money. I have never looked back – well, there was that one time in a hot, windy, dusty park in Kansas at the end of a blistering July en route from Colorado to Missouri during the Great Flood of '93 —but that's another story. It was too late to turn back, it only lasted a moment and there's never been a similar moment since.

"You must start somewhere."
- Winston Churchill

Santa Fe duffel bag

Janet Ghio
Janet Ghio Designs

This is a story about dreams coming true, about doing what you love, about trusting your intuition and synchronicity…

In 1999, a wonderful, magical, exciting thing happened to me. I was invited to show my art quilts in a brand new art quilt gallery in Santa Fe called Thirteen Moons. It's a fairy tale come true. How did it happen? This is my story…

From 1991–1996, I worked as a career counselor at a community college in Arizona, teaching classes in career development and counseling students to "follow their passion." One book we sometimes used in the career planning class was a book called "Do What You Love and the Money Will Follow." While I liked the concept, I wasn't really sure that you could *really* do what you loved and the money would follow. Those stories were about other people, not me. I had a great job, made good money and worked with people I really liked, so what did I have to complain about? But something was missing. I had no time or money to create anything that was not job-related. You know how it is—you work all day, get home, fix dinner, take care of your kids if you have them, etc. etc., and then collapse on the couch. The weekends are even worse with errand running. I had always been a creative person and was always "making something": knitting, crocheting, sewing, embroidery, needlepoint, cross-stitch, dolls, jewelry, paper, etc. I even made a "real quilt" back in the '70's—the bear paw pattern. This was back in the old days before rotary cutters, when you traced around each template and cut each piece out with scissors and got a big dent in the side of your thumb from the pressure of cutting so many pieces. Then you had to match all those points and sew all the pieces together, then the blocks together and quilt it. I vowed *never* to make another quilt!

Anyway, this yearning to create something, (I didn't know what it would be) kept gnawing at me and that, coupled with several life circumstances, caused my husband and I to decide to make some drastic changes in our lives. I decided to take a leap of faith. I quit my job and we moved back to Missouri. Our children were grown up, we paid off any debts we had and talked about what compromises we were willing to make. People thought we were crazy! "What are you going to do?" they asked. "I don't know. We'll get part-time jobs and I'll make art." (Whatever that was supposed to be…)

When I got back to Columbia, I was adopted by a group of women in a fiber study group that my mother had been part of. This group was the rebel group of The Columbia Weavers and Spinners—we were the fiber artists, papermakers and basket makers—all very interested in trying different surface design techniques. We spent lots of time during our meetings dyeing and embellishing pieces of fabric, which I neatly folded up and put into a drawer wondering what I would ever do with them. Periodically, I took them out and admired them. In the meantime, I was making a little bit of this and that and selling a few items here and there, but nothing to write home about.

In the summer of 1998, while visiting in Arizona, an astrologer friend told me that according to my horoscope, the first quarter of 1999 would be an auspicious time to market any artwork that I had. I filed this tidbit away. That was the year I was making collage boxes and I was sure that they were going to be my ticket to fame and fortune.

That fall, I had dyed some more fabric with the fiber group and there was this one piece that kept haunting me. Every time I looked at it I thought it looked like a sky with lightning bolts in it. Shortly after Christmas, I took that piece of fabric out and decided to make a small picture out of it with a magical woman walking in the woods. I had so much fun making it that I quickly made two more—a mermaid and a little crony woman I named "Queen Mab"… my first "art quilts."

Now, I didn't know that these were "Art Quilts." I didn't know there was such a thing! I called them "little wall hangings." They were put together like quilts with three layers, but didn't have much quilting on them, because as I told people: "I am not a quilter. I can't make those tiny, even stitches and I didn't know how to make a binding correctly. *I don't do quilts*."

In January of 1999, I showed these wall hangings and my collage boxes to my friend Gloria Page who has a card business and sells her work in Santa Fe. We talked about "how fun it would be to go to Santa Fe together sometime." She knew people in Santa Fe and maybe we could find a store that might like to sell my collage boxes. Maybe I would bring along a couple of quilts, too. We didn't have a definite plan…

I have an interesting connection with the Southwest. My grandfather, C.A. Seward was one of the Kansas Prairie Printmakers and his many trips to New Mexico inspired many of his lithographs. For as long as I can remember, my mother, a weaver and basket maker, had traveled to the Southwest and collected Navajo rugs and other Native American art. The first time I saw New Mexico it had a profound effect on me, as it does for many others. As Georgia O'Keeffe said: "If you ever see New Mexico, you will never lose the itch."

In the meantime, I decided that I needed to have a studio space where everything would be in one place (oh joy!) instead of running from the spare bedroom up to the attic and then down to the basement twenty times a day. So we decided to remodel the attic room upstairs and convert it into a studio with the intention that someday it would truly be a "working" studio.

In mid-March, Gloria called and said: "I know it's kind of short notice, but I'm going to Santa Fe in two weeks. Do you want to go?" Remember what the astrologer said: "market your work in the first quarter of 1999." Well, it was now or never. I said yes, still thinking that my primary things to market were the collage boxes.

I put several boxes and four small quilts into a navy blue duffel bag and we set out for New Mexico. Santa Fe has the reputation of being one of the most prestigious art centers in the United States. People come from all over the world to spend money and buy art in Santa Fe. No artist in his or her right mind would go there carrying artwork in a *duffel* bag, with no portfolio and no slides and expect to sell anything. If I had really thought about what I was actually *doing*, I probably would have never had the nerve, but my friend Gloria was going to be along, so it couldn't be too bad!

Gloria, her mother and I spent several days walking around Santa Fe in the drizzling cold rain, going in and out of shops where I would timidly at first, later more boldly, go up to salesclerks and ask if they "would like to see these collage boxes that I make or these little wall hangings?" I seemed to get more response to the quilts than the boxes, so I decided to concentrate on them. I even had a storeowner approach me in one of my favorite stores in Santa Fe and ask me what was in my duffel bag. She loved the quilts and told me to come back in the morning and see her store manager. I was so excited! To have something in my favorite store in Santa Fe—*Wow*! I went back for my appointment the next day and I waited to see the manager. And waited. And I waited some more. I waited for over an hour and she never showed up. I was so humiliated! I felt like such a fool! As I left, I wasn't sure at that point if I wanted to take that chance again…

The next day, my cousin and I decided to give it a rest and we would just have a day of fun, so I left my duffel bag at home. We went to a small shop that sold handwoven clothing. My cousin started whispering in my ear to "ask the woman who owns the shop if she can recommend any place in Santa Fe that might be interested" in looking at my quilts. Still licking my wounds from the day before, I hesitantly told her my story. She said: "Do you know about the new art quilt gallery that just opened up on Canyon Road?" My heart starts to beat a little faster. "No, I haven't heard of it." "Well," she said, "it's only been open for three weeks, but you might go talk to them."

The next day, armed with my duffel bag, I set out for Canyon Road and Thirteen Moons Gallery. As luck would have it, I stopped at another store along the way and was chatting with the saleswoman and mentioned where I was going. "Oh," she said, "my friend Sukie works there, ask for her and tell her I said 'hi!'" There's nothing better than having the name of the person you want to talk to and being able to make a personal connection as you go in the door. I walked in, and there were these fabulous quilts by Therese May hanging on the walls. I knew that this was the place I wanted to show my work if I could. I showed Sukie and another saleswoman my quilts—they liked them and gave me a lot of great advice—but they said I would need to talk to KC Willis, the gallery director, and she wasn't in. I would need to call her. They gave me her number. Again, luck or fate was with me, because she answered the first time I tried and I made an appointment to see her the day before I was going home. She also liked my quilts, but said the gallery *owner* had to have final approval and that she presently was in South America. They already had shows booked through the rest of 1999, but asked that I send slides of my work when I got home.

Well, after that conversation I was like a bird dog on point: someday I was going to be in that gallery—I was determined. Before I left Santa Fe, I took a photograph of the outside of the gallery and put it on a bulletin board in my new studio space for inspiration. I had slides taken of the five quilts I had made and sent them, along with a letter, to Thirteen Moons. I started making new quilts in anticipation of the day when I would be invited to show in their gallery, never dreaming that it would happen much sooner than I expected! As a former career counselor, I knew that it was important to follow up with a call soon after you have sent a resume to a future employer, so I decided to bite the bullet and follow up with the gallery to make sure they had received my slides, did they have any questions and so forth. I dreaded making that call, thinking they were going to say "…well, thanks but no thanks—we made a big mistake…" But I did it—I made that call anyway. I had to leave a message. Towards the end of April, KC Willis called me and I was invited to be in a four-woman show at the end of August! I would be one of the new "emerging artists" and could I please send "between eight and twelve quilts?" Yes! and *YES*! (I only had five quilts at this point and ones that I thought needed more work on them at that.) I was so excited I thought I would have a heart attack! I hardly knew what to do first—at least it was very clear that I had to get busy sewing in order to have that many quilts by mid-August.

In the meantime, I got on the Internet and looked at other people's art quilts. Mine didn't look like anyone else's—they weren't variations of patterns, abstract, or stitched with all kinds of fancy stitches on the sewing machine. My quilts told stories, were hand-stitched and a cross between folk art and art quilt. Maybe the gallery *had* made a mistake! Could they really want my little quilts? I worked diligently in my attic studio, planned my trip back to Santa Fe for the opening, and shipped my quilts off. The night before I was to leave, I got an e-mail from KC. It read: "…Everyone at the gallery is so excited about your quilts. Each one is a little treasure and we can hardly wait to show them to the world." I was on Cloud Nine!

The day of the opening came. My intention was not to go to the gallery until that evening for the reception, but I was out with some friends and my curiosity got the better of me—we decided to stop by for just a few minutes. Imagine my surprise when I walked back to the room where my quilts were and discovered that seven of the nine quilts I had sent already had SOLD signs on them! Needless to say, I was so thrilled and excited.

Thirteen Moons continues to sell my quilts. I have received commissions through the gallery and have been invited to participate in other shows. It is a dream come true. Now I can say with conviction: It is true. "Do what you love and the money will follow."

I'd Rather Be Stamping!

Brenda (BJ) Thompson
I'd Rather Be Stamping (Store)

In 1991 my older sister Sue (a missionary in Hong Kong) asked if rubber stamping was popular in the States. I went to the local craft store to check it out and found only a handful of small cartoon stamps. I came to the conclusion that stamping was just for kids. Later that year Sue came for a visit and I took her to Branson, Missouri. We walked into a mall and by surprise happened to walk into a rubber stamp store. As I looked around the many shelves, I realized that this was *not* just for kids!

The sales lady demonstrated heat embossing to us. I thought this was neat but it wasn't until I looked up on one wall and saw a large butterfly stamped on a t-shirt that I got hooked. We left after spending $150. That night in the hotel room all I could think about was what I could do with stamping and all these wonderful tools! So of course, before we left town the next day, I *had* to stop again and this time spent $70 more.

Once home I realized I was in a stamp wasteland. I found myself trying to convince my children how much *they* really wanted to go to Branson to see the sights every few months. That way, on the way out of town, we could stop by the stamp store and I could satisfy my stamp cravings and get my "fix." (It didn't take them long to figure me out.)

For a couple of years I kept my eyes open when on vacation and found stamp stores in Las Vegas and San Diego. That's where I found my first stamp magazine filled with mail order companies—that allowed me to order from home. At that time my fiancé (now my husband) and I were talking about my frustration at not being able to find items I needed and surely there must be others in the same boat we thought. So I started a home business, taught classes and carted boxes of stamps and accessories to craft shows. It wasn't long before we realized we couldn't take everything stampers wanted or needed to craft shows and the house was definitely not big enough for a store. It was time to consider the next step.

We prayed and sought God's direction and to our surprise people would come up to me at craft stores and just happen to mention that they wished there was a place to buy better stamps. I didn't know these people and they didn't know that I did stamping. I felt this was a nudge from God and things started falling into place.

After spending 20 years in Respiratory Therapy, my husband Dennis was looking for new challenges. Since he had a 3-year history as a hard lines manager in a retail store and a degree in sales and marketing, he agreed to open and run the store. I would stay working at the hospital and would go in after my "day job," give classes and finish up the day at the store. On August 1, 1995 we opened a full service stamp and stencil retail business—our very own store in a shopping area called Bernadette Square, across the street from the Columbia Mall. It has been a great deal of work and commitment. Most of the time we find ourselves working well into the wee hours of the morning, but it has been worth it. We have met so many wonderful people through this art medium and have watched beginners blossom into artists.

I look at my house, at stores and the whole world differently now, always looking for something to stamp on or stamp with. Tissue boxes are purchased because the design on the box can later be used to stamp on or cut and be used in a collage. Cotton from aspirin bottles is saved to dab in ink and stipple a background on cards. *YES*, I am a pack rat—if only I could organize everything so that I could find things easier!

I have never thought of myself as being creative but realize that God sees creativity in all of us. My sole reason for stamping and stenciling is to encourage and uplift others. Between my husband and I, we have over 51 years of experience in Health Care. We've seen lots of sickness and dying. We know that receiving a handmade card or note may be just what a person needs to lift his or her spirits. When we demonstrate a stamping or stenciling technique in the store, we usually save the demo to make a card to send to someone on our prayer list.

Looking at all the hobbies and crafting I have done over the years, I have to say that stamping has been the most enjoyable. It is an art form in which each person can develop a completely unique style, whether you are in China, Missouri or anywhere else in the world. To relieve some of the stresses and pressures that come from just being alive, I know that stamping is a wonderful, natural remedy that can help along the way. I set up a little area with "toys of all kinds" and get ready to ink up. I can truly and happily say:

"I'd Rather Be Stamping!"

Mountains to Climb

Lara K. Birkes
Sendable Wearable Art

The driving force behind my business was, in short, a mountain in Alaska. When my Mom and I began our business I was fourteen years old and my primary interest was mountaineering. This was an activity my Dad and I enjoyed and did together throughout the year. Though I was a relatively inexperienced climber at the time, I loved mountains and my goal was to someday climb North America's tallest peak, Mt. McKinley. The more I read about this endeavor, the more I realized I needed a means of revenue exceeding that of the average fourteen-year-old. It was my Mom who helped me design a way, and the result was our business: "Sendable Wearable Art."

Beginning with a postage stamp, the business progressed from there. My Grandfather's extensive stamp collection had exposed me to an eclectic selection of stamps from around the world. It was from admiring these small works of art that my Mom and I agreed there was potential for a business. After much experimentation, we decided to incorporate both stamps and stationary, a creative and logical link we thought! My Mom water-colored, by hand, a scene for each card that complemented a particular postage stamp, and I worked with the postage stamps themselves, mounting them on mat board, decorating edges, adding a sealer and pin back. The finished "stamp jewelry" was fixed to the hand-painted card, which could easily be removed and worn upon receipt, and there you had it: "Sendable Wearable Art!"

Sales of our cards began on a small scale in my hometown of Columbia, Missouri. We started at The Columbia Art League. This allowed me to slowly increase my sales locally and gradually work up to higher levels of production. By the next summer we had a big enough customer base and had produced enough cards to enter "Art in the Park," a summer art fair sponsored by The Columbia Art League. This was my first experience with volume sales and from that time on I realized that art fairs would be the most profitable way for me to sell my cards. This method was very appealing to me as a student because it meant working primarily in the summer, during the holiday season and on weekends, allowing me to focus on school during the weekdays and most of the year.

Sales drastically increased in the summer of 1994 when our local paper, The Columbia Tribune, did a feature article in their Scene Magazine on our business. We had been selling our cards for well over a year, and it was after this publication that our card business really began to take off. Several other local stores in addition to The Art League were now carrying my cards, and adding these sales together with art shows throughout the state of Missouri, we had as many orders as we could possibly handle!

We ran the business this way for four years—filling orders, participating in art fairs, and selling to local retailers. These four years were not only lucrative for me as a high school student, but also provided me with insightful exposure to the business world and invaluable experience in dealing with people. Now that I have graduated from college (The University of Montana) with a degree in International Business and Management, I realize just how valuable my early business experiences were, and I am appreciative of the support I received from my many faithful customers. Thank you.

The thirtieth of June, 1997, was a memorable day for many reasons. "Sendable Wearable Art" had in fact financed my Alaskan expedition, and my Dad and I stood on the summit of Mt. McKinley. Having been able to pay for my own equipment, training, and the expedition itself, made the climb all that much more rewarding for me. We were able to safely reach the summit after fifteen days of climbing, and through a radio call that our guide placed from the summit, a message of our success was relayed to my Mom and two-year-old brother in Missouri.

I tell this story to give special thanks to all those who were supportive of "Sendable Wearable Art," and also to encourage others to undertake similar business ventures. Though I am initially inclined to boast of the simplicity of such a business endeavor (as a point of encouragement for you), I would be remiss to take full credit. This was *our* business, not mine alone. I want to attribute its success to my Mom, her creative eye, patient nature and countenance, all qualities that have made my adventures and our business possible.

In loving memory of my Mother, Carolyn McLaughlin Birkes, my biggest fan and greatest supporter, a note of thanks could never be enough. You are with me everyday in all the mountains that I climb.

"Gratitude"
Dedicated to Carolyn Birkes

Part Five

dream machine

I like people who think big and I like being around them even more. One time I read something along the lines of "men think beyond the cave and women tend to want to decorate it." I laughed and reflected at the same time. What about the men who are fabulous architects and interior designers, and the women who fly NASA space shuttles and climb the highest mountains? Our personal dream machines can accommodate a wide spectrum of aspirations, it seems to me, even within the same human being.

A memory surfaces of being in 5th grade in 1964... Daydreaming one day, I was connected enough to reality to note that I was sitting in the 5th seat in the 5th row in the 5th grade, contemplating a monumental, historical decision: in the very big scheme of things, when I grow up, which is more important: To be the First Woman President of the United States or to be the First American Woman Astronaut to go into space with a Russian Woman Cosmonaut? Pretty tough choice for a little ten-year-old girl to make... there she was, seated in a small Catholic elementary school staring out the window at autumn trees. Decisions, decisions…

As it all turned out, the closest I ever got to a "position" in Washington was an appointment with the Smithsonian Graphic Art Department, and the only thing slightly resembling orbiting with Russians was a recent babysitting experience I had with my little nephew Nick. He was adopted in Russia and his energy level puts him at mach speeds most of every waking day. I am satisfied with these experiences.

The fact that I do not have an office in the West Wing and have never counted down in a space shuttle does not mean that I give up on my dreams—they just may take different forms over time. Sometimes all I want to do is decorate "my cave," yet my head always seems to be poked out the door checking for shooting stars. I am a daydream believer. I find that for me, there are two variations on the theme and I dovetail them— dreaming in practical, down-to-earth terms and dreaming in way-out-there cosmic realms.

This is the shortest section of the book, but potentially the biggest in reality since this is the inauguration, the launching pad to the great unknown: the future.

It can get downright scary

It is such a fabulous way to think and live—to actively, consciously believe that dreams do come true and to act accordingly. The counterpart to that is that at times, attempting to put such a belief firmly in place and maintaining momentum seem utterly impossible and it can get downright scary—scary financially, scary emotionally, and just plain nerve-wracking in general. We can completely romanticize this notion of throwing off the shackles of a boring, un-creative job and lifestyle and deciding to do what you love, praying like crazy that money and good fortune will follow you out the door as you slam it behind you. I am not one, however, for romantic, unrealistic wishful thinking that leads to poverty. But I'll tell you what—I am even less interested in something that scares me even more than taking a chance on a dream—the regret that comes from not trying.

Daytime talk shows are not my usual thing. I've heard of great episodes on *Oprah*, but I don't sit down and watch TV at that time of day, and I need to pick my kids up from school in the middle of the show anyway. Today my intuition, clear as a voice, told me to just *turn it on* while you eat your way-too-late lunch. Okay—I did it. It was perfect. Two women were featured, chosen from among those people who responded to the question: "What is your biggest regret in life?" One woman regretted the fact that she compromised her dream of working at Sea World with Orcas and dolphins. The other woman regretted that she had not followed her dream of joining the circus and had turned down a job offer with Barnum and Bailey's Ringling Brothers Circus when she was quite young. They both settled for office jobs that gave them security and approval—but not their dreams.

I caught the magic of Oprah's popularity when I found myself engrossed in the excitement of watching these two people on camera, totally surprised at work when they were invited into their own past-wishes, finding the joy of hugging dolphins or dressing for the Big Top Show. It killed me to have to leave and miss the whole wrap-up, all the crying and laughing, and I do wonder if they got new jobs or went back to work as usual. Was it a flashback and a temporary panacea/aspirin experience or did something change?

It is understandable to make choices based on fear and getting approval from others. Contemplating money, especially the lack of it, can be scary and I will be the first to say that from experience. The "starving artist syndrome?" It's pretty real, although the starvation is not so much about food as it is about life's material pleasures. Does it make me nutty sometimes that I have to calculate expenditures? Is it a little embarrassing to admit that I wish *I* was the one who found the quarter on the ground instead of my son? I could use it for parking. It is important to be honest. Sometimes it is hard. But I don't have to be on a TV show for my shot at "what it would be like to live the life of an artist with a home business all her own," for one fairy-tale, manufactured day. This little business that I have built, this is *my* show, which at times feels a lot like a circus, but I have no regrets. I can give it up anytime or I can keep going—it is a wide-open choice.

I know people who are struggling, others who are comfortable and there are those who are making a lot of money in their own businesses. There are times when we as individuals phase in and out of those zones over time. Is it possible to "make it big?" Sure. Yet here is the bottom line for us: living to make dreams come true is downright inspiring. It is life. I want to be a person who can make the leap and jump for joy! Those two women beamed, *sparkled*, when they were doing what they love. It's their call now. A second chance is very rare and a genuine gift. Another chance after that? Beyond rare.

When you start dreaming in French

I got off the boat and stopped speaking English. That was a cute, romantic move since I didn't speak anything else without the help of a phrase book. There are times when you just have to cut off the past in order to become new. To be in France meant to "be French." The capital is "Pahrrrree" not "Peariss," mon amie. I made myself speak, think, read, drink, eat and in every conceivable way become immersed in the land I had chosen to call home for a time. I slept on the ground to feel it and smell it, I ate sweet fresh white and black figs straight from the trees warmed by the French sun, and rubbed lavender leaves on my wrists instead of buying Chanel No.5—free, less marketing, packaging, and middlemen involved. Finally, one day after many months, it happened—I got into my tent at the base of the French Alps, snuggled into my orange down mummy sleeping bag, fell asleep in English and dreamed *in French*. In the morning I was totally transformed. How *splendide*. I had finally arrived. No longer a visitor—I was French.

When I got off another boat later in Dover, England, I reverted back to English, awkwardly, and laughed out loud at the way I put my adjectives into French context. My mouth was "funny talking." I flashed back to my childhood lingo... Giving up your native tongue or boring, familiar, same-old-same-old life and attitudes for a while, even for one day… It's a good place to break the molds—more concrete than a vaporous dream.

The Southwest Chief
On track to new horizons

We got on the train in Kansas City in the middle of the night after sleeping on a flat bicycle box at the base of a Christmas tree with our pillows and blankets held close. Chicago was a gigantic ice cube buried in snow, and the Southwest Chief had to melt miles and miles of icy tracks to connect the two cities and eventually get my family and me to Lamy, New Mexico for the Holidays—crazy and memorable story at the same time. Thank goodness my kids saw it the same way that I was trying to see it. The trip was stretched out but we made it, and of course it became a legend in the family archives.

Amtrak is good for me. I like to travel by train especially with my children. We are on the ground and have a sense of distance. It takes time to get from the Midwest to the Southwest. It is far. The formation of the land changes subtly and you can talk about what you observe as you settle into your seats in the Observation Car. It isn't exactly like traveling by covered wagon, but you find that you start talking about such things as you sense the distance, realize you have time to talk, and make the attitude as well as altitude adjustments en route. There can also be a distance between who you are—and want to be.

It was a round-trip experience that went way beyond the steel tracks and ties that took us there, and back. I went as a cardmaker trying so hard to write a book. The return trip found me a *designer* and a *writer* who is finishing a book—I could see the process and knew that I would get there. It is good to take trips away from your everyday life, whether it is on a boat, train, bicycle, or simply a mental flight of fancy. My train trip was short, yet to have some distance from the mountains of tasks at hand grants the possibility of a new perspective. I know now, I am *convinced*, that I am on track to new horizons. Before the Southwest Chief pulled out of Kansas City, it was all wishful thinking.

Just start talking
The value of setting things in motion and networking

Ideas come and ideas go. Such is the human mind. What we *do* with our ideas determines our destiny. There is a point when thinking is necessary, at other times enjoyable, and then there is a point when thinking too much makes you nuts. Right before I get to that point—hopefully—I start *talking*. In the beginning that may translate into talking out loud to myself which indeed may be a little nuts, but no one is around to take notes and contact the appropriate authorities. So I happily chatter away.

I wanted to write a book. My whole *life* I've wanted to write a book. I talked to myself and then I started talking to other people—*bingo*. Things started to line up—a momentum was created. The more I talked and the more I substantiated my ideas on paper, the more I physically and substantially *wrote* the book, the more help was coming my way. I had a "Velcro-mindset" in place—all the right things were coming along and sticking. I was tuned in enough to recognize what otherwise might have just passed right on by me. It is an amazing phenomenon and one of the most natural things in the world. (Note: Late nights *after* conferences can be the big highlight—communicating ideas.)

Networking is not a complex science. It is people, services and products connecting with each other. It is a fabulous synergistic flow of materials, ideas, spirit and goals. *Networking* is an active verb, and the more you put out, the more comes back. I could not be*lieve* how many times a question was in my mind, a problem needed to be solved, or information just seemed to elude me and then I opened my mouth, put a voice and words to my situation, and found that the exact person to help out just happened to be standing right in front of my face—listening and smiling. Then it was my turn to listen and take notes, primed and ready to follow through. At other times, in other conversations, I am stunned to discover that *I* am the unsuspecting answer to someone's prayer. The right person at the right time and place—it goes both ways. Create a stir; make a connection.

Think, talk, do. Thinking is good. Talking is next. Doing is best.

Think, talk, and do. I try to keep that in a kind of flowing motion and know from personal experience that it is a good idea to give the whole process and myself a break and rest from time to time. After a great tennis match, there is nothing like a splash of ice water on your face, a cold drink, and a solid nap.

So, just start talking, but be ever aware of the truth of this Chinese Proverb:
Talk doesn't cook rice.

Putting it all in the mix
…facing a challenge and gathering resources, both internal and external…

Do I run and hide from things occasionally? Yes. Some challenges seem way too big and complex in the moment—that may be the initial perception anyway. When I am willing to simply stand still in the open vs. running and hiding, there is hope. It is then time to put ideas and options on the table, talk, listen and actively engage in making decisions and exploring possibilities. There is a good chance of advancing to a new place at that point. My once seemingly nemesis challenge is manageable after all.

I call the process "putting it all in the mix." Gather from the internal well of resources from past experience, research who and what are available around me, put it all into play and see what happens. It is a matter of combining a lot of individual and unique ingredients—a tossed salad comes to mind. The more interesting the components, the more texture and flavor make it to the plate. "Put it all in the mix" and innovative solutions and exotic new dishes are on the menu.

Skipping stones

If you were to scuba dive in Lake Congamond where we had our summer cottage during the growing-up years, I am convinced that you would find a mountain peak of smooth, flat stones that had been skipped on the surface of the water many years ago. Endless competitions for the smoothest stone, most skips, farthest throw—all basically in the same general area of the lake. We always stood by a certain railing to throw rocks…

I think of my business using these images at times. I am skipping stones. Personal style in hand positioning and foot stance are important. There is a meditative pause in the act of preparing and aiming for the goal. I take the "handstamped bookmark" stone and let it fly, counting the skips, observing the ripples. It has its journey, goes into the depths and settles. I search the beach and come up with a bigger stone: "handmade cards." I skip it in the same part of the lake, noticing that this one goes much farther, deeper, and the splash/rippling effect is broader. Let's see: "handmade tiles." For this idea I am going to pick up a whole handful of rocks and let them rain on the surface of the water, laughing at the tinkling sounds of all the "plunks." "Write a book." I've carried that stone in my pocket for a very long time. It is smooth—looks like a good one.

Once the surface of the lake is sliced open, the skipping stones seem to disappear. I may never "see" them again, but they do exist underwater, building a structure unknown to me, yet nevertheless real and substantial—a foundation shifting itself slowly over time. There are layers and more layers. Whether with a pebble or boulder, smooth or rough— once tossed, the resulting splash may become a ripple and then a wave. The waves bring more stones to the water's edge. Searching once again, I bend down and pick up another.

I hear and I forget. I see and I remember. I do and I understand.

- *Chinese* Proverb

■

Happiness is when what you think,
what you say
and what you do are in harmony.

- *Gandhi*

269

Dreams

In the big picture of life, I have always had big dreams, idealistic longings and a pretty romantic view of what life could and should be like. If you were to observe my favorite movie choices, they would include: *The Sound of Music*, *It's a Wonderful Life*, *Remember the Titans*, *Gandhi*, movies based on book classics, history and biographies. *Chocolat* let me savor France again… My personal vision is uncomplicated—c'est moi.

For a few moments, I would like to play with a few of many fantasies. The focus will be on things related to "the art business" and possible directions, detours and adventures that may be in the future. It has been my experience that putting such things down on paper is good for the soul, as well as setting the very things you desire in motion—sometimes much sooner than you would expect.

I would just love to:

- trek to Taos and write my heart out (literally) in a class with Natalie Goldberg
- meet Sharilyn Miller in Santa Fe, take a workshop with her and go bead shopping
- have paint all over my hands, working side-by-side with Sherrill Kahn, on fabric
- be in the same room with Lynne Perrella, collage artist, absorbing, exploring
- go to Arizona someplace, anyplace, find a pottery workshop, a teacher, and hide out there for a while, making things I can't even imagine now, clay everywhere
- get aboard a Stamp Cruise ship to some islands somewhere and *play* non-stop

In other words, it would be just fabulous to be a student of these and so many artists I admire, many I have yet to discover. Learning is a huge part of my dream.

There are basically two different kinds of dreams: short-term realistic and way-out there fantastic. I believe that we need to have both types and to say it all out loud. My plan is to be available, to show up, to participate, to leap from one lily pad to the next. I am determined to get to the goals and when I get off-track or disoriented, I want to have the courage and love of life to get back on track and shoot higher than before.

Without having a clue as to how this book will be received, I already envision a second one. Call it: *Holy Cow! We actually did it!* or perhaps *Storytellers: Women Artists share their Favorite Stories*… whatever. The point is that I would like to be the Editor, the *reader* of the next book. As I found myself speaking at various places over the years, and as my own book came to be talked about even before going to print, people kept coming up to me, sharing their own stories—I want those written down and I want to treasure hunt for more. They are there. If you have a story, write it down and send it to me. I am serious. I can see many possibilities for chapter headings already. Among them:

- *My most successful failure*
- *Self-taught is cool*
- *What is "art" anyway?*
- *Why I stopped doing whatever the heck it was that I was doing and started…*
- *Now this was scary*
- *That one single person who believed in me when I did not believe in myself*
- *The point of no return—and no regrets either*, etc.

We shall see where this all leads. Now that you've read this book, let's do one together.

I would also like to be part of creating a resource center of information for artists to help each other find wholesale sources quickly. If it exists already, I'll jump in headfirst.

Coming from another angle, I am determined to delve into the world of licensing agreements, having signed my first exciting contract and, coming up, a second one with my favorite stamp company: a line of fabric stamps based on my handcarved blocks. The idea of licensing my tile designs has surfaced and the channels of exploration are open. More writing for magazines… Women artists are lining up with their stories already...

For the clay-aspect of my work, I will go three-dimensional with the tile work, and I will sit down at a potter's wheel and learn how to do that—there, I said it out loud. For whatever reason, I am scared of it, silly girl. Basketry beckons and I will heed the call.

As for the Smithsonian and other card accounts that I have kept active, I am going to go to new territories and experiment. It is time to re-think the designs.

Having said all of this *out loud*, the challenge is on, and I know darn well from experience that the twists and turns in the road ahead, the unexpected detours that lead to places unknown, are as much a part of the dream as the wishes I cast to fortune now. God knows I just want to have the courage, common sense and flexibility to face it all and *go*.

From the moment of putting pen to paper in 2000, certain ideas and goals that seemed very far-fetched have already happened and are now just a part of the past and pretty routine. That is the practical nature of dreams: they can actually come true.

It is good to be reminded that each of us
has a different dream.
- *Crow* Proverb

Memories

I have worked with my memories. Some were wrestled to the ground, others tossed to the wind or embraced, and still others were left entirely alone, thank you very much. Memories are like the skipping stones we have visited before. You pick one up, looking for just the right one. It has to fit your hand. You play with it for a while, eyeing the water and sensing the wind. No one wants to waste a good stone—no one wants to waste a good memory either. Reality sinks in that you have one shot and that's pretty much it. If any number of things goes wacky with your delivery, then it's bye-bye to the bottom of the lake or history.

Now the beautiful part of this whole story is: if the timing and any amount of magic whatsoever are in your dominion, the stone or memory, once released, will glide and sail, touching the surface of the water or people's minds more times than are countable. Once a story is told, it is told. Choosing the story, the timing and the toss, getting the "ride" is what it's all about. Could I skip enough, far enough to reach people and hit the mark? Did I pick up the ones that matter? I sure tried my best. Memories are the most valuable when they teach us about how special today is. There is a *Cherokee* saying that goes like this:

Don't let yesterday use up too much of today.

▪

We all have so many different kinds of memories.
I remind myself to gather the happy ones as if in a basket—all of these
early morning sparkles, dancing on the lake of my mind. - *Gloria Page*

BACKWARD
Writing this book: 2000 - 2001

Joni Mitchell wrote about being on a "carousel of time" and the fact that we can't go back in time, but are free to glance at the past, even as the present and future are upon us.

For the last two years I wrote my own words and lived them. It has been a great ride.

From the very outset, I had this idea fixed in my head that I wanted to self-publish for many reasons, including the fact that I wanted to be free to break conventions and not have anyone telling me things like: "That is a stupid title: change it," or "What are you talking about: a Foreword, a Forward, a Backward and an *Onward*? Forget it." I don't want to change it and I don't need to forget it. Here it is and here I am. My book is written and I did it in my own unique style—for you. No matter what my emotional mood happened to be during these years, whatever the surrounding situations were, writing came freely and brought with it… peace of mind and a smile.

During the whole process I wrote "notes to myself," chronicling experiences of the writing life in the midst of a hectic business and personal life. This became the closest thing to journaling I've done in way too long to mention. The ups were there as well as the downs, the victories, frustrations, dreams and mostly the everyday miracles that I tend to take for granted except when I am a "writer." There is a fabulous power over the ordinary that happens when you decide to tell your stories: you come to the extraordinary realization that everything is a story, and whether or not it turns out for the best has everything to do with attitude and heart. When something lousy was happening, I looked at it as "something for the book" and that made it a more tolerable annoyance because I didn't want to write a lousy ending—to laugh or celebrate made more sense than being embarrassed or upset. More than anything else, two things stood way above the crowd in my experience—the value of gratitude and a sense of humor—saving graces both.

I thought I could write this book in three months—oh, sure. When it stretched into a second year, I learned something about the writing life: *Life* does not go "on hold" so that it can be captured and packaged between the two covers of a book. It moves and churns; it tugs and pulls, is gentle once in a while and is always on the verge…of something new. I wanted to look at my business life in the arts and shake it up in my thinking—the past, the present and the future. I wanted to be real and honest, giving and challenging and above all, I wanted to shoot straight from the heart to anyone who wanted to listen.

Could I have said more… or less? Yes. Could I have said it differently? Definitely. If I were to start all over again today, would it be the same book? No, it would not. My business and I have changed over time, so that is no great surprise. That's why you write a second book, so I've been told. Looking backwards, I find myself to be a person who looks forward to so much. In your own reflections, my hope is that you find your own brand of peace and the strength, the lightness, and the dignity to dream. Looking back, you will clearly know the special people to thank, and please include yourself.

The world has cried together this year. May we laugh again with loving depth, actively creating a legacy that is not only worth writing about, but worth living in the purest, simplest moments that make a day and eventually, a life, complete… onward ho!

But to look back all the time is boring. Excitement lies in tomorrow.
- *Natalia Makarova* (Russian Ballerina)

ONWARD

One fine summer day, I met a boy who had some professional circus juggling toys and said to him: "When I grow up, I'd like to learn how to do that." He never missed a beat. "You are grown up already. How old are you anyway?" "I'm 47, but how do *you* know that I am grown up? Why? Because I have white hair? How old are *you*?" "I'm 10. Here, you can learn how to do this. You don't have to wait forever. I'll teach you now." "Thanks! This is great! I love it!" I wasn't very good at it, but it was so much fun to try.

Let's visit another fine summer day, a different year, place and child... My son Brandon, 11, wants to learn how to fish. Kentucky Lake holds promise, but time there is running short and then a great opportunity presents itself. My kids adopted Vinny as their own uncle, even though technically he isn't. "Uncle Vinny" was fishing with his own children and offered Brandon and little brother Bryan the chance to give it a try—they literally jumped at it, got a lesson and started casting away. Bryan proudly displayed the crawdad he caught and made a mobile aquatic environment. His fishing adventure was pretty much complete. I watched Brandon closely—his adventure had only just begun.

There was a flurry of activity and plans were flying all over the place, being changed left and right. Vinny's family was all set to head back home with a long drive ahead of them, but all of that was put on hold. He would stay—the fishing story was not over yet and he stayed with it. He kept giving. Over and over again, Brandon cast the line. Nothing. Over and over again, add the bait, cast again and again. It was getting later and darker. "What about your dinner?" "I'm not hungry. I want to keep fishing." Okay, that's fine." "Uncle Vinny, Dad and I are going to the other part of the lake to keep trying over there." "Sounds good. Good luck." Time was moving on, the sun was close to setting.

The bait was finally used up, the shop closed so you couldn't buy more, and still Brandon was casting over and over again—with *no bait*. Vinny's family prepared to get on the road, Dad stayed by the lake joined by the little brother, and Brandon kept casting with a bare hook. When asked about it, he quietly and simply said, "I'm practicing."

Something in the water... a snag maybe. Pull the line around a bit, perhaps just a branch, but Brandon knew it wasn't. He felt something *alive*! It splashed and pulled and so did he—it was a *big* one! Uncle Vinny came running down to the water; Brandon pulled in the biggest fish of the whole week—with absolutely nothing but perseverance. His practice turned into a victory. He was so surprised, the fish went wild in the air, they grabbed it, it slipped and splashed into the water, escaping in stunned joy, but the beauty of the story escaped no one there. What made that fish bite? Did the last of the evening sun glimmer just right on the hook? Was it the rhythm of the continuous splashing, cast after cast? Or did the fish just have to reward him for his spirit of never giving up...

In moving onward, I want to remember to keep things fresh and new and not be afraid to jump in there and learn to juggle. I want to remember that there is value in practicing, over and over, bait or no bait, fish or no fish. Victories come in time. Moving onward with just these simple attitudes makes the journey ahead so wonderfully inviting.

With all that you are juggling in life, go ahead... be a wild child!
Let us seize the day, embrace the possibilities. We will find out who we are... together.

CONNECTIONS

Gloria Page
ImpressionsArt Designs
www.holymolymackeroly.com
www.impressionsart.com

Sharilyn Miller
Editor of: *Somerset Studio*
and *Belle Armoire* magazines
To order magazines call US toll-free:
1-877-STAMPER
www.somersetstudio.com

Author of:
Stamp Art
The Stamp Artist's Project Book
(Rockport Publishers)
*The Complete Guide
    to Rubber Stamped Jewelry*
(North Light Books 2003)
Available through:
The Shoppe at Somerset
www.somersetstudio.com

Artist's Materials:
Daniel Smith
800-426-6740
www.danielsmith.com

Nasco Arts and Crafts
800-558-9595
www.enasco.com
(great prices on carving blocks)

Dick Blick Art Materials
800-723-2787
www.dickblick.com
(carry Daige Rollataq Adhesive Systems)

Plastic Sleeves for cards (packaging):
Impact Images
www.clearbags.com
East Coast (TN):   800-328-1847
West Coast (CA):   800-233-2630

Wholesale frames:
MCS Industries, Inc.
www.mcsframes.com
800-833-3058

Copyright-free Art Books:
Dover Publications, Inc.
www.doverpublications.com

Paper companies to get you started:

French Paper Co. (envelopes, too)
www.mrfrench.com

Shizen Design
N. Kansas City, Missouri
Tel: 816-221-1971
www.shizendesign.com

Stephen Kinsella, Inc.
(handmade, assorted art paper)
Olivette, Missouri
Tel: 800-445-8865

Golden Oak Papers (for businesses)
Spokane, Washington
Tel: 509-325-5456

East-West Hand Made Paper
Fort Jones, California
Tel: 800-542-4025

FLAX Art & Design
San Francisco, California
Tel: 888-727-3763
www.flaxart.com
(The Paper Catalog)

Ichiyo Art Center
Atlanta, Georgia
Tel: 800-535-2263
Fax: 404-233-8012
www.ichiyoart.com

Art Stamps featured in this book:
(trimmed, unmounted stamps)
Curtis' Collection
Midory Uyeda
3326 St. Michael Drive
Palo Alto, CA   94306

Good advice to prepare for Art Shows:

Be a Dynamic Craft Seller / audiotape
By: *Bruce Baker*
551 Munger St.
Middlebury, Vermont 05753
Tel: 802-388-3434
Fax: 802-388-7428
www.dbakerinc.com

The Best of Missouri Hands
(Organization of Missouri Artisans)
www.bestofmissourihands.com

Columbia Art League
(Annual juried outdoor art show,
gallery, gift shop, classes)
1013 E. Walnut St.
Columbia, Missouri 65201
Tel: 573-443-2131

Poppy (gift and card shop)
Barbara McCormick
914 East Broadway
Columbia, Missouri 65201
Tel: 573-442-3223
www.poppydowntown.com

I'd Rather Be Stamping
Dennis and BJ Thompson
2529 Bernadette Drive
Columbia, Missouri 65203
Tel: 573-446-5930
Fax: 573-445-8868

Ken Logsdon
Post-a-Quote
573-446-6625
www.postaquote.com

Kay Foley
Ampersand Cards
573-449-7504
www.ampersandcards.com

Lara K. Birkes
5400 Hayes Road
Columbia, Missouri 65201

Susan Taylor Glasgow
Taylor Glasgow Studios
www.taylorglasgow.com

Josephine Stealey
Jo Stealey Paperworks
460 County Rd. 328
Franklin, MO. 65250

Kate Gray
Gray Studios
573-443-7092

Janet Ghio
Janet Ghio Designs
www.quiltcollage.com

Lisa Christian
121 Burchwood Drive
St. James, Missouri 65559

The Story INDEX

Gloria Page is a wife, mom, artist and writer:
a creative kind of person.
In 1993 she started with a craft hobby,
and over time developed a home-based art business.
She loves her family, friends,
and the whole journey.

A handful of days
before going to print,
I learned something about Mr. Tamotzu,
my art teacher and apple-pie friend.
He frequently signed his artwork with the Japanese characters for
"The Ageless Wanderer."
May we all be ageless wanderers, filled with wonder.

One of his favorite quotations, displayed in his home for years and years,
was meant, I believe, for all of us. It goes like this:

"The Heavens Above
The Earth Below
I Stand Between
Alive, Unique—
Believe it."